ITALY

EXPORT-IMPORT, TRADE AND BUSINESS DIRECTORY

STRATEGIC INFORMATION AND CONTACTS

International Business Publications, USA
Washington DC, USA - Italy

ITALY

EXPORT-IMPORT, TRADE & BUSINESS DIRECTORY

STRATEGIC INFORMATION AND CONTACTS

UPDATED ANNUALLY

Cover Design: International Business Publications, USA

We express our sincere appreciation to all government agencies and international organizations which provided information and other materials for this directory

2018 Updated Reprint International Business Publications, USA
ISBN 0-7397-5865-9

This directory provides basic information for starting or/and conducting business in the country. The extraordinary volume of materials covering the topic, prevents us from placing all these materials in this directory. For more detailed information on issues related to any specific investment and business activity in the country, please contact Global Investment Center, USA
Please acquire the list of our business intelligence and marketing reports and other business publications. We constantly update and expand our business intelligence and marketing materials. Please contact the center for the updated list of reports on over 250 countries.

For additional analytical, business and investment opportunities information,
please contact Global Investment & Business Center, USA
at (703) 370-8082. Fax: (703) 370-8083. E-mail: ibpusa3@gmail.com
Global Business and Investment Info Databank - www.ibpus.com

Printed in the USA

For additional analytical, business and investment opportunities information,
please contact Global Investment & Business Center, USA
at (703) 370-8082. Fax: (703) 370-8083. E-mail: ibpusa3@gmail.com
Global Business and Investment Info Databank - www.ibpus.com

ITALY

EXPORT-IMPORT, TRADE AND BUSINESS DIRECTORY

STRATEGIC INFORMATION AND CONTACTS

TABLE OF CONTENTS

STRATEGIC AND BUSINESS PROFILES

STRATEGIC PROFILE

Capital and largest city	Rome 41°54′N 12°29′E
Official languages	Italian[a]
Religion	83.3% Christians 12.4% irreligious 3.7% Muslims 0.2% Buddhists 0.1% Hindus 0.3% other religions
Demonym	Italian
Government	Unitary constitutional parliamentary republic
• President	Sergio Mattarella
• Prime Minister	Paolo Gentiloni
• President of the Senate	Pietro Grasso
• President of the Chamber of Deputies	Laura Boldrini
Legislature	Parliament
• Upper house	Senate of the Republic
• Lower house	Chamber of Deputies
Formation	
• Unification	17 March 1861
• Republic	2 June 1946
• Founded the EEC (now the European Union)	1 January 1958
Area	
• Total	301,338 km^2 (116,347 sq mi) (71st)
• Water (%)	2.4
Population	
• 2016 estimate	60,589,445 ▲ (23rd)
• Density	201.3/km^2 (521.4/sq mi) (63rd)
GDP (PPP)	2016 estimate
• Total	$2.233 trillion (12th)
• Per capita	$36,823 (32nd)
GDP (nominal)	2018 estimate
• Total	2.050 trillion (9th)
• Per capita	$33,700 (27th)
Gini	33.1 medium
HDI (2015)	▲ 0.887 very high · 26th
Currency	Euro (€) (EUR)
Time zone	CET (UTC+1)
• Summer (DST)	CEST (UTC+2)
Date format	dd/mm/yyyy (AD)
Drives on the	right
Calling code	+39[c]
ISO 3166 code	IT
Internet TLD	.it[d]

Italy officially the **Italian Republic** is a unitary parliamentary republic in Europe. Located in the heart of the Mediterranean Sea, Italy shares open land borders with France, Switzerland, Austria, Slovenia, San Marino and Vatican City. Italy covers an area of 301,338 km^2 (116,347 sq mi) and has a largely temperate seasonal and Mediterranean climate. With around 61 million inhabitants it is the fourth most populous EU member state.

Since classical times, ancient Phoenicians, Carthaginians and Greeks established settlements in the south of Italy, with Etruscans and Celts inhabiting the centre and the north of Italy respectively and various ancient Italian tribes and Italic peoples dispersed throughout the Italian peninsula and insular Italy. The Italic tribe known as the Latins formed the Roman Kingdom, which eventually became a republic that conquered and assimilated its neighbors. Ultimately the Roman Empire emerged as the dominant power in the Mediterranean basin and became the leading cultural, political and religious centre of Western civilisation.

During the Early Middle Ages, Italy suffered sociopolitical collapse amid calamitous barbarian invasions, but by the 11th century, numerous rival city-states and maritime republics, mainly in the northern and central regions of Italy, rose to great prosperity through shipping, commerce and banking, laying the groundwork for modern capitalism. These mostly independent statelets, acting as Europe's main spice trade hubs with Asia and the Near East, often enjoyed a greater degree of democracy than the larger feudal monarchies that were consolidating throughout Europe. Part of central Italy was under the control of the theocratic Papal States, while Southern Italy remained largely feudal until the 19th century, partially as a result of a succession of Byzantine, Arab, Norman, Angevin and Spanish conquests of the region.

The Renaissance began in Italy and spread to the rest of Europe, bringing a renewed interest in humanism, science, exploration and art. Italian culture flourished at this time, producing famous scholars, artists and polymaths, such as Michelangelo, Leonardo da Vinci, Raphael, Galileo and Machiavelli. Since Middle Age, Italian explorers such as Marco Polo, Christopher Columbus, Amerigo Vespucci, John Cabot and Giovanni da Verrazzano discovered new routes to the Far East and the New World, helping to usher in the European Age of Discovery. Nevertheless, Italy's commercial and political power significantly waned with the opening of trade routes which bypassed the Mediterranean. Furthermore, the Italian city-states constantly engaged one another in bloody warfare, culminating in the Italian Wars of the 15th and 16th centuries that left them exhausted, with none emerging as a dominant power. They soon fell victim to conquest by European powers such as France, Spain and Austria.

By the mid-19th century, a rising movement in support of Italian nationalism and independence from foreign control led to a period of revolutionary political upheaval. After centuries of foreign domination and political division, Italy was almost entirely unified in 1871, creating a great power. From the late 19th century to the early 20th century, the new Kingdom of Italy rapidly industrialised, although mainly in the north, and acquired a colonial empire, while the south remained largely impoverished and excluded from industrialisation, fuelling a large and influential diaspora. Despite being one of the main victors in World War I, Italy entered a period of economic crisis and social turmoil, leading to the rise of a fascist dictatorship in 1922. Participation in World War II on the Axis side ended in military defeat, economic destruction, and an Italian civil war. Following the liberation of Italy and the rise of the resistance, the country abolished the monarchy, reinstated democracy, enjoyed a prolonged economic boom and, despite periods of sociopolitical turmoils, became a major advanced economy.

Today, Italy has the third largest nominal GDP in the Eurozone and the eighth largest in the world. As advanced economy the country has the sixth-largest worldwide national wealth and it is ranked third for its central bank gold reserve. Italy has a very high level of human development and it is sixth in the world for life expectancy. The country plays a prominent role in regional and global economic, military, cultural, and diplomatic affairs, and it is both a regional power and a great power.

Italy is a founding and leading member of the European Union and the member of numerous international institutions, including the UN, NATO, the OECD, the OSCE, the WTO, the G7, G20, the Union for the Mediterranean, the Council of Europe, Uniting for Consensus and many more. As a reflection of its cultural wealth, Italy is home to 53 World Heritage Sites, the most in the world, and is the fifth most visited country.

Location/Size: Southern Europe/301,230 sq km (186,763 sq mi, slightly larger than Arizona)
Major Cities: Rome (capital), Milan, Naples, Turin, Palermo, Genoa

Languages: Italian, German (parts of Trentino-Alto Adige region are predominantly German speaking), French (small French-speaking minority in Valle d'Aosta region), Slovene (Slovene-speaking minority in the Trieste-Gorizia area)
Ethnic groups: Italian (includes small clusters of German-, French-, and Slovene-Italians in the north and Albanian-Italians and Greek-Italians in the south)
Religion: predominately Roman Catholic with mature Protestant and Jewish communities and a growing Muslim immigrant community
Population : 57.6 million
Defense: Army, 165,600; Navy, 40,000; Air Force, 63,600; Paramilitary forces, 255,700; Conscripts, 134,100

Background: Italy became a nation-state belatedly - in 1861 when the city-states of the peninsula and Sicily were united under King Victor EMMANUEL. The Fascist dictatorship of Benito MUSSOLINI that took over after World War I led to a disastrous alliance with Nazi Germany and Italian defeat in World War II. Revival followed. Italy was a charter member of NATO and the European Economic Community (EEC) and joined the growing political and economic unification of Western Europe, including the introduction of the euro in 2004. Persistent problems include illegal immigration, the ravages of organized crime, corruption, high unemployment, and the low incomes and technical standards of southern Italy compared with the more prosperous north.

GEOGRAPHY

Location: Southern Europe, a peninsula extending into the central Mediterranean Sea, northeast of Tunisia
Geographic coordinates: 42 50 N, 12 50 E
Map references: Europe

Area:
total: 301,230 sq km
land: 294,020 sq km
water: 7,210 sq km
note: includes Sardinia and Sicily

Area - comparative: slightly larger than Arizona

Land boundaries:
total: 1,932.2 km
border countries: Austria 430 km, France 488 km, Holy See (Vatican City) 3.2 km, San Marino 39 km, Slovenia 232 km, Switzerland 740 km

Coastline: 7,600 km

Maritime claims:
continental shelf: 200-m depth or to the depth of exploitation
territorial sea: 12 nm

Climate: predominantly Mediterranean; Alpine in far north; hot, dry in south
Terrain: mostly rugged and mountainous; some plains, coastal lowlands
Elevation extremes:
lowest point: Mediterranean Sea 0 m
highest point: Mont Blanc (Monte Bianco) 4,807 m
Natural resources: mercury, potash, marble, sulfur, dwindling natural gas and crude oil reserves, fish, coal, arable land
Land use:
arable land: 31% *permanent crops:* 10% *permanent pastures:* 15% *forests and woodland:* 23% *other:* 21%
Irrigated land: 27,100 sq km

Natural hazards: regional risks include landslides, mudflows, avalanches, earthquakes, volcanic eruptions, flooding; land subsidence in Venice

Base 802446 (A04844) 3-96

Environment - current issues: air pollution from industrial emissions such as sulfur dioxide; coastal and inland rivers polluted from industrial and agricultural effluents; acid rain damaging lakes; inadequate industrial waste treatment and disposal facilities

Environment - international agreements:
party to: Air Pollution, Air Pollution-Nitrogen Oxides, Air Pollution-Sulphur 85, Air Pollution-Sulphur 94, Air Pollution-Volatile Organic Compounds, Antarctic-Environmental Protocol, Antarctic Treaty, Biodiversity, Climate Change, Desertification, Endangered Species, Environmental Modification, Hazardous Wastes, Law of the Sea, Marine Dumping, Nuclear Test Ban, Ozone Layer Protection, Ship Pollution, Tropical Timber 83, Tropical Timber 94, Wetlands, Whaling
signed, but not ratified: Air Pollution-Persistent Organic Pollutants, Climate Change-Kyoto Protocol

Geography - note: strategic location dominating central Mediterranean as well as southern sea and air approaches to Western Europe

PEOPLE

Population: 56,735,130
Age structure:
0-14 years: 14% (male 4,161,841; female 3,925,413)
15-64 years: 68% (male 19,205,293; female 19,285,848)
65 years and over: 18% (male 4,169,098; female 5,987,637)
Population growth rate: -0.08%

Birth rate: 9.27 births/1,000 population
Death rate: 10.28 deaths/1,000 population
Net migration rate: 0.17 migrant(s)/1,000 population

Sex ratio:
at birth: 1.06 male(s)/female
under 15 years: 1.06 male(s)/female
15-64 years: 1 male(s)/female
65 years and over: 0.7 male(s)/female
total population: 0.94 male(s)/female

Infant mortality rate: 6.3 deaths/1,000 live births

Life expectancy at birth:
total population: 78.51 years
male: 75.4 years
female: 81.82 years

Total fertility rate: 1.22 children born/woman

Nationality:
noun: Italian(s)
adjective: Italian

Ethnic groups: Italian (includes small clusters of German-, French-, and Slovene-Italians in the north and Albanian-Italians and Greek-Italians in the south)

Religions: Roman Catholic 98%, other 2%

Languages: Italian, German (parts of Trentino-Alto Adige region are predominantly German speaking), French (small French-speaking minority in Valle d'Aosta region), Slovene (Slovene-speaking minority in the Trieste-Gorizia area)

Literacy:
definition: age 15 and over can read and write
total population: 97%

male: 98%
female: 96% (1990 est.)

GOVERNMENT

Country name:

conventional long form: Italian Republic
conventional short form: Italy
local long form: Repubblica Italiana
local short form: Italia
former: Kingdom of Italy

Government type:

republic

Capital:

name: Rome
geographic coordinates: 41 54 N, 12 29 E
time difference: UTC+1 (6 hours ahead of Washington, DC, during Standard Time)
daylight saving time: +1hr, begins last Sunday in March; ends last Sunday in October

Administrative divisions:

15 regions (regioni, singular - regione) and 5 autonomous regions (regioni autonome, singular - regione autonoma)
regions: Abruzzo, Basilicata, Calabria, Campania, Emilia-Romagna, Lazio (Latium), Liguria, Lombardia, Marche, Molise, Piemonte (Piedmont), Puglia (Apulia), Toscana (Tuscany), Umbria, Veneto (Venetia)
autonomous regions: Friuli-Venezia Giulia; Sardegna (Sardinia); Sicilia (Sicily); Trentino-Alto Adige (Trentino-South Tyrol) or Trentino-Suedtirol (German); Valle d'Aosta (Aosta Valley) or Vallee d'Aoste (French)

Independence:

17 March 1861 (Kingdom of Italy proclaimed; Italy was not finally unified until 1870)

National holiday:

Republic Day, 2 June (1946)

Constitution:

previous 1848 (originally for Kingdom of Sardinia and adopted by Kingdom of Italy in 1861); latest enacted 22 December 1947, adopted 27 December 1947, entered into force 1 January 1948; amended many times, last in 2012 (2013)

Legal system:

civil law system; judicial review of legislation under certain conditions in Constitutional Court

International law organization participation:

has not submitted an ICJ jurisdiction declaration; accepts ICCt jurisdiction

Suffrage:

18 years of age; universal except in senatorial elections, where minimum age is 25

Executive branch:

chief of state: President Sergio MATTARELLA (since 3 February 2015)
head of government: Prime Minister Paolo GENTILONI (since 12 December 2016); the prime minister's official title is President of the Council of Ministers
cabinet: Council of Ministers proposed by the prime minister, known officially as the President of the Council of Ministers and locally as the Premier; nominated by the president
elections/appointments: president indirectly elected by an electoral college consisting of both houses of Parliament and 58 regional representatives for a 7-year term (no term limits); election last held on 31 January 2015 (next to be held in 2022); prime minister appointed by the president, confirmed by parliament
election results: Sergio MATTARELLA (PD) elected president; electoral college vote count in fourth round - 665 out of 1,009 (505-vote threshold)

Legislative branch:
description: bicameral Parliament or Parlamento consists of the Senate or Senato della Repubblica (322 seats; 315 members directly elected in single- and multi-seat constituencies by proportional representation vote to serve 5-year terms and 7 ex-officio members appointed by the president of the Republic to serve for life) and the Chamber of Deputies or Camera dei Deputati (630 seats; 629 members directly elected in single- and multi-seat constituencies by proportional representation vote and 1 member from Valle d'Aosta elected by simple majority vote; members serve 5-year terms)
elections: Senate - last held on 24-25 February 2013 (next to be held on 4 March 2018); Chamber of Deputies - last held on 24-25 February 2013 (next to be held on 4 March 2018); President MATTARELLA dissolved parliament on 28 December 2017, triggering an early election
election results: Senate - percent of vote by party - NA; seats by party - center-left coalition 123 (PD 111, SEL 7, SVP 2, other 3), center-right coalition 117 (PdL 98, LN 18, other 1), M5S 54, centrist coalition 19, other 2
Chamber of Deputies - percent of vote by party - NA; seats by party - center-left coalition 345 (PD 297, SEL 37, CD 6 SVP 5), center-right coalition 125 (PdL 98, LN 18, FdI-AN 9), M5S 109, centrist coalition 47, other 3

Judicial branch:
highest court(s): Supreme Court of Cassation or Corte Suprema di Cassazione consists of the first president (chief justice), deputy president, 54 justices presiding over 6 civil and 7 criminal divisions, and 288 judges; an additional 30 judges of lower courts serve as supporting judges; cases normally heard by 5-judge panels; more complex cases heard by 9-judge panels; Constitutional Court or Corte Costituzionale (consists of the court president and 14 judges)

judge selection and term of office: Supreme Court judges appointed by the High Council of the Judiciary, headed by the president of the republic; judges may serve for life; Constitutional Court judges - 5 appointed by the president, 5 elected by parliament, 5 elected by select higher courts; judges serve up to 9 years
subordinate courts: various lower civil and criminal courts (primary and secondary tribunals, courts, and courts of appeal)

Political parties and leaders:
Ruling left-center-right coalition: Civic Choice or SC [Enrico ZANETTI]
Democratic Centre or CD [Bruno TABACCI]
Democratic Party or PD [interim leader, Maurizio MARTINA]

Popular Alliance or AP [Angelino ALFANO] (formerly New Center-Right or NCD)
Union of the Center or UdC [Pier Fernando CASSINI]
Center-right opposition: Brothers of Italy-National Alliance or FdI-AN [Giorgia MELONI, Ignazio LA RUSSA, and Guido CROSETTO]
Forza Italia or FI [Silvio BERLUSCONI] (formerly People of Freedom or PdL)
Northern League or LN [Matteo SALVINI]
Other parties and parliamentary groups: Five Star Movement or M5S [Luigi DI MAIO]
Liberal Popular Alliance or ALA [Denis VERDINI]
Democratic and Progressive Movement or MDP [Roberto SPERANZA]
Sinistra Italiani or SI [Nicola FRATOIANNI] (formerly Sinistra Ecologia Liberta or SEL)
South Tyrolean People's Party or SVP [Philipp ACHAMMER]

Political pressure groups and leaders:
manufacturers and merchants associations: Confcommercio
Confindustria
organized farm groups: Confcoltivatori
Confagricoltura
major trade union confederations: Confederazione Generale Italiana del Lavoro or CGIL [Susanna CAMUSSO] (left wing)
Confederazione Italiana dei Sindacati Lavoratori or CISL [Raffaele BONANNI] (Roman Catholic centrist)
Unione Italiana del Lavoro or UIL [Luigi ANGELETTI] (lay centrist)
other: Roman Catholic Church

International organization participation:
ADB (nonregional member), AfDB (nonregional member), Arctic Council (observer), Australia Group, BIS, BSEC (observer), CBSS (observer), CD, CDB, CE, CEI, CERN, EAPC, EBRD, ECB, EIB, EITI (implementing country), EMU, ESA, EU, FAO, FATF, G-7, G-8, G-10, G-20, IADB, IAEA, IBRD, ICAO, ICC (national committees), ICCt, ICRM, IDA, IEA, IFAD, IFC, IFRCS, IGAD (partners), IHO, ILO, IMF, IMO, IMSO, Interpol, IOC, IOM, IPU, ISO, ITSO, ITU, ITUC (NGOs), LAIA (observer), MIGA, MINURSO, MINUSMA, NATO, NEA, NSG, OAS (observer), OECD, OPCW, OSCE, Pacific Alliance (observer), Paris Club, PCA, PIF (partner), Schengen Convention, SELEC (observer), SICA (observer), UN, UN Security Council (temporary), UNCTAD, UNESCO, UNHCR, UNIDO, UNIFIL, Union Latina, UNMOGIP, UNRWA, UNTSO, UNWTO, UPU, WCO, WHO, WIPO, WMO, WTO, ZC

Diplomatic representation in the US:
chief of mission: Ambassador Armando VARRICCHIO (since 2 March 2016)
chancery: 3000 Whitehaven Street NW, Washington, DC 20008
telephone: [1] (202) 612-4400
FAX: [1] (202) 518-2151
consulate(s) general: Boston, Chicago, Detroit, Houston, Miami, New York, Los Angeles, Philadelphia, San Francisco
consulate(s): Charlotte (NC), Cleveland (OH), Detroit (MI), Hattiesburg (MS), Honolulu (HI), New Orleans, Newark (NJ), Norfolk (VA), Pittsburgh (PA), Portland (OR), Seattle

Diplomatic representation from the US:
chief of mission: Ambassador Lewis EISENBERG (since 4 October 2017); note - also accredited to San Marino
embassy: Via Vittorio Veneto 121, 00187-Rome
mailing address: PSC 59, Box 100, APO AE 09624
telephone: (+39)06.46741
FAX: [39] (06) 4674-2244
consulate(s) general: Florence, Mi

Flag description:

three equal vertical bands of green (hoist side), white, and red; design inspired by the French flag brought to Italy by Napoleon in 1797; colors are those of Milan (red and white) combined with the green uniform color of the Milanese civic guard

note: similar to the flag of Mexico, which is longer, uses darker shades of red and green, and has its coat of arms centered on the white band; Ireland, which is longer and is green (hoist side), white, and orange; also similar to the flag of the Cote d'Ivoire, which has the colors reversed - orange (hoist side), white, and green

National symbol(s):

white, five-pointed star (Stella d'Italia)

National anthem:

name: "Il Canto degli Italiani" (The Song of the Italians)

ECONOMY

Italy's economy compromises a developed industrial north, dominated by private companies, and a less-developed, highly subsidized, agricultural south, with a legacy of unemployment and underdevelopment. The Italian economy is driven in large part by the manufacture of high-quality consumer goods produced by small and medium-sized enterprises, many of them family-owned. Italy also has a sizable underground economy, which by some estimates accounts for as much as 17% of GDP. These activities are most common within the agriculture, construction, and service sectors.

Italy is the third-largest economy in the euro zone, but its exceptionally high public debt and structural impediments to growth have rendered it vulnerable to scrutiny by financial markets. Public debt has increased steadily since 2007, reaching 131% of GDP in 2017. Investor concerns about Italy and the broader euro-zone crisis eased in 2013, bringing down Italy's borrowing costs on sovereign government debt from euro-era records. The government still faces pressure from investors and European partners to sustain its efforts to address Italy's longstanding structural economic problems, including labor market inefficiencies, a sluggish judicial system, and a weak banking sector. Italy's economy returned to modest growth in late 2014 for the first time since 2011. In 2015-16, Italy's economy grew at about 1% each year, and in 2017 growth accelerated to 1.5% of GDP. In 2017, overall unemployment was 11.4%, but youth unemployment remained high at 37.1%.

GDP (purchasing power parity):

$2.307 trillion (2017 est.)
$2.273 trillion (2016 est.)
$2.253 trillion (2015 est.)
note: data are in 2017 dollars
country comparison to the world: 13

GDP (official exchange rate):
$1.921 trillion (2017 est.)

GDP - real growth rate:
1.5% (2017 est.)
0.9% (2016 est.)
0.8% (2015 est.)
country comparison to the world: 172

GDP - per capita (PPP):
$38,000 (2017 est.)
$37,500 (2016 est.)
$37,100 (2015 est.)
note: data are in 2017 dollars

country comparison to the world: 49

Gross national saving:
19.6% of GDP (2017 est.)
19.6% of GDP (2016 est.)
18.8% of GDP (2015 est.)
country comparison to the world: 94

GDP - composition, by end use:
household consumption: 60.2%
government consumption: 18.7%
investment in fixed capital: 17.2%
investment in inventories: 0.1%
exports of goods and services: 31.8%
imports of goods and services: -28% (2017 est.)

GDP - composition, by sector of origin:
agriculture: 2.1%
industry: 24%
services: 73.9% (2017 est.)

Agriculture - products:
fruits, vegetables, grapes, potatoes, sugar beets, soybeans, grain, olives; beef, dairy products; fish

Industries:
tourism, machinery, iron and steel, chemicals, food processing, textiles, motor vehicles, clothing, footwear, ceramics

Industrial production growth rate:
0.8% (2017 est.)
country comparison to the world: 173

Labor force:
25.94 million (2017 est.)
country comparison to the world: 25

Labor force - by occupation:
agriculture: 3.9%
industry: 28.3%
services: 67.8% (2011 est.)

Unemployment rate:
11.4% (2017 est.)
11.7% (2016 est.)
country comparison to the world: 148

Population below poverty line:
29.9%

Household income or consumption by percentage share:
lowest 10%: 2.3%
highest 10%: 26.8% (2000 est.)

Distribution of family income - Gini index:
31.9 (2012 est.)
27.3 (1995 est.)
country comparison to the world: 122

Budget:
revenues: $884.4 billion
expenditures: $927.7 billion (2017 est.)

Taxes and other revenues:
46% of GDP (2017 est.)
country comparison to the world: 21

Budget surplus (+) or deficit (-):
-2.3% of GDP (2017 est.)
country comparison to the world: 94

Public debt:
131.2% of GDP (2017 est.)
132.5% of GDP (2016 est.)
note: Italy reports its data on public debt according to guidelines set out in the Maastricht Treaty; general government gross debt is defined in the Maastricht Treaty as consolidated general government gross debt at nominal value, outstanding at the end of the year, in the following categories of government liabilities (as defined in ESA95): currency and deposits (AF.2), securities other than shares excluding financial derivatives (AF.3, excluding AF.34), and loans (AF.4); the general government sector comprises the central government, state government, local government and social security funds
country comparison to the world: 5

Fiscal year:
calendar year

Inflation rate (consumer prices):
1.4% (2017 est.)
-0.1% (2016 est.)
country comparison to the world: 58

Central bank discount rate:
0.25% (31 December 2013 est.)
0.75% (31 December 2012 est.)
note: this is the European Central Bank's rate on the marginal lending facility, which offers overnight credit to banks in the euro area
country comparison to the world: 141

Commercial bank prime lending rate:
3.3% (31 December 2017 est.)
3.5% (31 December 2016 est.)
country comparison to the world: 167

Stock of narrow money:
$1.238 trillion (31 December 2017 est.)
$1.101 trillion (31 December 2016 est.)
note: see entry for the European Union for money supply for the entire euro area; the European Central Bank (ECB) controls monetary policy for the 18 members of the Economic and Monetary Union (EMU); individual members of the EMU do not control the quantity of money circulating within their own borders
country comparison to the world: 7

Stock of broad money:
$1.694 trillion (31 December 2017 est.)
$1.519 trillion (31 December 2016 est.)
country comparison to the world: 11

Stock of domestic credit:
$3.264 trillion (31 December 2017 est.)
$3.024 trillion (31 December 2016 est.)
country comparison to the world: 7

Market value of publicly traded shares:

$587.3 billion (31 December 2014 est.)
$615.5 billion (31 December 2013 est.)
$480.5 billion (31 December 2012 est.)
country comparison to the world: 20

Current account balance:
$52.83 billion (2017 est.)
$47.31 billion (2016 est.)
country comparison to the world: 10

Exports:
$499.1 billion (2017 est.)
$454.1 billion (2016 est.)
country comparison to the world: 10

Exports - commodities:
engineering products, textiles and clothing, production machinery, motor vehicles, transport equipment, chemicals; foodstuffs, beverages, and tobacco; minerals, nonferrous metals

Exports - partners:
Germany 12.6%, France 10.5%, US 8.9%, UK 5.4%, Spain 5%, Switzerland 4.6% (2016)
Imports:
$426.7 billion (2017 est.)
$387.1 billion (2016 est.)
country comparison to the world: 13

Imports - commodities:
engineering products, chemicals, transport equipment, energy products, minerals and nonferrous metals, textiles and clothing; food, beverages, tobacco
Imports - partners:
Germany 16.3%, France 8.9%, China 7.5%, Netherlands 5.5%, Spain 5.3%, Belgium 4.9%

Reserves of foreign exchange and gold:
$136 billion (31 December 2016 est.)
$130.6 billion (31 December 2015 est.)
country comparison to the world: 18

Debt - external:
$2.444 trillion (31 March 2016 est.)
$2.3 trillion (31 March 2015 est.)
country comparison to the world: 10

Stock of direct foreign investment - at home:
$495.2 billion (31 December 2017 est.)
$471.7 billion (31 December 2016 est.)
country comparison to the world: 18

Stock of direct foreign investment - abroad:
$607.8 billion (31 December 2017 est.)
$584.1 billion (31 December 2016 est.)
country comparison to the world: 16

Exchange rates:
euros (EUR) per US dollar -
0.885 (2017 est.)
0.903 (2016 est.)
0.9214 (2015 est.)
0.885 (2014 est.)
0.7634 (2013 est.)

ENERGY

Electricity - production:

299.3 billion kWh
country comparison to the world: 13

Electricity - consumption:

307.2 billion kWh
country comparison to the world: 13

Electricity - exports:

2.304 billion kWh
country comparison to the world: 42

Electricity - imports:

45.41 billion kWh
country comparison to the world: 3

Electricity - installed generating capacity:

124.2 million kW
country comparison to the world: 10

Electricity - from fossil fuels:

65% of total installed capacity
country comparison to the world: 120

Electricity - from nuclear fuels:

0% of total installed capacity
country comparison to the world: 111

Electricity - from hydroelectric plants:

18% of total installed capacity
country comparison to the world: 95

Electricity - from other renewable sources:

15.8% of total installed capacity
country comparison to the world: 13

Crude oil - production:

112,000 bbl/day
country comparison to the world: 48

Crude oil - exports:

6,300 bbl/day
country comparison to the world: 63

Crude oil - imports:

1.591 million bbl/day
country comparison to the world: 7

Crude oil - proved reserves:

521.3 million bbl (1 January 2013 est.)
country comparison to the world: 50

Refined petroleum products - production:

6,600 bbl/day
country comparison to the world: 107

Refined petroleum products - consumption:

1.454 million bbl/day
country comparison to the world: 15

Refined petroleum products - exports:

628,000 bbl/day
country comparison to the world: 12

Refined petroleum products - imports:

393,300 bbl/day
country comparison to the world: 15

Natural gas - production:

7.8 billion cu m
country comparison to the world: 47

Natural gas - consumption:

68.7 billion cu m
country comparison to the world: 10

Natural gas - exports:

324 million cu m
country comparison to the world: 48

Natural gas - imports:

67.8 billion cu m
country comparison to the world: 5

Natural gas - proved reserves:

62.35 billion cu m
country comparison to the world: 62

Carbon dioxide emissions from consumption of energy:

400.9 million Mt

COMMUNICATIONS

Telephones - main lines in use:

21.656 million
country comparison to the world: 13

Telephones - mobile cellular:

97.225 million
country comparison to the world: 14

Telephone system:

general assessment: modern, well-developed, fast; fully automated telephone, telex, and data services
domestic: high-capacity cable and microwave radio relay trunks
international: country code - 39; a series of submarine cables provide links to Asia, Middle East, Europe, North Africa, and US; satellite earth stations - 3 Intelsat (with a total of 5 antennas - 3 for Atlantic Ocean and 2 for Indian Ocean), 1 Inmarsat (Atlantic Ocean region), and NA Eutelsat

Broadcast media:

two Italian media giants dominate - the publicly owned Radiotelevisione Italiana (RAI) with 3 national terrestrial stations and privately owned Mediaset with 3 national terrestrial stations; a large number of private stations and Sky Italia - a satellite TV network; RAI operates 3 AM/FM nationwide radio stations; some 1,300 commercial radio stations

Internet country code:

.it

Internet hosts:

25.662 million
country comparison to the world: 4

Internet users:

29.235 million
country comparison to the world: 13

TRANSPORTATION

Airports:

129
country comparison to the world: 45

Airports - with paved runways:

total: 98
over 3,047 m: 9
2,438 to 3,047 m: 31
1,524 to 2,437 m: 18
914 to 1,523 m: 29
under 914 m: 11

Airports - with unpaved runways:

total: 31
1,524 to 2,437 m: 1
914 to 1,523 m: 10
under 914 m:
20

Heliports:

5

Pipelines:

gas 20,223 km; oil 1,393 km; refined products 1,574 km

Railways:

total: 20,255 km
country comparison to the world: 13
standard gauge: 18,611 km 1.435-m gauge (12,662 km electrified)
narrow gauge: 123 km 1.000-m gauge (123 km electrified); 1,290 km 0.950-m gauge (151 km electrified); 231 km 0.850-m gauge

Roadways:

total: 487,700 km
country comparison to the world: 14
paved: 487,700 km (includes 6,700 km of expressways) (2007)

Waterways:

2,400 km (used for commercial traffic; of limited overall value compared to road and rail)
country comparison to the world: 37

Merchant marine:

total: 681

country comparison to the world: 17
by type: bulk carrier 105, cargo 42, carrier 1, chemical tanker 164, container 21, liquefied gas 28, passenger 25, passenger/cargo 154, petroleum tanker 59, refrigerated cargo 4, roll on/roll off 39, specialized tanker 9, vehicle carrier 30
foreign-owned: 90 (Denmark 4, France 2, Greece 7, Luxembourg 14, Netherlands 2, Nigeria 1, Norway 6, Singapore 1, Sweden 1, Switzerland 13, Taiwan 10, Turkey 4, UK 2, US 23)
registered in other countries: 201 (Bahamas 1, Belize 3, Cayman Islands 7, Cyprus 6, Georgia 2, Gibraltar 4, Greece 5, Liberia 47, Malta 45, Marshall Islands 1, Morocco 1, Netherlands 6, Panama 25, Portugal 12, Russia 14, Saint Vincent and the Grenadines 4, Singapore 5, Slovakia 2, Spain 1, Sweden 5, Turkey 1, UK 3, unknown 1)

Ports and terminals:

major seaport(s): Augusta, Cagliari, Genoa, Livorno, Taranto, Trieste, Venice
oil terminals: Melilli (Santa Panagia) oil terminal, Sarroch oil terminal
container port(s) (TEUs): Genoa (1,847,648), Gioia Tauro (2,264,798), La Spezia (1,307,274)

MILITARY

Military branches:

Italian Armed Forces: Army (Esercito Italiano, EI), Navy (Marina Militare Italiana, MMI), Italian Air Force (Aeronautica Militare Italiana, AMI), Carabinieri Corps (Arma dei Carabinieri, CC) (2011)

Military service age and obligation:

18-25 years of age for voluntary military service; women may serve in any military branch; Italian citizenship required; 12-month service obligation

Manpower available for military service:

males age 16-49: 13,865,688
females age 16-49: 14,003,755

Manpower fit for military service:

males age 16-49: 11,247,446
females age 16-49: 11,348,695

Manpower reaching militarily significant age annually:

male: 288,188
female: 281,671

Military expenditures:

1.69% of GDP
country comparison to the world: 53
1.72% of GDP (2011)
1.69% of GDP (2010)

TRANSNATIONAL ISSUES

Disputes - international:

Italy's long coastline and developed economy entices tens of thousands of illegal immigrants from southeastern Europe and northern Africa

Refugees and internally displaced persons:

refugees (country of origin): 12,682 (Eritrea); 10,817 (Somalia); 6,695 (Afghanistan) (2013)
stateless persons: 470

Illicit drugs:

important gateway for and consumer of Latin American cocaine and Southwest Asian heroin entering the European market; money laundering by organized crime and from smuggling

IMPORTANT INFORMATION FOR UNDERSTANDING ITALY

PROFILE

OFFICIAL NAME: Italian Republic

Geography
Area: 301,225 sq. km. (116,303 sq. mi.); about the size of Georgia and Florida combined.
Cities: *Capital*--Rome (pop. 2.8 million). *Other cities*--Milan, Naples, Turin.
Terrain: Mostly rugged and mountainous.
Climate: Generally mild Mediterranean; cold northern winters.

People
Nationality: *Noun and adjective*--Italian(s).
Population: 57.8 million.
Annual growth rate: 0.28%.
Ethnic groups: Primarily Italian, but there are small groups of German-, French-, Slovene-, and Albanian-Italians.
Religion: Roman Catholic (majority).
Language: Italian (official).
Education: *Years compulsory*--18. *Literacy*--98%.
Health: *Infant mortality rate*--5.76/1,000 live births. *Life expectancy*--76.08 years for men; 83.0 years for women.
Work force (23.8 million): *Services*--57.6%; *industry and commerce*--28.9%; *agriculture*--4.2%; *unemployed*--9.2%.

Government
Type: Republic since June 2, 1946.
Constitution: January 1, 1948.
Branches: *Executive*--president (chief of state), Council of Ministers (cabinet), headed by the president of the council (prime minister). *Legislative*--bicameral parliament: 630-member Chamber of Deputies, 315-member Senate (plus a varying number of "life" Senators). *Judicial*--independent constitutional court and lower magistracy.
Subdivisions: 94 provinces, 20 regions.
Political parties: Forza Italia, Democratic Party of the Left, National Alliance, Northern League, United Christian Democrats, Democrats, Italian People's Party, Christian Democratic Center, Socialist, Communist Renewal, Social Democratic, Republican, Liberal, Greens, Italian Renewal.
Suffrage: Vote for House; universal over 18; vote for Senate; universal over 18.

PEOPLE AND HISTORY

Italy is largely homogeneous linguistically and religiously but is diverse culturally, economically, and politically. Italy has the fifth-highest population density in Europe--about 200 persons per square kilometer (490 per sq. mi.). Minority groups are small, the largest being the German-speaking people of Bolzano Province and the Slovenes around Trieste. There are also small communities of Albanian, Greek, Ladino, and French origin. Immigration has increased in recent years, however, while the Italian population is declining overall due to low birth rates. Although Roman Catholicism is the majority religion--85% of native-born citizens are nominally Catholic--all religious faiths are provided equal freedom before the law by the constitution.

Greeks settled in the southern tip of the Italian Peninsula in the eighth and seventh centuries B.C.; Etruscans, Romans, and others inhabited the central and northern mainland. The peninsula subsequently was unified under the Roman Republic. The neighboring islands came under Roman control by the third century B.C.; by the first century A.D., the Roman Empire effectively dominated the Mediterranean world. After the collapse of the Roman Empire in the West in the fifth century A.D., the peninsula and islands were subjected to a series of invasions, and political unity was lost. Italy became an oft-changing succession of small states, principalities, and kingdoms, which fought among themselves and were subject to ambitions of foreign powers. Popes of Rome ruled central Italy; rivalries between the popes and the Holy Roman Emperors, who claimed Italy as their domain, often made the peninsula a battleground.

The commercial prosperity of northern and central Italian cities, beginning in the 11th century, combined with the influence of the Renaissance, mitigated somewhat the effects of these medieval political rivalries. Although Italy declined after the 16th century, the Renaissance had strengthened the idea of a single Italian nationality. By the early 19th century, a nationalist movement developed and led to the reunification of Italy--except for Rome--in the 1860s. In 1861, Victor Emmanuel II of the House of Savoy was proclaimed King of Italy. Rome was incorporated in 1870. From 1870 until 1922, Italy was a constitutional monarchy with a parliament elected under limited suffrage.

20th-Century History

During World War I, Italy renounced its standing alliance with Germany and Austria-Hungary and, in 1915, entered the war on the side of the Allies. Under the postwar settlement, Italy received some former Austrian territory along the northeast frontier. In 1922, Benito Mussolini came to power and, over the next few years, eliminated political parties, curtailed personal liberties, and installed a fascist dictatorship termed the Corporate State. The king, with little or no effective power, remained titular head of state.

Italy allied with Germany and declared war on the United Kingdom and France in 1940. In 1941, Italy--with the other Axis powers, Germany and Japan--declared war on the United States and the Soviet Union. Following the Allied invasion of Sicily in 1943, the King dismissed Mussolini and appointed Marshal Pietro Badoglio as Premier. The Badoglio government declared war on Germany, which quickly occupied most of the country and freed Mussolini, who led a brief-lived regime in the north. An anti-fascist popular resistance movement grew during the last two years of the war, harassing German forces before they were driven out in April 1945. A 1946 plebiscite ended the monarchy, and a constituent assembly was elected to draw up plans for the republic.

Under the 1947 peace treaty, minor adjustments were made in Italy's frontier with France, the eastern border area was transferred to Yugoslavia, and the area around the city of Trieste was designated a free territory. In 1954, the free territory, which had remained under the administration of U.S.-U.K. forces (Zone A, including the city of Trieste) and Yugoslav forces (Zone B), was divided between Italy and Yugoslavia, principally along the zonal boundary. This arrangement was made permanent by the Italian-Yugoslav Treaty of Osimo, ratified in 1977 (currently being discussed by Italy, Slovenia, and Croatia). Under the 1947 peace treaty, Italy relinquished its overseas territories and certain Mediterranean islands.

The Roman Catholic Church's status in Italy has been determined, since its temporal powers ended in 1870, by a series of accords with the Italian Government. Under the Lateran Pacts of 1929, which were confirmed by the present constitution, Vatican City is recognized by Italy as an independent, sovereign entity. While preserving that recognition, in 1984, Italy and the Vatican updated several provisions of the 1929 accords. Included was the end of Roman Catholicism as Italy's formal state religion.

Italy's Cultural Contributions

Europe's Renaissance period began in Italy during the 14th and 15th centuries. Literary achievements--such as the poetry of Petrarch, Tasso, and Ariosto and the prose of Boccaccio, Machiavelli, and Castiglione--exerted a tremendous and lasting influence on the subsequent development of Western civilization, as did the painting, sculpture, and architecture contributed by giants such as da Vinci, Raphael, Botticelli, Fra Angelico, and Michelangelo.

The musical influence of Italian composers Monteverdi, Palestrina, and Vivaldi proved epochal; in the 19th century, Italian romantic opera flourished under composers Gioacchino Rossini, Giuseppe Verdi, and Giacomo Puccini. Contemporary Italian artists, writers, filmmakers, architects, composers, and designers contribute significantly to Western culture.

GOVERNMENT

Italy has been a democratic republic since June 2, 1946, when the monarchy was abolished by popular referendum. The constitution was promulgated on January 1, 1948.

The Italian state is centralized. The prefect of each of the provinces is appointed by and answerable to the central government. In addition to the provinces, the constitution provides for 20 regions with limited governing powers. Five regions--Sardinia, Sicily, Trentino-Alto Adige, Valle d'Aosta, and Friuli-Venezia Giulia--function with special autonomy statutes. The other 15 regions were established in 1970 and vote for regional "councils." The establishment of regional governments throughout Italy has brought some decentralization to the national governmental machinery, and recent governments have devolved further powers to the regions. Many regional governments, particularly in the north of Italy, are seeking additional powers.

The 1948 constitution established a bicameral parliament (Chamber of Deputies and Senate), a separate judiciary, and an executive branch composed of a Council of Ministers (cabinet), headed by the president of the council (prime minister). The president of the republic is elected for seven years by the parliament sitting jointly with a small number of regional delegates. The president nominates the prime minister, who chooses the other ministers. The Council of Ministers--in practice composed mostly of members of parliament--must retain the confidence of both houses.

The houses of parliament are popularly and directly elected by a proportional representation system. Under 2005 legislation, the Chamber of Deputies has 630 members (12 of which are elected by Italians abroad). In addition to 315 elected members (six of which are elected by Italians abroad), the Senate includes former presidents and several other persons appointed for life according to special constitutional provisions. Both houses are elected for a maximum of five years, but either may be dissolved before the expiration of its normal term. Legislative bills may originate in either house and must be passed by a majority in both.

The Italian judicial system is based on Roman law modified by the Napoleonic code and subsequent statutes. There is only partial judicial review of legislation in the American sense. A constitutional court, which passes on the constitutionality of laws, is a post-World War II innovation. Its powers, volume, and frequency of decisions are not as extensive as those of the U.S. Supreme Court.

Principal Government Officials

Gentiloni Cabinet		
Ministry	Minister	Party
President of the Council (Prime Minister)	Paolo Gentiloni	PD
Secretary of the Council of Ministers	Maria Elena Boschi	PD
Ministers with portfolio		
Minister of the Interior	Marco Minniti	PD
Minister of Foreign Affairs	Angelino Alfano	AP
Minister of Defence	Roberta Pinotti	PD
Minister of Justice	Andrea Orlando	PD
Minister of Economy and Finance	Pier Carlo Padoan	Ind.
Minister of Economic Development	Carlo Calenda	Ind.

Minister of Infrastructure and Transport	Graziano Delrio	PD
Minister of Agriculture, Food and Forestry Policies	Maurizio Martina	PD
Minister of Education, Universities and Research	Valeria Fedeli	PD
Minister of Labour and Social Policies	Giuliano Poletti	PD
Minister of the Environment, Protection of Land and Sea	Gian Luca Galletti	CpE
Minister of Heritage and Cultural Activities and Tourism	Dario Franceschini	PD
Minister of Health	Beatrice Lorenzin	AP
Ministers without portfolio		
Minister for Parliamentary Relations	Anna Finocchiaro	PD
Minister for Simplification of Public Administration	Marianna Madia	PD
Minister for Regional Affairs	Paolo Gentiloni	PD
Minister for Territorial Cohesiveness and Southern Italy	Claudio De Vincenti	PD
Minister for Sport Affairs	Luca Lotti	PD

Italy maintains an embassy in the United States at 3000 Whitehaven Street, NW, Washington, DC 20008 (tel. 202-612-4400).

POLITICAL CONDITIONS

Politics of Italy is conducted through a parliamentary republic with a multi-party system. Italy has been a democratic republic since 2 June 1946, when the monarchy was abolished by popular referendum and a constituent assembly was elected to draft a constitution, which was promulgated on 1 January 1948.

The executive power is exercised collectively by the Council of Ministers, which is led by the Prime Minister, officially referred to as President of the Council (*Presidente del Consiglio*). Legislative power is vested in the two houses of the Italian Parliament primarily, and secondarily on the Council of Ministers, which can introduce bills and holds the majority in both houses. The judiciary of Italy is independent of the executive and the legislative branches. It is headed by the High Council of the Judiciary, a body presided over by the President of Italy, who is the head of state though his position is separate from all branches. The current Italian President is Sergio Mattarella and the current Prime Minister of Italy is Paolo Gentiloni. The Economist Intelligence Unit has rated the Italy as "flawed democracy" in 2016

Italy has a parliamentary government based on a proportional voting system. The parliament is perfectly bicameral: the two houses, the Chamber of Deputies (that meets in Palazzo Montecitorio) and the Senate of the Republic (that meets in Palazzo Madama), have the same powers. The Prime Minister, officially President of the Council of Ministers (*Presidente del Consiglio dei Ministri*), is Italy's head of government. The Prime Minister and the cabinet are appointed by the President of the Republic, but must pass a vote of confidence in Parliament to come into office. The incumbent Prime Minister is Paolo Gentiloni of the Democratic Party.

The prime minister is the President of the Council of Ministers—which holds effective executive power— and he must receive a vote of approval from it to execute most political activities. The office is similar to those in most other parliamentary systems, but the leader of the Italian government is not authorised to request the dissolution of the Parliament of Italy.

Another difference with similar offices is that the overall political responsibility for intelligence is vested in the President of the Council of Ministers. By virtue of that, the Prime Minister has exclusive power to: coordinate intelligence policies, determining the financial resources and strengthening national cyber security; apply and protect State secrets; authorise agents to carry out operations, in Italy or abroad, in violation of the law.

A peculiarity of the Italian Parliament is the representation given to Italian citizens permanently living abroad: 12 Deputies and 6 Senators elected in four distinct overseas constituencies. In addition, the Italian Senate is characterised also by a small number of senators for life, appointed by the President "for outstanding patriotic merits in the social, scientific, artistic or literary field". Former Presidents of the Republic are *ex officio* life senators.

Italy's three major political parties are the Lega Nord, Democratic Party and the Five Star Movement. During the 2018 general election these three parties won 614 out of 630 seats available in the Chamber of Deputies and 309 out of 315 in the Senate. Most of the seats were won by Luigi Di Maio's Five Star Movement with the rest going to Berlusconi's Forza Italia which formed a centre-right coalition with Matteo Silvani's Northern League and Giorgia Meloni's Brothers of Italy, beyond these the rest were taken by Matteo Renzi's Democratic Party along with Achammer and Panizza's South Tyrolean People's Party & Trentino Tyrolean Autonomist Party in a centre-left coalition and the independent Free and Equal party.

Law enforcement in Italy is an exclusive function of the State. While organisations and companies may have "security guards" (called "Guardie Giurate"), investigation and police duties are carried by national law enforcement bodies. In a general overview, the most common definition and idea of "police" can be applied only to two forces, Polizia di Stato and Carabinieri: both of them have full power in the investigation, public safety duties, road patrols and others. Nevertheless, other forces exist, focusing on specifical and distinguished duties (for example the finance and economy police called "Guardia di Finanza" [roughly, Customs, Excise and Fraud Squad - see below], the prison guards agency of "Polizia Penitenziaria" and, up to 2016, when it was absorbed in the Carabinieri, the environment and forestry police guard of "Guardia Forestale").

Italy divides law enforcement into Military and Civil forces, distinguishing each "agency" by duties and jurisdictions. All law enforcement officers are considered "Pubblico Ufficiale" [Public Functionary] and but not all officers belonging to police forces are "Agente di Pubblica Sicurezza" [Public Safety officer] as the latter gives the authority to arrest, investigate and patrol in the whole national territory and in all situations.

In a different way from other countries (such as the United States), Italy does not have multiple specialised agencies for immigration, drug, patrolling and etc, but each "subject" is investigated by a dedicated section of each national agency (as for example Polizia Stradale [highway patrol] is a section of "Polizia di Stato" with focus on road patrolling and various crimes committed on national and local roads.), making it easier to collaborate in the same investigation implying different sections.

All police are under the Ministero dell'Interno for the public order tasks (the highest police and public safety authority, which - through the Department of Public Safety - coordinates the enforcement. Locally, Polizia di Stato [National Police] is under the Authority of the Prefetto, who collaborates with the Questore (the local chief of Polizia di Stato, with technical jurisdiction on all forces) to organise law enforcement activities.

Borders and Maritime patrolling is a specifical duty of Guardia Costiera agency called "Corpo delle Capitanerie di Porto", but officers - who are in facts members of Italian Navy, have not full powers as Polizia or Carabinieri.

Working local and minor tasks, from traffic (in the minor cities and towns) to drug dealing and abusive camping or other (in major cities, as for Milan, Rome, Naples and others) municipal police can be found on duties. This means that each City or town has its own police department but the latter is limited in jurisdiction and duties: i.e. Local officers can control driver licences, respect of municipal laws and authorisations and investigations for robbery and little offences, but they can never form a "riot squad" or interfere with homicide or general investigation by Police and Carabinieri. Each Polizia Locale, in fact, is under the authority of the respective local mayor, but the officers' mandate is valid only during duty time and in the town borders, whereas Carabinieri, Polizia di Stato and Guardia di Finanza are always formally "on duty", even during leave and vacations.

During 2005 in Italy, the number of active police officers from all agencies totaled **324,339**, the highest number in the European Union both overall and per capita, twice the number of agents in the similarly sized United Kingdom.[1] However, in this numbers are included the members of the Arma dei Carabinieri, one of the four Italian Armed Forces, that does not only have a law enforcement role.

Political Parties

Italy's dramatic self-renewal transformed the political landscape between 1992 and 1997. Scandal investigations touched thousands of politicians, administrators, and businessmen; the shift from a proportional to majoritarian voting system--with the requirement to obtain a minimum of 4% of the national vote to obtain representation--also altered the political landscape.

Party changes were sweeping. The Christian Democratic party dissolved; the Italian People's Party and the Christian Democratic Center emerged. Other major parties, such as the Socialists, saw support plummet. A new populist, and free-market orientated movement, Forza Italia, gained wide support among moderate voters. The National Alliance broke from the neofascist Italian Social Movement. A trend toward two large coalitions--one on the center-left and the other on the center-right--emerged from the April 1995 regional elections. For the 1996 national elections, the center-left parties created the Olive Tree coalition while the center right united again under the Freedom Pole. The May 2001 elections ushered into power a refashioned center-right coalition dominated by Berlusconi's party, Forza Italia. The April 2006 elections returned the center-left to power under the Union coalition, a successor to the Olive Tree. Freedom House now sits in the opposition. This emerging bipolarity represents a major break from the fragmented, multi-party political landscape of the postwar era, although it appears to have reached a plateau, since efforts via referendums to further curtail the influence of small parties were defeated in 1999 and 2000.

The largest parties in the Chamber of Deputies are Olive Tree (31.3%), now a party within the broader Union coalition comprised of the Democrats of the Left, the Daisy Party, and the European Republican Movement; Forza Italia (23.7%); the National Alliance (12.3%); the Union of Christian and Center Democrats (6.8%);

and the Communist Refoundation Party (5.8%). Similar rankings generally apply in the Senate, in which the Olive Tree and Forza Italia are the dominant parties.

ECONOMY

Currency	Euro (EUR), except in Campione d'Italia (CHF)
Fiscal year	calendar year
Trade organisations	EU, WTO (via EU membership), OECD
	Statistics
GDP	$2.129 trillion (2014 estimate by IMF)(nominal) 8th $2.065 trillion (2014 estimate by IMF) (PPP; 12th)
GDP rank	8th (nominal) / 12th (PPP)
GDP growth	▼-0.1% Q3 2014
GDP per capita	▲$35,512 nominal (2014)$34,455 PPP (2014)
GDP by sector	agriculture: 1.8%; industry: 25%; services: 73% (2010 est.)
Inflation (CPI)	0,6 CPI, (april . ISTAT estimate)
Population below poverty line	8% 4,814,000 people below absolute line of poverty (about €520/month)
Gini coefficient	36
Labour force	▲22.4 million (est.)
Labour force by occupation	services (68%), industry (28%), agriculture (4%)
Unemployment	12.3% (ISTAT estimate)
Average gross salary	▲€2,378/$3,270,
Average net salary	▲€1,898/$2,610, Average net income monthly €1472/$2003 (2014)
Main industries	tourism, communications, machinery, steel, chemicals, pharmaceuticals, food processing, textiles, motor vehicles, home appliances, clothing, fashion
Ease-of-doing-business rank	73rd
	External
Exports	▲$483 billion (est.) (+3.2%)
Export goods	engineering products, textiles and clothing, production machinery, motor vehicles, transport equipment, chemicals; food, beverages and tobacco; minerals, and nonferrous metals
Main export partners	Germany 13%, France 11%, United States 6.6%, Switzerland 6%, United Kingdom 5%, Spain 4.8%,
Imports	▲$470 billion
Import goods	engineering products, chemicals, transport equipment, energy products, minerals and nonferrous metals, textiles and clothing; food, beverages, and tobacco
Main import partners	Germany 15.7%, France 9%, China 7%, Netherlands 6%, Spain 4.8%, Belgium 4%,
FDI stock	▲$369.5 billion
Gross external debt	▲$2.493 trillion
	Public finances
Public debt	▲134,6 % of GDP
Revenues	$956.6 billion
Expenses	$1.014 trillion
Economic aid	donor: $2.48 billion, 0.15% of GDP
Credit rating	Standard & Poor's: BBB- (Domestic)

	BBB- (Foreign) AAA (T&C Assessment) Outlook: Stable Moody's: BAA2 Outlook: Stable Fitch: BBB+ Outlook: Stable
Foreign reserves	▲US$152.689 billion

Italy has a diversified industrial economy with high gross domestic product (GDP) per capita and developed infrastructure. According to the International Monetary Fund (see List of countries by past and future GDP (nominal)) Italy in 2014 is the 8th-largest economy in the world, the 4th-largest in Europe and in the EU and the 3rd-largest in the Eurozone in terms of nominal GDP, and the 12th-largest economy in the world and 5th-largest in Europe in terms of purchasing power parity (PPP) GDP.

Italy is a member of the G7 and the G8 industrialized nations, the European Union and the OECD.

The Italian economy has changed dramatically since the end of World War II. From an agriculturally based economy, it has developed into an industrial state ranked as the world's sixth-largest market economy. Italy belongs to the Group of Eight (G-8) industrialized nations; it is a member of the European Union and the Organization for Economic Cooperation and Development (OECD).

Italy has few natural resources. With much land unsuited for farming, Italy is a net food importer. There are no substantial deposits of iron, coal, or oil. Proven natural gas reserves, mainly in the Po Valley and offshore Adriatic, constitute the country's most important mineral resource. Most raw materials needed for manufacturing and more than 80% of the country's energy sources are imported. Italy's economic strength is in the processing and the manufacturing of goods, primarily in small and medium-sized family-owned firms. Its major industries are precision machinery, motor vehicles, chemicals, pharmaceuticals, electric goods, and fashion and clothing.

Italy is in the midst of a slow economic recovery from the aftermath of September 11, 2001, and the global economy's tailspin. While Italy's economic growth averaged only 0.66% for the last five years, 2006 GDP growth should reach 1.5%, largely due to growth in the Euro zone area.

Italy continues to grapple with excessive budget deficits and high public debt--4.3% and 108% of GDP expected in 2006, respectively. Italy joined the European Monetary Union in 1998 by signing the Stability and Growth Pact, and as a condition of this Euro Zone membership, Italy must keep its budget deficit beneath a 3% ceiling. In June 2006, the European Commission warned Italy it must bring the deficit down to that level by 2007. Italy must either cut its spending dramatically and/or raise new revenue; most such measures will require real political will and buy-in from the Italian public. The rise in public debt has also caused some credit rating agencies to lower Italy's sovereign debt rating.

Italy's closest trade ties are with the other countries of the European Union, with whom it conducts about 54.4% of its total trade (2002 data). Italy's largest EU trade partners, in order of market share, are Germany (15.5%), France (11.6%), and the United Kingdom (5.9%). Italy continues to grapple with the effects of globalization, where certain countries (notably China) have eroded the Italian lower-end industrial product sector.

The Italian economy is also affected by a large underground economy--worth some 27% of Italy's GDP. This production is not subject, of course, to taxation and thus remains a source of lost revenue to the local and central government.

U.S.-ITALY ECONOMIC RELATIONS

The United States and Italy cooperate closely on major economic issues, including within the G-8. With a large population and a high per capita income, Italy was the United States' eleventh-largest trading partner in 2005, with total bilateral trade of $42.5 billion comprised of exports to Italy totaling $11.5 billion and imports from Italy worth $31.0 billion. The U.S. ran a $19.5 billion deficit with Italy in 2005, up from $17.4 billion in 2004. Part of this imbalance has been due to a strong dollar. Significant changes are occurring in the composition of this trade. Value-added products such as office machinery and aircraft are becoming important U.S. exports to Italy. U.S. foreign direct investment in Italy at the end of 2004 exceeded $33.3 billion.

Labor

Unemployment is a regional issue in Italy--low in the north, high in the south. The overall national rate is at its lowest level since 1992. Chronic problems of inadequate infrastructure, corruption, and organized crime act as disincentives to investment and job creation in the south. A significant underground economy absorbs substantial numbers of people, but they work for low wages and without standard social benefits and protections. Women and youth have significantly higher rates of unemployment than do men.

Unions claim to represent 40% of the work force. Most Italian unions are grouped in four major confederations: the General Italian Confederation of Labor (CGIL), the Italian Confederation of Workers' Unions (CISL), the Italian Union of Labor (UIL), and the General Union of Labor (UGL), which together claim 35% of the work force. These confederations formerly were associated with important political parties or currents, but they have evolved info fully autonomous, professional bodies. The CGIL, CISL, and UIL are affiliated with the International Confederation of Free Trade Unions (ICFTU) and customarily coordinate their positions before confronting management or lobbying the government. The confederations have had an important consultative role on national social and economic issues. Among their major agreements are a 4-year wage moderation agreement signed in 1993, a reform of the pension system in 1995, and an employment pact, introducing steps for labor market flexibility in economically depressed areas, in 1996. In April 2002, unions held a general strike to protest against labor reforms proposed by Prime Minister Berlusconi.

Agriculture

Italy's agriculture is typical of the division between the agricultures of the northern and southern countries of the European Union. The northern part of Italy produces primarily grains, sugarbeets, soybeans, meat, and dairy products, while the south specializes in producing fruits, vegetables, olive oil, wine, and durum wheat. Even though much of its mountainous terrain is unsuitable for farming, Italy has a large work force (1.4 million) employed in farming. Most farms are small, with the average farm only seven hectares.

FOREIGN RELATIONS

Italy was a founding member of the European Community--now the European Union (EU). Italy was admitted to the United Nations in 1955 and is a member and strong supporter of the North Atlantic Treaty Organization (NATO), the Organization for Economic Cooperation and Development (OECD), the General Agreement on Tariffs and Trade/World Trade Organization (GATT/WTO), the Organization for Security and Cooperation in Europe (OSCE), and the Council of Europe. It chaired the CSCE (the forerunner of the OSCE) in 1994, the EU in 1996, and the G-8 in 2001 and served as EU president from July to December 2003.

Italy firmly supports the United Nations and its international security activities. Italy actively participated in and deployed troops in support of UN peacekeeping missions in Somalia, Mozambique, and East Timor and provides critical support for NATO and UN operations in Bosnia, Kosovo, and Albania. Italy deployed 1,000 Alpini troops to Afghanistan in support of Operation Enduring Freedom (OEF) in February 2003. Italy also supports international efforts to reconstruct and stabilize Iraq through its military contingent of some 2,800 troops, as well as humanitarian workers and other officials. The troops remain in Iraq under UN mandate and at the request of the sovereign Iraqi Government.

The Italian Government seeks to obtain consensus with other European countries on various defense and security issues within the EU as well as NATO. European integration and the development of common defense and security policies will continue to be of primary interest to Italy.

U.S.-ITALY RELATIONS

The United States enjoys warm and friendly relations with Italy. Italy is a leading partner in the war against terrorism. The two are NATO allies and cooperate in the United Nations, in various regional organizations, and bilaterally for peace, prosperity, and security. Italy has worked closely with the United States and others on such issues as NATO and UN operations as well as with assistance to Russia and the New Independent States; the Middle East peace process; multilateral talks; Somalia and Mozambique peacekeeping; and combating drug trafficking, trafficking in women and children, and terrorism.

Under longstanding bilateral agreements flowing from NATO membership, Italy hosts important U.S. military forces at Vicenza and Livorno (army); Aviano (air force); and Sigonella, Gaeta, and Naples--home port for the U.S. Navy Sixth Fleet. The United States has about 16,000 military personnel stationed in Italy. Italy hosts the NATO War College in Rome.

Italy remains a strong and active transatlantic partner which, along with the United States, has sought to foster democratic ideals and international cooperation in areas of strife and civil conflict. Toward this end, the Italian Government has cooperated with the United States in the formulation of defense, security, and peacekeeping policies.

Principal U.S. Officials
chief of mission: Ambassador Lewis EISENBERG (since 4 October 2017);

Deputy Chief of Mission--Anna Borg

Economic Affairs--Kathleen Reddy
Political Affairs--David Pearce
Consular Affairs--Barbara Cummings
Public Affairs--John P. Dwyer
Commercial Affairs--vacant
Regional Security Affairs--Nancy Rolph-O'Donnell
Agricultural Section--Geoffrey Wiggin
Defense Attache--Col. Rolf Yngve

Consular Posts
Consul General, Florence--Nora Dempsey
Consul General, Milan--Deborah Graze
Consul General, Naples--Suneta Halliburton

The U.S. Embassy in Italy is located at Via Veneto 119, Rome (tel. (39)(06) 46741.

TRAVEL AND BUSINESS INFORMATION

The U.S. Department of State's Consular Information Program provides Consular Information Sheets, Travel Warnings, and Public Announcements.

Consular Information Sheets exist for all countries and include information on entry requirements, currency regulations, health conditions, areas of instability, crime and security, political disturbances, and the addresses of the U.S. posts in the country. **Travel Warnings** are issued when the State Department recommends that Americans avoid travel to a certain country.

Public Announcements are issued as a means to disseminate information quickly about terrorist threats and other relatively short-term conditions overseas that pose significant risks to the security of American travelers. Free copies of this information are available by calling the Bureau of Consular Affairs at 202-647-5225 or via the fax-on-demand system: 202-647-3000. Consular Information Sheets and Travel Warnings also are available on the Consular Affairs Internet home page: http://travel.state.gov. Consular Affairs Tips for Travelers publication series, which contain information on obtaining passports and planning a safe trip abroad, are available on the Internet and hard copies can be purchased from the Superintendent of Documents, U.S. Government Printing Office, telephone: 202-512-1800; fax 202-512-2250.

Emergency information concerning Americans traveling abroad may be obtained from the Office of Overseas Citizens Services at (202) 647-5225. For after-hours emergencies, Sundays and holidays, call 202-647-4000.

The National Passport Information Center (NPIC) is the U.S. Department of State's single, centralized public contact center for U.S. passport information. Telephone: 1-877-4USA-PPT (1-877-487-2778). Customer service representatives and operators for TDD/TTY are available Monday-Friday, 8:00 a.m. to 8:00 p.m., Eastern Time, excluding federal holidays.

Travelers can check the latest health information with the U.S. Centers for Disease Control and Prevention in Atlanta, Georgia. A hotline at 877-FYI-TRIP (877-394-8747) and a web site at http://www.cdc.gov/travel/index.htm give the most recent health advisories, immunization recommendations or requirements, and advice on food and drinking water safety for regions and countries. A booklet entitled Health Information for International Travel (HHS publication number CDC-95-8280) is available from the U.S. Government Printing Office, Washington, DC 20402, tel. (202) 512-1800.

Information on travel conditions, visa requirements, currency and customs regulations, legal holidays, and other items of interest to travelers also may be obtained before your departure from a country's embassy and/or consulates in the U.S. (for this country, see "Principal Government Officials" listing in this publication). U.S. citizens who are long-term visitors or traveling in dangerous areas are encouraged to register their travel via the State Department's travel registration web site at https://travelregistration.state.gov or at the Consular section of the U.S. embassy upon arrival in a country by filling out a short form and sending in a copy of their passports. This may help family members contact you in case of an emergency.

ITALY IN THE MEDITERRANEAN AND IN EUROPE

GEOGRAPHICAL POSITION AND GEOPOLITICAL FUNCTION

Italy is situated on the southern border of Europe and her peninsula, with surrounding islands, reaches almost to the coast of Africa. Just because of this geographical position, Italy has direct contact with the main ethnic and cultural areas of the Old World (neo-Latin, Germanic and Slav-Balkan) as well as, through the North Africa countries, with the world of Arab-Islamic civilization.

Consequently, while remaining firmly anchored in the world of western or European civilization, which was the direct heir of the Graeco-Roman culture that developed and flourished on this very peninsula for over a millennium, Italy seems to stretch out na turally towards the opposite shore of the Mediterranean, practically dividing its western and eastern basins. Thus Italy can be considered the most logical link between Europe and the peoples of Africa and Asia, bordering as they do on the same sea and sh aring over many centuries both historical events and cultural influences.

Still today, with the present international situation of unrest and open conflict in some Mediterranean areas, Italy, with her renewed productivity and a policy of peaceful co-existence with all countries, provides a source of stability and moderation wit hin the political context of this part of the Old World.

EXTENT AND BORDERS

The territory of the Italian Republic covers 301,278 sq km (including the enclave of Campione in Switzerland and the states of the Republic of San Marino and of the Vatican City, measuring together 61 sq km). This is equal to a 35th part of Europe and slightly more than a five-hundredth of all the world's landmass. In Europe, excluding the Soviet Union, Italy's territorial extent is cons iderably smaller than that of France, Spain and Sweden, while only being slightly less than that of Finland, Norway and Poland.

Italy lies between the northern latitudes of 47°05'29" (m 2,837 from the Testa Gemella Occidentale/Westl. Zwillingsköpfe in the Aurine Alps on the Austrian border) and 35°39'26" (Punta Pesce Spada on the island of Lampedusa to the south of Sicily), and the eastern longitudes from Greenwich of 6°37'32" (m 3,178 from the minor peak north of the Rocca Bernauda in the northern Cottian Alps, upper Val di Susa, on the French border) and 18°31'13" (Capo d'Otranto on the Salentina Peninsula).

The territory of the Republic of Italy coincides amolst precisely with the geographically defined Italian region. Its northern border corresponds with the Alpine watershed and it also physically includes the Istrian peninsula, the island of Corsica, the S wiss territories of Canton Ticino, Val Bregaglia and Val di Poschiavo and the Maltese Islands, while excluding Pantelleria and the Pelagian Islands (Lampedusa and Lampione), which emerge from the African continental platform. Altogether, the Italian physi cal region measures some 324,000 sq km.

Politically the territory of the Italian Republic has its northern border along the Alpine arc. This touches on France, Switzerland, Austria and Yugoslavia and is some 1,900 km long, generally following the watershed of the mountain chain except where it moves far away as in the Swiss and Yugoslavian sections. The remaining Italian territorial limits are maritime and, except for the territorial seas, they have usually been fixed with the countries concerned: Yugoslavia and Albania in the Adriatic, Greece in the Ionian, Malta, Libya and Tunisia in the Sea of Sicily, Tunisia and Algeria in the Channel of Sardinia, Spain in the Sea of Sardinia and France in the Ligurian and upper Tyrrhenian Seas.

The structure of the Italian territory differs considerably. Besides the continental section (Alps and Po-Venetian Plain), there is a long and indented peninsula that is almost completely occupied by the Apennine chain, the two large islands (Sicily and Sardinia) marking the borders of the Tyrrhenian Sea and many other minor island groups (Tuscan Archipelago, Lipari Islands, etc.). This produces long distances between the country 's extremities. In fact, along the Trieste parallel this is of some 540 km, while along that of Otranto, to the western coast of Sardinia, it is some 845 km. Finally, the greatest latitudinal distance is measured along the meridian of the Pelagian Islands for some 1,290 km.

It should also be noted that the geographical form of Italy favours the maritime. Indeed, the most inland zones of the peninsula are little more than 100 km from the sea (the peninsula's widest point, between the Argentario Promontory and Mount Conero, do es not exceed 240 km) and on the two largest islands is rarely greater than 50 km. Even for continental Italy the zone furthest from the sea (the Spluga Pass in the Lombard Alps) is only just 230 km away. Finally to the land borders should be added some 7 ,500 km of coasts, over half of which belong just to the islands. In particular, Sicily has a perimeter of 1,115 km, Sardinia 1336 km and the minor islands 1,734 km.

THE REPUBLIC OF SAN MARINO

This tiny ancient European State, whose earliest statutes date back to 1263, was recognized by Napoleon in 1797 and by the Congress of Vienna in 1815. San Marino maintains diplomatic and consular relations with a number of European and American countries, mints its own coins, issues its own postage stamps and grants honours of merit. Legislative power is exercised by the Grand Council of 60 members and the executive by a State Congress divided into ministries, renewed with each legislature. The Capitani Reggenti have a representative mandate and are elected twice yearly, in April and October.

Surface: 60.57 sq.km.

Population: 19,149 (1976 census), 21,240 (1982 estimate), of which 4,344 in San Marino, the capital, on Mount Titano, the remainder living in various small localities. Some 20,000 San Marino citizens live abroad.

Language: Italian (the local dialect is Romagnolo).

Religion: Roman Catholic (diocese of San Marino-Montefeltro).

Economic resources: Agriculture (wheat, wine), industry and tourism (3,500,000 tourists in 1980). Vehicles: 16,085 (1984), of which 14,794 are cars. Currency: Italian lira.

THE VATICAN

With the Treaty of 11th February 1929, Italy recognized the right of the Holy See to full powers and exclusive rights with sovereign jurisdiction over the Vatican and all it contains, as presently constituted, thus creating the Vatican City. Although St. Peter's Square lies within Vatican City, it is normally open to the public and comes under Italian police authority.

Surface: 0.44 sq.km.

Population: 731 (1978).

The Pontiff: John Paul II (Karol Wojtyla), the 266th pope, born in Wadowice (Poland), became Pope on 16th October 1978 and head of the Roman Catholic Church, which he governs flanked by the Sacred College of Cardinals.

The Pope is elected by an assembly of cardinals in secret conclave, under strictly observed severe rules, on a majority vote of two thirds plus one.

The Sacred College of Cardinals: consists of 146 cardinals (August 1986), of whom 112 are electors.

Secretary of State: Cardinal Angelo Sodano.

Vehicles: 235, including 194 cars (1984).

ITALIAN ADMINISTRATIVE STRUCTURE: REGIONS AND PROVINCES

ABRUZZO

Abruzzo holds a record: 30 per cent of its territory is protected by environmental legislation. No other region in Europe can boast as much. Not without good reason is it known as "the region of parks". Three national parks, a regional park and many protected sites and nature reserves. In a region like this, it seems natural that the regional capital is called L'Aquila ('The Eagle').

Dominated by an imposing sixteenth-century castle (which houses the National Museum of Abruzzo), L'Aquila has splendid civic and religious monuments from the medieval and renaissance eras. On the coast of Abruzzo (which vaunts popular bathing areas) one of the most popular locations is Pescara, birthplace of Gabriele D'Annunzio. The house where he was born is now a small and evocative museum.

At Chieti there is an important National Archaeological Museum, well-known for the modernity and effectiveness of its exhibitions (for which it has won prizes). The "show piece" of the museum is the Warrior of Capestrano, a funerary statue of the sixth century B.C., found in the province of L'Aquila in 1934.At Teramo the stupendous fifteenth-century Antepedium (inside the cathedral) made by the great goldsmith of Abruzzo, Nicola da Guardiagrele, should not be missed. But Abruzzo is surprisingly rich in architectural and artistic treasures, almost as much as it is full of natural treasures and folk traditions (such as the "festival of the serpents" in Cocullo, which brings thousands of people to this tiny village on the first Sunday of May).

APULIA

In Bari - Apulia's capital city - they say: "If Paris was by the sea, it would be like a small Bari". Presumption or arrogance? No, just pride (for which these people are famous, apart from their strong sense of humour). The pride of living in a city that successfully blends art and deep historic roots with a very modern spirit of business enterprise. Traditionally the "land's end" that bridged Italy with the worlds of Greece and the Middle East, Bari enjoyed its "golden age" during medieval times. The Cathedral and Church of St. Nicholas with their Romanesque forms, bear majestic witness to that period. Traces of the ancient trading and social contacts with the Greek world can be seen in the Archaeological Museum.

The blend of history and art that characterizes the monuments of Bari is reflected in many areas of Apulia, where you will often discover cathedrals built during the medieval era such as in Brindisi, Andria, Barletta, Trani, Ruvo di Puglia, Lucera, Troia, Manfredonia, Otranto, and Gallipoli. Belonging to another era yet equally precious and extraordinary is the flourishing of the baroque architecture in the town of Lecce. In Taranto, the Archaeological Museum has sections of the more remote past. And Alberobello, in the province of Bari, is the capital of the Trulli, singular domains dating back to pre-history no less. As to nature's wonders, Apulia offers an extraordinary intermingling of mountains, woods and uncontaminated sea, for which the promontory of the Gargano in the province of Foggia is so well renowned.

BASILICATA

A piece of prehistory in the modern world.. This is found at Matera, the second main city of Basilicata, and UNESCO, the UN organisation that deals with education, science and culture, has proclaimed it to be the "heritage of humanity". It is the "caves of Matera", one of the most peculiar, ancient and extraordinary human settlements in the world, which have drawn the attention of scholars and artists from all over the world (the Italian writer Carlo Levi spoke of them in his famous book "Christ stopped at Eboli").

In the "caves", the houses have been dug out of the tufa rock and the walls constructed with the excavated material. Inhabited until recently, the "caves" are now empty and have become the object of projects of cultural and touristic revaluation and restoration. A visit to the "caves of Matera" is a truly unique experience. But it is not the only reason to come to this small, secluded, and beautiful region boarded by two seas: the Tyrrhenian and the Ionian. In Basilicata there are Greek ruins (Metaponto), medieval churches and castles (Melfi, Lagopesole), beautiful beaches (Maratea), and unspoilt countryside (Basilicata shares the splendid park of Pollino with Calabria).

And Matera does not only have its "caves": the remarkable blend of Romanesque and Baroque styles in the Church of S. Francesco, for example, is also fascinating. Finally, why not plan a visit to Venosa, birthplace of the great and wise Latin poet Horace? Here, among other attractions, it is possible to admire the medieval Abbey of SS. Trinità and other interesting monuments. In the regional capital, Potenza, ancient and recent earthquakes have seriously damaged the historic centre. But the archaeological museum merits a visit.

CALABRIA

Eternal gratitude is due to the Riace Bronzes, the two stupendous Greek statues dredged from the sea and exhibited, from the early 1980s, in the Museo Nazionale della Magna Grecia in Reggio Calabria. Thanks to the irresistible attraction exercised by the two masterpieces (one of which is attributed to Fidia, the master Greek sculptor of the fifth century B. C.), hundreds of thousands of visitors arrived in Calabria. And in this way many of them finally discovered, as a joyous and marvellous surprise, a beautiful country, an unspoilt sea, a lush and sometimes wild countryside, with numerous architectural and artistic masterpieces of unexpected quality.

Extraordinary, fascinating Calabria, a land of a thousand surprises. Of exquisite beauty, for example, is the Codex Purpureus, a rare sixth-century Greek gospel conserved in the Museo Diocesano in Rossano, with silver lettering and illustrated with splendid elegant figures and religious scenes. A breathtaking surprise, for those who see it for the first time, is the picturesque and spectacular coast of Tropea, on the Tyrrhenian sea (Calabria is also boarded by the Ionian). But it bears repeating that in Calabria, the surprises never end.

CAMPANIA

The Neapolitan dialect is said to be the best known of the Italian language in the world. This comes as no surprise: music, as we know, is a universal language and it is easy to remember the accompanying lyrics. And Neapolitan songs are known throughout the world. Who has not heard or sung "O sole mio" at least once? And yet, the diffusion of the Neapolitan dialect hides another truth: Neapolitan is not a dialect, it is a true and proper language that expresses and transmits an autonomous culture, formed and consolidated over the centuries. Naples, in short, has a history apart.

And it is for this that it is so well-known, beloved and visited: because there is no other city like it in the world, with its inimitable characteristics. It fascinates and conquers whoever stays therefore even for a short time. And how could it be otherwise when confronted with the beauty of its sea, the fascination of its history, the good humour of its people, and the beauty of the innumerable architectural treasures of all eras and all styles that grace the city?

A fascination and ability to enchant, throughout the whole of Campania, the region of which Naples is the capital: in the splendid Neapolitan islands of Capri, Ischia, Procida, on the spectacular Amalfi coast, in the magnificent Reggia di Caserta, in the archaeological site of Paestum (in the province of Salerno) and so many other beautiful centres of Campania. The ancients called this land "felix" (happiness) with good reason.

EMILIA-ROMAGNA

The porticoes that shelter and shade your way through the streets of the historic centre of Bologna; the infinite, multicoloured sea of umbrellas on the sunny beaches of Romagna. The modern, dynamic and wealthy city, which at the same time is capable of preserving its "human face". The lengthy coastline, crowded with tourists drawn by the irresistible trinity sun-sea-fun. Is this Emilia-Romagna? Yes, it is all this. And much much more, starting from its extraordinary historic, artistic and cultural heritage.

One of the richest regions of Italy, Emilia-Romagna is a gigantic treasure house filled with architectural gems and artistic masterpieces, with ancient and famous universities, and modern centres of artistic and cultural learning. In Bologna, the home of the most ancient Italian university (eleventh century), the monuments of great artistic value are truly countless. Here we shall mention just the two ancient spectacular towers of the Asinelli and the Garisenda, both leaning, and Piazza Maggiore, with its great medieval buildings, and the gothic duomo of S. Petronio, where Charles V was crowned emperor in 1530.

Outside Bologna, you should not miss the Byzantine masterpieces of Ravenna, the medieval baptistery of Benedetto Antelami in Parma, the Tempio Malatestiano in Rimini, the Romanesque church of S.Mercuriale in Forlì, the ancient Palazzo comunale in Piacenza, the seventeenth-century Sanctuary of the Madonna della Ghiara in Reggio Emilia, the splendid Galleria Estense in Modena, or the harmonious and well-preserved historic centre of Ferrara. And 'enjoy your meal!'. Why? Go into any restaurant of Emilia-Romagna and you will understand.

FRIULI-VENEZIA GIULIA

The last Doge of Venice, Ludovico Manin, retired to this area at the end of the eighteenth century when the Venetian Republic fell to the blows of Napoleon Bonaparte. These days, whoever visits Villa Manin in the province of Udine, detects a hint of twilight in the air, almost as if the memory of the old gentleman who came here to pass the autumn of his life was influencing the visitors and inducing a melancholic mood in them. But this is a pleasant sensation, that leads to a more intimate and intense kind of aesthetic enjoyment.

The same sensation recurs all over this beautiful and severe border region, where almost every town boasts a museum (those of Udine, Tolmezzo, Pordenone, Cividale del Friuli, Gorizia, and Aquileia are particularly important and interesting), and is able to surprise with the plurality of architectural styles (in the centre of Udine the Venetian Gothic of the Palazzo del Comune faces the beautiful twentieth-century Art Deco Caffé Contarena) and cultural attractions (at Udine again, there are galleries of historic and modern art).

Highly suggestive is the Basilica in Aquileia, now a small town but once an important city of the Roman Empire. Trieste, in Venezia Giulia, the most "middle-European" of Italian cities, rich in history and culture, with its important ancient and modern artistic heritage, has been loved and represented by great literary figures (James Joyce, Italo Svevo, Umberto Saba and many others). Grado in the province of Gorizia is the favourite of many tourists who regularly return for its sea and particularly healthy climate.

LATIUM

The regional capital of Latium is Rome. Everybody knows it: the pull of the Eternal City is great and irresistible, the capital of the Christian world, the seat of the Papacy, the incomparable home of architectural and artistic masterpieces of the ancient world. Is it possible to resist the fascination of Rome? It may be difficult, but why not try to spend a few days "exploring" Latium? In this way you would discover a region of fascinating nature and environment, with an extraordinary variety of landscape: wide beaches, great pinewoods, mountains like Terminillo (an excellent ski resort), gentle hills and expansive plains. A region rich in artistic monuments that bring to mind the long and extraordinary history of this region in the most immediate fashion.

At Tarquinia, Cerveteri and Tuscania, necropolises and museums bear evidence of ancient and mysterious Etruscan people (seventh to sixth centuries B.C.) who ruled central Italy before the rise of Rome. There are countless testimonies of the Roman and later historical eras outside Rome, in the other provinces of Latium and in the local centres: Rieti, Viterbo, Latina and Frosinone.

It is enough to think of the splendid and grandiose Villa Adriana in Tivoli (where the renaissance Villa d'Este can also be found), the seventeenth-century Palazzo Barberini in Palestrina, and the Cathedral in Anagni. The same grandiose style of the Roman religion seems to be projected and duplicated outside Rome: in the abbeys of Montecassino, Casamari, and Fossanova and in the monasteries of Subiaco, places dear to Saint Benedict of Norcia. Latium, therefore, is not just Rome. And Rome is also Latium.

LIGURIA

A spectacular land of mountains descending sharply to the sea. Mountains and cliffs that seem to rise directly out of the Tyrrhenian Sea, in the far northern reaches of the Mediterranean . This is the dominant landscape of Liguria, fascinating and breathtaking, which induces an intensity of emotions and sensations in the visitor that will never leave during a tour through this region, so full of historic memories and a dynamic and severe (the mythical Genoese thrift) participation in the modern world.

The regional capital is Genoa, one of the main ports of the Mediterranean, the birthplace of Christopher Columbus, the great navigator who discovered America. A powerful marine city since the Middle Ages, Genoa preserves the traces of its great history to a remarkable extent. Imposing buildings, sumptuous aristocratic houses and great churches testify to the splendour of the past and integrate perfectly with the fabric of the modern city. In the other provinces of Liguria (Imperia and the other two important port cities of the region, La Spezia and Savona) there are countless natural and artistic attractions.

The peninsula of Portofino and the Cinque Terre are exceptional examples of lush and intact Mediterranean landscape; just as Portovenere is a small, exemplary jewel of the Mediterranean coast and Sanremo (where the vastly hugely Festival of the Italian Song is held in the casino every year) is one of most typical and famous seaside towns in Italy. Among the many monuments of great historical-artistic worth, we will limit ourselves to the example of the splendid Benedictine abbey of S. Fruttuoso, in Camogli. The pleasure of discovering the others is yours.

LOMBARDY

The richest, most highly developed and most densely populated region of Italy. And it is precisely for this that it is one of most surprising and unexpected for the tourist who arrives there knowing little of its historic, architectural, artistic and natural heritage. Let us take Milan, the great city of industry and commerce. Here everything that is modern and advanced finds its home: from technological innovation to fashion, from advertising to design, from ways of life to political “experiments”. Milan sets the trend. Yet, beneath its thick aspect of a dynamic and modern metropolis projected towards the future, Milan conceals extraordinary architectural and artistic treasures.

There is only the embarrassment of choice: the Duomo, the Castello Sforzesco, the La Scala theatre and the Brera picture gallery. And in the rest of Lombardy there are many splendid natural landscapes (the lakes, the Stelvio national park), and monuments and works of art of considerable value. At Monza, Varese, Como, Bergamo, Brescia, Lodi, Cremona, and Pavia, every era has made its cultural and artistic mark: in the urban structures, in the churches, in the civic buildings. >From the Romanesque to the Gothic, from the Renaissance to the Baroque, up to the most daring and innovative architectural and artistic solutions of the modern and contemporary eras: Lombardy boasts an impressive cultural and artistic heritage. And many people have yet to discover all this.

MARCHE

It is a matter of fact: Italy possesses the most remarkable artistic and cultural heritage in the world. And this is not all: its heritage is not just to be found in the great artistic cities, but is diffuse, “spread” throughout national territory as in no other country. The proof? Le Marche. A region in which a rich and varied countryside (the Adriatic sea, with its flat and sandy coast interrupted at intervals by rugged, rocky precipices; the harmonious agricultural landscape of its gentle hills; the deep and mysterious caves; the protected areas of natural beauty) is enriched with towns, villages, palaces, and religious buildings, all of them of important architectural and artistic value.

This is the case with the cathedral of Ancona, the regional capital and an important Adriatic port, or the cathedral of Pesaro. In Urbino, the Ducal Palace is a stupefying testimony of Renaissance grandeur. If you find yourself in Macerata during the summer it is an unpardonable not to book a seat at the majestic Sferisterio theatre for a play or musical performance. At Ascoli Piceno the blend of medieval and renaissance architecture (S. Francesco, Loggia dei Mercanti, Piazza del Popolo, etc.) arrests the attention of even the most distracted visitor. But in almost all the centres of Le Marche, even the smallest, there are many genuine artistic treasures. It is difficult to single out one without doing the others an injustice. We will make an exception for Recanati, the birthplace of the most beloved Italian poet of all time: the tender, bitter, unhappy and sublime Giacomo Leopardi (1798-1837). It is difficult not to feel moved when visiting the building where the poet spent his childhood and adolescence. An emotion which is felt, in a rather different way, by the visitor to the Santa Casa at Loreto, the destination for continuous crowds of pilgrims.

MOLISE

We shall hazard a slogan for this small and delightful region of the southern Adriatic: “Pay a visit, before it becomes fashionable”. Ah yes, because it is not difficult to predict the mass discovery of this land where everything still has the “flavour” of old times: from the splendid landscapes to the folk traditions, from the gastronomic attractions (fabulous cheeses, among the many other typical products) to the community life, from the hospitality of the inhabitants to the unspoilt sea, from the craftsmanship (the bells of Agnone are famous) to the quiet life in the villages of the interior.

It is a genuine pleasure to visit Molise. Starting from the regional capital, Campobasso, with its evocative tangle of historic streets and the fifteenth-century Monforte castle. At Termoli, the most important town of the province of Campobasso, the Mediterranean sunshine illuminates the ancient walls constructed by Emperor

Frederick and the massive sixteenth-century castle that looms over the sea. And everywhere in Molise, nature seems to keep watch over history, preserving memories.

As in the esplanade at Sepino, whose archaeological zone testifies to the ancient Roman colony, and in the vicinity of Pietrabbondante, where another interesting archaeological site recalls the remote existence of the Sannites, an ancient Italic people which dared to challenge and fight the power of Rome. And again, in the province of Isernia (the second city of Molise, with a beautiful Cathedral and fourteenth-century fountain), where the ancient abbey of S. Vincenzo al Volturno rises, solitary and majestic. A visit to Molise really is worthwhile, then. Before it becomes fashionable.

PIEDMONT

Turin, the regional capital of Piedmont, is reputed to be a magical city. And it can only be by magic that a city, considered to be the capital of Italian heavy industry (FIAT, one of the biggest automobile producers in the world, is based here), is also one of the main tourist attractions of Italy. Of course, there are good reasons for this. In the cathedral of Turin is kept the Holy Shroud, the ancient linen winding-sheet in which, according to the tradition, the body of Christ was wrapped after his crucifixion. At Turin there is also the Egyptian Museum, which contains an extraordinary collection of art from Ancient Egypt, and the Sabauda Gallery, full of masterpieces by great European artists.

Finally, at Turin there are some great monumental testimonies to the important role played by Piedmont in modern Italian history, as the seat of the House of Savoy (the reigning dynasty of Italy until 1946) and the first capital of the Kingdom of Italy: the Royal Palace, Palazzo Madama, the Mole Antonelliana, and the Royal Villa at Stupinigi. Throughout the rest of Piedmont, in the cities and provinces of Novara, Vercelli, Cuneo, Alessandria, and Asti, there are numerous civic and religious edifices which bear witness to the past: fortresses, basilicae, convents. Too many to give even a few examples. The natural landscape is splendid and varied: mountains, valleys, hills (the Langhe are famous as the setting for many stories by Cesare Pavese and Beppe Fenoglio, famous writers from Piedmont), lakes (Maggiore, d'Orta, di Viverone), and the Valgrande National Park. The gastronomic and wine-producing culture is rich and prestigious (some of the great Italian wines are from Piedmont).

SARDINIA

David Herbert Lawrence, the famous English writer, loved Italy. He travelled through it far and wide, often on foot. Sardinia inspired him and he dedicated his fine book to it, “Sea and Sardinia”, where he wrote: “Sardinia is left outside of time and history”. Of course, nowhere is left outside of time and history. But Lawrence's affirmation has a certain “poetic” truth, which captures and sums up a sensation which unites everyone who goes to Sardinia: the sensation of finding oneself in a region where the stunning beauty of nature, the limpid waters of the sea, the reserved and genuine character of the people, the exquisiteness of the many typical dishes, the ancient traditions, and the various expressions of Sardinian culture, will never change.

In spite of the twists and turns of history, and in spite of the passing of time. The Phoenicians, Carthaginians, Romans, Arabs, Byzantines and Spanish all arrived in this splendid island: Sardinia assimilated and reinterpreted all these different influences, integrated them into its own culture, but did not allow its heart, its own profound way of feeling, to be touched or changed.

Just as the physical heart of Sardinia, the area of Gennargentu (now a splendid National Park), has always been inaccessible to foreigners. All this gives a unique and original flavour to a holiday in Sardinia. The visitor feels reassured, “guaranteed” by this sensation of unchangeability: as if here, even in the most modern and built-up areas of the island, everything continues to be more authentic, more genuine than elsewhere. It is so at Cagliari as it is at Nuoro, at Sassari as it is at Oristano, at Alghero as it is on the Emerald Coast: wherever the tourist chooses to enjoy the magnificent sea or visit museums, to study the mystery of the “nuraghi” or to try a delicious typical dish. Wherever you are, you will feel that you are doing the right thing, at the right time, in the right place.

SICILY

Do you want to learn about Greece? So come to Sicily. It is a paradox, for sure, but only to a certain extent. The Greek cities of Sicily (Agrigento, Selinunte, Segesta, Syracuse, to mention the most important) were among the most beautiful of the Hellenic world. Nowadays, to visit the Valley of Temples at Agrigento or to watch a summer performance in the great Greek Theatre of Syracuse is to plunge yourself into the remote Hellenic past. And this is also true in Sicily for many other historical eras and civilisations, from the Spanish to the French. With the sole exception of Arab rule, which has left scarce physical testimony. Sicily is a book of history and art history, a compendium of the greatest civilisations and cultures of all time. A sunny island whose landscape is rich in contrasts, with a splendid coastline and a refined, delicious and varied cuisine of traditional flavours and exquisite aromas: the quintessence of Mediterranean culture, yet also dense with intellectual complexity and refinement, so well represented by the literary masterpieces of Luigi Pirandello, Giuseppe Tomasi di Lampedusa, Leonardo Sciascia, Gesualdo Bufalino and today, Andrea Camilleri.Every style, every movement in art is richly represented in Sicily. In cities like Palermo, Catania, Caltanissetta, Enna, Syracuse, Ragusa, Trapani, Agrigento, and Messina. And in small towns, like Cefalù, clustered around its Norman cathedral, or Noto, with its extraordinary Baroque cathedral, or Taormina, with its splendid Greco-Roman theatre.

TUSCANY

Modern Italian was born in Tuscany, from the great literature of Dante, Petrarch and Boccaccio. Can there be a deeper bond, a greater and more noble debt owed by a nation to one of its regions, than that of the common language? But the whole of Europe is in debt to Tuscany for its extraordinary contribution to European culture. It was in Tuscany between the fourteenth and sixteenth centuries that the great era of humanism and the Renaissance was born and developed, movements which radically renewed the culture and art of the time, leaving a profound and indelible mark on the common civilisation of Europe.

Of that extraordinary period of history, Tuscany, starting from the regional capital Florence, bears the greatest witness. Great works of civic and religious architecture, sculpture and paintings of extraordinary artistic value, testify to the creative genius of great artists: Leonardo da Vinci, Michelangelo Buonarroti, and Filippo Brunelleschi.

But Tuscany is not just Florence. There is Siena too, with its Piazza del Campo, the theatre each summer for its famous Palio. In the province of Siena (also famous for its great wines, such as Chianti and Brunello) Montepulciano and Pienza stand out, extraordinary gems of renaissance art, and San Gimignano, with its famous towers and turreted houses. Then there is Pisa with its world-famous leaning tower; Carrara, with its Duomo clad in the precious marble that takes the name of the city; and also Lucca, Pistoia, Arezzo, Grosseto, Livorno, and Prato, that all boast churches and other monuments of great architectural and artistic value. The beauties of the Tuscan countryside are innumerable. Above all, its landscape: the typical, unique, gentle and warm Tuscan countryside.

TRENTINO-ALTO ADIGE

Apples, for example. Or the green of the valleys, the candour of the snow-capped mountains, or perhaps the placid lakes. Trentino-High Adige/Südtirol is a region that irresistably evokes images of genuineness, naturalness and quiet. [I took out a sentence at this point the meaning of which baffles me]. So whether your holiday will be spent on the banks of Lake Garda, in the Stelvio National Park, among the spectacular Dolomites Mountains, in one of the many verdant valleys, or skiing at Madonna di Campiglio or San Martino di Castrozza, you are sure to find exactly what you're looking for: splendid nature, excellent hospitality, excellent food and wine. For lovers of culture and history, this area has much in store: the provinces of Trento or Bolzen (both provinces with their own special autonomy) have their fair share of historic sites and monuments to admire. Trento's Romanesque/Gothic Cathedral dating from 1545 to 1563 hosted the most famous Council of Christianity. Also, the town of Rovereto vaunts two particular points of architectural interest, both dating back to the 15th century: the Castle and the Church of St. Mark.

On the hill of Miravalle, the great Bell of those fallen in war provides the suitable occasion for a civil pilgrimage. In Bolzen, a city where Italian and German cultures seamlessly blend together, between the many architectural sites we recommend beginning from a "lesser" work, yet one which have a great symbolic interest: the Porta del Vino (the “Wine Gate”) inside Bolzen's gothic Cathedral, artistically engraved with images of peasants at the work between the vines. A homage to wine, which here is produced with excellent results – just one more reason for this region's appeal. Not to be missed is the Domenican Church, with its 14th century fresco on the "Triumph of Death" in clear Giotto style. Finally, Merano is a pretty and highly popular tourist centre with ancient porticoes and a suggestive historic centre.

UMBRIA

Perhaps it is the evocative nature of the place, or a certain enchanted air (we might almost say “mystic”) that you breathe to some extent everywhere, but sooner or later whoever visits Umbria ends up thinking: Saint Francis, that great, gentle, tender and poetic Saint of happiness and meekness could only have been born here in Umbria. In this place of ever-green, enchanted and radiant nature. In these towns the concept of “historic centre” seems inadequate and reductive, so widespread is the monumental and artistic component in the towns of Umbria. Perugia, for example, the regional capital. Just to describe it is to lose oneself in the richness, complexity and magnificence of its architectural and artistic treasures: from the Etruscan walls to the splendid Palazzo Gallenga, seat of the prestigious university for foreigners, and many other buildings and historic monuments that lead out from the central Piazza IV Novembre, itself dotted with architectural and artistic jewels such as the Great Fountain and the magnificent Palazzo dei Priori.

The same is true for splendid Gubbio, rich with Franciscan memories and monuments from the medieval and renaissance eras. And then Todi, Spello, Spoleto, Orvieto, Città di Castello and many other small towns: all magnificently enriched by monuments, palaces and churches of high artistic merit. Even Terni, a modern industrial city, boasts jewels such as the churches of S. Salvatore and S. Francesco and, close by, the masterpiece of nature that is the Waterfall of Marmore. Finally Assisi, the town where Saint Francis was born (as was Saint Clare, founder of the Poor Clares), one of the best-known Christian destinations frequented by pilgrims. You have to see it for yourself.

IMPORTANT BUSINESS CONTACTS

ITALIAN TRADE OFFICES IN THE US

ITALIAN TRADE COMMISSION – ATLANTA

233 Peachtree Street. N.E.
Peachtree Center - Harris Tower
Suite 2301
Atlanta, GA 30343
Tel.: 404/525-0660
Fax: 404/525-5112
atlanta@atlanta.ice.it

Antonio Avallone
Trade Commissioner

Geographic territory:
Alabama, Arkansas, Florida, Georgia, Louisiana, Mississippi, North Carolina, South Carolina, Oklahoma, Tennessee, Virginia, West Virginia and Jamaica

Products responsible for:

AGRICULTURAL MACHINERY AND EQUIPMENT
CARPETS
CONSTRUCTION AND EARTHMOVING EQUIPMENT
EDUCATIONAL AND DIDACTIC EQUIPMENT AND MATERIALS
FUNERARY ARTICLES
GIFTWARE
HANDICRAFTS
HOUSEHOLD APPLIANCES
HOUSEWARES
LEATHERWORKING AND SHOEMAKING EQUIPMENT

PAPER PRODUCTS
PET PRODUCTS
RECREATIONAL BOATING
COMMERCIAL SHIPBUILDING
RUGS
STATIONARY AND STATIONERS SUPPLIES
TEXTILE MACHINERY
TEXTILE FINISHING EQUIPMENT
TEXTILE LAUNDERING EQUIPMENT
UPHOLSTERY FABRICS
WOOD PRODUCTS
WOODWORKING EQUIPMENT

ITALIAN TRADE COMMISSION – CHICAGO

Italian Trade Commission - Chicago
401 North Michigan Avenue
Suite 3030
Chicago, IL 60611
Tel.: 312/670-4360
Fax: 312/670-5147
chicago@chicago.ice.it

Geographic territory: Illinois, Indiana, Iowa, Kansas, Kentucky, Michigan, Minnesota, Missouri, Nebraska, North Dakota, Ohio, South Dakota, , Wyoming

AUTOMOBILES
AUTOMOTIVE ACCESSORIES
AUTOMOTIVE PARTS
AUTOMOTIVE SERVICE STATION AND REPAIR EQUIPMENT
BOOKS AND PUBLISHING
CATERING EQUIPMENT
INSTITUTIONAL KITCHENS
INDUSTRIAL REFRIGERATION
ELECTRICAL GENERATORS AND TURBINES
FOOD PROCESSING EQUIPMENT
GASKETS & SEALS
HARDWARE AND TOOLS
INDUSTRIAL CLEANING MACHINERY
INDUSTRIAL OVENS
INDUSTRIAL PAINTING EQUIPMENT
INDUSTRIAL PUMPS
INDUSTRIAL SUBCONTRACTING
MACHINE TOOLS AND METALWORKING MACHINERY
MATERIALS HANDLING AND WAREHOUSING EQUIPMENT
MOTORS
PACKAGING PRODUCTS
PACKAGING EQUIPMENT
PAPERMAKING EQUIPMENT
PLASTICS AND RUBBER MANUFACTURING EQUIPMENT
PNEUMATIC AND HYDRAULIC EQUIPMENT
PRINTING MACHINERY
PROCESS CONTROLS
PROFESSIONAL DRY-CLEANING AND LAUNDRY EQUIPMENT
STEEL AND IRON
TRANSMISSIONS
VALVES AND TURBINES
VENDING MACHINES
WELDING EQUIPMENT
WINE INDUSTRY EQUIPMENT
WIRE MACHINERY

ITALIAN TRADE COMMISSION - LOS ANGELES

1801 Avenue of the Stars
Suite 700
Los Angeles, CA 90067
Tel.: 323/879-0950
Fax: 310/203-8335
losangeles@losangeles.ice.it
Fortunato Celi Zullo
Trade Commissioner

Geographic territory: Arizona, California, Colorado, Nevada, New Mexico, Texas, American Samoa, Guam, Palau, The Northern Marianas.

Products responsible for:

AMUSEMENT PARK EQUIPMENT, FITNESS CENTER
EQUIPMENT
AUDIO/VISUAL EQUIPMENT
BICYCLES
BEAUTY SALOON EQUIPMENT
BUILDING & CONSTRUCTION SUPPLIES
CERAMIC TILE MANUFACTURING EQUIPMENT
CHEMICAL AND PHARMACEUTICAL PLANT EQUIPMENT (EXCEPT PACKAGING)
CHEMICALS
CONSTRUCTION
COSMETICS
FERTILIZERS
FILM AND TELEVISION PRODUCTS AND SERVICES
FLAT GLASS
FRAMES AND EYEWEAR
GLASSWORKING MACHINERY
HEATING, VENTILATION AIR CONDITIONING AND
COOLING (HVAC)
JEWELRY (FINE AND COSTUME)
JEWELRY MAKING MACHINERY
KITCHEN AND BATHROOM PRODUCTS
LABORATORY EQUIPMENT
MARBLE AND GRANITE
MEDICAL APPLIANCES AND EQUIPMENT
MINERAL PRODUCTS
MINING AND QUARRYING EQUIPMENT
MOTORCYCLES
MUSICAL INSTRUMENTS
PAINTS
PATENTS & COPYRIGHTS
PERFUMES
PETROLEUM EXTRACTION AND REFINERY EQUIPMENT
PHARMACEUTICALS
PLUMBING HARDWARE
PUMPS & VALVES (NOT INDUSTRIAL)
SIGNAGE
SLATE
SPORTING GOODS
WIGS

ITALIAN TRADE COMMISSION - NEW YORK

499 Park Avenue
6th Floor
New York, NY 10022
Tel.: 212/980-1500
Fax: 212/758-1050
newyork@newyork.ice.it
Roberto Luongo
Trade Commissioner
Executive Director for the U.S.A.

Geographic territory: Connecticut, District of Columbia, Delaware, Maine, Maryland, Massachusetts, New Hampshire, New Jersey, New York, Pennsylvania, Rhode Island, Vermont, Bahamas, Bermuda, Puerto Rico, US Virgin Islands

Products responsible for: '

AGRICULTURAL PRODUCTS
ANTIQUES
APPAREL
APPAREL ACCESSORIES (INCLUDING HATS &
UMBRELLAS)
APPAREL TEXTILES AND YARNS.
ART WORK
BEVERAGES
CERAMIC TILES
FLOWERS AND PLANTS
FOODSTUFFS
FOOTWEAR AND ACCESSORIES
HOME TEXTILES AND YARNS
INDUSTRIAL PATENTS
LEATHER GOODS, FURS AND HIDES
LIVE ANIMALS AND ANIMAL FEEDS
SPIRITS
WINE
US DIRECT IVENSTMENTS IN ITALY
ITALIAN INVESTMENTS IN THE USA

ITALIAN TRADE COMMISSION - SEATTLE

U S Bank Center
1420 Fifth Avenue
Suite 2670
Seattle, WA 98101
Tel.: 206/398-0530
Fax: 206/398-0532
seattle.seattle@ice.it
Pasquale Bova
Trade Commissioner

Geographic territory: Alaska, Hawaii, Idaho, Montana, Oregon, Utah, Washington and Wyoming

Products responsible for:

AVIATION & SPACE TECHNOLOGY
SOFTWARE & TECHNOLOGY PRODUCTS
ADVANCED MATERIALS (PLASTICS, CERAMICS,
COMPOSITES, ETC.)
AEROSPACE
ARTIFICIAL INTELLIGENCE
BANK EQUIPMENT
BIOTECHNOLOGY
CIRCUIT BOARD MACHINERY
COMMUNICATIONS EQUIPMENT
CONSUMER ELECTRONICS
E-COMMERCE
ELECTRONIC COMPONENTS
FIRE SAFETY EQUIPMENT
FRAMES & EYEWEAR
INFORMATION SERVICES
OFFICE MACHINES AND EQUIPMENT
OPTICS AND LASERS
PHOTOGRAPHIC EQUIPMENT
POLLUTION ABATEMENT EQUIPMENT
RECYCLING EQUIPMENT
SAFETY PRODUCTS & EQUIPMENT
SOFTWARE
TELECOMMUNICATIONS EQUIPMENT
TELEPHONE EQUIPMENT (CONSUMER)
TOYS & GAMES

US AND COUNTRY CONTACTS

U.S. EMBASSY TRADE PERSONNEL

Embassy Web Site: www.usis.it

Margaret Dean
Minister Counselor for Economic Affairs
American Embassy
Via Vittorio Veneto 119/A
00187 Rome, Italy
Tel: 39-06-4674-2107
Fax: 39-06-4674-2230

Eric Weaver
Minister Counselor for Commercial Affairs
Tel: 39-06-4674-2202
Fax: 39-06-4674-2113
Rome.Office.Box@mail.doc.gov

Elizabeth Berry
Minister Counselor for Agricultural Affairs
Tel: 39-06-4674-2362
Fax: 39-06-4788-7008
AgRome@fas.usda.gov

Gregory Delawie
Economic Counselor
Tel: 39-06-4674-2233
Fax: 39-06-4674-2389

Brian McCleary
Commercial Counselor
Tel: 39-06-4674-2382
Fax: 39-06-4674-2113
Rome.Office.Box@mail.doc.gov

Clay Hamilton
Agricultural Attache
Tel: 39-06-4674-2362
Fax: 39-06-4788-7008
AgRome@fas.usda.gov

CONSULATE PERSONNEL

Maria Andrews
Principal Commercial Officer
American Consulate Milan
Via Principe Amedeo 2/10
20121 Milan, Italy
Tel: 39-02-659-2260
Fax: 39-02-659-6561
Milan.Office.Box@mail.doc.gov

Jay Field
Commercial Officer
American Consulate Milan
Tel: 39-02-659-2260
Fax: 39-02-659-6561
Milan.Office.Box@mail.doc.gov

Barbara Lapini
Commercial Representative
American Consulate Florence
Lungarno A. Vespucci 38
50123 Florence, Italy
Tel: 39-055-211-676
Fax: 39-055-283-780
Florence.Office.Box@mail.doc.gov

Susanna Lezzi
Commercial Specialist
American Consulate Genoa
Via Dante 2
16121 Genoa, Italy
Tel: 39-010-543-877
Fax: 39-010-576-1678
Genoa.Office.Box@mail.doc.gov

Albina Parente
Commercial Assistant
American Consulate Naples
Piazza della Repubblica
80122 Naples, Italy
Tel: 39-081-583-8206
Fax: 39-081-761-1592
Naples.Office.Box@mail.doc.gov

ITALIAN GOVERNMENT AGENCIES

Bank of Italy
Credit Institutions Supervision Service
Via Nazionale 187
00184 Rome
www.bancaitalia.it

CONSOB (Securities Regulatory Agency)
Via Isonzo 19
00198 Rome
Fax: 39-06-841-6703/8417707
www.consob.it
consob@consob.it

The Italian Embassy
Commercial Section
1601 Fuller Street, NW
Washington, DC 20009
Tel: (202) 328-5558
Fax: (202) 328-5593
www.italyemb.org/

Italian Government Tourist Board (ENIT)
630 Fifth Avenue, Suite 1565
New York, NY 10111
Tel: (212) 245-5095
Fax: (212) 586-9249
www.enit.it
enitny@bway.net

The Italian Trade Commission
(Assists in locating Italian suppliers and products.)
Offices are located in the follow-ing cities:

Peachtree Center
Harris Tower
233 Peachtree Street, NE
Suite 2301
Atlanta, GA 30343
Tel: (404) 525-0660
Fax: (404) 525-5112
www.italtrade.com/ice/index.html
itc@italtrade-atlanta.com

401 North Michigan Avenue
Suite 3030
Chicago, IL 60611
Tel: (312) 670-4360
Fax: (312) 670-5147
ital1@italtrade-chicago.com

1801 Avenue of the Stars
Suite 700
Los Angeles, CA 90067
Tel: (323) 879-0950
Fax: (310) 203-8335
italcomm@itc-ice-la.com

499 Park Avenue
6th Floor
New York, NY 10022
Tel: (212) 980-1500
Fax: (212) 758-1050
www.italtrade.com
NewYork@italtrade.com

US Bank Center
1420 Fifth Avenue
Suite 2670
Seattle, WA 98101
Tel: (206) 398-0530
Fax: (206) 398-0532
itc@italtrade-seattle.com

Dipartimento della Dogana
(Department of Customs)
Via M. Carucci 71
00143 Roma
Tel: 39-06-50241
Fax: 39-06-5095-7346
dogane_dc_ssdoganali@finanze.it

Istituto Nazionale per il Commercio Estero (ICE)
Viale Liszt, 21
00144 Rome
Tel: 39-06-59921
Fax: 39-06-5992-6899
www.ice.it
ice@ice.it

Ente Nazionale Italiano di Unificazione (UNI)
(Italian National Bureau of Standards)
Via Battistotti Sassi, 11/B
20133 Milan
Tel: 39-02-700-241
Fax: 39-02-7010-5992/6106
www.uni.com
uni@uni.com

Comitato Elettrotecnico Italiano
(Electrical standards and certification)
Viale Monza, 259
20126 Milan
Tel: 39-02-257-73257/259
Fax: 39-02-2577-3222

www.ceiuni.it
ceiuni@ceiuni.it

Ministero dell'Industria e Commercio
Ufficio Centrale Brevetti per Invenzioni
(Patent and trademark applications and inquiries)
Modelli e Marchi
Via Molise, 19
00187 Rome, Italy
Tel: 39-06-47051
Fax: 39-06-4705-3035
www.minindustria.it
www.european-patent-office.org/it/
cccmail@minindustria.it

Presidenza del Consiglio dei Ministri
Ufficio del Proprietà Letteraria, Artistica e Scientificia
(Applications and inquires concerning copyrights)
Via Boncompagni, 15
00187 Rome, Italy
Tel: 39-06-487-971
Fax: 39-06-4879-7727
www.palazzochigi.it/
urpdie@palazzochigi.it

AGRICULTURAL CONTACTS

Istituto per il Commercio Estero
(Italian Trade Commission)
Contact: Paolo Angelini, Vice-Director, Food/Agriculture Product Division
Via Liszt, 21
00144 Rome (EUR)
Tel: 39-06-59929506
Fax: 39-06-59647364
www.ice.it
ice@ice.it

Ministero delle Politiche Agricole
(Ministry of Agriculture)
Contact: Pasquale Mainolfi, Director, Agr. Production
Via XX Settembre, 20
00187 Rome
Tel: 39-06-4884293
Fax: 39-06-4814628

Ministero della Sanita'
(Ministry of Health)
Romano Marabelli, Director General, Nutrition, Food, and Public Health Dept.
Piazzale Marconi, 25
Palazzo Italia
00144 Eur-Rome
Tel: 39-06-59943946
Fax: 39-06-59943217

ITALIAN TRADE ASSOCIATIONS

GENERAL/INDUSTRIAL:
American Chamber of Commerce in Italy
Via Cantu', 1
20123 Milan
Tel: 39-02-869-0661
Fax: 39-02-805-7737
www.amcham.it
amcham@enter.it

Associazione Bancaria Italiana
(Association of Italian Banks)
Piazza del Gesu, 49
00186 Rome
Tel: 39-06-67671
Fax: 39-06-676-7457
www.abi.it
abi@abi.it

Associazione Imprenditrici e Donne Dirigenti d'Azienda (AIDDA)
(Association of women mangers and entrepreneurs)
Associazione Nazionale del Commercio con l'Estero (AN-CE)
(National Association for Foreign Trade)
Corso Venezia, 49
20121 Milan
Tel: 39-02-775-0320/775-0321
Fax: 39-02-775-0329
www.aidda.org
www.ance.it
ance.italy@iol.it

Associazione Nazionale fra le Imprese Assicuratrici
(National Association of Business Insurance)
Via della Frezza, 70
00186 Rome
Tel: 39-06-326-881
Fax: 39-06-322-7135
www.ania.it
info@ania.it

ANFIA - Associazione Nazionale fra Industrie Automobilistiche
(Auto Industry Association)
Corso Galileo Ferraris 61
10128 Turin (TO)
Tel: 39-011-545160/545057
Fax: 39-011-545464
Contact: Dr. Aldo Malandra, Director
www.anfia.it
info@anfia.it

ASTER S. cons.a.r.l

(Agency for the Development of Technology in Emilia-Romagna. This agency promotes use of new technologies and international trade in the Region.)
Via Morgani 4
40122 Bologna
Tel: 39-051-236-242
Fax: 39-051-227-803
Contact: Debora Facchini
www.aster.it
info@aster.it

CESVIT S.p.A. / M.Cube
(M. Cube is part of the European Union's Esprit project to promote the development of the multimedia sector in Italy.)
Via Giovanni del Pian dei Carpini 28-30
50127 Florence
Tel: 39-055-429-4261
Fax: 39-055-429-4220
Contact: Paolo Martinez
www.mcube.org
martinez@cesvit.it

Confederazione Generale dell'Industria (Confindustria)
(Confindustria is the general confederation of Italian industry and
principal trade association in Italy acting as an umbrella organization covering numerous industry trade associations.)
Viale dell'Astronomia, 30
00144 Rome
Tel: 39-06-59031
Fax: 39-06-591-9615
www.confindustria.it
confindustria@confindustria.it

Confederazione Generale Italiana dell'Artigianato
(General confederation of handicrafts associations.)
Via San Giovanni in Laterano 152
00187 Rome
Tel: 39-06-703-741
Fax: 39-06-7045-2188
www.confartigianato.it
confartigianato@confartigianato.it

Confederazione Generale dell'Agricoltura Italiana
Corso Vittorio Emanuele II, 101
00186 Rome
Tel: 39-06-690151
Fax: 39-06-6830-8578/686-1726

Confederazione Generale Italiana del Commercio e del Turismo (Confcommercio)
(Confcommercio is an umbrella trade association affiliated with industry groups in commerce and tourism.)
Pazza G. G. Belli, 2
00153 Rome
Tel: 39-06-58661
Fax: 39-06-580-9425
www.confcommercio.it
confcommercio@confcommercio.it

Confederazione Italiana della Piccola e Media Industria (CONFAPI)
(Industry confederation serving small- and medium-size firms.)
Via della Colonna Antonina, 52
00186 Rome
Tel: 39-06-690151
Fax: 39-06-679-1488
www.confapi.it
mail@confapi.it

Lega Nazionale Cooperative e Mutue
(National Cooperative and Mutual League)
Via Guattani, 9
00161 Rome
Tel: 39-06-844-391
Fax: 39-06-8443-9406/8443-9216
www.legacoop.it/home.htm
presidenza@legacoop.it

Promo Firenze
(Special Agency of the Florence Chamber of Commerce for the promotion of international trade)
Via Por Santa Maria
angolo Via Volta dei Mercanti 2
50123 Florence
Tel: 39-055-267-141
Fax: 39-055-267-1607
Contact: Dante Cecchini
www.promofirenze.com
promofirenze@promofirenze.com

punto.it
(a "virtual" organization with no fixed address that promotes electronic commerce and internet use)
www.puntoit.org

Unione Italiana delle Camere di Commercio Industria Artigianato e Agricoltura
(responsible as umbrella organization for all chambers of commerce in Italy)
Piazza Sallustio, 21
00187 Roma
Tel: 39-06-47041
Fax: 39-06-470-4342
www.unioncamere.it
unionecamere@unioncamere.it

UCINA - National Union of Italian Shipyards, Nautical Industries and Related Sectors

Piazzale J F. Kennedy 1
16129 Genoa (GE)
tel; 39/010/5769811
fax: 39/010/5531104
internet: www.ucina.it
e-mail: ucina@ucina.it
Contact: Eng. Andrea Gasparri, Director General

AGRICULTURAL:

Associazione Italiana Allevatori
(Breeders)
Dr. Bonizzi, Director
Via Tomassetti 9
00161 Rome
Tel: 39-06-854-5118
Fax: 39-06-8545-1252
www.aia.it
info@aia.it
spag@aia.it

Associazione Italiana Industria Olearia
(Veg Oil)
Giorgio Cilenti, Director Generale
Piazza Campitelli 3
00186 Rome
Tel: 39-06-6994-0058
Fax: 39-06-6994-0118
assitol@foodarea.it

A.I.S.S.
(Seed Industry Assoc)
Marco Nardi, Secretary
Piazza della Costituzione, Galleria del Reno, Scala C
40128 Bologna
Tel: 39-051-850-3881
Fax: 39-051-355-166

Associazione Nazionale Allevatori Bovini della Razza Bruna
(Brown Swiss Breeders)
Giuseppe Santus, Director
Via Locatelli 20
37122 Verona
Tel & Fax: 39-030-364-280

Associazione Nazionale Allevatori Razza Frisona Italiana
(Holstein Frisian Breeders)
Giancarlo Lanari, President
Via Bergamo 292
21626 Cremona
Tel: 39-037-412-521
Fax: 39-037-474-203

Associazione Nazionale Allevatori Suini
(Swine Breeders)
Giancarlo Cintoli
Via G.B. De Rossi 3
00161 Rome
Tel: 39-06-844-9106
Fax: 39-06-844-3471

Associazione Nazionale Bieticoltori
(Beet Growers)
Luciano Biasco, Director General
Via D'Azeglio 48
40123 Bologna
Tel: 39-051-334-884
Fax: 39-051-331-403

Associazione Nazionale Cerealisti
(Grain Traders)
Lorenzo Fineschi, Director
Via Po 102
00198 Rome
Tel: 39-06-841-6554
Fax: 39-06-884-0877

ASSALZOO
(Compound Feed)
Emilio Minetti, Secretary General
Via Lovanio 6
00198 Rome
Tel: 39-06-854-1641
Fax: 39-06-854-1641

ANEIOA
(Nat'l Imp/Exp Hort Assoc)
Pino Calcagni, President
Via Sabotino 46
00195 Rome
Tel: 39-06-3751-5147
Fax: 39-06-372-3569

ANIPO
(Nat'l Imp Hort Assoc)
Fausto Ratto, Secretary General
Largo Brindisi 5
00182 Rome
Tel: 39-06-7049-7472
Fax: 39-06-700-4428

FEDERCOMLEGNO
(Wood Trade Federation)
Alfonso Froncillo, President
Via G. d'Arezzo 16
00198 Rome
Tel: 39-06-841-7195
Fax: 39-06-8530-1785

FEDERORTOFRUTTA
(Fruit Trade Assoc)

Paolo Antenore
Via Gigli d'Oro 21
00186 Rome
Tel: 39-06-689-3414
Fax: 39-06-689-3409

FEDERVINI
(Wine Trade Assoc)
Federico Castellucci
Via Mentana 2B
00185 Rome
Tel: 39-06-494-1630
Fax: 39-06-494-1566

ITALMOPA
(Millers Assoc)
Fabrizio Vitali, Deputy President
Via Crociferi 44
00187 Rome
Tel: 39-06-678-5409
Fax: 39-06-783-054
www.italmopa.it
italmopa@foodarea.it

UNA
(Poultry Union)
Rita Pasquarelli, Secretary General
Via V. Mariano 58
00189 Rome
Tel: 39-06-325-4015
Fax: 39-06-3325-2427

UNAPROL
(Olive Oil Producers Assoc)
Paolo Nigro, President
Via Rocca di Papa 12
00197 Rome
Tel: 39-06-784-6901
Fax: 39-06-7834-4373
unaprol@tin.it

UNICEB
(Livestock Meat Traders)
Renzo Fossato, Director
Via dei Campioni 13
00144 Rome
Tel: 39-06-592-1241/592-1239
Fax: 39-06-592-1478/591-4843
uniceb@tin.it

UNIPI
(Pasta Traders Assoc)
Giuseppe Menconi, President
Via Po 102
00198 Rome
Tel: 39-06-854-3262
Fax: 39-06-841-5132
www.unipi-pasta.it
unipi@foodarea.it

ITALIAN MARKET RESEARCH FIRMS

Addressvitt S.r.l.
Via Anna Kuliscioff 38
20152 Milan
Tel: 39-02-483-361
Fax: 39-02-4830-1355
Contact: Dr. Marida Cagnoli
www.addressvitt.it
info@Addressvitt.it

Commark - Communicazione e Marketing S.r.l.
Via Isonzo 25
00198 Rome
Tel: 39-06-855-8748/854-9394
Fax: 39-06-841-6677

Databank
Corso Italia 8
20122 Milan
Tel: 39-02-8052-855
Fax: 39-02-865-579
Contact: Mrs. Daniella Bosio

Directa S.r.l.
Via Solari 8
20144 Milan
Tel: 39-02-4819-3581
Fax: 39-02-4801-2277
Contact: Dr. Giorgio Calo'

Executive Services Business Centres S.r.l.
Via V. Monti 8
20123 Milan
Tel: 39-02-4819-4271
Fax: 39-02-48013233

Loverso Dr. Alfredo
Via Morosini 39
20135 Milan
Tel: 39-02-55011554
Fax: 39-02-72002889

Nielsen
Via G. di Vittorio 10
20094 Corsico (MI)
Tel: 39-02-451-971
Fax: 39-02-4510-1068/4586-6235

Palandri Horwath S.r.l.
Piazza Navona 49
00186 Rome
Tel: 39-06-686-7841

Fax: 39-06-689-6075
Contact: Dr. Aldo Sanchini

Reseau
Ricerche e Studi su Elettronica & Automazione
Via S. Vittore 39
20123 Milan
Tel: 39-02-4819-3800
Fax: 39-02-439-0535

Serin S.r.l.
Viale Beatrice d'Este 37
20122 Milan
Tel/Fax: 39-02-5832-2635

WASHINGTON-BASED USG COUNTRY CONTACTS

---TPCC Trade Information Center
Tel: 1-800-USA-TRADE

U.S. Department of Commerce
Market Access Compliance Office
David DeFalco, Italy Desk Officer
Room H-3042
14th Street and Constitution Ave, NW
Washington, DC 20230
Tel: (202) 482-2178
Fax: (202) 482-2897
www.mac.doc.gov

U.S. Department of State Office of Business Affairs
2201 C Street, NW
Washington, DC 20520
Tel: (202) 646-1625
Fax: (202) 646-3953

U.S. Department of Agriculture
Foreign Agricultural Service
14th St. & Independence Ave. S.W.
Washington, DC 20250
Trade assistance and promotion office:
Tel: (202) 720-7420

Overseas Private Investment Corporation
1100 New York Avenue, NW
Washington, DC 20527
Tel: (202) 336-8799
Fax: (202) 408-9859
www.opic.gov
info@opic.gov

U.S. - BASED MULTIPLIERS RELEVANT FOR ITALY

GENERAL

National Italian American Foundation (NIAF)
(NIAF conducts cultural and educational events, sponsors exchange programs, works to enhance cultural, political, and economic relations between the United States and Italy and serves as an advocacy group.)
1860 19th Street, NW
Washington, DC 20009
Tel: (202) 387-0600
Fax: (202) 387-0800
www.niaf.org

Italy-America Chamber of Commerce
1825 I Street N.W.
Suite 400
Washington, D.C. 20006
Tel: (202) 429-2068
Fax: (202) 429-9574
www.iaccmd.com
info@iaccmd.com

Delegation of the European Community
2300 M Street NW
3rd Floor
Washington, DC 20037
Tel: (202) 862-9500/1/2
Fax: (202) 429-1766

AGRICULTURAL

Alaska Seafood
Marketing Institute
J.C. Power, Exec Director
P.O. Box DX
Juneau, Alaska
99811-0800
Tel: (907) 586-2902

American Hardwood Export Council
Kathleen Landauer, Exec Director
1250 Conn Ave, Suite 200
NW463-2720
Washington, DC 20037
Tel: (202)463-2785

American Quarter Horse Association
Gary Griffith, Director of Field Operations
2701 I-40 East
P.O. Box 8112
Amarilly, Texas 79168
Tel: (806) 376-4811
Fax: (806) 376-8112

American Seed Trade Assoc
Jack W. Wells, Int'l Mktg
Suite 964
1030 15th St, NW
Washington, DC 20005

Tel: (202) 223-4080
Fax: (202) 293-2617

American Soybean Assoc
Tom Brennan, Div Manager Europe
P.O. Box 27300
St. Louis, MO St. Louis, MO
Tel: (314) 576-1770
Fax: (314) 576-2786

California Prune Board
Richard Peterson, Exec Director
5990 Stoneridge Drive, Suite 101
Pleasanton, CA 94588-2706
Tel: (510) 734-0150
Fax: (510) 734-0525

California Walnut Commission
Nathan Hollerman, Marketing Director
1540 River Park Drive, Suite
Sacramento, CA 95815
Tel: (916) 646-3807
Fax: (916) 923-2548

Cotton Council International
K. Adrian Hunnings, Exec Director
Suite 964
1110 Vermont Ave NW
Washington, DC 20005
Tel: (202) 331-2943
Fax: (202) 331-0622

Hardwood Plywood Manufacturers Association
E.T. Altman, President
P.O. Box 2789
Reston, Virginia 22090
Tel: (703) 435-9200
Fax: (703) 435-2537

Leather Industries of America
Charles Myers, President
1000 Thomas Jefferson Street N.W., Suite 515
Washington, D.C. 20007
Tel: (202) 342-8086
Fax: (202) 342-9063

MIATCO
Drayton C. Mayers, Executive Director
820 Davis Street, Suite 212
Evanston, IL 60201
Tel: (708) 866-7300
Fax: (708) 866-7413

Michigan Bean Shippers Association
James E. Byrum
P.O. Box 473
Leslie, MI 9688

Tel: (517) 790-3010
Fax: (517) 790-3742

Mohair Council of America
Brian J. May, Exec Director
P.O. Box 5337
San Angelo, TX 76902
Tel: (915) 655-3161
Fax: (915) 655-4761

Nat'l Assoc of Animal Breeders
Gordon A. Doak, President
P.O. Box 1033
Columbia, MO 65205
Tel: (314) 445-4406
Fax: (314) 446-2279

National Dry Bean Council
Philip Kimball
Suite 700
1101 Conn Ave, NW 857-1169
Washington, DC 20026
Tel: (202) 429-5154

National Honey Board
Mary R Humann, Exec Director
421 First St, Suite 203
Longmont, CO 80501-1421
Tel: (303) 776-2337
Fax: (303) 776-2337

National Forest Products Assoc
Steve Lovett, Vice President
Suite 200
1250 Conn Ave, NW
Washington, DC 20036
Tel: (202) 463-2723
Fax: (202) 463-2785

National Peanut Council
Jeannette Anderson, Director
1500 King Street, Suite 301
Alexandria, VA 22314
Tel: (703) 838-9500
Fax: (703) 838-9508

Northwest Horticultural Council
Christian Schlect, President
P.O. Box 570
Yakima, WA 98907
Tel: (509) 453-3193
Fax: (509) 453-4880

Southern U.S. Trade Association
Scott Hansen, Exec Director
World Trade Center, Suite 1540
2 Canal Street
New Orleans, LA 70130-1408

Tel: (504) 568-5986
Fax: (504) 568-6010

Tobacco Associates
Kirk Wayne, President
1725 K St, NW
Suite 512
Washington, DC 20006
Tel: (202) 828-9144
Fax: (202) 828-9149

USA Dry Pea & Lentil Council
Harol Blaine, Administrator
5071 Hwy West
Moscow, ID 83843-4023
Tel: (208) 882-3023
Fax: (208) 882-6406

USA Rice Council
Bill J. Goldsmith, Exec Vice Pres
PO Box 740123
Houston, TX 77274
Tel: (713) 270-6699
Fax: (713) 270-1146

U.S. Hide, Skin & Leather Association
Jerome J. Breiter, President
1700 North Moore
Suite 1600
Arlington, VA 22209
Tel: (703) 841-5485
Fax: (703) 841-9656

U.S. Wheat Associates
Winston L. Wilson, President
1620 I St, NW
Suite 801
Washington, DC 20006
Tel: (202) 463-0999
Fax: (202) 785-1052

Western Wood Products Association
H.A. Roberts, President
522 SW Fifth Ave
4th Floor
Portland, OR 97204-2122
Tel: (503) 224-3930
Fax: (503) 224-3934

Wine Institute
John A. De Luca, President
425 Market St
Suite 1000
San Francisco, CA 94105
Tel: (415) 512-0151
Fax: (415) 442-0742

BANKS WITH CORRESPONDENT U.S. BANKING ARRANGEMENTS

A large number of Italian banks have correspondence relationships with U.S. banks. Below is a listing of Italian banks with branch offices in the U.S.

Istituto Bancario San Paolo di Torino S.p.A.
Piazza San Carlo, 156
10121 Turin
Tel: 39-011-5551
Fax: 39-011-555-6650
www.sanpaolo.it

444 South Flower Street
45th Floor
Suite 4550
Los Angeles, CA 90071
Tel: (213) 489-3100
Fax: (213) 622-2514
losangeles.us@sanpaolo.com

245 Park Avenue, Suite 3500
New York, NY 10167
Tel: (212) 692-3000
Fax: (212) 599-5303/599-5304
Newyork.us@sanpaolo.com

Banca di Roma
Via Marco Minghetti, 17
00187 Rome
Tel: 39-06-670-71
Fax: 39-06-678-1929
www.bancaroma.it

34 East 51st Street
New York, NY 10022
Tel: (212) 407-1600/407-1707/407-1746
Fax: (212) 407-1677
Bdrny@earthlink.net

225 West Washington Street, Suite 1200
Chicago, IL 60606
Tel: (312) 368-8855
Fax: (312) 726-3058
Bdrchicago@aol.com

One Market Stewart Tower, Suite 1000
San Francisco, CA 94105
Tel: (415) 357-0800
Fax: (415) 357-9869
Bdrsf@opticmail.com

CARIPLO - Cassa di Risparmio delle Provincie Lombarde S.p.A.
Via Monte di Pietà, 8
20121 Milan
Tel: 39-02-886-61
Fax: 39-02-8866-2302
www.cariplo.it
scrivici@cariplo.it

190 South La Salle Street, Suite 2890
Chicago, IL 60603
Tel: (312) 444-1500
Fax: (312) 444-1501

One Embarcadero Center, Suite 2820
San Francisco, CA 94111-3717
Tel: (415) 439-6780
Fax: (415) 439-6785

Banca Nazionale del Lavoro BNL S.p.A.
Via V. Veneto, 119
00187 Rome
Tel: 39-06-470-21
Fax: 39-06-470-7298
www.bnl.it

25 W. 51st Street
New York, NY 10019
Tel: (212) 581-0710
Fax: (212) 489-9088
comdiv@bnlny.com

Xerox Center 55 West Monroe Street, Suite 3490
Chicago, IL 60603
Tel: (312) 444-9250, 444-9251, 444-9252, 444-9253, 444-9254
Fax: (312) 444-9410
BNLChicago@aol.com

Banca Commerciale Italiana S.p.A.
Piazza della Scala, 6
20121 Milan
Tel: 39-02-88501
Fax: 39-02-8850-3026
www.bci.it

1 William Street
New York, NY 10004
Tel: (212) 607-3500
Fax: (212) 809-2124

150 North Michigan Ave., Suite 1500
Chicago, IL 60601
Tel: (312) 346-1112
Fax: (312) 346-5758

55 S. Flowers Street, Suite 4300
Los Angeles. CA 90071
Tel: (213) 624-0440
Fax: (213) 624-0457

Banco di Napoli S.p.A.
Via Toledo, 177/178
80132 Naples
Tel: 39-081-792-1111
Fax: 39-081-580-1343
www.bancodinapoli.it

4 East 54th St.
New York, NY 10022
Tel: (212) 872-2400
Fax: (212) 872-2426

Banco di Sicilia S.p.A.
Via Generale Vincenzo Magliocco, 1
90141 Palermo
Tel: 39-91-608-1111
Fax: 39-91-608-5964/3227
www.bancodisicilia.it
sicilbanco@bancodisicilia.it

Credito Italiano
Direzione Centrale
Piazza Cordusio
20123 Milan
Tel: 39-02-88621
Fax: 39-02-837-0161
www.credit.it
info@credit.it

375 Park Avenue
New York, NY 10152
Tel: (212) 546-9600
Fax: (212) 546-9675

Two Prudential Plaza
180 North Stetson Suite 1310
Chicago, IL 60601-6713
Tel: (312) 946-1-111
Fax: (312) 946-1-112
unicrechgo@aol.com

Monte dei Paschi di Siena
Piazza Salimbeni, 3
53100 Siena
Tel: 39-0577-294-111
Fax: 39-0577-294-653
www.mps.it

55 East 59th Street
New York, NY 10022-1112
Tel: (212) 891-3600

Fax: (212) 891-3661/30

MAJOR ITALIAN NEWSPAPERS AND BUSINESS JOURNALS:

AVVENIRE
Piazza Carbonari, 3
20125 Milano
tel. 39-02-67801
fax. 39-02-678-0208
www.avvenire.it
lettere@avvenire.it

CORRIERE DELLA SERA
Via Solferino, 28
20121 Milano
tel. 39-02-6339/628-27246
fax. 39-02-2900-9668/2900-9705
www.corriere.it/
astroni@rcs.it

LA DISCUSSIONE
Piazza del Gesú, 46
00186 Roma
tel. 39-06-6902-0931/679-6564
fax. 39-06-6920-9333

IL FOGLIO
Viale Milano Fiori, STR.3. Pal. B/10
20090 Assago (MI)
tel. 39-02-575771
www.ilfoglio.it/
lettere@ilfoglio.it

LA GAZZETTA DEL MEZZOGIORNO
Viale Scipione l'Africano, 264
70124 Bari
tel. 39-080-547-0400
fax. 39-080-547-0488
gazz@interbusiness.it

GAZZETTA DEL SUD
Via Ubeto Bonino, 15/C
98124 Messina
tel. 39-090-2261
fax. 39-090-2936-359/2932-063
www.gazzettadelsud.it
info@gazzettadelsud.it

GIORNALE DI SICILIA
Via Lincoln, 21
90133 Palermo
tel. 39-091-662-7111
fax. 39-091-662-7280/617-7517
www.gds.it
info@quotidianodelsabato.it

IL GIORNALE
Via Gaetano Negri, 4
20123 Milano
tel. 39-02-85661
fax. 39-02-7202-3859/80

IL GIORNO
Piazza Cavour, 2
20123 Milano
tel. 39-02-77681
fax. 39-02-7600-6656
http://ilgiorno.monrif.net/

IL MANIFESTO
Via Tomacelli, 146
00186 Roma
tel. 39-06-687-191
fax. 39-06-689-2600/6871-9573
www.ilmanifesto.it
redazione@ilmanifesto.it

IL MATTINO
Via Chiatamone, 65
80121 Napoli
tel. 39-081-794-7111
fax. 39-081-794-7288
www.ilmattino.it

IL MESSAGGERO
Via del Tritone, 152
00187 Roma
tel. 39-06-47201
fax. 39-06-472-072
www.ilmessaggero.it/indexmsgr.htm

LA NAZIONE
Via Ferdinando Paolieri, 2
50121 Firenze
tel. 39-055-87951
fax. 39-055-234-3646
http://lanazione.monrif.net/

L'OSSERVATORE ROMANO
Via del Pellegrino
00120 Citta' del Vaticano
tel. 39-06-6989-9310
fax. 39-06-6988-3675
www.vatican.va/news_services/or/home_ita.html
ornet@ossrom.va

IL PICCOLO
Via Guido Reni, 1
34123 Trieste
tel. 39-040-373-3111
fax. 39-040-373-3283

www.ilpiccolo.it
piccolo@ilpiccolo.it

IL POPOLO
Via del Gesú, 62
00186 Roma
tel. 39-06-695071
fax. 39-06-6994-2377

LA REPUBBLICA
Piazza Indipendenza, 11/b
00185 Roma
tel. 39-06-49821
fax. 39-06-4982-2923
www.repubblica.it
larepubblica@repubblica.it

IL RESTO DEL CARLINO
Via Mattei, 106
40138 Bologna
tel. 39-051-536-111/530-202
fax. 39-051-532-990
www.ilrestodelcarlino.monrif.net

IL SECOLO XIX
Piazza Piccapietra, 21
16121 Genova
tel. 39-010-53881
fax. 39-010-538-8426
www.ilsecoloXIX.it
redazione@ilsecoloxix.it

LA SICILIA
Viale Odorico da Pordenone, 50
95126 Catania
tel. 39-095-330-544
fax. 39-095-338-073/336-466

IL SOLE-24 ORE
Via Lomazzo, 52
20154 Milano
tel. 39-02-31031
fax. 39-02-3454-9701
www.ilsole24ore.it
info@ilsole24ore.it

LA STAMPA
Via Marenco, 32
10126 Torino
tel. 39-011-65681
fax. 39-011-655-306/310-0759
www.lastampa.it
online@lastampa.it

IL TEMPO
Piazza Colonna, 366
00187 Roma
tel. 39-06-675-881
fax. 39-06-675-8869/315

L'UNITÀ
Via dei Due Macelli, 23/13
00187 Roma
tel. 39-06-699-961
fax. 39-06-678-3555
www.unita.it/
posta@unita.it

MAJOR ITALIAN BUSINESS JOURNALS:

L'ESPRESSO
Via Po, 12
00198 Roma
tel. 39-06-84781
fax. 39-06-884-5167
www.espressoedit.kataweb.it/

ITALIA OGGI
Via Marco Burigozzo, 5
20122 Milano
tel. 39-02-582-191
fax: 39-02-5831-7559
www.italiaoggi.it
italiaoggi@class.it

MILANO FINANZA
Via Puligozzo, 5
20122 Milano
tel. 39-02-582-191
fax: 39-02-5831-7518
www.milanofinanza.it
mf-milanofinanza@class.it

PANORAMA
Viale Mondadori 1
20090 Segrate (MI)
tel. 39-02-75421
fax. 39-02-7542-2769
www.mondadori.com/panorama

IL MONDO
Via Angelo Rizzoli, 2
20132 Milano
tel. 39-02-25841
fax. 39-02-2720-1158
www.ilmondo.rcs.it
ilmondo@rcs.it

Largest Advertising Agency Trade Association:
ASSAP –
Associazione Italiana Agenzie di Pubblicita' a Servizio Completo
Via Larga, 19
20122 Milano
Tel: 011/39/02 5830-7450

Fax : 011/39/025830.7147
www.assocomunicazione.it

ADVERTISING AGENCIES:

Armando Testa
Via Luisa del Carretto, 58
10131 Torino
Tel. 011/39-0118810111
Fax: 011/39-0118810367
www.testa.it

Young & Rubican Italia
Piazza Eleonora Duse, 2
20122 Milano
Tel: 011/39/027732.1
Fax: 011/39/027600.0904
www.yr.com

McCann-Erickson Italiana S.p.A.
Via Albricci, 10
20122 Milano
Tel: 011/39/028529.1
Fax: 011/39/0285292557
www.mccann.com
194.244.76.3

BGSD'ARCY
Corso Galileo Ferraris, 24/A
10121 Torino
Tel: 011/39-0115601911
Fax: 011/39-0115175300

Via Correggio, 18
20149 Milano
Tel: 011/39/02/4679.1
Fax: 011/39/02/4818633

J. Walter Thompson S.p.A.
Via Paolo Lomazzo, 19
20154 Milano
Tel: 011/39/02/336341
Fax: 011/39/02/33634400
www.jwalterthompson.com

Lowe Lintas Pirella Gottsche
Piazzale Biancamano, 8
20121 Milano
Tel: 011/39/02/290281
Fax: 011/39/02/6597722

Milano & Grey S.p.A.
Via Bertani, 6
20154 Milano
Tel: 011/39/02/349761
Fax 011/39/02/34530785
Leo Burnett Company
Via Fatebenefratelli, 14
20121 Milano
Tel: 011/39/02/6354.1
Fax: 011/39/02/2900.5229
www.leoburnett.it

Euro RSCG
Via Dante, 7
20123 Milano
Tel: 011/39-02802021
Fax: 011/39-0272000027

Saatchi & Saatchi
Corso Monforte, 52
20122 Milano
Tel: 011/39-0277011
Fax 011/39-02781196
www.saatchi_saatchi.it

ITALIAN CONSULATES IN THE U.S.

Italian Embassy - Consular Section
WASHINGTON, D.C.
3000 Whitehaven street, N.W.
Washington, D.C., 20008
Homepage: www.italyemb.org

Gli uffici della sezione consolare sono aperti al pubblico dalle ore 10:00 alle ore 12:30 dal lunedi' al venerdi'. L'ufficio visti e' aperto al pubblico dalle ore 10:00 alle ore 12:30 il lunedi', il mercoledi' ed il venerdi`.

The consular section is open to the public from 10:00 am to 12:30 pm from Monday until Friday. The visa office is open to the public from 10:00 am to 12:30 pm on Mondays, Wednesdays, and Fridays.

Visa Office
Tel (202) 612-4405 / 612-4407
Fax (202) 518-2141
visa@itwash.org

Citizenship, Vital Records, Marriages/Stato Civile
Tel (202) 612-4422
Fax (202) 518-2141
statocivile@itwash.org

Military Draft, Pensions, Assistance, Waiver J1/Leva, Pensioni, Assistenza
Tel.: (202) 612-4423
Fax: (202) 518-2141

Legalizations, Notary/Legalizzazioni, Notariato
Tel.: (202) 612-4406
Fax: (202) 518-2141

Passports/Passaporti
Tel.: (202) 612-4408
Fax: (202) 518-2141
passaporti@itwash.org

For further information and/or suggestions - Per ulteriori informazionei e/o suggerimenti:
affariconsolari@itwash.org

Jurisdiction:
District of Columbia
Maryland: *only Montgomery and Prince George Counties (all other counties are under the jurisdiction of the Italian Consulate General in Philadelphia)*
Virginia: *only Arlington and Fairfax Counties (all other counties are under the jurisdiction of the Italian Consulate General in Philadelphia)*

A titolo puramente indicativo (questa Ambasciata non assume alcuna responsabilità sulla qualità del servizio o sulle parcelle richieste), si elencano qui di seguito dei nominativi di alcuni professionisti italiani o che parlano italiano:

AVVOCATI: Sig.Joseph LAMARI, Attorney at law, (tel.301-762.2018)
Sig.Angelo CASTELLI, " " " , (tel.301-441.4900)
Sig.Frederick TRONCONE, " " ", (tel.202-232.5100)

TRADUTTORI: Sig. Mark PISONE, (tel. 301-897.3728)
Sig.ra Giovanna CAVAGNA, (tel. 301-384.9243)

Il Dott. Giovanni IMPEDUGLIA (tel. 301-681.7101) è il **medico di fiducia dell'Ambasciata.**

Italian Consulate General
BOSTON
100 Boylston Street
Suite 900
Boston, MA 02116

Tel (617) 542-0483/4 main number
Fax (617) 542-3998
Homepage: www.italconsboston.org
E-mail: it.conbos@ix.netcom.com

Jurisdiction:
Maine, Massachusetts, New Hampshire, Rhode Island, Vermont.

Italian Consulate General
CHICAGO
500 North Michigan Avenue
Suite 1850
Chicago, IL 60611

Tel (312) 467-1550/1/2 main number
Fax (312) 467-1335
Homepage: www.italconschicago.org

Jurisdiction:
Colorado, Illinois, Iowa, Kansas, Minnesota, Missouri, Nebraska, North Dakota, South Dakota, Wisconsin, Wyoming.

Italian Consulate
DETROIT
Buhl Building
535 Griswold
Suite 1840
Detroit, MI 48226

Tel (313) 963-8560 main number
Fax (313) 963-8180
Homepage: www.italconsdetroit.org
E-mail: inform@italconsdetroit.org

Jurisdiction:
Indiana, Kentucky, Michigan, Ohio, Tennessee

Italian Consulate General
HOUSTON
1300 Post Oak Boulevard
Suite 660
Houston, TX 77056

Tel (713) 850-7520 main number
Fax (713) 850-9113
Homepage: www.italconshouston.org
E-mail: italyconsulate@pdq.net

Jurisdiction:
Arkansas, Louisiana, Oklahoma, Texas

Italian Consulate General
LOS ANGELES
12400 Wilshire Boulevard
Suite 300
Los Angeles, CA 90025

Tel (310) 820-0622/826-6207 main number
Fax (310) 820-0727
Homepage: www.conlang.com
E-mail: cglos@aol.com

Jurisdiction:
Arizona, California (following counties: Imperial

Valley, Kern, Los Angeles, Orange, Riverside, Santa Barbara, San Bernardino, San Diego, San Louis Obispo, Ventura), New Mexico, Nevada.

Italian Consulate General
MIAMI
1200 Brickell Avenue
7th Floor
Miami, FL 33131

Tel (305) 374-6322 main number
Fax (305) 374-7945
Homepage: www.italconsmiami.com
E-mail: italcons@netrox.net

Jurisdiction:
Alabama, British Virgin Islands, Cayman Islands, Florida, Georgia, Island of Saba, Mississippi, Puerto Rico, St. Maarten, St. Eustatius, South Carolina, Turks and Caicos, U.S. Virgin Islands.

Italian Consulate General
NEW YORK
690 Park Avenue
New York, N.Y. 10021

Tel (212) 737-9100 main number
Fax (212) 249-4945
Homepage: www.italconsulnyc.org
E-mail: italconsNY@aol.com

Jurisdiction:
Connecticut, New Jersey [following counties(*): Bergen, Essex, Hudson, Morris, Passaic, Sussex, Union, Warren], New York.
Bermuda.

(*) For visas only. For any other requests, residents of these counties must contact the Italian Vice Consulate in Newark, NJ.

Italian Vice Consulate
NEWARK
744 Broad Street
Suite 2800
Newark, NJ 07102

Tel (973) 643-1448 main number
Fax (973) 643-3043
Homepage: www.reference.it/vcnewark
E-mail: ITALVCNK@ix.netcom.com

Jurisdiction:
New Jersey [only following counties (*): Bergen, Essex, Hudson, Morris, Passaic, Sussex, Union, Warren].

(*) For visas residents of the above counties must contact Italian Consulate General in New York.

Italian Consulate General
PHILADELPHIA
1026 Public Ledger Building
100 South 6th Street
Philadelphia, PA 19106-3470

Tel (215) 592-7329 main number
Fax (215) 592-9808
Homepage: http://www.op.net/~conphila
E-mail: conphila@op.net

Jurisdiction:
Delaware, Maryland (except Montgomery and Prince Georges Counties), New Jersey (following counties: Atlantic, Burlington, Camden, Cape May, Cumberland, Gloucester, Hunterdon, Mercer, Middlesex, Monmouth, Ocean, Salem, Somerset), Pennsylvania, North Carolina, Virginia (except Arlington and Fairfax counties), West Virginia

Please note that Maryland residents (except residents of Montgomery and Prince Georges counties), may deal directly with the Italian Honorary Consulate in Baltimore.

Italian Consulate General
SAN FRANCISCO
2590 Webster Street
San Francisco, CA 94115

Tel (415) 292-9210/931-4924 main numbers
Fax (415) 931-7205
Homepage: www.italcons-sf.org

Jurisdiction:
Alaska, California (except for the following counties: Imperial Valley, Kern, Los Angeles, Orange, Riverside, Santa Barbara, San Bernardino, San Louis Obispo and Ventura which are under the jurisdiction of Italian Consulate General in Los Angeles), Idaho, Montana, Oregon, Utah, Washington, Hawaii.
American Territories of Samoa, Guam, Marshall Islands, Caroline, Yap, Palau, Marianne Islands.

CHAMBERS OF COMMERCE IN ITALIAN PROVINCES

Agrigento CCI
Representing business in Agrigento
P; Gallo 317
92100 AGRIGENTO
Italy
Telephone: 0922 490211
Fax: 0922 28508

President
Paolo Di Betta

General Secretary
Francesco Capitano

Status: Public
International services?: Yes

Alessandria Chamber of Commerce & Industry
Representing Businesses in Alessandria, Italy
v. S. Lorenzo, 21
15100 ALESSANDRIA
Italy
www.al.camcom.it/

Telephone: 39-0131-3131
Fax: 39-0131-43186
Email: camera.commercio@al.camcom.it

President
Dr. Renato VIALE

Secretary General
Dr. Bruno Fara

Number of members: 35000
International services?: Yes

Ancona Chamber of Commerce and Industry
Representing Business in Ancona, Italy
P. XXIV Maggio, 1
60100 ANCONA
Italy
www.an.camcom.it/

Telephone: 39-071-58981
Fax: 39-071-2073907
Email: camcom@an.nettuno.it

President
Libero Lucconi

Secretary General
Dr.Franco DEL MASTRO

Status: Public
International services?: No

Aosta CCI
Representing business in Aosta
P.zza A. Deffeyes
11100 AOSTA
Italy
Telephone: 0165 273111
Fax: 0165 238529

President
Demetrio Mafrica

General Secretary
Nadia Betterle

Status: Public
International services?: Yes

Arezzo Chamber of Commerce and Industry
Representing Businesses in Arezzo, Italy
Viale Giotto 4
52100 AREZZO
Italy
www.ats.it/camcom/

Telephone: 39-0575-3030
Fax: 39-0575-300953

President
Pietro Faralli

General Secretary
Lodovico Lodovichi

International services?: No

Ascoli Piceno Chamber of Commerce and Industry
Representing Businesses in Ascoli Piceno, Italy
Via L. Mercantini 25
63100 ASCOLI PICENO
Italy
www.rinascita.it/PROVIAP/cameic/camcomap.ht
m

Telephone: 39-0736-27-91
Fax: 39-0736-26-21-44

President
Sauro Ramadori

General Secretary
Francesco Di Matteo

International services?: No

Asti Chamber of Commerce & Industry
Representing Businesses in Asti, Italy
P.zza Medici, 8
14100 Piemonte ASTI
Italy
www.at.camcom.it/

Telephone: 39-0141-535211
Fax: 39-0141-535200
Email: studi@at.camcom.it

President
Salvatore Garipoli

Secretary General
Dr.ssa Maria Erminia ZOTTA

International services?: No

Bari Chamber of Commerce and Industry
Representing Businesses in Bari, Italy
14100 ASTI
Italy
www.pug.camcom.it/IT221000.html

Telephone: 39-080-2174201

President
Dr. G. Mazzitello

International services?: No

Italo - Cipriota Chamber of Commerce and Industry
Representing Business between Cyprus and Sicily, Italy
Via F. Caracciolo,118
96011 SR AUGUSTA
Italy
www.gbella.it/cycamcom

Telephone: 39-0931-523051
Fax: 39-0931-522810
Email: cycamcom@gbella.it

Director of Delegation
Giovanni Bella

Status: Public
Established: 1998
International services?: No

Avellino CCI
Representing business in Avellino
V. le Cassitto 7
83100 AVELLINO
Italy
Telephone: 0825 31091
Fax: 0825 37252

President
Elio Ianuzzi

General Secretary
Antonio D'Ascoli

Status: Public
International services?: Yes

Camera di Commercio, Industria, Artigianato e Agricoltura
Representing business in Bari
Corso Cavour 2
70121 BARI
Italy
www.pug.camcom.it/IT221000.html

Telephone: 39080 2174111
Fax: 39080 2174228

President
Giuseppe Mazzitello

Director General
Giuseppe Liantonio

Status: Public
International services?: Yes

Unione delle Camere di Commercio Pugliesi

Representing Businesses in Pugliesi (Apulian Region), Italy
BARI
Italy
www.pug.camcom.it/

Telephone: 39-080-2174243
Fax: 39-080-2174259

International services?: No

Verbano Chamber of Commerce & Industry
Representing Businesses in Verbania Cusio Ossola, Italy
S.S. Sempione 4
28042 BAVENO
Italy
www.vb.camcom.it/

Telephone: 39-0323-925277
Fax: 39-0323-922054

President
Cav. Giuseppe MORONI

Secretary General
Dr. Mauro TEMPERELLI

International services?: No

Belluno CCI
Representing business in Belluno
Piazza S. Stefano 15
32100 BELLUNO
Italy
www.bl.camcom.it

Telephone: 0437 955135
Fax: 0437 955250
Email: melita.troian@bl.camcom.it

President
Paolo Terribile

General Secretary
Giuseppe Trevisiol

Status: Public
International services?: Yes

Benevento CCI
Representing business in Benevento
P. IV Novembre
82100 BENEVENTO
Italy
Telephone: 0824 300111
Fax: 0824 47424

President
Roberto Costanzo

General Secretary
Giuseppe Greco

Status: Public
International services?: Yes

Bergamo Chamber of Commerce & Industry
Representing Businesses in Bergamo, Italy
L.go B. Belotti, 16
24100 BERGAMO
Italy
www.bg.camcom.it/

Telephone: 39-035-4225111
Fax: 39-035-226023
Email: docstudi@cciaabg1.inet.it

President
Dr. Roberto SESTINI

Secretary General
Mario Pomesano

International services?: No

Biella Chamber of Commerce & Industry
Public Law Body representing Commerce, Industry, Handicraft, Agriculture in northern Italy
Via N. Sauro, 1
13051 Piemonte BIELLA
Italy
www.bi.camcom.it/

Telephone: 39-015-3599311
Fax: 39-015-2522215
Email: promozione@bi.camcom.it

President
Dr. Gianfranco DE MARTINI

Secretary General
Dr. Livio CALBI
Tel: 39-015-3599322
Fax: 39-015-2522215
Email: livio.calbi@bi.camcom.it

Status: Public
Established: 1994
Number of members: 19940

Number of employees: 35
International services?: Yes

Bologna Chamber of Commerce and Industry
Representing Businesses in Bologna, Italy
Piazza Mercanzia 4 - Pal. Mercanzia
40125 BOLOGNA
Italy
www.bo.camcom.it/

Telephone: 0039/051/6093111
Fax: 0039/051/6093451-225
Email: segreteria.generale@bo.camcom.it

President
Giancarlo Sangalli

Foreign Trade Department Officer
Dr. Giuseppe Rocco
Fax: 0039/051/6093225
Email: commercio.estero@bo.camcom.it

Status: Public
Number of members: 80000
International services?: Yes

Unione delle Camere di Commercio dell'Emilia-Romagna
Representing Businesses in Emilia-Romagna, Italy
40121 Bologna BOLOGNA
Italy
www.rer.camcom.it/

Telephone: 39-051-6566011
Fax: 39-051-6566050
Email: staff@rer.camcom.it

President/CEO
Giampaolo Montaletti

International services?: No

Bolzano Chamber of Commerce
Representing business in the autonomous provine of Bolzano/Bozen
via Perathoner 8b/10
39100 South Tyrol BOLZANO - BOZEN
Italy
www.hk-cciaa.bz.it

Telephone: 0039-0471-945511
Fax: 0039-0471-945620
Email: info@hk-cciaa.bz.it

President
Benedikt Gramm

Director of export
Petra Seppi
Tel: 0039-0471-945645
Fax: 0039-0471-945620
Email: eic@hk-cciaa.bz.it

Status: Public
Established: 1820
Number of members: 38000
Number of employees: 120
International services?: Yes

Brescia Chamber of Commerce & Industry
Representing Businesses in Brescia, Italy
V.L Einaudi 23
25122 Lombardia BRESCIA
Italy
www.bs.camcom.it/

Telephone: 39-030-37251
Fax: 39-030-3725222
Email: brescia@bs.camcom.it

President
Dr. Francesco BETTONI

Secretary General
Dr. Carmelo ANTONUCCIO

International services?: No

Brindisi
Representing business in Brindisi
V. Bastioni Carlo V, 4
72100 BRINDISI
Italy
Telephone: 0831 2201
Fax: 0831 220210
Email: www.pug.camcom.it/br/pagbr1.html

President
Andrea Gentile

General Secretary
Isabella De Carlo

Status: Public
International services?: Yes

Campobasso CCI
Representing business in Campobasso
P. della Vittoria 1
86100 CAMPOBASSO

Italy
Telephone: 0874 4711
Fax: 0874 90034

President
Enrico Colavita

General Secretary
Giovanni Scordamaglia

Status: Public
International services?: Yes

Caserta Chamber of Commerce
Representing Businesses in Caserta, Italy
Via Roma 97
81100 CASERTA
Italy
www.ce.camcom.it/

Telephone: 39-0823-325366
Fax: 39-0823-320418
Email: camcomce@caserta.peoples.it

President
Ferdinando Tamburrino

General Secretary
Guido Perrotta

International services?: No

Catania Chamber of Commerce
Representing Businesses in Catania, Italy
95124 CATANIA
Italy
Telephone: 39-095-321155
Fax: 39-095-321110

International services?: No

Catanzaro
Representing business in Catanzaro
V. Minniti Ippolito 16
88100 CATANZARO
Italy
Telephone: 0961 721224
Fax: 0961 721236

President
Alfonso Muleo

General Secretary
Raffaele De Franco Paladini

Status: Public
International services?: Yes

Chieti CCI
Representing business in Chieti
P.G. Battista Vico 3
66100 CHIETI
Italy
Telephone: 0871 354306
Fax: 0871 330913

President
Palmerindo Roselli

General Secretary
Ettore Lalli

Status: Public
International services?: Yes

Como Chamber of Commerce & Industry
Representing Businesses in Como, Italy
Via Parini, 16
22100 COMO
Italy
www.co.camcom.it/

Telephone: 39-031-256-111
Fax: 39-031-240-826
Email: como@co.camcom.it

President
Rag. Marco CITTERIO

Secretary General
Dr. Sergio RIGAMONTI

International services?: No

Cosenza Chamber of Commerce and Industry
Representing Business in Cosenza, Italy
Via Calabria 33
87100 COSENZA
Italy
cs.camcom.it/

Telephone: 39-0984-8151
Fax: 39-0984-815284
Email: camera97@antares.it

President
Ernesto Marano

General Secretary
Aleardo Forleo

International services?: No

Cremona Chamber of Commerce & Industry
Representing Businesses in Cremona, Italy
Piazza Cavour, 5
26100 CREMONA
Italy
www.cr.camcom.it/

Telephone: 39-0372-4901
Fax: 39-0372-21396
Email: cremona@cr.camcom.it

President
Gino Villa

Secretary General
Dr. Massimo DESTER

International services?: No

Cuneo Chamber of Commerce & Industry
Representing Businesses in Cuneo, Italy
Via E. Filiberto, 3
12100 CUNEO
Italy
www.cn.camcom.it/

Telephone: 39-0171-318711
Fax: 39-0171-696581
Email: info@cn.camcom.it

President
Dr. Ferruccio DARDANELLO

Secretary General
Dr. Vittorio SABBATINI

International services?: No

Ferrara Chamber of Commerce and Industry
Representing business in Ferrara
Largo Castello 10
Via Borgoleoni 11
44100 FERRARA
Italy
Telephone: 0532 783711
Fax: 0532 240204

President
Carlo Alberto Roncarati

General Secretary
Giuseppe Sansoni

Status: Public
International services?: Yes

Firenze Chamber of Commerce and Industry
Representing Businesses in Firenze, Italy
P. dei Giudici 3
50122 FIRENZE
Italy
www.fi.camcom.it/

Telephone: 39-055-2795-1
Fax: 39-055-2795-259
Email: cciaafi@saatel.it

President
Alberto Carmi

General Secretary
Francesco Barbolla

International services?: No

Foggia Chamber of Commerce and Industry
Representing Businesses in Foggia, Italy
Via Dante 27
71100 FOGGIA
Italy
www.pug.camcom.it/IT223000.html

Telephone: 39-0881-7971
Fax: 0881-726046

President
Luigi Lepri

General Secretary
Guzzardo Calogero

International services?: No

Forli Chamber of Commerce and Industry
Representing Businesses in Forli, Italy
Corso della Repubblica 5
47100 FORLI
Italy
Telephone: 39-0543-713111
Fax: 39-0543-713502

President
Sergio Mazzi

General Secretary
Ettore Neri

Number of members: 30000
International services?: No

Forll-Cesena Chamber of Commerce and Industry
Representing Businesses in Forll-Cesena, Italy
47100 FORLL
Italy
www.fo.camcom.it/

Telephone: 39-0543-713111
Fax: 39-0543-713502

International services?: No

Frosinone Chamber of Commerce and Industry
Representing Business in Frosinone, Italy
Via A. de Gasperi 2
3100 FROSINONE
Italy
www.fr.camcom.it/

Telephone: 39-0775-2131
Fax: 39-0775-853105
Email: segreteria@fr.camcom.it

President
Luigi Annunziata

General Secretary
Matteo Piemontese

International services?: No

Genova Chamber of Commerce and Industry
Representing Businesses in Genova, Italy
Via Garibaldi, 4
16124 GENOVA
Italy
www.lig.camcom.it/cciaa_ge/default.htm

Telephone: +39 01027041
Fax: +39 0102704300
Email: camera.genova@ge.camcom.it

President
Paolo Cesare Odone

Secretary General
Guido Molinari

Status: Public
International services?: No

Gorizia CCI
Representing business in Gorizia
Via F. Crispi 10
34170 GORIZIA
Italy
Telephone: 0481 3841
Fax: 0481 533176

President
Enzo Bevilacqua

General Secretary
Giuliano Bigoni

Status: Public
International services?: Yes

Grosseto Chamber of Commerce and Industry
Representing Businesses in Grosseto, Italy
Via Cairoli 10
58100 GROSSETO
Italy
www.gol.grosseto.it/puam/cciaa/

Telephone: 39-0564-430111
Fax: 39-0564-415821
Email: cciaagr@gol.grosseto.it

President
Mario Gennari

General Secretary
Luciano Spaziani

International services?: No

Imperia Chamber of Commerce and Industry
Representing Business in Imperia, Italy
Viale Matteotti 48
18100 IMPERIA
Italy
www.lig.camcom.it/

Telephone: 39-0183-7931
Fax: 39-0183-275021
Email: marco.stefanolo@im.cciaa.net

President
Gianfranco Cozzi

General Secretary
Alessandro Scajola

International services?: No

Isernia CCI
Representing business in Isernia
C. so Risorgimento 302
86170 ISERNIA

Italy
Telephone: 0865 4551
Fax: 0865 235024

President
Agostino Angelaccio

General Secretary
Carmine Spensieri

Status: Public
International services?: Yes

Spezia Chamber of Commerce and Industry
Representing Businesses in Spezia, Italy
Via Veneto 28
19100 LA SPEZIA
Italy
www.sp.camcom.it/

Telephone: 39-0187-728111
Fax: 39-0187-777908
Email: info@laspeziainvest.com

President
Pier Gino Scardigli

Technical Manager
Gabriele Boni
Tel: 39-0187-728225
Fax: 39-0187-777961
Email: euroinfosp@sp.camcom.it

Number of employees: 6
International services?: No

L'Aquila CCI
Representing business in L'Aquila
V. del Guastatore 7
67100 L'AQUILA
Italy
Telephone: 0862 6671
Fax: 0862 413543

President
Benito Bove

General Secretary
Mario Santucci

Status: Public
International services?: Yes

Latina CCI
Representing business in Latina
Via Umberto I, 84
4100 LATINA
Italy
Telephone: 0773 6721
Fax: 0773 693003

President
Alfredo Loffredo

General Secretary
Erasmo Fiumara

Status: Public
International services?: Yes

Lecce Chamber of Commerce and Industry
Representing Businesses in Lecce, Italy
V. le Gallipoli 39
73100 LECCE
Italy
www.pug.camcom.it/le/pagle1.html

Telephone: 0832 6841
Fax: 0832 684260-79

President
Salvatore Leone de Castris

General Secretary
Francesco Ciardo

International services?: No

Lecco Chamber of Commerce & Industry
Representing Businesses in Lecco, Italy
Via Amendola, 4
22053 LECCO
Italy
www.lc.camcom.it/

Telephone: 39-0341-292-111
Fax: 39-0341-292-220-30
Email: lecco@lc.camcom.it

President
Ing. Vico VALASSI

Secretary General
Dr.ssa Rossella PULSONI

International services?: No

Livorno CCI
Representing business in Livorno
P. del Municipio 48
57123 LIVORNO
Italy

Telephone: 0586 231111
Fax: 0586 886689

President
Ernesto Laviosa

General Secretary
Renzo Pratesi

Status: Public
International services?: Yes

Livorno CCI
Representing business in Livorno
P. del Municipio 48
57123 LIVORNO
Italy
Telephone: 0586 231111
Fax: 0586 886689

President
Ernesto Laviosa

General Secretary
Renzo Pratesi

Status: Public
International services?: Yes

Lodi Chamber of Commerce & Industry
Representing Businesses in Lodi, Italy
Via Haussmann, 11
20075 LODI
Italy
www.lo.camcom.it/

Telephone: 39-0371-45051
Fax: 39-0371-431604
Email: info@lo.camcom.it/

President
Dr. Francesco FERRARI

Secretary General
Maurizio Falcone

Status: Public
Established: 1995
Number of employees: 30
International services?: Yes

Lucca Chamber of Commerce and Industry
Representing Businesses in Lucca, Italy
Corte Campana 10
55100 LUCCA
Italy
www.lunet.it/enti/cciaa/welcome.html

Telephone: 39-0583-976635
Fax: 39-0583-976629
Email: cameracommercio@lu.cciaa.net

President
Claudio Guerrieri

General Secretary
Roberto Camisi

International services?: No

Macerata CCI
Representing business in Macerata
V. Tommaso Lauri 7
62100 MACERATA
Italy
Telephone: 0733 2511
Fax: 0733 230839

President
Ernesto Guizzardi

General Secretary
Mario Guadagno

Status: Public
International services?: Yes

Mantova Chamber of Commerce & Industry
Representing Businesses in Mantova, Italy
Via P. F. Calvi, 28
46100 MANTOVA
Italy
www.mn.camcom.it/

Telephone: 39-0376-2341
Fax: 39-0376-234234
Email: mantova@mn.camcom.it

President
On. Prof. Antonino ZANIBONI

Secretary General
Dr. Enrico (f.f.) MAROCCHI

International services?: No

Massa Carrara Chamber of Commerce and Industry
Representing Business in Massa Carrara, Italy
Piazza 2 giugno
54033 MASSA CARRARA

Italy
www.ms.camcom.it/

Telephone: 39-0585-7641
Fax: 39-0585-776515
Email: cciaams@iclab.it

President
Giuseppe Tramonti

General Secretary
Alberto Ravecca

International services?: No

Matera CCI
Representing business in Matera
Via Lucana 82
75100 MATERA
Italy

President
Francesco Manfredi

General Secretary
Salvatore Bucceri

Status: Public
International services?: Yes

Messina Chamber of Commerce and Industry
Representing Businesses in Messina, Italy
98100 MESSINA
Italy
Telephone: 39-090-777211
Fax: 39-090-674644

International services?: No

Unioncamere del Veneto
Representing Businesses in Veneto, Italy
30172 MESTRE (VENEZIA)
Italy
www.gpnet.it/unioncamere/

Telephone: 39-041-932555
Fax: 39-041-933336
Email: uvcamcom@gpnet.it

International services?: No

Camera di Commercio Industria Artigianato e Agricoltura di Milano - Milan Chamber of Commerce
The Milan Chamber of Commerce is a public law body which supports and promots the companies' interests in the province where it is located. The mission includes the issuing of companies' certifcates, promotion, training and development actions as well as information supply. The Milan Chamber of Commerce has launched numerous initiatives to favour especially small and mediumsized companies, culturally and economically on a worldwide scale.
Via Meravigli, 9/b-11
20123 MILAN
Italy
www.mi.camcom.it/

Telephone: 39-02-8515-1
Fax: 39-02-85154232
Email: infohighway@mi.camcom.it

President
Dr. Carlo SANGALLI

Secretary General
Dr. Pier Daniele MELEGARI

Status: Public
Established: 1786
International services?: Yes

Unione delle Camere di Commercio della Lombardia
Representing Businesses in Lombardia, Italy
20121 MILAN
Italy
www.lom.camcom.it/

Telephone: 39-02-29010201
Fax: 39-02-29010203
Email: info@lom.camcom.it

International services?: No

American Chamber of Commerce in Italy
Representing Businesses in Italy and the United States
Via Cantu 1
20123 MILAN
Italy
www.amcham.it

Telephone: 39-02-8690661
Fax: 39-02-8057737
Email: amcham@enter.it

Managing Director
Sergio Minoretti

Number of members: 1000
International services?: Yes

French Chamber of Commerce and Industry in Italy
Representing French Business interests in Italy
Via Cusani 5
20121 MILAN
Italy
www.contacsfrancoitaliens.it

Telephone: (39 02) 72 53 71
Fax: (39 02) 86 55 93
Email: cfci@seicom.it

President
Didier LARTILLEUX

Secretary General
Christine PICHLER

Status: Public
International services?: Yes

Swiss Chamber of Commerce in Italy - Camera di Commercio Svizzera in Italia
Representing Swiss Businesses in Italy
via Palestro 2
20121 MILAN
Italy
www.ccsi.it

Telephone: 39-02-76003606
Fax: 39-02-781084
Email: ccsi@iol.it

Secretary General
Alessandra Modenese Kauffmann

Number of members: 550
Number of employees: 6
International services?: Yes

Modena Chamber of Commerce and Industry
Representing Businesses in Modena, Italy
Via Ganaceto 134
41100 MODENA
Italy
www.mo.camcom.it/

Telephone: 059 208111
Fax: 059 211035
Email: cciaamo@mo.nettuno.it

President
Antonio Camellini

General Secretary
Claudio Fornasari

International services?: No

Napoli Chamber of Commerce and Industry
Representing business in the system of factories of Province of Napoli.
Piazza Bovio
80133 Naples, Italy NAPOLI
Italy
www.na.camcom.it

Telephone: +390817607111
Fax: +390815526940
Email: webmaster@na.camcom.it

Presidente
Lucio Barone Lumaga

Funzionario
Elisabetta Gilenti
Tel: +390817607632
Fax: +39081285465
Email: elisabetta.gilenti@na.camcom.it

Status: Public
Established: 1899
Number of members: 30
Number of employees: 200
International services?: Yes

Novara Chamber of Commerce & Industry
Representing Businesses in Novara, Italy
V.degli Avogadro, 4
28100 Piemonte NOVARA
Italy
www.no.camcom.it/

Telephone: 39-0321-338211
Fax: 39-0321-338338

President
Alberto Macchi

Secretary General
Dr. Franco LAMONARCA

International services?: No

Padova Chamber of Commerce & Industry
Representing Businesses in Padova, Italy
Via E. Filiberto, 34
35122 PADOVA
Italy
www.pd.camcom.it/

Telephone: 39-049-8208111
Fax: 39-049-8208290
Email: chamberpadova@pd.camcom.it

President
Comm. Gianfranco CHIESA

Secretary General
Dr. Alessandro SELMIN
Tel: 39-049-8208111
Fax: 39-049-8208290
Email: segreteria@pd.camcom.it

Status: Public
Established: 1811
Number of members: 96000
Number of employees: 134
International services?: Yes

Palermo Chamber of Commerce and Industry
Representing Businesses in Palermo, Italy
90139 PALERMO
Italy
Telephone: 39-091-589922
Fax: 39-091-582338

International services?: No

Parma Chamber of Commerce and Industry
Promoting general interests of the enterprises (especially SME) localized in the area served through 1) managing administrative procedures provided by the law to enter business; 2) providing services and techical assistance 3) carrying out actions in order to develop foreign trade and international business cooperation
Via Verdi 2/a
43100 PARMA
Italy
www.pr.camcom.it

Telephone: 39-0-521 2101
Fax: 39-0-521 282168
Email: isabella.benecchi@pr.cciaa.net

President
Cesare Gherri

General Secretary
Daniele Alfieri

Number of members: 40000
International services?: No

SELECTED EXPORT-IMPORT OPPORTUNITES AND CONTACTS[1]

NEW SYSTEM FOR QUALIFYING CONSTRUCTION FIRMS

1. On January 21, 2000, the Italian government approved a decree establishing a new system of qualifying construction firms bidding on public works. It is anticipated that the decree will be published in the Official Gazette at the end of February.

Among other things, the decree introduces SOAs (Societa' Organismo di Attestazione), and dictates the rules governing their establishment and operations. SOAs is the acronym for the privately owned firms which, under the new system, will certify that a construction company wanting to bid on public works is qualified, that is, complies with all financial, as well as technical, requirements and has the required experience. These specialized certification firms will operate in a manner similar to that of auditing firms.

The new system of qualification based on certification by SOAs will replace the previous system, centralized and public, based on listing in the ANC (Albo Nazionale Costruttori, that is, National Register of Constructors), which has been in force from 1962 through the end of 2004. Until the decree establishing the new qualification system is officially published, decree 502 (published in December, 2004) provides interim rules for qualifying construction firms wanting to bid on public works.

This report will briefly outline the overall content of the decree approved on January 21 and will then focus on SOAs, which will constitute the keystone of the new qualification system, as well as on the business potential for these new certification firms.

2. The decree establishing the new system of qualification of contractors bidding on public works consists of 34 articles and several attachments. In a nutshell, the decree provides for:

- the definitions of 34 general and special public works categories, and of 8 classes (that is, levels of expenditures)
- the specifications of the general, as well as the special, qualifications required for bidding on public works
- the rules governing the qualification of consortia of enterprises
- the compulsory, although gradual, introduction of ISO 9000 quality certification as a qualification requirement
- the establishment and duties of the Authority supervising public works and SOAs
- the establishment of SOAs and the rules governing their operations and fees
- the requirements for the technical directors of construction firms bidding on public works
- the requirements for qualification of construction firms applicable in the years 2000 and 2001, waiting for the new qualification system to become fully operational

The new qualification system will apply to construction companies of all sizes from January 1, 2002. During the two years of transition, entities contracting public works will conduct the assessment of the required qualifications directly. However, contractors bidding on projects in excess of Lire 10 billion (or approximately USD 5 million), will need to be certified by a SOA by March 2001, a year after the new decree will come into force.

[1] This section based in part on the materials of the US Trade Office in Italy

The new system is said to increase competition. In particular, contractors which were not listed in the ANC will have access to public works bids, provided they comply with the necessary requirements.

Contractors from countries belonging to the European Union are not subject to the new qualification system (unless they elect to seek qualification under it), but rather to the regulations governing qualification for public works in their home country.

Among the general requirement, one states that technical directors of construction firms seeking qualification for bidding on public works, as well as directors representing the firm, must have Italian citizenship, or that of a country belonging to the European Union. Third country nationals are also accepted, provided they reside in Italy and are citizens of countries granting reciprocity treatment.

It should be noted that, as a result of the new regulation, the public works sector will become one of the few sectors in Italy in which quality certification according to ISO 9000 will become a requirement for qualification, except for small projects.

3. Articles of the decree from 7 to 14 deal with the SOAs, the new firms which will certify construction companies wanting to bid on public works. Unlike the old qualification procedure carried out by ANC, the SOAs' qualification procedure will require in-depth assessment of the investigated construction firm's structure, organization, technical and financial standing, expertise and background. Such an assessment may include inspections of the branch offices and construction yards.

SOAs will be permitted to perform only those activities that are directly related to the certification of the qualification requirements. As an exception, accredited firms engaged in the certification of quality systems (ISO 9000) will be eligible to be authorized to also certify the qualification requirements for public works. SOAs must be joint stock corporations with a minimum capital of Lira 1 billion (or USD 500 million) and must be headquartered in Italy. Furthermore, they must be authorized by the Authority monitoring public works and included in an official list.

Detailed rules are aimed at assuring objective assessments by SOAs. To that purpose, organizations having an interest in the outcome of such assessments are prevented from participating in the SOAs' capital. An exception are the Italian associations of constructors, which are permitted to participate in the SOAs' equity capital, but only up to a maximum of 10 percent and provided that also the Italian associations of entities contracting public works participate in the same amount.

SOAs must be properly staffed. The minimum staff configuration will have to include: a technical director with a degree in engineering or architecture and enrolled in the official register of engineers or architects, 10 years professional experience, of which, at least five years are in public works; three employees with a degree in, respectively, engineering or architecture, law, and economics; and at least six employees with adequate professional qualifications. SOAs will not be permitted to outsource any activities.

SOAs will have to conduct their assessments within 90 days from the date of the contract with the construction companies. Certifications will be valid for 3 years.

4. The certification of qualification requirements for public works will generate new significant business. Sectoral experts conservatively estimate that SOAs' revenues will be at least Lira 350 - 400 billion per year (or USD 175 - 200 million). These estimates assume that about 20,000 construction firms (out of the approximately 50,000 which were qualified under the previous ANC

system) are likely to seek qualification under the new system, while the SOAs' fees will range from a minimum of Lira 20 million (for smaller construction firms seeking qualification in three or four categories) up to Lira 100 million and more for large companies.

It is expected that most SOAs will be established by banks, insurance companies, and ISO 9000 quality certification organizations

ADVERTISING REGULATIONS

For many years, the use of comparative advertising in the American market has been accepted and utilized as a legal and useful form of comparison. In the USA, an advertiser may develop a campaign that identifies competitors by name, trademark, or other distinctive features.

In Italy the situation is very different and the Italian courts and the Giuri - an arbitral panel established by the advertising industry's code of self-regulation - share a generally unfavorable opinion of American-style comparative advertising, which, in the Italian view, promotes more discord than benefit.

COMPARATIVE ADVERTISING IN ITALY

The Italian courts adjudicate the propriety of comparative advertising under article 2598 of the Codice Civile, which classifies as unfair competition the dissemination of "information and opinions about a competitor's products and activities, tending to bring them into discredit . . ."

Alternatively, the Giuri - an arbitral panel established by the advertising industry's code of self-regulation - decides comparative advertising disputes where the parties have bound themselves to abide by the Codice di Autodisciplina Pubblicitaria ('CAP').
In recent years the Giuri's decisions have gained increasing importance.
Thus, although the courts pay lip service to the principle that Article 2598 of the Codice Civile does not prevent advertisers, consistent with standards of "professional correctness," from making truthful comparative references to competitors, in practice, legal challenges to comparative advertising are frequently successful. In marked contrast with American law, Italian courts often consider illegal a comparative advertisement on the ground that it is "tendentious."

With regard to the Giuri, the CAP itself generally prohibits direct comparative advertising, that is, advertising that identifies a competitor by name or mark. Moreover, the CAP permits indirect comparative advertising - in which the advertiser compares its product or service with a generic competitive product or service - only "when useful to illustrate from a technical and economic point of view the objectively relevant and verifiable characteristics and advantages of the goods and services advertised."
This antagonism toward aggressive comparative advertising leads to the suppression of advertisements and television commercials that would be considered as innocuous fair competition in the United States.

EXAMPLES OF ILLEGAL ADVERTISING

There are several examples on the Italian market of advertisements considered illegal by the Italy Court.

On the complaint of the glass manufacturers' association, the Tribunale (Italy's court of general jurisdiction) ordered cessation of a trade magazine advertisement for a polyethylene container that touted the synthetic product as a "light, unbreakable and noiseless organic glass." The Court held that in describing its product as "organic glass," the advertiser provoked an unjust comparison with real glass containers by "tendentiously" underscoring that real glass was breakable and neither light nor noiseless.

The worldwide cola wars between Coca Cola and Pepsi Cola have prompted two significant Giuri decisions regarding the limits of comparative advertising.
In 1991, Coke's Italian subsidiary challenged the Pepsi subsidiary's television commercial - aired in many other countries featuring rap star M.C. Hammer at a fake concert. In the commercial, Hammer loses his

energy when he mistakenly drinks an unnamed "other" cola and lapses into a Perry Como style of singing. Only an infusion of Pepsi jolts Hammer back into rapping again.

Pepsi argued that the commercial dealt only with subjective taste, not a comparison of objectively measurable qualities, and was obviously surreal. The Giuri ordered Pepsi to withdraw the advertisement. In the Giuri's view, the commercial conveyed an irrational message because it was not objectively relevant and verifiable that Hammer needed Pepsi to sing rap. The Giuri also found the commercial impermissibly "suggestive" in representing Pepsi as more suitable for young, energetic consumers.

In 1993, Coke and Pepsi were again in front of the Giuri. Pepsi's Italian subsidiary had aired a commercial, also shown in the United States, in which a young, muscular motorcyclist stops at a run-down gas station in the middle of the desert. Upon being told that only Coke was available and that it was 50 miles to the next store selling Pepsi, the biker hesitates for a moment, but then continues on his way across the desert. The commercial ends with the biker happily drinking Pepsi in a clean, modern gas station and the message "Farther ahead, there's Pepsi."

The Giuri again sustained the Coca Cola complaint. In the Giuri's view, the advertisement drew an unfair comparison between the young, modern lifestyle of the Pepsi-drinking motorcyclist and the old, out-of-date of the Coke-drinking desert characters. The Giuri also held that the advertisement denigrated Coke by suggesting that it was better to drive 50 miles under the desert sun than quench an overwhelming thirst with Coca Cola.

Italy's New Law on Comparative Advertising

Recently a new decree, Legislative Decree No 67 of February 25, 2000 (LD 67), published on March 27, 2000 has been implemented to amend Directive 97/55/EC concerning misleading advertising. (Attachment #1)
Since 1992, the Authority has been responsible for enforcing the Decree, in implementation of a European Community Directive, whose objective is the introduction of a legislation prohibiting **misleading advertising** in Italy.
On April 11, 2000 the Legislative Decree no. 67 has entered into force, which gives the Authority responsibility for ruling on comparative advertising. It is the task of the Authority to ascertain the lawfulness of the advertising comparison. Generally, two conditions are to be respected:

- the comparative advertisment must not be misleading,
- and it has not to be unfair.

Any advertising is deemed to be "**misleading**" when, in any way whatsoever, including its presentation, **it deceives or it is likely to deceive** those to whom it is directed and, as a consequence, **it is likely to affect their economic behaviour or cause harm to a competitor**.

The notion of advertising is very broad, and even includes the packaging of products.
Under Section 1 of the Decree, advertising must be "**clear, truthful and fair.**" In particular refers to the **transparency** of advertising, which must be "**clearly recognisable**" as such.

The purpose of this decree is to protect everybody against misleading advertising and its unfair consequences, and to lay down conditions under which comparative advertising is lawful.

Particular emphasis is placed on advertisements relating to products that might damage consumer health and which may reach children or adolescents.
The Italian Antitrust Authority will be competent for controversies arising from comparative advertising. However, the Authority cannot take action on its own initiative but may only act on the basis of a complaint, which may be filed following the rules set out in the Presidential Decree no. 627/96, Section 2, by:

a) private consumers,
b) consumer associations,
c) competitors of companies disseminating allegedly misleading advertisements,

d) the Ministry of Industry or any public agency or authority which may be interested in relation to its institutional objectives, even following a public complaint.

The sectoral Directorates deal with other Government departments and agencies: in particular **they work jointly**, in areas laid down in the Act, **with the Autorità per le garanzie nelle comunicazioni (the National Regulator for Communications)** which, after the Antitrust Authority has completed its investigation, expresses its own non-binding opinion on misleading advertisements which have been broadcast or disseminated in the press, and on the lawfulness of comparative advertisements

CIVIL AVIATION

The Italian Civil Aviation market is facing a period of difficult decisions which will probably lead to major changes in the near future: on one side, Alitalia, the national flag carrier, is seeking its own way among the competing giant airline combinations and therefore is endeavoring to pursue strategic alliances worldwide; on the other hand, Finmeccanica, the financial holding with substantial interests in the Aerospace sector with industries like Alenia and Agusta, is in the middle of political and industrial changes, and is seeking to maintain and develop its presence in the European aerospace sector (in particular the Airbus Consortium), where Italy ranks fourth, while keeping its industrial identity. Finmeccanica management is well aware that to achieve this second goal it is necessary to strengthen the cooperation with the U.S. industry. U.S. companies seeking to penetrate or to expand their existing market in Italy should therefore closely follow both Alitalia's policy developments and Finmeccanica's medium term industrial plans.

In the past few years, the Italian Civil Aviation sector has seen important changes, and is undergoing a significant restructuring, which has lead to lay-offs of almost 15,000 people, down to the actual 34,000, mainly in the manufacturing industry, which is now concentrated in two industrial poles: Finmeccanica and Fiat. As regards Alitalia, it has reached a joint venture agreement with the Dutch KLM and the American Northwest. This agreement will help optimize resources and create operational synergies in order to better compete against other giant alliances worldwide. The Civil Aviation market is therefore showing signs of recovery after a period of general contraction which also affected the national economic scenario.

As of January, 1998, Alitalia's fleet comprised 148 airplanes, 81 of which were operated by Alitalia, and the rest by its related companies Alitalia Team (54) and Alitalia Express (13). The majority of these aircraft were MD-80 (90), while the balance included: A-321 (20); B-747 (11); ATR-42 (9); MD-11 (8); B-767 (6) and ATR-72 (4). Average age of these aircraft is 8.6 years, which makes the fleet one of the youngest in Europe. In the latest shareholder meetings held last June, Alitalia management announced the purchase of five new B747s, to be delivered by the first half of 2001, and the company's interest in acquiring a number of new 50/70 seater regional-jets, some of which as substitutes for older ATR-42.

Other national companies (Air-One, Meridiana, Azzurra, Lauda Air, Air Europe, Med Airlines, and Air Sicilia and several smaller ones), together operate nearly 150 additional aircraft, mostly on national routes or charter connections with foreign destinations.

Furthermore, by the end of 1998, there were in Italy approximately 900 airplanes belonging to aeroclubs and about 650 owned by private associations. As for business planes, Italy ranks among the top countries in Europe, with over 300 aircraft in use (turbofan, turbojets and turboprops).

The increasing demand for regional and national flights has been influenced by the dissatisfaction of many business users with the state-owned railways, which offer below standard services. Many of these short routes are actually covered by a small fleet of ATR-42s and ATR-72s turboprops, which are manufactured by Alenia in cooperation with Aerospatiale and have gained a very positive reputation. However, the need for increased passenger capacity as well as higher flexibility and speed has led both the industry and the air carriers to seek possible alternatives. Alenia, in particular, has been seeking, so far unsuccessfully, European partners for the co-production of 70/100 seater class jet-propelled airplanes. This could provide an opportunity to U.S. manufacturers.

U.S. manufacturers have virtually abandoned the market for small, single engine aircraft, leaving the French to dominate this sector of the market, with the Germans specializing in turbo engines. However, the U.S. know-how remains unparalleled, and there is still a broad range and a fairly large number of U.S. aircraft in use. U.S. companies producing light aircraft, jet engines and piston and turboprop engines of innovative design still have good opportunities in this expanding market, provided that the following conditions are met: availability (possibly in Italy) of after-sale services, and the possibility to set up medium to long term financing (generally 36 to 60 months) at competitive rates. There are also aeronautical financial services companies which can provide leasing terms that respond to the needs of the market.

KEY CONTACTS

AIAD (Italian Industries Association for Aerospace, Systems and Defense)
Via Nazionale, 200
00184 Roma
tel: 39/064880247
fax: 39/064827476

RAI Registro Aeronautico Italiano (Italian Airworthiness Authority)
Via del tritone, 169
00187 Roma
tel: 39/06675841
fax: 39/066781318

IBAA (Italian Business Aviation Association of end-users)
Viale dell'Aviazione, 65
20138 Milano
tel: 39/027560621
fax: 39/027560621

Alitalia S.p.A.
Via della Magliana, 88600148 Roma
Tel: 39/0665621
Fax: 39/0665625631

Air One
Via Sardegna, 14
00187 Roma
tel: 39/06478761
fax: 39/064885986

Alenia S.p.A.
Via G.V. Bona, 85
00156 Roma
tel: 39/06417231
fax: 39/064114439

Fiat Avio S.p.A.
Via Nizza, 312
10127 Torino
tel: 39/0116858111
fax: 39/0116859382

COMPUTER AND RELATED SERVICES

Ministero per i Beni e le Attività Culturali
Ufficio del responsabile per i Sistemi informativi automatizzati
via del Collegio Romano 27
00186 Roma
Tel.: 066 72 35 96
Fax: 066 72 34 14
ITALY

VITAMINS & MINERALS SUPPLEMENTS

The combined Italian market for nutritional supplements, homeopathic remedies, teas and herbs in 2004 is estimated at $250 million dollars and represents 16% of the European market. As Italy is a strong producer and exporter of vitamins and minerals in bulk and in manufactured form, U.S. companies will need to focus on price to develop their market share. In addition, U.S. companies need to pay close attention to product specifications since vitamins and minerals in the form of capsules, tablets, liquid form, etc. produced in the United States often contain ingredients in quantities which exceed the limits set by the Ministry of Health for nutritional supplements, and consequently would be classified as pharmaceuticals in Italy. As pharmaceuticals, they would require marketing authorizations prior being placed on the market, a long and costly procedure which many importers prefer to avoid, and their sales would be confined to pharmacies. The appointment of a local distributor and importer is recommended in any case.

DEFINITIONS AND REGULATIONS

There is no specific European or Italian law which regulates vitamin and minerals in the form of tablets, capsules, powder and liquid form, known as nutritional supplements or integrators. European community directive 89/398 EEC on the Approximation of the laws of the Member States relating to foodstuffs intended for particular nutritional uses, implemented through Italian law decree 111 of January 27, 1992 is generally interpreted to provide the basic directorylines for the marketing, distribution and labeling of vitamin and nutritional supplements as well as for the nine categories of foodstuffs it specifically addresses, i.e. babies' formulas, baby foods, low-sodium and salt substitutes, gluten-free foods, artificial sweeteners, weight-control meal substitutes and energy-enhancing beverages and preparations.

Guidelines not provided for in Law decree 111 have been supplemented by the Ministry of Health in informal instructions** (see translation in the Attachment). Essentially, the Ministry aims to differentiate between nutritional supplements or integrators whose active ingredients are within the limits designated for safe consumption by the U.S. Food & Drug Administration as the recommended daily intake (RDA) and by Italy in its own version LARN (Livelli di Assunzione Raccomandati di Nutrienti) and those surpassing the recommended daily intake, and which are considered medicinal products. (There is no distinction between natural and synthetic ingredients. The RDA/LARN limits apply in either case.)

** Note: The Ministry of Health has announced that it is revising the instructions translated in Attachment. The Commercial Service in Rome will provide the necessary updates, when available.

Different types of marketing authorizations and retail distribution rules apply, depending on the nature and composition of the product:
-For nutritional supplements, (i.e. those which do not exceed the RDA/LARN limits and which are without medical attributes): a copy of the label or of the retail packaging must be transmitted to the Ministry of Health concurrent with their being placed on the market. If no objections or exceptions are raised by the Ministry of Health within 90 days, the product can be considered approved. The Ministry, however, reserves the right to recall the product for further examination and eventual withdrawal if the information placed on the packaging or on the label does not correspond with the contents, or if it is found that the product is unsafe. There is no restriction on advertising, and nutritional supplements may be sold in food and health stores, supermarket chains, department stores, etc.;
- For vitamins and minerals which exceed the RDA/LARN limits and claim medical attributes: Laws pertaining to over-the-counter (OTC) pharmaceuticals, apply.

OTCs may only be sold in pharmacies and must have special Ministry of Health marketing authorizations prior to their being placed on the market. Unlike for subscription medicines, advertising for OTCs is permitted. (For information on how to apply for marketing authorizations for pharmaceuticals, see Industry Market Insight of July 21, 1998).

Two other categories of products share similarities with the two categories described above:

Homeopathic remedies: At present these are regulated by European Union directive 92/73/EEC, implemented through Law decree 185 of March 17, 1995. The decree differentiates between homeopathic medicines subject to a simplified registration procedure and those which must undergo more complicated pharmacological, toxicological and clinical tests. The decree also states that homeopathic remedies on the Italian market as of June 6, 1995 could remain on sale until June 2000 pending their reassessment. Sales are now restricted to pharmacies (some 7,500 out of Italy's 16,000 pharmacies specialize in homeopathy) and advertising is not permitted. Reassessment may classify a number of homeopathic remedies as herbal preparations;
Herbal preparations. i.e. teas, tisanes, and herbs sold mainly in herbalists'shops or erboristerie: As in the case of homeopathic remedies, some products are due for reassessment. A decree law on herbal preparations was approved by the Lower Chamber in February 2000 and is due to be examined by the Senate for final approval. It should define the products which can be sold at herbal shops and those to be marketed in pharmacies.

Overall, this is a complex sector which requires clearer guidelines. This situation is not peculiar to Italy since the European Commission is recognizing the need for uniformity and clarity and is proposing common rules in the European Union on the sale of vitamin and mineral supplements aiming to give consumers clearer information about safe consumption levels and potential risks of excess doses. Under the proposals, labels on vitamin and mineral supplements would include recommendations on a daily intake (as determined by EU scientists), a warning about possible health risks of excess use, and a statement that the product should not be used as a substitute for a balanced diet. Claims that a product can prevent or cure illness, or any suggestion that a balanced, varied diet did not provide necessary amounts of essential nutrients, would be banned.

MARKET ASSESSMENT

The total Italian market for vitamins and minerals, OTC nutritional supplements, homeopathic preparations, herbs and teas, is estimated at $250 million, and represents 16% of the European market. Sales of vitamins and minerals in retail outlets (40% of buyers purchase them in supermarkets) during 2004 are estimated at $90 million; OTC vitamins and minerals for self-medication, sold at pharmacies, accounted for $140 million; homeopathic remedies accounted for $5 million in sales, and, teas, herbs and herb-based preparations sold in health shops and herbalists' stores were estimated at $15 million. Most sectors reported growth in 2004: sales of vitamins and minerals increased by 10%, homeopathic remedies by 27%, and herbal preparations grew by 15%.

END USER PROFILE

In surveys of product awareness, 21% of the Italian population of 57.6 million, aged 15 to 64, stated to be habitual users of nutritional supplements. The largest consumption was reported in the North-West: (26%), and in the North-East: (26%), while Central Italy accounted for 22% of consumption , and Southern Italy and the Islands for12%.

Income plays a significant part in consumption: of the 663 individuals interviewed, 171 (or 35%) were high income earners: 214 (24%) were middle income earners, and 139 (14%) were low-income earners.

COMPETITIVE SITUATION AND U.S. MARKET POSITION AND PROSPECTS

The Italian market for nutritional supplements is mature and highly competitive.
Italy is a strong producer and exporter of vitamins and medicinal plant extracts. 1998 production amounted to 42,227 kilograms for vitamins, an increase of 36% from 1997; and 1,332,189 kilograms for medicinal plant extracts, an increase of 13.4 from 1997. In the period 1969-1998, production of vitamins rose by 374% and medicinal plant extracts by 82%.

Italian manufacturers lead the local market for OTC vitamins and minerals, followed by multinationals Roche, Boots and Whitehall. Smaller manufacturers and exporters from the European Union have also successfully entered the Italian market benefiting from experience in their own countries (consumption of vitamins and minerals is more common in Northern than in Southern Europe) and taking advantage of the trading regime in the European Union which exempts members from customs duties.

In order to be competitive, U.S. companies will have to focus on price and to develop their market share. Flexibility is also recommended:vitamin and mineral capsules and tablets produced in the United States often exceed the recommended daily intake permitted for unrestricted sale in Italy, resulting in their qualification as pharmaceuticals. Marketing authorization for pharmaceutical products is a costly and lengthy procedure which few importers/distributors are willing to confront for non-innovative drugs. Therefore, it is recommended that U.S. manufacturers scale down their formulations, whenever possible, in order to benefit from the simpler procedure reserved for nutritional supplements.

APPOINTING A DISTRIBUTOR OR AN AGENT; U.S. DEPARTMENT OF COMMERCE SERVICES

The appointment of a resident representative or distributor is extremely important for companies operating in this sector. For business promotion, market knowledge, and familiarity with bureaucratic procedures, there is no effective alternative. It is, in fact, mandatory for applications for marketing authorizations of OTCs to be filed by a person domiciled in Italy or in the European Market. (Italy is a signatory to the Mutual Recognition Agreement and therefore automatically recognizes marketing authorizations for pharmaceuticals issued in other EU countries). In addition, the person responsible for placing the products on the market (and whose contact information must be recorded on the packaging or label) must domiciled in the European Community.

The U.S. Department of Commerce has numerous services for American companies wishing to expand their international activities and needing to appoint a foreign distributor or an agent, such as the Agent/Distributor Service and the Gold Key service. For further information, please contact the nearest Export Assistance Center of the U.S. Department of Commerce.

Exhibitions are a cost-effective method to enter the Italian market and meet a wide range of buyers interested in a particular industry sector. Also, fairs are useful for finding an agent, distributor, or representative. The U.S. Department of Commerce, through the Foreign Commercial Service in Italy and in collaboration with the U.S. Agricultural Service, organizes a U.S. pavilion at SANA, a trade show dedicated to herbal, natural and environmentally friendly products. The next edition will be held in Bologna, September 14-17, 2000. (A smaller version will be held in Naples in September 2001).

For further information, contact:
Maria Andrews, Commercial Officer (e-mail: Maria.Andrews@mail.doc.gov)
or Piera Gattinoni, Commercial Specialist (e-mail: Piera.Gattinoni@mail.doc.gov)
U.S. Foreign Commercial Service
Via Principe Amedeo 2
20121 Milan
tel. 39 02 6592260; fax 02 6596561.

KEY CONTACTS

Ministero della Sanita'
Dr. Roberto Copparoni
Viale della Civilta' Romana 7
00144 Rome
tel. 39 06 5994 3697

Mariella Stannus
Pharmaceuticals Specialist
U.S. Foreign Commercial Service
Via V. Veneto 119/a
00187 Rome
tel. 39 06 4674 2250, fax 39 06 4674 2113, e-mail: Mariella.Stannus@mail.doc.gov

MARKETING AUTHORIZATION AND PHARMACEUTICAL REGISTRATION CONSULTANT

Dr. Sante Di Renzo
Di Renzo s.n.c.
Viale Manzoni 59
00185 Rome
tel. 39 06 704581; fax 39 06 474067

TRADE ASSOCIATIONS

Federsalus Federazione Nazionale Prodotti Salutistici
(Association of Health Products' Manufacturers)
Dr. Minasi, President
Via Toscanini 1/i
04011 Aprilia (Latina)
tel. 39 06 9206 0056; fax 39 06 920 60667

Assosalute (OTC Association)
Dr. Garlaschini (tel. 39 02 268 10252)
Via Accademia 33
20131 Milan
tel. 39 02 268101; fax 39 02 26810348.

IMPORTERS/DISTRIBUTORS

Just Natural s.r.l.
Via Luigi Bertelli 14
00141 Rome
tel. 39 06 82 002 058; fax 39 06 83083357, website: www.justnatural.com

La Strega s,.r.l.
Via San Damaso 23a
00165 Rome
tel. 39 06 632192; fax 39 06 632196, e-mail: strega@lastrega.com,
website: http://www.lastrega.com

Borri s.a.s.
Via Tropea 18/20
00178 Rome
Tel. 39 06 71888841

Ass. Orya
20124 Milan
tel. 39 02 29513459; fax: 39 02 29513459, e-mail: orya.benessere@digibank.it

Vaas s.r.l.
Via Siena 2568
47032 Capo Colle di B. Fo
tel. 39 0543 462411, fax: 0039 0453 448644

Il Fiore di Loto
Corso Adriatico 347/12
10095 Grugliasco (Turin)
tel. 39 011 4018511; fax 011/4037186; e-mail: marketing@fiordiloto.it
website: www.fiordiloto.it

IVC Italia s.r.l. Italia Vitamins Corporation
Via Falcone 212
40018 San Pietro in Casale (Bologna)
tel. 39 051 818481, fax 39 051 818481 e-mail: geminitc@tin.it

PUBLICATIONS

Erboristeria Domani
(monthly)
Annuario Italiano di Erboristeria
(year book)
Studio Edizioni s.a.s.
Piazza Wagner 1
20145 Milan
tel. 39 02 481 8684, fax 39 02 4817843, website: http://www.erbe.it

TRANSLATION OF LISTING PROVIDED BY THE MINISTRY OF HEALTH, MAY 2000

These preparations come in the form of tablets, capsules, powder and liquid (e.g. in vials) etc. and are specifically formulated to combine the supplement of vitamins and/or minerals and are devoid of other significant nutritional contents.

VITAMINS REFERENCE VALUE

Vitamin A 800 mcg *
Vitamin D 5 mcg *
Vitamin E 10 mg *
Vitamin K 70 mcg **
Vitamin C 60 mg *
Thiamine (vitamin B1) 1.4 mg *
Riboflavin (vitamin B2) 1.6 mg *
Niacin 18 mg *
Vitamin B6 2 mg *
Folacin (folic acid) 200 mcg *
Vitamin B12 1-2 mcg *§
Biotin 0.15 mg *
Pantothenic acid 6 mg *

MINERALS

Calcium 800 mg *
Phosphorus 800 mg *
Iron 14 mg *
Magnesium 300 mg *
Zinc 15 mg *
Iodine 150 mcg *
Copper 1.2 mg §
Fluorine 1.5-4 mg ***
Selenium 55 mcg §
Manganese 1-10 mg **
Chromium 50-200 mcg ***
Molybdenum 75-250 mcg ***
Minimum daily quantity of potassium 200 mg

* values foreseen by the provision regarding nutritional labeling
** values proposed by the EU Scientific Committee
*** values taken from the 1989 U.S. RDA
§ LARN 1996
For others, e.g. nickel, cobalt, boron, tin, vanadium, the most recent published data is being re-examined for a more precise evaluation of their nutritional value.

DAILY INTAKE

Vitamin-mineral supplements: from 30% to 150% of the reference value

Vitamin E and vitamin C supplements: max. 300% of the reference value, taking their anti-oxidizing activity into consideration

Nutritional factors, for which there is no RDA value or suggested daily intake, should preferably not be proposed as single supplements but used in rational quantities in order that the purpose be understood by users.

It is important to differentiate between VITAMIN AND MINERAL SUPPLEMENTS AND FOOD ENRICHED WITH VITAMINS AND MINERALS.

The parameter foreseen for supplements (from 30% to 150% of the RDA on the suggested intake) is not directly applicable to enriched foods, in which the usual quantity eaten of the enriched product must be taken into account preceding the addition of vitamins and/or minerals. It is not acceptable to propose quantities of enriched foods to be eaten that are arbitrary or out of proportion to those usually consumed in order to arrive at a significant vitamin/mineral intake.

It is preferable not to enrich foods with vitamins and minerals when their usual intake is a few grams and they are eaten in extremely variable quantities by each individual.
This is because of a shortage of basic criterion for determining the quantity to be added, given by the usual quantity eaten of the chosen food.

OTHER VITAMIN-LIKE FACTORS

Daily Intake maximum
Beta-carotene 15 mg (300% RDA
as an equivalent of vitamin A)
Coenzyme Q 20 mg
Taurine 500 mg
Choline 900 mg

PABA undefined intake
Pangamic acid (Vitamin B15)
Bioflavonoid
Inositol

OTHER NUTRITIONAL FACTORS

Betaine undefined intake
Nucleic acids

AMINO ACIDS

Estimated requirements of essential amino acids for an adult weighing 70kg (mg/kg of the PRI of each essential amino acid X 70)

Daily recommended consumption of protein:
70 g per adult (1 g/kg for an adult weighing 70 kg)

AMINO ACID COMPOUNDS

They must contain all of the essential amino acids (hystidine may be considered optional) which must be substantially present in the proportions indicated above.
They may also contain non-essential amino acids and other nutrients.

Given the supplementary role of these products at the daily doses indicated on the label, the intake must not cover the entire requirement.

Indications should be as follows:
Integrator of essential amino acids, indicated to supply a supplement of these nutrients to complement the protein intake of a dietary plan.

If the compound does not contain all the essential amino acids, the label may not state the phrase supplement of essential amino acids.

GROUPING OF AMINO ACIDS

Only those for which written nutritional evidence exists are acceptable.

It must be clear from their presentation that they are not supplements which aim to fulfill the total intake of nitrogenous requirements since in this case, a balanced composition of amino acids is required.

Specific references to nutrients are allowed if they are supported by current scientific documentation.

For example, products intended for trophism of the skin and similar conditions, which contain, as stated in the daily dose indicated on the label, sulphured amino acids in quantities equal to at least 25% of the daily recommended intake, may state the following on the label:
This product is a dietary supplement of sulphured amino acids (and, if applicable, of other nutrients with antioxidant properties). suitable for providing a supplement of these nutrients and useful for trophism of the skin, and other tissues such as hair, nails, etc.

For amino acids and/or collagen hydrolysed substances, reference to derma trophism is allowed.

In any case, the suggested intake must not represent a large part of the daily protein/amino-acidic ration since these compounds are incomplete.

It is believed that a compoun containing only ramified amino acids should be reserved to sports people or prescribed by a physician.

SINGLE AMINO ACIDS

Trophic and/or functional effects, which can be unequivocally supported by scientific evidence, may be stated on the label so that the consumer may be aware that their use is intended for physical or sports activities which involve intense muscular performance. The daily recommended intake must be within the nutritional limits.

In any event, only form L amino acids may be used, with the exception of methionine, which may be used in DL form.

AMINO ACID DERIVATIVES OF NUTRITIONAL RELEVANCE

Carnitine

Daily intake: 200 mg

Recommendations:
Carnitine is an energy enhancer for cells carrying fatty acids into areas delegated to their metabolic utilisation.

Creatine

Daily intake: max 3 g

Recommendations:
Creatine is a derivative of amino acids. It is naturally produced by the human body and is also contained in various foodstuffs. Transformed into its phosphorylated form, it is employed in maintaining cellular energy reserves.

Glutathione

Daily intake: max 50 mg

Recommendations:
Glutathione is a derivative of amino acids and is naturally produced by the human body. It has anti oxidizing properties.

Carnosine

Nutritional intake and indications to be defined

PROTEIN AND/OR ENERGY-ENHANCING SUPPLEMENTS

In order to be admitted as supplements other than within the groups listed in Appendix 1 of law 111/92, it is considered necessary that the daily intake indicated on the label provide no more than:
max 35 g of protein
(half of the recommended intake for an adult)

the minimum recommended consumption should be at least 7 g
(10% of the recommended intake)

max 600 kcal.
(25% of the total daily calories needs, equal to 2400 kcal)

the minimum calories supplied should be no less than
5% of the total energy daily requirement

These products may make references to conditions, with the exception of sports activities, where a reduced or increased intake of proteins and/or calories are advisable. Preliminary authorization from the Ministry of Health is required before marketing.

LIPIDIC SUPPLEMENTS

Phospholipidic supplements (derived from soy-beans): must provide at least 3 grams of phospholipids daily in order to make claims to their usefulness in controlled diets prescribed for individuals affected by lipidic metabolic disorders.

LCP-n3 supplements: in order for integrators to be destined to individuals with lipidic metabolic disorders, they must provide a minimum daily supply of 1 g. of EPA+DHA = ; EPA >DHA

Other fatty acid supplements

BIOLOGICAL VITAMIN SUPPLEMENTS

If these supplements contain Saccaromyces cerevisiae, it is advisable that they supply a dose of at least 100,000,000 live cells per unit.
If they contain lactic ferments, a dose of hundreds of millions per unit is desirable.
Indications must make reference to rebalancing of bacterial, intestinal flora through vitamin integrators. Products containing only one microbic component and of no nutritional effect are not considered food supplements.

FIBER SUPPLEMENTS

A daily intake of 4g of fiberis required for these supplements.
Supplements based on insoluble fiber are advised in cases where reduced fiber ingestion results in a slow bowel passage.
Supplements based on soluble fiber, containing at least 2 g of such fiber, taken before the two main meals (1.5g for glucomannan), are advisable in order to:
Bring about a sensation ion of fullness in controlled or weight-reduction diets.
slow down the absorption of nutrients by individuals affected by lipidic and glucidic metabolic disorders.
If lactulose is present in these products, the intake of disaccharide must not exceed 4g.

SUPPLEMENTS WITH A HEALTH COMPONENT

Herbs traditionally known for their pharmacological activity (i.e. herbs that cannot be sold other than in pharmacies) are not acceptable as ingredients in food products, including those which may be sold according to the provisions in Art. 7 of law 111/92.

Products which only contain herbs, even if they are suitable for nutritional use, are not to be considered food supplements.

Herbs present in food supplements must be suitable for nutritional use and be devoid of concentrations of substances which would result in pharmacological effects.

Glandular and organic extracts and hormonal substances

Present scientific knowledge maintains that products containing the above stated substances as ingredients do not meet the specifications of dietetic products or food supplements.

Enzymes

Present scientific knowledge maintains that enzymes may not be used as ingredients in day to day foods. For this reason, they may not be sold as food supplements.

ELECTRICITY DISTRIBUTION AND CONTROL APPARATUS

ACEA SpA
piazzale Ostiense 2
00154 Roma
Tel.: 06 57 99 34 39
Fax: 06 57 99 31 29
ITALY

ELECTRICITY LIBERALIZATION

The Italian electricity sector is heading towards the gradual opening of its market, a move which goes along with recent trends in European institutions. The regulatory changes implemented during the '90s, the gradual opening of the generation market to many operators and the establishment of a sector Authority, represent important steps towards this liberalization.

The recently approved Italian government decree enacting European Directive 96/92/EC of the European Parliament and Council (the Bersani Decree) containing the common norms for the internal electricity market is essential in the liberalization process.

For Italy, the implementation of Directive 96/92/EC represents the opportunity to liberalize and modernize the sector, while respecting consumer rights as well as protecting the environment. In addition, the liberalization process is intended to reduce the cost of services while stimulating investment, thereby spurring economic growth. Privatization of the sector in Italy basically means the privatization of the giant state electricity monopoly ENEL. This privatization entails the implementation of economic and institutional measures to foster the development of free enterprise and increased competition, in order to prevent ENEL's privatization from simply changing the public monopoly into a private one. Last but not least, the creation of a free market should provide excellent opportunities for interested U.S. companies.

BACKGROUND

As of today, there are 50 municipal utilities operating outside the ENEL monopoly: they control four percent of Italy's installed capacity and seven percent of electricity distributed; many of these companies also own generation facilities (self producers). To foster the development of new technologies, electricity conservation and alternative energy sources, the GOI enacted, in 1992 the CIP-6 program that forced ENEL to offer above-market tariffs for electricity generated by producers using renewable sources. As a result, the GOI has committed to purchase, by 2002 some 19,000 MW of electricity from independent producers at preferential rates. (Italy has a total of 72,000 MW of installed capacity.)

The GOI therefore succeeded in diversifying the electric power sources and the electricity generated by self producers reached 22% of the total. ENEL's purchases from self-producers increased by over 40%. ENEL, however, still maintains a complete monopoly over transmission and cross-border trading and virtually a monopoly over distribution. Imports make up approximately 15% of Italy's electricity use, most of which is imported from French nuclear power plants (despite the fact that since 1985 Italy has banned the operations and constructions of nuclear power plants on the Italian territory.)

The creation (1997) of the Authority for Electricity and Gas (the Energy Authority) to oversee Italian electricity production, supply and tariffs, was followed by the so-called Bersani Decree, issued for the implementation of the European Union Directive Concerning Common Rules for the Internal Market in Electricity (the EU Directive.)

HIGHLIGHTS OF THE BERSANI DECREE

On February 19, 2004, meeting the EU's deadline, the Parliament passed the Bersani Decree into a law which became effective April 1, 2004. This law provided that:

generation, imports, exports and the purchase and sale of power are all liberalized;
transmission and dispatching are reserved to the state and granted to the Transmission System

Operator (TSO)
distribution is carried out under a concession granted by the Minister of Industry

ENEL

ENEL will be transformed into a holding company in charge of setting strategic guidelines and coordinating individual companies. ENEL will set up separate companies for: a) power generation; b) power distribution and sales to captive market clients; c) power sales to eligible clients; d) ownership of the transmission network.
A new company will be created for the decommissioning of nuclear power plants.

Generation

As of January 1, 2003, no operator will be allowed to import or generate more than 50% of the total electricity imported or generated in Italy. By that date, ENEL will have to sell at least 15,000 MW of its own installed capacity. Further, ENEL must put together a plan for the sale of power generation plants in adequate market conditions. The plan will have to consider business plans, employment level, research, innovation and internationalization.

Transmission and Dispatching

Transmission and Dispatching, reserved to the state, are granted to a joint stock company (Transmission System Operator), in charge of managing the national network. The TSO will manage the energy flow and makes decisions on network maintenance and development. Besides the network, all of ENEL's transmission business will be transferred to the TSO. The TSO defines, co-ordinates and supervises the maintenance and development of the transmission network. For the access and usage of the national transmission network, the TSO receives a compensation, the amount of which is determined by the Authority for Electricity and Gas.

Distribution

Companies currently distributing electricity under Ministry of Industry's concessions issued by March 31, 2001, will continue to do so until December 31, 2030. As of this date (3/31/01), distribution service will be awarded on the basis of tenders, respecting national and EU public contract regulations. In the meantime, the Ministry of Industry will determine the ways, conditions and criteria, including the remuneration for investment made by the previous licensee, for issuing new concessions effective from 2031. Each concession must service one or more municipal territories, and cannot distribute electricity to more of 25% of all end-users. Only one concession per municipality can be issued. There are municipalities where more than one distributor operates: in cities like Milan, Rome or Turin some consumers are served by ENEL, others by the local power companies. In these cases, the distributors are encouraged to merge into one company.

ENEL's distribution network, currently covering 90% of distribution to end-users, will be transferred to a separate ENEL-owned company.

The Single Buyer

The Single Buyer is a single market operator entrusted with the task of guaranteeing that captive market clients have a continuous, safe and efficient supply of electricity. The Single Buyer must also warrant equal treatment, and draw up sales contractswith distributors based on electricity demand projections.

The Bersani Decree exceeds the EU Directive's requirement: while the Directive requires that consumers making up approximately 33 percent of aggregate electricity demand be free to choose their electricity supplier, the Bersani Decree requires that ENEL's market shares do not exceed 50% by 1/1/03. In order to meet this objective, the Bersani Decree requires ENEL to sell, by the same date, 15,000 MW of its 59,000MW of installed capacity (this deadline is extendable for one year if considered necessary by the energy and antitrust authorities.)

CURRENT SITUATION

After more than one year, the process of liberalization and the first structural changes have gone forward, although the impact of these changes has yet to be felt by the consumer. An entity which will become the System Operator has been created as an ENEL subsidiary, while the Single Buyer will be created later this year. The Single Buyer, however, will only contract with producers and will not solicit competitive bids, at least until electricity suppliers in the Italian market are in such number as to ensure effective competition. In the meantime, the Single Buyer will mostly be a clearing house to which ENEL the producer sells electricity and from which ENEL the distributor buys it back.

Although electricity prices paid by consumers in 2004 increased, ENEL predicts that in 2000 there will be a reduction in tariff revenues over 1998. The Energy Authority estimates that ENEL's revenue will decrease by 17 percent by 2003, i.e., during the time before ENEL divestiture.

MARKET OPORTUNITIES

The development of the Italian electricity market will create several market entry opportunities. Electricity demand grew on average 2.4 percent each year from 1994 to 1998. ENEL and market experts predict 2.5 percent growth in 2000-2001 and thereafter.

ENEL will sell turn-key assets already connected to the transmission network for a total of 15,000 MW. To do that, ENEL has recently selected some thermal and Hydro plants and passed them to three different holding companies. The process is now stalled waiting for the GOI instructions as to the modality of the divestiture (stock offering, direct negotiation, or a combination of the two). ENEL privatized approximately 30 percent of the company through a public offering in 2004. A number of Italian and foreign companies, including some U.S. companies, have showed interest in acquiring ENEL's assets.

In order to follow the E.U. directive, the Bersani decree requires that by 2002 two percent of the electricity provided by major producers and importers must derive from renewable energy sources. Since the energy generation under the CIP-6 program will mainly come from co-generation plants that do not qualify as renewable sources under the decree, a niche-market should emerge.

Presently ENEL has no plan to increase generation capacity after the 15,000 MW divestiture. Consequently, the growing increase in demand will have to be met by different sources. However, installed or scheduled capacity in Italy is predicted to be sufficient for the next few years. (The actual installed or scheduled capacity includes ENEL's residual 44,000 MW, its to-be-divested 15,000 MW, GOI CIP-6 commitments of 19,000 MW and about 6,000 MW in municipal non-CIP/non-ENEL production.)

The majority of the independent companies in the market entered through the CIP-6 project with its fifteen-year price guarantee, which will continue to be applied under the new regime. Energy producers seeking to enter the Italian market without the benefit of the incentives provided by CIP-6 (price guarantees, eligibility for the renewable energy set-aside) should address the Pool

Market. The pool will include all suppliers wishing to provide electricity, after January 1, 2001, to the Single Buyer, which will supply power to the small and medium consumers at prices to be set by the Energy Authority.

Starting from 4/1/99 eligible customers in Italy could choose to contract with any electricity supplier. Once the pool market becomes fully operational, traders also will be free to supply the Single Buyer. ENEL has already formed a trading subsidiary. As the Italian market evolves and increasingly smaller end-users are able to choose their own suppliers, a demand for energy consultants and energy resellers will certainly grow.

As regards basic electricity supply, short-term market entry opportunities are limited. Consequently, unless demand increases, new suppliers would need to bring in electricity from outside Italy, since ENEL has yet to complete the process of divestiture of 15,000 MW. The Bersani Decree ended ENEL's monopoly on electricity imports. However, there was no apparent change in the import market in the first year of liberalization.

Italian imports make up approximately 41 TWh of the 270 TWh annual electricity consumption (15 percent of the total electricity consumed). More than half of ENEL's electricity imports are pursuant to long-term contracts still ineffect. It is likely that ENEL will have to assign these contracts to the Single Buyer. However, the transmission capacity they represent will remain dedicated to existing contracts.

Municipal utilities which remained outside the ENEL monopoly, in some cases overlap with ENEL in energy distribution. The Bersani Decree requires the consolidation of all such areas of duplication by offering the local municipality the possibility of buying the local ENEL distribution assets. Each municipality will eventually have a single distributor, licensed for thirty years. The deadline for the distribution plan (31/3/2000) is forcing many municipalities to reconsider their role and presence in the electricity market. Companies interested in entering the market have the opportunity to offer supply/service/billing packages to the Italian electricity consumers.

KEY CONTACTS

The Commercial Service
Embassy of the United States of America
Via Vittorio Veneto 119/a
00187 Rome
Contact: Cristiano Sartorio
Tel: 39/0646742252
Fax: 39/0646742113
e-mail: cristiano.sartorio@mail.doc.gov

Ministry of Industry
Direzione Generale delle Fonti di Energia
e delle Industrie di Base
Via Molise, 2
00100 Rome
Tel: 39/06462723

ENEL Ente Nazionale per l'Energia Elettrica
Via Palmiano, 101
00138 Rome
Contact: Ing. Vittorio De Martino
Tel: 39/0681655370
Fax: 39/0681655241
e-mail: demartino.vittorio@grtn.it

ENI S.p.A. Ente Nazionale Idrocarburi
Piazzale E. Mattei, 1
00144 Rome
Tel: 39/0659821
Fax: 39/0659822141

ENEA National Board for New Technologies, Energy and Environment
Viale Regina Margherita
00198 Roma
Tel: 39/0630484089
Fax: 39/0630484643

ASSOCARBONI Italian Association of Coal Importers and Traders
Via Parigi, 11

00185 Roma
Contact: Dott. Andrea Clavarino
Tel: 39 064818941
Fax: 39/064885258

ANIE National Association of Electric and Electronic Industries
Via Algardi, 2
20148 Milano
Tel: 39/0232641
Fax: 39/023264212

ASSOMINERARIA National Association of Mining and Petroleum Industries
Via A. Bertoloni, 31
00197 Roma
Tel: 39/068073045
Fax: 39/068073385

UNAPACE National Association of Energy Self-Producers
Via Ombrone 2/g
00100 Roma
Tel: 39/068540935
Fax: 39/0685356495

MARKET FOR INSURANCE SERVICES

According to ANIA (Italian Association of Insurance Companies), total direct insurance premiums (exclusive of re-insurance) collected in Italy increased by 9.3 percent in the year 2000 totaling approximately $62.4 billion, largely attributable to the 11.5 percent growth in the sale of life insurance which surpassed for the third consecutive time even the total amount of casualty insurance premiums and represented almost 59% of the entire Italian insurance business. Although the annual increase in demand for insurance products was not as spectacular as the average annual 20 percent increases of recent years, it nonetheless reflects the continued uncertainties over the guarantees offered by the Italian state pension and health systems.

Among the factors which contributed to keep up the demand is the necessity of Italian households to increase the proportion of savings set aside for retirement needs, and their reduced preference for cash assets (a result of the drop in interest rates and poor results of the financial markets). In addition to the greater attention paid by the population to welfare problems, the continued growth in life insurance is also due to the variety of distribution channels and the expansion of index-linked and unit-linked policies.

Among the first top ten companies operating in the sector are eight large Italian insurance companies led by "Assicurazioni Generali". Foreign-owned insurance companies, which have been quite aggressive in the market, maintain an estimated market share of 30 percent.

The handful of U.S. companies presently doing business in Italy are estimated to have increased their performance by 12.5%, but only still represent approximately 0.3 percent of the market. Nonetheless, U.S. companies are expected to take advantage of greater opportunities in Italy due to the liberalization of the EU insurance services market, as well as to the newly-introduced Italian fiscal incentives for insurance covers involving individual supplemental allowance and long term care plans (Italian Legislative Decree 47/2000 effective as of January 1, 2001).

The insurance industry will thus be playing a major role in Italy's financial markets, both as a source of capital and management for the newly created private pension funds and as a complementary system for the national pension and health systems. U.S. firms, which have operated in highly competitive environments, and have a long history and expertise, especially in life insurance, pension funds, individual retirement accounts, and health insurance, should take advantage of increased Italian need for insurance products. Italy allows non-EC based insurance companies access to its market through local subsidiaries, branches or representative offices.

Thus, in order to sell insurance products, a U.S. insurance company must set up in Italy at least a representative office which has to be authorized by ISVAP (Supervisory Institute of private and public-interest Insurance companies which monitors insurance activities in Italy). The license can normally be obtained in six months.

MARKET FOR NATIVE AMERICAN HANDICRAFTS

Italy is an interesting niche market for Native American handicrafts and giftware from the United States. This report provides a market overview and a guide for U.S. exporters of Native American handicrafts.

2. MARKET DEMAND

General Market Overview

Italy is the world's sixth largest industrial economy, and an important member of the European Union (EU). Within Europe, Italy is one of the continent's largest economies, about equal to that of the United Kingdom in GDP and other economic measures.

In general, the Italian market is mature and highly competitive, and demands quality products. Italian consumers are very open to U.S. items, particularly innovative and niche market products.

Ethnic items, in particular Native American products, recently have been growing in popularity in Italy. While statistical information on this niche within the giftware sector remains scarce, there is clear evidence of great interest in these products. It is important to note that the giftware and handicraft sectors are closely linked in Italy, and a large percentage of giftware items sold in Italy are hand-crafted. A growing number of stores sell ethnic items or other gift items in special Native American sections, even as the presence of such items in the general marketplace is still very limited. So far, there are few Italian retailers fully specialized in Native American products, and the majority of these have opened their doors within the last three years. The number of Italian companies selling Native American items is expected to increase in the next few years.

As a result of this increasing interest in Native American items in Italy, local importers are interested in developing more contacts with Native American artisans and manufacturers.

The popularity of Native American items was particularly clear at the U.S. Pavilion at the CHIBI&CART trade show organized by the U.S. Commercial Service Italy (CS), the export-promotion arm of the U.S. Department of Commerce, in Milan in January '99. All participants displaying Native American products made significant sales at the event, which for most marked their entry into the Italian market.

Native American items, especially quality jewelry at moderate prices, are "best sellers" in Italy, and should offer the best future market potential.

Market Entry Considerations

Sellers of Native American items should be aware that Italy is one of the most challenging marketing environments in Europe because of the traditionally strong sense of fashion and style. Italian consumers are extremely fashion conscious, and style and uniqueness often justify the additional cost of quality imported products.

Selling in Italy means dealing with very sophisticated consumers, looking for novelties and trendy items. U.S. exporters should be aware that success in Italy is reached by establishing linkages with Italian representatives or partners, and flexiblity in approaching the market.

Competition from third country imports is severe. Much of what is sold in Italy as Native American (as much as 90 percent, according to some importers) is, in fact, made in developing countries with low labor costs. This competition hurts the market position of more expensive authentic Native American items, which tend to be hand-crafted and made from fine materials.

When providing the Italian buyer with a price quote, American firms should provide a C.I.F. (cost, insurance, and freight) quote that includes sales price plus packing costs, insurance, and freight to the named point of destination. Such quotes can be obtained from most freight forwarders in the U.S. With a C.I.F. price, Italian importers can then usually determine the charges for customs, taxes, and local transportation and arrive at the final, or landed, cost to the importer. The customary terms of sale in Italy are either cash on delivery (which is rare) or settlement 60-120 days after invoice date (more common).

Import duty is charged on the C.I.F. value (cost, insurance and freight). In addition there is a 20 percent sales tax, which is eventually passed on to the consumer in form of the value-added tax (VAT) and is charged on the C.I.F. value plus duty. VAT applies to both imports and domestically produced goods. There are no other non-tariff trade barriers or limitations on the import of American gift/handicraft items.

3. DISTRIBUTION/BUSINESS PRACTICES

In general, giftware items and handicrafts are distributed in Italy through three major channels:

-Importers/distributors
-Sales representatives
-Direct sales

Importers/distributors:

Importers/distributors generally take actual possession and stock goods to be sold. U.S. manufacturers of Native American items may use specialized importers/ distributors to market and sell their products. Thus, U.S. companies can take advantage of the distributor's expertise, his/her sales force and existing distribution channels. Distributors call on giftware retailers, purchasing groups and department stores. They usually also handle smaller orders. The distributors' mark-up varies depending on the item, but generally is between 40% and 80%.

Commission agents/Sales representatives:

Comission agents and sales representatives generally only take and transmit orders to U.S. suppliers for a fee, generally a percentage. Commission agents provide U.S. companies with direct access to the Italian market and better direct control. These agents normally work on a percent commission and operate on a regional basis. They concentrate on retailers, purchasing groups and department stores.

Direct Sales :

The direct sales approach calls for U.S. manufacturers to sell directly to retailers. U.S. companies interested in establishing business contacts with major retailers may also chose the direct sales approach. Department stores in particular prefer to deal directly with manufacturers. If a department store decides to import a particular giftware item, it places bulk rather than small orders.

Native American items can be sold through the traditional distribution channels described above; however, direct sales from manufacturers to retailers are more common in this sector. There are approximately 20 Italian retailers specialized in Native American products. Generally, this specialization indicates a good deal of knowledge about Native American culture and craftsmanship by the retailer and a willingness or even eagerness to work directly with manufacturers or specialized dealers from the U.S. There are also a couple of large distributors of Native American products in Italy.

In conclusion, direct sales to a specialized retailers/distributors may be the easiest way to enter the Italian market for Native American handicrafts, rather than using a commission sales agent.

The following is a partial list of Italian distributors specialized in Native American products:

IMPORTERS/DISTRIBUTORS (OF NATIVE AMERICAN ITEMS)

MEXICO E NUVOLE
Via G. Papini, 10
50135 Firenze
Tel. 01139/055-606630

Fax 01139/055-609841
Contact: Stefano Cruciani

SENTIERI DEL VENTO
Via Manzoni, 14
20121 Milano
Tel. 01139/02-796136
Contact: Mr. Roger Imer

TIKAL
Corso Garibaldi 133/B
20025 Legnano MI
Tel. 01139/0331/549750
Fax 01139/0331/549750
Contact: Mr. Marco Campigotto

FIRST NATIONS
Viale Milano 47
47036 Riccione
Phone: 39/0541604348
Fax: 39/0541604348
Contact: Marcello Balbi

4. TRADE PROMOTION OPPORTUNITIES

In Italy, trade fairs play a major role in product marketing. U.S. companies seeking to penetrate the Italian market are encouraged to exhibit in, or at least to visit, a specialized Italian fair. Exhibiting at fairs can bring direct sales, but more significantly, can be one of the best ways to test the market's receptivity to a firm's products and to assess the strength and scope of the competition. It also helps companies establish contact with others "in the trade" and, from these contacts, a U.S. firm can gather substantial valuable information about marketing products in Italy and Europe.

The most important trade fair for the giftware/handicraft sector is:

CHIBI&CART
International exhibition of gift articles, perfumery, items, costume jewelry, handicrafts and smoker's supplies

Date: January 18-21, 2001
Site: Milan
Organizer: Fiera Milano International
Palazzina Fmi
Largo Domodossola, 1
20145 Milano
Tel: +39-02-48550.331
Fax: +39-02-4980199
E-mail: chibicart@fmi.it
Web site: http://chibicart.fmi.it

CHIBI&CART is the premier event in Italy and one of the largest shows in Europe covering the giftware, handicrafts, stationary, and jewelry sectors; it has generated business for several U.S. exporters new to market at past editions. CHIBI&CART provides a special opportunity for American companies to crack the Italian market and establish relationships with major distributors and potential business partners in Italy and throughout the rest of Europe.

With 800 exhibitors in all fields and over 60,000 visitors each year, CHIBI&CART offers a unique - and affordable - opportunity for Native American products to gain exposure to thousands of potential buyers, distributors, and other interested parties from throughout Europe. This show has a strong concentration in hand-crafted items: fifty-one percent of the exhibitors represented the hand-crafted sector, while only 29 percent represented the industrial sector. U.S. products are in demand here, and some of the best sellers include giftware, novelty items, new age products and Native American handicrafts.

Given the importance of this exhibition, the U.S. Commercial Service (CS) in Milan and Florence will organize again a U.S. Pavilion at CHIBI&CART 2001. Participants will have the possibility to come to Milan and take a booth within the U.S. Pavilion. The CS is offering a broad range of services to the U.S. exhibitors, including extensive marketing of their presence at the exhibition, interpreters, business related services and a business lounge serving refreshments.

The 2001 show will be the third edition of the U.S. Pavilion at CHIBI. Past editions of the U.S. Pavilion at CHIBI&CART have brought Native American craftsmen as well as U.S. manufacturers of novelties, greeting cards, and other gift items to Italy to increase their international sales. Attendance at the show and the great interest of many trade operators in the U.S. exhibit confirmed the Commercial Service's assessment that excellent prospects exist for American products here - particularly Native American items. This exhibition proved to be an excellent venue for the many American firms which participated in the U.S. Pavilion at the show. To date, 10 distribution agreements have been reported as a direct result of the U.S. Pavilion.

For further information please contact:

Annalena Anselmini, Commercial Specialist
American Consulate General
Via Principe Amedeo 2
020121 Milan, Italy
Phone: 01139/02/6592260
Fax: 01139/02/6596561
E-mail: Annalena.Anselmini@mail.doc.gov

Barbara Lapini, Commercial Specialist
American Consulate General
Lungarno Vespucci 38
50123 Florence, Italy
Phone: 01139/055/292266
Fax: 01139/055/283780
E-mail: Barbara.Lapini@mail.doc.gov

PLEASURE BOATING

In 2004, the Italian market for pleasure boats, marine equipment and accessories totaled approximately $756 million, according to industry sources (research carried out by the Italian Marine Industry Association UCINA). Imports increased by 17 percent and accounted for 42 percent of Italian market demand. U.S. producers, historically Italy's principal foreign suppliers, dramatically increased sales in Italy by 67 percent during 2004, reaching approximately $53 million, or 17 percent of all Italian imports in this sector. In particular, sales of U.S. pleasure boats in Italy have more than doubled during the past year (up 140 percent), and covered almost a third of the import market.

In spite of the fact that Italy has the longest coastline in the Mediterranean, the current ratio of boat ownership to population is 1 to 70, compared to the U.S. ratio of 1 to 16. Recently-introduced boating industry friendly legislation, coupled with a Government of Italy (GOI) commitment to create 35,000 new mooring spaces within the next three years, and to double the size of new marine infrastructure to 200,000 mooring spaces within ten years, are expected to boost sales in the Italian marine leisure market.

2. MARKET PROFILE:

ITALIAN PLEASURE BOAT PRODUCTION AND EXPORTS:

The latest statistics presented by UCINA in October 2000 at Genoa's annual International Boat Show showed Italian overall pleasure boat sales of approximately $716 million for 2004, an increase of 16.5 percent compared to 1998. While domestic sales by Italian manufacturers amounted to some $150 million (a 15.7 percent increase from the previous year), exports remained the principal driving force and a critical element for Italian boat builders. Exports, which have more than doubled during the past five years, accounted for 79 percent of Italian production, with sales of approximately $566 million (16.7 percent growth from 1998 to 2004).

Specifically, inboard and stern-drive boat sales remain the backbone of Italian watercraft production, accounting for $499 million (88 percent) in export sales. This situation reflects continued strong foreign demand for medium-to-large size Italian boats. Domestic sales of Italian inboard and stern-drive boats also increased 16.5 percent (to $68 million). Meanwhile, Italian outboard motorboats fared remarkably well with increases of 29.4 percent in domestic sales (reaching $35.4 million), and of 31 percent in export sales (to $28 million).

While exports of Italian-built sailboats rose by 55 percent, domestic sales were stable (approximately $14 million) and covered only 30 percent of Italian market demand.

Italian inflatable boat builders increased their domestic sales by 8.7 percent ($32 million) and export sales by 4 percent ($13.8 million).

MARKET DEMAND AND IMPORTS:

According to an UCINA statistical survey of the industry, 1,389 pleasure boats were registered in Italy during 2004 (a 12 percent increase over the previous year). Of these, over 44 percent were inboard motorboats, 29 percent stern-drive motorboats, 6 percent outboard motorboats, 17 percent sailing boats and 4 percent motor-sailers. The relatively low number or registrations can be attributed to the fact that there is no registration obligation for motorboats up to 7.5 meters in length, or for sailboats of up to 10 meters long. Approximately 60 percent of registered boats were 7.5 to 12 meters in length, followed by the class 12 to 16 meters (24 percent of new registrations). Boats longer than 16 meters constituted 6 percent of new registrations and those below 7.5 meters maintained stable at 8 percent of new registrations. About 83 percent of newly bought units were fiberglass construction. Cabin cruisers represented 62 percent of new registrations. Although sailboats represent only a very small percentage of the market in terms of value, in terms of new registrations, they recorded an increase of 17 percent from 1998.

The Italian pleasure boat market rose by 25.7 percent through 2004 compared with 1998, reaching total sales of $280 million -- finally surpassing 1991, the previous record year for sales, (with approximately $262 million).

According to UCINA figures, in 2004 Italian sales of inboard and stern-drive-powered boats grew 31 percent to $169 million. Imports of these products increased 42 percent compared to the previous year, and met over half (60 percent) of market demand. Import figures have topped the 1991 record-high in value terms. Imports from the U.S. accounted for 25.5 percent of import market share.

Total Italian 2004 pleasure boat imports soared 39.4 percent to $130 million, or 46.5 percent of the market. Although no hard figures are yet available for the year 2000, industry sources believe that pleasure boating is definitely on the rise in Italy, becoming a growth market once again. U.S. pleasure boat exports to Italy have more than doubled (up 140 percent) during the past year. The U.S. is Italy's principal foreign supplier of pleasure boats, and currently holds almost a third (26 percent share) of the import market.

Sales in Italy of outboard-powered craft increased by a healthy 30 percent during 2004-- reaching $47 million. Imports also increased 31 percent and represented 24 percent of market demand. Imports from the U.S. covered 21 percent of the import market share.

In 2004, Italian demand for sailboats increased 20 percent, reaching $28 million. The market peak for sailboat demand was in 1990, with sales of $44 million. Imports were up 49 percent from the previous year and accounted for half of market demand. U.S. suppliers held 4 percent of the import market share for sailboats.

In unit terms, inflatable boats and rigid-hull inflatable boats (RIBs) are considered "best-sellers" in Italy. The Italian market for these products is generally believed to be the best in Europe. Because of this popularity, Italy has a large number of inflatable/RIB manufacturers (about 75). The 2004 market demand was worth $36 million (up 6.4 percent). Imports experienced a decrease of 9 percent and accounted for only about 11 percent of the market. U.S. suppliers held a 10 percent share of the import market.

MARINE ENGINES AND ACCESSORIES:

In the equipment sector, Italy runs a sizeable trade deficit in engines. 2004 sales in Italy of pleasure boat motors amounted to $110 million (down 0.4 percent), of which 85 percent were imports (up 2.3 percent). Imports consisted almost exclusively of inboard diesel engines and outboard gasoline-fueled engines. Belgium, where major U.S. companies have engine manufacturing facilities, is the top supplier of pleasure boat engines to Italy.

Sales of marine accessories in Italy were $366 million (up 9.3 percent), only 26 percent of which were imports (up 10 percent). This is largely due to strong vertical integration between accessory suppliers and Italian shipyards, which absorb a very high portion of domestic output (70 percent). Furthermore, international statistics report that Italy has the second largest industry in the world for the production of accessories, next to the United States. Major imported products include: electronic instrumentation, docking equipment, marine paint, engine spare parts and marine hardware. U.S. exports in this sector are estimated to consist of at least 12 percent of the import market.

3. FACTORS AFFECTING PLEASURE BOATING IN ITALY:

CURRENT SITUATION:

According to the International Council of Marine Industry Associations (ICOMIA), Italy ranks third worldwide (behind the U.S. and the U.K.) in terms of pleasure boat industry turnover and first in the production of mega-yachts. Pleasure boating is especially popular in New Zealand, Norway, Sweden and Finland, where the ratio of boats to population is one boat for every six or seven persons. In other words, one family out of two owns a boat in those countries. Boating is also quite common in Canada, the United States, Denmark, United Kingdom, Australia, the Netherlands and France (an average of 1 boat per 50 inhabitants). In Italy, however, the ratio is 1 boat per 70 inhabitants.

Industry sources maintain that the popularity of pleasure boating worldwide is dependent on four factors: the wealth of the population; geographic conditions facilitating boating; the availability of pleasure boating facilities; and the country's seafaring tradition. In most of the countries where pleasure boating is very popular, purchasing power is indeed higher than average (Norway, Netherlands, Denmark, France, Italy, Switzerland, Canada and the U.S.). In those countries in which per capita wealth is below average, pleasure boating has developed largely because of these countries' favorable geographic positions and the existence of navigable lakes and rivers and large numbers of harbors, marinas and moorings. In some countries, such as Sweden and Finland, a long sailing tradition contributes to the success of pleasure boating as a popular social activity. On the other hand, lack of a seafaring tradition and unfavorable geographical conditions limit the spread of pleasure boating. This is the case even for countries with high per capita wealth, such as Germany, Austria, Belgium and Japan.

Existing boat moorings in Italy are estimated at approximately 800,000 pleasure units - - 70,531 are registered pleasure boats, 320,000 non-registered craft and 400,000 canoes, kayaks, boards, and other small craft. The 1 to 70 ratio of boats to inhabitants is rather low for a country which ranks among the top seven industrialized nations in the world, has an extensive Mediterranean coastline (almost 5,000 miles of navigable coastline, plus 2,500 miles of shoreline on inland waterways), and enjoys relatively favorable year round weather. During the first half of the 1990s the lack of adequate infrastructure to support pleasure boating, and onerous Italian government fiscal rules and boating regulations hindered pleasure boating expansion. Many of these regulations, however, have been modified in recent years, thereby creating better conditions for the boating industry in Italy.

GOVERNMENT REGULATIONS:

Several GOI 'boating-friendly' regulations have recently been adopted, in order to revitalize a highly fragmented industry which, nonetheless, provides almost 100,000 jobs.

The most important change resulted from a new law which made adoption of boat length and motor size (if applicable), instead of tonnage, the key criteria for classification. This law classifies as "small craft" all motorboats up to 7.5 meters and all sailboats up to 10 meters. As mentioned previously, because registration of these small boats is optional, and therefore rarely done, boats of this size result in significant savings in both mooring taxes and registration fees for owners.

There are now fewer mandatory safety features and equipment required onboard. Previously, safety equipment was based on the boat's classification (length and motor size) but is now based on the type of navigation intended (i.e. distance from the coast; day or night navigation, or navigation in inland/open waters). This means that boats used only for navigation a mile from the shore are no longer required to be equipped with the same safety features as a boat traveling 3, 6, or 12 miles from the coast. Other changes in regulations have made VHF radios more affordable and easier to operate, especially for link calls with shore-stations.

In January 1998, a GOI decree extending the coastal limit for smaller craft from six to twelve miles was issued. This measure effectively means that small boats can legally go just about everywhere on the Italian coast, and represents a major boost to recreational boating.

Ministerial decrees promulgated in December 1997 and April 1998 have also streamlined procedures for marina development. As a result, marina development is expected to take a little more than a year from start to finish, as opposed to the ten years it took previously. The Ministry of Transportation committed to doubling the present size of marine mooring spaces to approximately 200,000 within the next ten years, and to increase the number of affordable berths and marinas, making pleasure boating more accessible.

In December 2004 the Italian government waived the annual license fees and most importantly eliminated the mooring tax for small craft. UCINA's next goal is for further simplification of safety regulations and the elimination of multiple checks at sea. Such measures should spur the demand for both domestically produced and imported boats.

Both Italian and foreign pleasure boat producers should be aware of EC Directive 94/25, implemented in Italy as of June 16, 1998. This directive requires the CE mark on all new pleasure craft between 2.5 and 24 meters in length, and all used boats entering from all non-EU members. The CE mark certifies that the construction of pleasure craft complies with basic safety requirements and is compulsory for the marketing of boats within the EU.

GENOA'S ANNUAL INTERNATIONAL BOAT SHOW:

In October every year Genoa hosts one of the most important (and largest) boat shows in the world. By virtue of its international standing, the Genoa Boat Show is considered one of the best market indicators for the industry. The latest (40th) edition of the show was held October 14th to 22nd, 2000 and was completely sold out. The show attracted over 350,000 visitors from about 80 countries and featured 1,468 exhibitors, with 38 countries represented. The U.S. again had the largest foreign participation (26 percent of all non-Italian participants). There were 1,909 boats on display (including two 'Sea Pavilions'). Motorboats represented 51 percent of the total number of boats on display; sailboats 10 percent; and inflatables, canoes, personal water craft, work-boats and multi-hulls the remaining 39 percent. Interestingly, the display of marine accessories and electronic instrumentation again covered almost 40 percent of the exhibition.

5. U.S. CATALOG EXHIBIT AT GENOA INTERNATIONAL BOAT SHOW:

Capitalizing on this renewed dynamism in the market, Commercial Service Genoa organized, for the third time, a U.S. Catalog Exhibit at the October 2000 Genoa Boat Show. The Exhibit featured 34 U.S. companies, and was promoted in collaboration with Jerry Martin's Global Marine Network, a leading public relations agency entirely dedicated to the marine industry. More than 800 persons visited the Commercial Service booth at the show, resulting in almost 600 trade leads for the participating firms.

COMMENTS:

PROSPECTS FOR U.S. FIRMS:

U.S. producers, traditionally Italy's principal foreign suppliers, can expect to benefit from the Italian Government's renewed interest in reinvigorating and expanding the pleasure boat industry.

Participation in the Genoa International Boat Show is a "must for U.S. boat and marine accessory producers wishing to expand in Italy and Europe. Since it is held in the fall, trade participation is high and a sizeable amount of annual business is traditionally transacted in Genoa, as dealers build stock for the spring season.

PARTICIPATION IN SHOW:

The next edition of the show is scheduled in Genoa, October 13 - 21, 2001. The U.S. Commercial Service in Italy (CS Italy) plans to expand its presence in the show to include a larger scale event. U.S. suppliers wishing to investigate market potential for their products or to participate in this CS initiative should contact the U.S. Commercial Service office in Genoa: Tel: 39/10/543877, fax: 39/10/5761678;
E-mail: genoa.office.box@mail.doc.gov Internet: www.usatrade.gov/italy

WASTE ELECTRICAL AND ELECTRONIC EQUIPMENT

The electric and electronic waste sector in Italy has been regulated by a particularly complex set of regulations that the Italian Government is currently attempting to consolidate with legislative Decree 22/97, which implemented European Union (EU) Directives 91/56 on waste, 91/689 on hazardous waste, and 94/62 on waste packaging. This Italian law, published in the Official Gazette no. 22, dated February 15, 1997, is commonly referred to as the "Decreto Ronchi."

The Ronchi Decree abrogated a substantial number of laws that previously regulated waste disposal in Italy, and simplified procedures with top priority to waste minimization, re-use, recycle, recovery and disposal in landfill. The decree defines program accords to encourage enterprises to adopt production processes that prevent or reduce the quantity of waste and relative level of danger. Article 44 of the Ronchi Decree regulates the following end-of-life electrical and electronic equipment: refrigerators, freezers, television sets, clothes, dish washers, and air-conditioning equipment. It also defines a system for takeback, collection, recovery, and recycling of end-of-life electric and electronic equipment.

In particular, the decree also lays down for the creation (within three years) of a WEEE (waste of electrical and electronic equipment) program agreement between government and industry. To date, no agreement has been reached, despite three years of meetings between the Italian Ministry of Environment, the Ministry of Industry and Commerce, the Environmental Association, and the Electrical and Electronic Manufacturers Association.

Currently, the following Italian laws regulate WEEE:

Legislative Decree no. 22/97, article 44 (Decreto Ronchi) - Management of Waste of Electrical and Electronic Equipment (WEEE);

Ministerial Decree 05/02/98 - Technical Regulations for the Recovery of WEEE (Hazardous and Non-Hazardous Substances);

Presidential Decree no. 203/88, Ministerial Decree 12/07/90, Ministerial Decree 503/97 (attachment 4) - Atmosphere Emission Limits;

Law 549/93 - Measures to Protect the Ozone (with subsequent modifications); and

Ministerial Decree 141/98 - No disposal in Landfills of Waste Containing CFCs (Chlorofluorocarbons).

The rapid growth of WEEE in Italy, as well as general waste, represents one of the most serious problems Italy must confront and has been recognized as a top priority by the Government. Every year, Italy generates approximately 64 million tons of special waste, of which 3.6 million tons is hazardous. At present, Italy has the capacity to manage and dispose properly of only 30 percent of the waste it generates. Italy has not been able to develop adequate waste treatment and disposal programs. Waste recovery and recycling practices, in spite of their growing importance, still have a minimal impact on waste management. Italy disposes over 50 percent of its WEEE in landfills. According to the Italian Association of Household Appliance Manufacturers, out of 1 to 1.2 million units of end-of-life refrigerators and freezers, equivalent to 50,000-60,000 tons, 25 percent is collected by municipalities, 15 percent is landfilled, 40 percent is returned to the retailer, and 15-20 percent is discarded or sold as second-hand products. In 1998, discarded computers amounted to 708,000 units and to 800,000 units in 2004, in which they end up being stored by the distributor or owner.

There is EU-proposed legislation on the prevention, recovery, re-use and recycling of WEEE and a proposal on the restriction of the use of certain hazardous substances in electrical and electronic equipment. The proposal on WEEE is applied to a wide range of electrical and electronic equipment. The proposed legislation is designed to tackle the vast stream of electrical and electronic equipment and compliment other existing measures on landfill and incineration of waste. The increased recycling of such equipment will limit the total quantity of waste going to final disposal. Producers will be responsible for taking back and recycling electrical and electronic equipment. This will most probably provide incentives to design equipment in an environmentally more efficient way that takes waste management aspects fullly into account.

For additional information on both Directives currently under consideration in the European Parliament, you may wish to contact the United States Commercial Service, United States Mission to the European Union, Rue Zinner 13, 1000 Brussels, Belgium, Tel: (32) (2) 5082111, Fax: (32) (2) 5131228.

In conclusion, developments within this industry are driven largely by implementation of environmental legislation that will likely open potential market opportunities for U.S. firms, especially those engaged in waste management, recycling and waste recovery technologies, new product development/technological innovations, and consulting services.

KEY CONTACTS IN ITALY:

Ministero dell'Ambiente
(Ministry of Environment)
Via Cristoforo Colombo, 44
00187 Rome
Tel: (39) (06) 57221; Fax: (39) (06) 57288513

AssoAmbiente
(Association of Italian Environmental Service Companies)
Via del Poggio Laurentino, 11
00144 Rome
Tel: (39) (06) 5921076; Fax: (39) (06) 5919955

ANIE
(Italian Federationi of Electrotechnical and Electronics Industries)
Via Gattamelata, 34
20149 Milan
Tel: (39) (02) 32641; Fax: (39) (02) 3264212

GROWTH TREND IN GOLF MARKET

Based on one of Italy's leading newspapers, "Il Sole 24 Ore," experts expect the number of Italian golfers to approximately double from the current 54,000 players to 110,000 players within the next three years. Alongside the rapid growth in the number of players, golf course construction in Italy is also on the rise. The Italian Golf Federation organized a nationwide campaign this past summer of 2004 to actively introduce the sport to the Italian public by offering complimentary lessons and golf course usage at certain locations. Both the increase in popularity of golf and the Italian Golf Federation's promotions present a prime opportunity for US firms to penetrate the Italian market with high-quality golf equipment and accessories, as well as golf course design, construction and management.

2. THE ITALIAN GOLF MARKET: GENERAL OVERVIEW

Considering the fact that there were less than 1500 golfers in Italy during the 1950s, the nation has recently seen a large increase in both the numbers of golf players and courses. The current number of players (54,000) is expected to double (110,000) within a three-year period. Italy now has 252 courses in total:
18 or more holes (88 courses or 35%)
9 holes (73 courses or 29%)
Practice or promotional use (91 courses or 37%)
[30 courses currently under construction]

Although the fact that Italy having greater numbers of golfers than baseball players promises the potential growth of the sport, Italy at the moment still has very few golfers compared to other European nations:
United Kingdom (3,500,000)
Sweden (400,000)
Germany (350,000)
France (261,000)
Spain (130,000)
Italy (54,000)

A US-based firm, Golf Research Group, further comments on the general golf trend in Europe:

"Population per 18 holes is a useful benchmark of supply levels. Europe averages 77,000 people per eighteen holes (pp18h). In comparison the US is better supplied with 23,000 pp18h. Scotland, with nearly 7,500 holes and a population of just over 5 million, enjoys the best supply level in Europe with 12,000 pp18h... the mainland is very poorly supplied with 139,000 pp18h, Italy being the worst with 443,000 pp18h."

Prices of golf club memberships and construction costs may explain the reasons as to why Italy still falls behind in the number of golfers. Based on a study conducted by Federgolf, membership fees run between 5 million and 15 million lire. In comparison to the 25 million golf players in the United States, golf in Italy is still regarded as a sport for the elite.

Operational fees of golf courses in Italy are also quite high. For example, current construction costs average six to eight billion lire per hole for the three, new 18-hole courses near Rome. Golf courses in Italy are presently valued at 2 trillion lire in total (approx. 8 billion lire per course) and total golf club membership is valued at 162 billion lire.

The fixed costs for golf course development in Italy is certainly not the most economical. However, one should consider the fact that Italy's rapid increase in the number of golfers and courses is worth the investment for the United States in a long perspective, since it directly establishes new opportunities in other business sectors such as eco-tourism, hotel/resort development, and tournament/event development. A recent survey further suggests golf's importance in today's society viewed by American business executives:

Almost half of the respondents of the survey said that the golf is a way with which one operates in the business world.
89% said that golf is a method to build a new business relationship.
35% assured that many business decisions were "concluded on the green."

Italy's high regard for US-made golf equipment and America's exceptional know-how of golf course management and development provide additional reasons for US firms to take active participation in penetrating the current Italian market.

KEY CONTACTS

FEDERAZIONE ITALIANA GOLF – F.I.G.
National Italian Golf Association
Att: Dr. Roberto Livraghi, President
Dr. Stefano Manca, Secretary General
Viale Tiziano, 74
00196 Roma
Phone: 011/39/06-3231825
Fax: 011/39/02/3220250

TRADE ASSOCIATIONS

ASSOSPORT
National Sporting Goods Association
Att: Dr. Alberto Borella, Secretary General
Via Petitti, 16
20149 Milano
Phone: 011/39/02/33001135
Fax: 011/39/02/311182

ADAS - ASSOCIAZIONE DETTAGLIANTI ARTICOLI SPORTIVI
Association of Sporting Goods Retailers
Attn. Dr. Sergio Lolli, Secretary General
Corso Venezia, 47/49
20121 Milano
Tel. 011/39/02/7750272
Fax 011/39/02/7750480

ANRAAS-ASSOCIAZIONE NAZIONALE RAPPRESENTANTI AGENTI ARTICOLI SPORTIVI
National Agents/Distributors Sporting Goods Association
Attn. Mr. Maurizio Governa, President
Via Palestro, 24
20126 Milano
Tel.011/39/02/7750
Fax 011/39/02/783008
CONCLUSION:

Prospective U.S. exporters of golf products are encouraged to explore the Italian market. While the Italian sporting goods and sportswear industry is holding on to its position of world leadership, sources contacted indicate that quality products with an American look may have good potential in the market. The Italian consumer is extremely fashion conscious and more and more attracted by American brands. The "made in U.S.A." label is considered an important factor in buying decisions, especially for younger consumers.

The Commercial Service (CS) in Italy, the export-promoting arm of the U.S. Department of Commerce, has a variety of services to help American exporters interested in the Italian market. Excellent trade promotion opportunities are available to U.S. companies wishing to export their products. These include participation in Commercial Service trade events. For more information on trade opportunities in the Italian sporting goods market, firms should contact Principal Commercial Officer Maria Andrews or Commercial Specialist Annalena Anselmini at CS Milan: tel- 01139/02/659-2260 fax- 01139/02/659-6561; mailing address: Commercial Service,
American Consulate General - Milan
PSC 59, Box M
APO AE 09624.

E-mail address:
Milan.office.box@mail.doc.gov

THE E-MARKET FOR SPORTING GOODS

Italy's geography offers outstanding opportunities for sports: seacoasts for water sports, mountains with some of the most extensive ski areas in Europe, and a diversity of landscapes and climates for fans of hiking, mountain biking, mountaineering, whitewater sports, and other activities. In Italy, as in the U.S.A., the active, sporting lifestyle is ever more popular, and the sporting goods business is capitalizing on the growing interest. Thirty-nine percent of Italians are actively involved in at least one sport. The market for sporting goods, apparel and footwear in Italy is estimated at US$4.7 billion, making Italy the world's fourth largest market and the second largest market in Europe, after Germany.

E-business capabilities have created new market opportunities for U.S. sporting goods companies in Italy, who can enter the market through this new channel and boost sales in Italy. In fact, the Italian e-sporting goods market is extremely receptive to American products due to their reputation as innovative and of high quality, critical features for success in the Italian market.

LIFESTYLE TRENDS

The number of Italians actively participating in sports activities increased considerably between 1980-2000. According to SITA-Nielsen, (a market research company), 39 percent of Italians over the age of four, or 21.5 million, practice at least one sport. Of these potential consumers, 30 percent practice two or more sports. The sporting goods market is divided among clothing (72.7 percent, including licensed products), footwear (23 percent), and equipment (4.3 percent.)

DISTRIBUTION IN THE ITALIAN MARKET

Distribution channels for sporting goods constantly evolve, and recently well established chains and large buying groups, have had a market advantage. However, the Internet is creating a new "virtual" distribution channel with forecasts for larger on-line sales. Market specialists claim this will accelerate the reduction of small independent retailers, and their market share will be taken over by the "virtual retailers". E-business is a new phenomenon in the Italian market but local manufacturers and distributors are quickly taking advantage by launching new web sites. An recent example is the Giacomelli group , an Italian sporting goods distribution chain that has recently launched a very successful web site (www.giacomellisport.com). Through the site Giacomelli has increased its sales by 5 percent and is expected to reach 15-20 percent growth in the next two years.

GOOD PROSPECTS FOR U.S. SPORTING GOODS COMPANIES

In conclusion, although the Italian market is very competitive, U.S. exporters with innovative products may find sales opportunities and growth using the e-business channel to sell in Italy. Leading market experts in the recreation industry are optimistic about e-commerce in the sporting goods sector, expecting increased sales in 2001. These indicators suggest that U.S. products could assume a larger market share.

POSITIONING OF GLOBAL DISTRIBUTION SYSTEMS

Global Distribution Systems (GDS) offer real-time booking management systems to tourism services suppliers such as airlines, hotel chains, tour operators, and car rental agencies.

These booking systems are technologically sophisticated, using satellite technologies for data transmission. The wealth of information and optimal speed allow both suppliers and users to save significant time in their booking and ticketing activities. GDS are important for travel agencies, as they allow fast and reliable service to customers, and can compete with the direct booking possibilities offered through the internet.

This report gives an overview of the services available from the 4 GDS present in the Italian market, and their market position in Italy.

THE PLAYERS

There are four GDS operators - Amadeus, Sabre, Sigma and Worldspan – that operate in the Italian market. These companies rent to travel agencies their own point of sale (POS) terminals through which the majority of airlines bookings and ticketing are carried out. Sales of travel packages through the GDS are becoming increasingly popular, and for many Italian tour operators and cruise lines, these electronic sales surpassed phone transactions.

Italian GDS operators Sigma SpA, the developer of the technology, and Sigma Travel System SpA, the distributing company, have the highest market penetration in Italy. In 2004, Sigma reported 200 billion lira (approx $ 91 million) turnover. It is affiliated with Galileo International, the second largest GDS worldwide with $1.3 billion in consolidated sales.
Sigma's main shareholder is Racom Teledata (92%) a company of the Alitalia Group. Sigma has negotiated contracts with the following travel agencies networks: Buon Viaggio, Sestante- Hit, CTS, CIT, Carlson Wagon Lit, American Express, Uvet, BTI, Cisalpina, Gruppo Fabretto, Robintour, and Gruppo Marsupio.

The second most common GDS is Sabre Italia srl, a subsidiary of Sabre Inc. Sabre is the largest GDS worldwide, with approximately $ 2.1 billion in consolidated sales in 2004. Sabre is quoted on the New York Stock Exchange. Sales data in Italy are not available. Sabre Italia has announced contracts with the following Italian travel networks: Giramondo, Gruppo Fabretto, ITN, Sima, Travel Company, Uvet, and Viaggi & Vacanze.

Amadeus Marketing Italia, of the Amadeus Global Travel Distribution group, is the third largest GDS per number of affiliated agencies both in Italy and at a worldwide level. Amadeus' main shareholders are the European Airlines Lufthansa, Air France and Iberia, each with 25% of shares, while the remaining 25% is publicly held and is quoted on the European Stock Exchange. Amadeus has agreements with the following retail organizations: Cisalpina, Le Marmotte, Touring Club, Kuoni Gastaldi, Cimair, Silverado.

Worldspan Services Ltd is the GDS with the smallest presence in the Italian market. Worldspan is owned by Northwest Airlines (34%), Delta Air Lines (40%) and TWA (26%), and has agreements with the travel agency networks CIT Italia, and CTS (Youth travel organization).

All GDS suppliers rent the hardware, charge a monthly subscription fee, and offer specific training for users on both hardware and software, provide hardware/user assistance, as well give incentives for electronic ticketing.

The table below indicates the market position of these GDS suppliers.

	Amadeus	Sabre Italia	Sigma/Galileo	Worldspan

Years present in Italy	7	12	18	9
Travel agencies and terminals	1100 agencies, 2700 terminals	2200 agencies 4500 terminals	4065 agencies 10805 terminals	780 agencies
MKT Share in Italy*	17%	24%	64%	12%
Mkt share worldwide	34%	40%	31%	20%
Employees in Italy	52	53	260	20
Employees Worldwide	3000	11000	3000	3000
Internet site	www.amadeus.net www.amadeusitalia.it	www.agentexplorer.sabre.com	www.sigma.it	Www.worldspan.com
Access reserved to travel agents	Public access +special Sections for agents	Agents only + free of charge	Agents can have a booking section for their clients on Sigma's web	Public access but only for information. Agents can book through the web
Italian TOs Represented	Alpitour, Aviomar, Bini, Columbus, Comitour, Eurotravel, Going, Kuoni Gastaldi, Orizzonti, Teorema, Transalpino, Viaggi del Ventaglio, Viaggidea, Karambola, Francorosso.	Alpitour, Francorosso, Sportime, I Viaggi del Ventaglio, Aviomar, Eurotravel	Alpitour, Atitur, Aviomar, Bini Viaggi, Columbus, Comitours, Costa Crociere, Distal & ITR Group, Eden, Eurotravel, Going, Francorosso, I Viaggi del Turchese, I Viaggi del Ventaglio, Imperatore Travel, Italiatour/Offshore, Karambola, Libarna, Orizzonti, Polycastrum, Settemari, Springtours, Teorema, Transalpino, Turisanda, Valtur, Veratour, Viaggidea, Viloratour, Wasteels.	Alpitour, Francorosso, Karambola, Aviomar, Idee per viaggiare, Teorema.
Other services offered	Travel insurance	Theater tickets (Broadway + London)	Travel Insurance, Theater tickets, financial products	None

* Frequently a travel agency is a client of more than one GDS, resulting in total market share over 100%.

THE INTERNET CHALLENGE

GDS operators created separate procedures to allow easy booking through the internet so as to not lose market share. Airlines, hotel chains, car rentals, and cruise lines, all offer websites with direct booking capabilities, for both trade and consumers. In order to guarantee commissions to their subscribers, GDS have two separate sections for consumers and travel agents. In general, the travel agents section is more complete and accessible only with a password, and while consumers are allowed to make their own reservations through the web, they need to indicate a travel agent in order to conclude the transaction and collect the travel documents. In this way, GDS systems allow the travel agent to maintain part of its business. A slightly different approach was chosen by Sigma Travel System. It recently launched a special program – Sigma Gift - that allows the agent to include the special reservation module in the agent's website, thus granting the agent's customer better service, without taking away clients.

CONTACTS

Amadeus Marketing Italia
Via Solferino 7
20121 Milano
Tel. 39/02725471
Fax 39/0286458501

Sabre Italia srl
Via Vittore Pisani 19
20124 Milano
Tel 39/02667361
Fax 39/026693696

Sigma Travel System
Via Alessandro Marchetti 111
00148 Roma
Tel 39/06659641
Fax 39/0665964533

Worldspan
Viale Ferdinando di Savoia 2
20124 Milano
Tel 39/0267070994
Fax 39/0267071047

THE CHARTER FLIGHT MARKET

Italian charter flight companies are gaining overall travel market share at the expense of international charter competitors in the outbound market segment. The charter market, especially in the medium-haul segment, is steadily increasing with 16% growth in 2000. However, charters to North America decreased by 40% in 2000
.

THE ITALIAN OPERATORS

Charter flights boomed in Italy in 2000, reaching 8.5 million passengers transported to and from Italy, and 69,219 flights. Italian carriers enjoyed the most significant growth, increasing market share to 38 % of the market. The market leader was Eurofly with 713,000 passengers, followed by Volare (671,000) and Air Europe (650,000). After the acquisition of Air Europe by Volare, the Volare Group becomes the largest charter operator in Italy with more than 1.3 million passengers and 8,500 flights. Volare is the market leader for outbound flights to Egypt, Greece, and Cape Verde. Operator Blue Panorama grew the most in 2000; a record +86%. With this it became the fourth largest Italian charter operator, with 450,000 passengers transported mainly to Israel and Spain.

Outbound charter flights to North America decreased dramatically from 30 to 10 flights in 2000. Charter flights to the U.S. are not attractive due to strong competition from reduced fares available on scheduled flights. Furthermore, Italians visiting the U.S. prefer to build their own travel itinerary and therefore prefer to use scheduled flights as opposed to charters. Jubileum celebrations in 2000 accounted for the increase of international charter flights to Italy, primarily from the U.S. and Canada.

FUTURE TRENDS

According to executives at Blue Panorama, the the Italian carriers' growth is due to improved service. The Italian traveler is more and more sophisticated, and demands convienient flight scheduling, and premium service on-board. Italian tour operators reinforced alliances with Italian charter carriers to better satisfy their customers, especially those travelling from the largest Italian cities. International operators tend to serve the lower end of the outbound market, fly to less important destinations, and depart from smaller Italian airports. These executives also conceeded that Italian charter companies are practically inactive in organizing incoming flights.

According to the association of Italian tour operators, the increased number of flights in 2000 did not increase the profits of tour operators and charter companies. Excess capacity in 2000 considerably lowered prices, and flights were filled using super-discounted last-minute trips with major repercussions on Italian tour operators' profitability. Operators are optimistic for increased profits in 2001, as capacity has been slightly reduced, and Italian customers are responding well to new advance booking policies implemented by most Italian operators.

AIR CONDITIONING EQUIPMENT FOR RESIDENTIAL USE

MARKET HIGHLIGHTS & BEST PROSPECTS

MARKET PROFILE

In 1998, the residential A/C market was estimated at 700 million USD, an increase of 12 percent over 1997 figures. The end of a severe recession in 1998, Italy's entry in the Euro, controlled inflation and government incentive plans are all factors which have helped to shape this market and contributed to an overall rise in consumer confidence. A favorable summer season in 1998 also contributed to an increases in sales, allowing for a sell-off of overstocks bringing them back to near normal levels.

As the economy continues to recover, and with the expectation that the government will continue with incentive programs for renovation as it has in the recent past, sector experts are confident that the market will provide the right conditions for the market to expand further.

There is a close relationship between sales of residential A/C equipment and activity in the construction industry, which has picked up after having remained stagnant in the early 90s. In particular, government incentive programs for the renovation of homes have encouraged homeowners to refurbish their apartments and homes. This increase in residential renovation during the last few years is a direct cause of the increase in demand for A/C equipment. Local production – which saw an increase of 28 percent last year -- sped up to meet this demand, and imports also saw substantial growth, valued at 695 million USD in 1998.

Another positive factor is changing consumer preferences. While Italians are generally not air conditioner fanatics, preferences are beginning to change. Air-conditioned environments are becoming more popular, and the trend is towards small units offering energy savings and climate control: air-conditioning units which allow for finely-tuned temperature control, perhaps allowing reversal of heat and cold, with minimal energy consumption.

In terms of imports and market share, U.S. products have historically been one of the most consistent in this sector, enjoying excellent reputation in the marketplace. Assuming the current trend continues, U.S. products should continue to enjoy a relatively important market share.

Mono-split and multi-split units are particularly widespread among Italian households. Mono-split units are comprised of one internal unit (containing the battery and fan) and one external unit(containing a battery, fan and compressor). Multi-split units consist of one external unit and two or more internal units. The market for split units saw a rapid expansion in Italy (and in general in all of Europe) after Japanese producers introduced basic technological innovations. The aggressive marketing strategies adopted by oriental manufacturers during the early 1990's provoked the prompt reaction of Italian producers (including those firms with foreign capital) who adjusted their technology in order to remain competitive.

Portable systems: The portable units, which are very popular in Italy and in Europe in general, consist of one single block containing all of the parts making up the internal and external units of the split systems. These portable systems are called portable because they can be transported from one room to another for the simple reason that they are on wheels.

Historically, Italian constructors consider themselves the inventors of this type of unit, which only began to make up a substantial market share when several of the more important Italian manufacturers took interest in this model. Since there were virtually no foreign competitors in the early stages, the Italian constructors at first held nearly the entire market share and sales took off, reaching elevated figures. The Italian style and simplicity of these units found no comparable product manufactured by foreigners and, therefore, rapidly became popular in other foreign markets. The simplicity of installation has distinguished this model in the Italian market especially among users who have found this to be a key factor in the purchase of such models and, especially, have boosted unprogrammed purchases during unexpected heat waves.

COMPETITIVE ANALYSIS

1. Domestic Production

The Italians are the third most important producers of A/C for residential use after the U.S. and Japanese. Italian producers have a reputation for being among the most technologically advanced and are known for their after-sales-service network.

Italian manufacturers have undergone a process of improvement and innovation in their production and must continue in this vein mainly due to strict new legislation at the European Community level, forcing them to commit to more investments and technological improvements.

Local production saw a 28 percent increase in 1998, with over 220,000 units produced. Major domestic producers include Riello Condizionatori, holding approximately 20 percent of the market; Marelli Clima; Officine di Seveso; RC Condizionatori; and Climaveneta. These companies export a great portion of their production, and their markets include North Africa, the Middle East, Europe and the U.S. This is reflected in local production and export figures which indicate that domestic production is almost equal to exports. At the same time, some of the products imported (in the lower price range) are being re-exported to third countries.

Other small manufacturers have cut down production and are shifting to imports of complete units and/or parts from Japan and the Far East. These firms tend to distribute small units for domestic use and for exportation to third countries.

2. Third-Country Imports

Imports represent an important portion of the total Italian market and, when compared to local production and the market itself, have shown remarkable growth. In the past years, Japanese industries have aggressively marketed their products in Europe, including Italy, with the majority having opened local production facilities. Japanese manufacturers have expanded their operations and will likely continue to do so in the future. Firms including Hitachi, Daikin, Fuji Electric, Mitsubishi Electric, Sharp and Toshiba make up over 30 percent of the import market. The Japanese products are well-known and have a very good reputation for being compact and reliable, and their technical support is very effective through a major network of dealers, distributors and installers which covers major cities and rural areas.

Other major exporters to Italy include Germany (Vortex, Wolf Klimatechnik), France (Saunier-Duvall) and Spain (Roca), each holding approximately 10 percent of the import market share. The remaining share of imports is divided up among other European and Far Eastern suppliers.

U.S. Market Position

U.S. manufacturers of HVAC equipment have made marginal gains since 1993, maintaining a fairly important market share. Trade sources indicate the U.S. holds approximately 22 percent of the market. It is expected that U.S. manufacturers' presence in Italy will continue to grow at an estimated growth rate of 7 percent over the next 2 years.

Growth has been favored by the strong presence of old and well-established multinationals. Considering that in the recent past this sector has undergone a difficult period, this performance can be considered a success. U.S. manufacturers such as Carrier, York, Trane and McQuay have long-established Italian subsidiaries and are well known throughout the country.

Competitive Factors: Quality and after-sales-service are two factors of equal importance for the successful marketing of A/C equipment in the Italian market. The presence of a nationwide service organization which can guarantee installation and maintenance will prove a definite advantage. Price has comparatively limited bearing as compared with other goods.

Other competitive factors include: ease of installation and low operating costs; technical factors include limiting noise pollution and ensuring energy saving qualities (high cost of electricity and limitations of 3 kw/hour per household). In
addition, residential A/C units should be of attractive design to meet Italian sophisticated taste, and, at the same time, of small dimensions to minimize space requirements in small apartments, shops or studios.

END-USER ANALYSIS

As mentioned earlier, Italian preferences are changing. More and more Italians are opting for climate controlled environments. The typical end-user purchasing air conditioning units for the home belongs to the middle and upper-class who enjoy the comforts of life, including air conditioning in their car (which has just about become standard equipment) and home. End-users tend to buy in both small shops and specialized electronic and consumer goods retail outlets. Some department stores and hypermarkets are now also selling consumer electronics and appliances, including air conditioners. Prices of residential AC units in Italy are dramatically more expensive than in the U.S. and range from 2,000.00 - 3,800.00 USD.

While this study covers the residential sector, it should be noted that there are other end-users of small A/C units, including the service sector (hotels, health spas, hospitals and banks), small businesses and manufacturing plants. The public sector, including ministries and other government entities, is also an end-user of small units. Some government offices are still undergoing renovation and it can be expected that they will be upgrading or installing AC units.

MARKET ACCESS

1. Import Climate

No trade restrictions or other non-tariff barriers exist on the import of air conditioning equipment. A substantial reduction in tariffs on some A/C products took place as a result of GATT negotiations and were implemented in 1995. Tariffs for residential air conditioning units are in the range of 2.2 - 2.7 percent.

Chlorofluorocarbons (CFCs) have been a major issue of the recent years in the worldwide campaign to eliminate ozone-depleting chemicals. A law was passed on December 28, 1993, containing all the regulations regarding CFCs and also HCFCs, which are to be eliminated in Europe by 2008. This law complies with EU regulations no. 594/91 and no. 3952/92. With only minor exceptions, the sale, import/export and use of CFCs has been progressively limited, and their production prohibited as of December 31, 1994. Under the same law, the production, use, sale, import and export of HCFCs will be forbidden after December 31, 2004. The Ministry for the Environment has created a special agency, the National Agency for Environmental Protection, to control and enforce this law.

In addition, new European regulations are expected which will update European directive no. 3093/94. It is expected that R22 refrigerants will necessarily have to be replaced by new refrigerants (R410A, R407,

R404, etc.) which will necessitate the redesigning of air conditioning machines. It is anticipated that American and Japanese competitors will have the advantage since new refrigerants are already in use in their respective countries. For this reason national industry associations are actively lobbying at both the local and EU levels to bring about a change so that standards and regulations become harmonized throughout the world.

Italian regulations fully comply and sometimes exceed the standards regarding safety and dependability established by the Committee for European Regulation (CEM). Standards enforced in the U.S. and set by the American Society of Heating, Refrigeration and Air-conditioning Engineers (ASHRAE), are usually stricter than those set by EU countries. These standards are followed by The Italian Association of Air Conditioning, Heating and Refrigeration (AICARR), which, in turn, is a member of ASHRAE. Therefore, increased restrictions will certainly impact A/C technology but should not result in a major poblem for U.S. manufacturers. For further technical clarifications, exporters may find it useful to contact ASHRAE (see Key Contacts section).

The National Center for Standards and Certification Information (NCSCI), a U.S. Government agency, which is part of the Department of Commerce's National Institute of Standards and Technology (NIST), should be a first point of contact for U.S. companies attempting to determine which Italian standard or EU directive may be applicable to their products. NIST maintains standards information for all ISO (International Organization for Standardization) countries, including Italy. See the Key Contacts section for contact information on this organization.

The U.S. Commercial Service's branch office at NIST in Gaithersburg is another valuable source of information and assistance for U.S. firms with questions about Italian and EU standards. Contact information can be found in the Key Contacts
section at the end of this report

Labeling requirements: The EU directive 92/75 of Sept. 22, 1992 regarding labeling requirements governs this sector. Only those products bearing the required "CE" mark are allowed to be sold in Europe. General information on the EU directives and CE mark regulations can be obtained from the Office of European Union and Regional Affairs (OEURA) (see Key Contacts section).

OEURA staff can provide the latest information on CE mark requirements, including the so-called (new approach(to CE mark conformity, copiesof directives, availability of standards, lists of (notified(bodies, interpretive guides and other commercial information.

Another source of information is the American National Standards Institute (ANSI) in New York. ANSI is the official U.S. depository for all ISO member-countries and has English translations of foreign standards. U.S. firms may request a standard search for a fee.

In some cases, Underwriters Laboratories Inc. in the United States can assist U.S. manufacturers and exporters in understanding and complying with foreign national and international standards and certification requirements and
procedures. UL's TATE (Technical Assistance To Exporters) program, can provide technical information about standards in many foreign countries. UL has agreements with a number of foreign agencies, including Italy's IMQ, for conducting product testing and factory evaluations. U.S. firms wishing to avail themselves of the UL TATE program may contact the TATE coordinator. (See the Key Contacts section).

2. Distribution/Business Practices

As stated above, major multinational companies have long established direct presence in Italy. U.S. companies who do not wish to operate with a direct presence should have an agent or distributor, or contact the various installer associations, which are active in all 95 Italian provinces. The Italian association for air conditioning, heating and refrigeration (AICARR, see contact information in the key contacts section) can provide a list of these associations.

The system of retail and wholesale distribu-tion in Italy centers on small family-operated stores, although the supermarket-type operation has gained importance and there are a number of substantial department store operations. The retail distribution sector is large in total sales and serves the consumer at the retail level through numerous small, family-owned, retail outlets rather than large, mass market operations. Many large retail stores have recently been opening on Sundays. Recent legislation has liberalized the range of products and hours of operation permitted at retail outlets and should promote a more modern, competitive retail system.

In terms of existing points of sale, there is a trend away from the family-type stores and street vendors to the distribution chains. Italian distribution outlets include small family-owned stores, street vendors, hypermarkets, shopping malls, specialty stores and discount stores. Specialty stores selling air conditioning equipment also carry heating units, dehumidifiers and other related products.

Horizontal points of sale such as general stores, which had experienced boom conditions in the early 1980s, have begun to lose ground to specialty stores, franchising chains, and hypermarkets. In order to create a unique busi-ness identity, department stores have begun a process of realignment and now tend to attract the more affluent, quality-oriented consumers, as well as compete on price and product selection. Supermarket chains now look toward further expansion, particularly in creating and operating large shopping malls. Where such shopping centers exist, they are proving to be successful.

It is common business practice among local manufacturers to grant discounts to wholesalers (up to 50-60 % off the price list). Agent and distributor commissions normally are in the range of 5-6 percent.

FINANCING

Financing and trade practices in this sector adhere to normal Italian business standards. The majority of financial transactions are handled through private agreements and banking institutions. While some U.S. manufacturers request payment upon receipt of the goods, more successful sellers are offering offering terms allowing settlement of the account from 60 to 120 days following date of invoice, which is the most common practice in Italy.

The use of irrevocable letters of credit for the Italian market has declined appreciably in recent years. Although such instruments are still required by American exporters, especially when the Italian customer's credit reputation is not well known, the growing reluctance of Italian firms to provide letters of credit has required American exporters to turn to other methods to assure payment or lose the sale to other suppliers in the competitive Italian market. The Italian businessperson is reluctant to pay a high fee for a letter of credit when other suppliers or means of payment are available. American firms have put to greater use the export credit insurance and guarantee programs available through the Foreign Credit Insurance Association (FCIA).

KEY CONTACTS FOR THE INDUSTRY

U.S. Commercial Service Italy
c/o American Embassy
Via Veneto 119/A
00187 Rome
Tel: 39-06-4674-2382
Fax: 39-06-4674-2113
Web site: http://www.usis.it/fcs/
E-mail: mailto:Rome.Office.Box@mail.doc.gov
mailto:fcs@usis.it

ITALIAN GOVERNMENT

Ministero dell'Industria, del Commercio e dell'Artigianato
(Ministry for Industry, Commerce and Handicrafts)
Via Molise 2

00187 Rome
Tel: 39-06-47051
Fax: 39-06-47887773
Web site: http://www.minindustria.it/

Ministero dell'Ambiente
(Ministry for the Environment)
Via Cristoforo Colombo 44
00147 Rome
Tel: 39-06-57221
Fax: 39-06-57288513
Web site: http://www.scn.minambiente.it/

TRADE ASSOCIATIONS AND GOVERNMENT AGENCIES

ASHRAE
American Society of Heating, Refrigeration and Air-conditioning Engineers
1791 Tullie Circle NE
Atlanta, GA 30329
Toll free: (800) 527-4723
Tel: (404) 636-8400
Fax: (404) 321-5478
Web site: http://www.ashrae.org/

NCSCI - National Center for Standards and Certifiction Information
NIST - National Institute for Standards and Technology
TRF Room A 163
Gaithersburg, MD 20899
Tel: (301) 975-4040
Fax: (301) 975-2128 or 926-1559
Web site: http://ts.nist.gov/htdocs/210/217/bro.htm

U.S. Commercial Service
Gaithhersburg Branch Office
c/o NIST Building 411
Gaithersburg, MD 20899
Contact: Mr. Stephen B. Hall, Trade Specialist
Tel: (301) 978-3904

OEURA
Office of European Union and Regional Affairs
U.S. Department of Commerce
14th and Constitution Avenue, N.W. Room 3036
Washington, D.C. 20230
Tel: (202) 482-5276
Fax: (202) 482-2155

ANSI
American National Standards Institute
11 West 42nd Street, 13th Floor
New York, NY 10036
Tel: (212) 642-4900
Fax: (212) 302-1286
Web site: http://web.ansi.org/default.htm

OFFICE IN BRUSSELS:

ANSI
American National Standards Institute
c/o American Chamber of Commerce
Ave. des Arts 50
B-1040 Brussels, Belgium
Tel: 011-32-2-5136892
Fax: 011-32-2-5137928

UL
Underwrites Laboratories
International Compliance Services Department
333 Pfingsten Road
Northbrook, IL 60062
Tel: (708) 272-8800
Fax: (708) 272-9562
Web site: http://www.ul.com/

ANIMA
Federazione delle Associazioni Nazionali dell'Industria Meccanica Varia ed Affine
(Federation of National Associations of various mechanical industries)
Contact: Dott. Ing. Enrico Malcovati (Mr.), Secretary General
Via Luisa Battistotti Sassi 11/B
20133 Milan
Tel: 39-02-73971
Fax: 39-02-739-7316
Web site: http://www.anima-it.com
E-mail: mailto:anima@anima-it.com

A.I.CARR
Associazione Italiana Condizionamento dell'Aria, Riscaldamento, Refrigerazione
(Italian Association of Air Conditioning, Heating and Refrigeration)
Contact: Ing. Sanzio Boldrini (Mr.), Secretary General
Viale Monte Grappa 2
20124 Milano
Tel: 39-02-2900-2369
Fax: 39-02-2900-0004
Web site: http://www.aircarr.it
E-mail: mailto:aicarr@aicarr.it

ANGAISA
Associazione Nazionale Commercianti Articoli Idro Sanitari, Climatizzazione, Pavimenti, Rivestimenti ed Arredobagno
(National association of Traders in hydro-sanitary, climatization, flooring, coverings and bathroom fittings)
Contact: Dott. Arch. Gianni Mari (Mr.), President
Via Pelizza da Volpedo 8
20149 Milano
Tel: 39-02-48591611/43990459
Fax: 39-02-4859-1622
Web site: http://www.angaisa.it

ASSITAL
Associazione Nazionale Costruttori di Impianti
(National Association of Industrial Plant Builders and Constructors)
Contact: Dott. Nicola Cianitto (Mr.), Direttore
Via Serbelloni 4
20122 Milan
Tel: 39-02-7600-2894
Fax: 39-02-7601-3014
Web site: http://www.assistal.it

A.T.I.
Associazione Termotecnica Italiana
(Italian Thermoelectric Association)
Contact: Prof. Giancarlo Chiesa (Mr.), Secretary
Piazzale Morandi
40136 Milan
Tel: 39-02-2399-5110
Web site: http://www.ingegneria.unige.it/strutture/ati/ati.html

QUALIFIT
Istituto Nazionale per la Qualificazione e la Certificazione dei Costruttori e Installatori di Impianti Tecnici
(National Institute for Quality Control and Certification of Manufacturers and Installers of Technical Equipment)
Contact: P.Ind. giampiero Baldassari (Mr.) & Comm. Carlo Perucconi (Mr.), Vice Presidents
Via Ramazzini 2
20129 Milan
Tel: 39-02-2940-1364
Fax: 39-02-2940-1847
Web site: http://www.qualifit.it

UNI
Ente Nazionale Italiano di Unificazione
(Italian National Institute for Harmonization)
Contact: Ing. Paolo Morelli (Mr.), Managing Director
Via Battistotti Sassi 11
20133 Milan
Tel: 39-02-700241
Fax: 39-02-70105992
Web site: http://www.uni.unicei.it/

C. PUBLICATIONS

L'Installatore Italiano
(The Italian Installer)
Monthly magazine
Publisher: Editoriale PEG S.p.A.
Contact: Dott. Sanguinetti (Mr.), Owner
Via Fratelli Bressan 2
20126 Milan
Tel: 39-02-2479841
Fax: 39-02-2552779

Il Corriere Termo Idro Sanitario
(The Thermal Hydro-sanitary Courier)

Monthly magazine
Publisher: Editoriale PEG S.p.A.
Contact: Dott. Sanguinetti (Mr.), Owner
Via Fratelli Bressan 2
20126 Milan
Tel: 39-02-2479841
Fax: 39-02-2552779

RCI - Riscaldamento, Climatizzazione, Idraulica
(Heating, refrigeration, hydraulics)
Publisher: Tecniche Nuove S.p.A.
Contact: Mr. Enzo Guaglione, Mr. Antonio Briganti (editors)
Via Ciro Menotti 14
20100 Milan
Tel: 39-02-75701
Fax: 39-02-7570373

Condizionamento dell'Aria, Riscaldamento e Refrigerazione
(Air Conditioning, Heating and Refrigeration)
Monthly magazine
Publisher: Editoriale PEG S.p.A.
Contact: Dott. Sanguinetti (Mr.), Owner
Via Fratelli Bressan 2
20126 Milan
Tel: 39-02-2479841
Fax: 39-02-2552779

Suppliers (domestic, U.S. and third country)

PORTABLE UNITS

DELCHI CARRIER S.P.A.
Via R. Sanzio 9
20058 VILLASANTA (Milano)
TEL.: 39-039-3636
FAX: 39-039-3636555

GALLETTI SPA
Via L. Romagnoli 12/A
40010 Bentivoglio (Bologna)
TEL.: 39-051-6640457
FAX: 39-051-6640680

R.B.L. RIELLO BRUCIATORI LEGNAGO SPA
Via degli Alpini 1
37045 LEGNAGO (Verona)
TEL.: 39-0442-630111
FAX: 39-0442-22510

RICAGNI CONDIZIONATORI S.P.A.
Via L. da Vinci 4
20068 PESCHIERA BORROMEO (Milano)
TEL.: 39-02-516621
FAX: 39-02-55301148

RIELLO CONDIZIONATORI S.P.A.
Via Roma 44
37040 BEVILACQUA (Verona)
TEL.: 39-0442-633111
FAX: 39-0442-93630

SANYO ARGO CLIMA S.R.L.
Via Varese 90
21013 GALLARATE (Varese)
TEL.: 39-0331-791120
FAX: 39-0331-784513

YORK INTERNATIONAL S.P.A. div. SEVESO CLIMA
Via XXV Aprile 29
20030 BARLASSINA (MI)
TEL.: 39-0362-5381
FAX: 39-0362-565493

SPLIT UNITS

ACCORRONI S.R.L.
Via Pignocco 25
60027 OSIMO (Ancona)
TEL: 39-071-723991
FAX: 39-071-7133153

APEN GROUP S.P.A.
Via Provinciale 85
20060 PESSANO CON BORNAGO (Milano)
TEL: 39-02-95742671
FAX: 39-02-95742797

CLIVET S.R.L.
Zona Ind.le Villapaiera
32030 VILLAPAIERA-FELTRE (Belluno)
TEL: 39-0439-3131
FAX: 39-0439-81404

DELCHI CARRIER S.P.A.
Via R. Sanzio 9
20058 VILLASANTA (Milano)
TEL: 39-039-3636
FAX: 39-039-3636555

GALLETTI SPA
Via L. Romagnoli 12/A
40010 Bentivoglio (Bologna)
TEL: 39-051-6640457
FAX: 39-051-6640680

HIROSS S.P.A.
Via L. da Vinci 8
35028 PIEVE DI SACCO (Padova)
TEL: 39-049-9719111
FAX: 39-049-5841421

INTERKLIM SISTEMI S.R.L.
Via R. Bricchetti 7
27100 PAVIA
TEL: 39-0382-5131
FAX: 39-0382-529130

JUCKER S.P.A.
Via Verdi 9
22050 LOMAGNA (Lecco)
TEL: 39-039-59181
FAX: 39-039-5301286

MC QUAY ITALIA S.P.A.
Via Piani di S. Maria 72
00040 ARICCIA (Roma)
TEL: 39-06-9374055
FAX: 39-06-9374014

MTA SRL
Via dell'Artigianato 2
35026 CONSELVE (Padova)
TEL: 39-049-9500590
FAX: 39-049-9500580

R.B.L. RIELLO BRUCIATORI LEGNAGO SPA
Via degli Alpini 1
37045 LEGNAGO (Verona)
TEL: 39-0442-630111
FAX: 39-0442-22510

R.C. CONDIZIONATORI S.P.A.
Via Roma 5
27010 VALLE SALIMBENE (Pavia)
TEL: 39-0382-587147
FAX: 39-0382-587148

RICAGNI CONDIZIONATORI S.P.A.
Via L. da Vinci 4
20068 PESCHIERA BORROMEO (Milano)
TEL: 39-02-516621
FAX: 39-02-55301148

RIELLO CONDIZIONATORI S.P.A.
Via Roma 44
37040 BEVILACQUA (Verona)
TEL: 39-0442-633111
FAX: 39-0442-93630

SABIANA SPA
Via Piave 53
20011 CORBETTA (Milano)
TEL: 39-02-9777021
FAX: 39-02-9777282

SANYO ARGO CLIMA S.R.L.
Via Varese 90
21013 GALLARATE (Varese)
TEL: 39-0331-791120
FAX: 39-0331-784513

YORK INTERNATIONAL S.P.A. div. SEVESO CLIMA
Via XXV Aprile 29
20030 BARLASSINA (Milano)
TEL: 39-0362-5381
FAX: 39-0362-565493

TRADE PROMOTION OPPORTUNITIES

The Mostra Convegno Expocomfort is the most important specialized trade show for the HVAC sector in Italy. This show is held biennially on even-numbered years at the Milan International Fairgrounds. The last edition, which was held March 25-29, 1998, had over 150,000 visitors of which 30,000 were from 117 foreign countries. A total of 2,707 companies were represented.

The 32nd edition of the show will be held March 21-25, 2000, and will feature, among others, pavilions dedicated to sanitary installations and cogeneration.

Organizer: Fiera Milano International SpA
Largo Domodossola 1
20145 Milan
Tel: 39-02-485501
Fax: 39-02-4800-5450
Web site: http://www.fieramilano.it

U.S. companies interested in participating may contact the Milan Fairgrounds "International Sales Force" at mailto:mce@planet.it or through their U.S. locations:

Fiera Milano Office
Italy-America Chamber of Commerce West, Inc.
10350 Santa Monica Boulevard - Suite 210
Los Angeles, CA 90025
Toll free: 1-800-343-7264
Tel: (310) 557-3017
Fax: (310) 557-1217
Web site: http://www.italchambers.net
E-mail: mailto:fiera.losangeles@italchambers.net

Fiera Milano Office
Italy-America Chamber of Commerce, Inc.
730 Fifth Avenue - Suite 600
New York, NY 10019
Toll free: 1-800-343-7264
Tel: (212) 459-0044
Fax: (212) 459-0090
Web site: http://www.italchambers.net
E-mail: mailto:fiera.newyork@italchambers.net

Fiera Milano Office
Italy-America Chamber of Commerce of Chicago
30 S. Michigan Avenue – Suite 502
Chicago, IL 60603
Toll free: 1-800-343-7264
Tel: (312) 553-9137
Fax: (312) 553-9142
Web site: http://www.italchambers.net
E-mail: mailto:fiera.chicago@italchambers.net

Climatec is another important trade show which is held in conjunction with the SAIE trade fair, one of the top international exhibitions in Italy specializing in various sectors of the construction/building materials sector, and one of the most important shows in the field in Europe. Climatec, in particilar, focuses on air conditioning, heating, refregeration, and air water treatment. this pavilion is held every other year during the SAIE trade show. The 2004 edition of SAIE/Climatec
was held October 13-17, and the Commercial Service Italy organized a catalog show at this event. For more information on the next edition of SAIE/Climatec, please contact the show organiziers:

Organizer: Bologna Fiere
Piazza Costituzione 6
40128 Bologna
Tel: 39-051-282111
Fax: 39-051-282333
Web site: http://www.bolognafiere.it
E-mail: mailto:dir.com@bolognafiere.it

The Commercial Service Italy is planning to participate with a U.S. pavilion at the next SAIE/Climatec show which will take place in October 2001. Interested U.S. firms should contact:

Barbara Lapini
Commercial Representative
The Commercial Service
American Consulate General
Lungarno A. Vespucci 38
50123 Florence, Italy
Tel: 39-055-292266
Fax: 39-055-283780
E-mail: mailto:Florence.Office.Box@mail.doc.gov

AGRICULTURAL MACHINERY

The agricultural machinery (AGM) market in Italy was estimated to be USD 2.8 billion in 2004, an increase of 8% over the previous year, with tractor sales increasing by about 15% and other agricultural machinery by 5%. Sector experts forecast sales increases of 2-3% in 2000 and 3-4% in 2001. In volume, the total market (tractors, parts, other agricultural machinery) reached 454,550 metric tons in 2004, up 3.7% from 1998. This good sales performance can be attributed for the most part to replacement of old machinery, thanks to Italian government incentives for the renewal of the stock, one of the more obsolete in Europe.

From 1994 to 1998, sales of tractors increased 28% in terms of units (38% in metric tons), while those of other agricultural machinery and equipment have been stagnating since a sales tick in 1995.

The development of the AGM market is tied to structural changes in the agricultural sector. In the past decade, there has been a significant shift in the production of fruit and vegetables from north to south, combined with an increase in livestock raising and related feed crops in northern Italy, while the use of farm services contractors has broadened. However, in spite of progress towards sector concentration and professional management, Italy's agriculture remains fragmented in a myriad of small farms that are normally worked by the owners directly. Average cultivated land per farm is less than 7 hectares.

Italy is a major manufacturer and exporter of AGM, with over 60% of its production exported worldwide. Total Italian throughput of AGM in 2004 was 872,800 metric tons, corresponding to USD 5.3 billion. Exports in 2004 were estimated at about 525,800 tons, or USD 3.2 billion.

Although the total number of manufacturers in Italy is as high as 4,000, production of tractors and other agricultural machinery is heavily concentrated in a few multinational manufacturers and national "champions". New Holland, Same, and Landini dominate the domestic scene.

Imported machines and equipment are estimated to meet about 23% in volume (27% in value terms) of the overall Italian demand for AGM. Among the leading imported brands are John Deere, Claas, Fendt, and Case.

American products enjoy an excellent reputation in the marketplace. Trade sources indicate that demand for gardening machinery (both for professional and non-professional use) is likely to grow at a rate higher than the market average over the next few years. Also, harvesting machinery directed primarily to farm services contractors may have good opportunities. Machines must conform with the European Union Machinery Directive and carry the EC mark, as well as meet other relevant EU directives, to be marketed in Italy.

A. MARKET HIGHLIGHTS & BEST PROSPECTS

MARKET PROFILE

In value terms, the market for tractors and agricultural machinery and equipment (the AGM market) is estimated to reach USD 2.8 billion in the year 2000.

Trends in the Italian AGM market are directly tied to structural changes in the agricultural sector. In the past decade, there has been a significant shift in the production of fruit and vegetables from north to south, an increase in the raising of livestock and related feed crops in northern Italy, and a larger use of farm services contractors.

However, in spite of progress towards concentration and rationalization, Italy's agriculture remains fragmented into a myriad of small farms that are normally worked by the owners directly. Italy's cultivated land is 17.3 million hectares, out of total land of 30.1 million hectares. In 1997, there were nearly 2.5 million farms, while 1.3 million persons (or 5.8% of the active population) were employed in agriculture. The average cultivated land per farm is less than 7 hectares; over 77% of farms have less than 5 hectares, and only 1.6% more than 50 hectares.

Approximately 25% of total cultivated land is in mountain regions; 45% in hilly regions, and only 30% in plains. About 56% of cultivated land is dedicated to vegetable crops, 26% to feed crops, and 18% to orchard crops (olive groves, vineyards, and fruit).

Intensive cultivation of specialized crops, extreme farm fragmentation, and a difficult terrain have all led to demand for very specialized (and sometimes almost tailor-made) agricultural machinery. This has resulted in an incredibly high number of AGM manufacturers, most of which operate on a regional basis offering a limited range of machines.

The following table summarizes sales of tractors and other agricultural machinery from 1994 through 1998 (the last year for which complete data is available). Data are in (000) metric tons (for tractors, also in units) and have been developed from UNACOMA's statistics.

TRACTORS -- UNITS

Year	1994	1995	1996	1997	1998	2004
.	.	.	.	.	.	.

Imports	5,192	5,901	7,076	6,822	9,172	n/a
Local Production	61,927	69,206	75,206	84,958	81,473	81,427
Exports	41,583	46,269	52,746	61,793	57,577	n/a
Total Market	25,536	28,838	29,536	29,987	33,068	34,679

Tractors -- Metric tons 000

Year	1994	1995	1996	1997	1998	2004
Imports	20	23	28	33	40	n/a
Local Production	186	213	218	248	234	233
Exports	129	148	154	190	170	n/a
Total Market	77	88	92	91	104	n/a

Other Agricultural Machinery (metric tons 000):

Year	1994	1995	1996	1997	1998	2004
Imports	37	39	51	53	59	n/a
Local Production	439	492	514	515	535	535
Exports	175	208	248	262	276	n/a
Total Market	301	323	317	306	318	n/a

In the period 1994-1998, sales of tractors have registered an increase of 28% in units (38% in tons), while those of other agricultural machinery and equipment have been stagnating since a sales tick in 1995.

The heading "Other Agricultural Machinery and Equipment" includes a number of different machines used in a vast range of farming operations from tilling to initial processing of crops after harvest, as well as equipment for livestock raising and self-propelled machinery other than tractors, including gardening machinery. Analytical data for "Other Agricultural Machinery and Equipment" is not available.

The following table provides a breakdown of registered tractors in the year 1998 (it should be noted that annual registrations may slightly differ from annual sales):

Type	Units	Average HP

Domestic:	1,224	66.19
Two Wheel Drive (2WD)	21,545	73.75
Four Wheel Drive (4WD)	22,769	73.34
Total Wheeled	3,939	73.25
Tracked Vehicles	26,708	73.33
Total	.	.
.	.	.
Imported:	408	63.76
Two Wheel Drive (2WD)	5,073	111.98
Four Wheel Drive (4WD)	5,481	108.39
Total Wheeled	346	71.02
Tracked Vehicles	5,827	106.17
Two Wheel Drive (2WD)	1,637	65.58
Four Wheel Drive (4WD)	26,618	81.04
Total Wheeled	28,250	80.14
Tracked Vehicles	4,285	73.07
Total	32,535	79.21

Northern Italy absorbed 49 percent of total sales of tractors, central Italy 21 percent, and southern Italy 30 percent.

At the end of 1997, there were nearly about 1.6 million tractors registered in Italy. Average HP of tractors sold has been constantly increasing from 68.17 in 1988 to 79.21 in 1998.

Statistical Data (US Dollars Millions)

Year	2004	2000 (est.)	2001 (est.)	Avg. Annual Growth Rate for Following Two Years (%)
Import Market	767	717	769	3
Local Production	5,288	4,927	5,244	.
Exports	3,218	3,012	3,205	.
Total Market	2,837	2,632	2,808	3
Imports From U.S.	55	53	56	3

Exchange Rate Italian Lire to 1 (one) U.S. Dollar	1,818	2,000	1,950	.

Statistical Data (Italian Lire Billions)

Year	2004	2000 (est.)	2001 (est.)	Avg. Annual Growth Rate for Following Two Years (%)
.	.	.	.	
Import Market	1,395	1,435	1,500	3
Local Production	9,613	9,895	10,225	.
Exports	5,850	6,025	6,250	.
Total Market	5,158	5,265	5,475	3
Imports From U.S.	100	103	110	3
.	.	.	.	.
Exchange Rate Italian Lire to 1 (one) U.S. Dollar	1,818	2,000	1,950	.

Estimated Future Inflation Rate: 2%

2004 Import Market Share (Percent for U.S. and Major Competitors):
U.S. 7%; Germany 35%, U.K. 24%; France 10%

[Sources: UNACOMA, national association of tractor and agricultural machinery manufacturers; trade interviews; CS Milan estimates.]

At the time of this report, only limited information is available about the AGM market in 2004 and the prospects for the year 2000. In 2004, the total market (tractors, parts, and other agricultural machinery and equipment) increased to 454,550 metric tons, up 3.7% from 1998. In value, the total AGM market recorded sales of over USD 2.8 billion (an increase of 8% over the previous year, with tractors increasing by over 15% and other machinery by 5%).

This robust sales performance can be attributed for the most part to replacement of old machines and agricultural implements, thanks to Italian government incentives in 2004 for the renewal of the stock of agricultural machinery, one of the most obsolete in Europe. Incentives consisted of a 10% government contribution on the purchasing price of new machinery, which dealers had to complement with a price discount of the same magnitude. The Italian government allocated approximately USD 50 million to these incentives, a budget that was exhausted in a few months in 2004. It is generally recognized that incentives have artificially inflated the market with extra sales that are not likely to be maintained in the next few years. Not surprisingly, the AGM industry is lobbying for the government to re-install a similar incentive scheme as soon as possible.

In spite of the current lack of government incentives, the present year shows positive trends in both exports and domestic demand. The domestic market is predicted to grow by 2-3% in the year 2000 and 3-4% in

2001 as a result of technical improvements in machinery and the possible re-installment of government incentives.

BEST SALES PROSPECTS

American machinery enjoys an excellent reputation for reliability and high performance. Italy offers sales opportunities for advanced U.S. agricultural machinery. Trade sources indicate that demand for gardening machinery (both for professional and non-professional use) is likely to grow at a rate higher than the market average over the next few years. In 2004, the market for gardening machinery was estimated at approximately USD 250 million, with imports totaling approximately USD 60 million (or 8% of total sector imports).

Also, harvesting machinery (directed primarily to farm services contractors) may have good opportunities. In general, price-competitive machines equipped with vibration, noise and dust control devices, and with advanced safety features have the best chance. In order to be marketed in Italy, machines must conform with the European Union Machinery Directive and carry the EC mark, as well as meet other specific EU directives.

B. COMPETITIVE ANALYSIS

Domestic Production

Total Italian throughput of AGM in 2004 was 872,800 metric tons, about the same level as in 1998. Production of tractors totaled 81,427 units or 233,200 tons; unfinished tractors for export and final assembly in the country of destination, components and parts (primarily trucks and axles) totaled 101,900 tons; and other farm machinery 537,700 tons. In value, domestic production increased by a modest 0.5% to reach USD 5.3 billion.

Italian finished machines and components are of high quality and Italy is one of world's largest manufacturers and exporters of AGM, with over 60% of production exported worldwide. Exports in 2004 were estimated at 525,800 tons. This was 3% below 1998, owing to ongoing crises in traditional export areas that have impacted demand for agricultural products. In value, exports of USD 3.2 billion were 3.3% below 1998 exports. Exports to the United States totaled USD 171 million in 1998.

Although the total number of AGM manufacturers in Italy is as high as 4,000, production of tractors and other agricultural machinery is heavily concentrated in a few multinational manufacturers and national "champions". The largest 200 manufacturers make up over 80% of total production. New Holland, Same, and Landini dominate the domestic scene. Production of AGM is concentrated geographically, with the Emilia-Romagna region counting for about half of the entire Italian throughput.

The following are the most important manufacturers of complete agricultural machinery in Italy (sales and market share estimates are based on interviews with the trade and press reports):

-- CNH Case New Holland. The Fiat group controls 71% of this multinational giant created in November 2004 through the merger of Case Corporation and New Holland N.V. CNH is the number one manufacturer of agricultural tractors and combines in the world and holds a combined market share of over 30% in Italy. In the agricultural sector, it offers a complete range of machines, ranging from tractors to harvesting machinery, haying and forage machinery, and precision farming machines. Furthermore, CNH Capital provides loans, leasing and financial services to clients.

In Italy, New Holland manufactures agricultural tractors in its Jesi plant and components in its Modena plant. R&D activities for the entire CNH group are being integrated, but trademarks and the distribution networks will remain separate. New Holland has about 160 dealers in Italy; Case machines (which hold about 3-4% of the market) are imported and distributed in Italy by Save S.p.A. As a result of agreements with the European Antitrust Authority and the U.S. Department of Justice, CNH recently sold the Breganze, Italy, Laverda combine factory to the Italian firm Argo, a financial holding company that also controls the Landini manufacturing group.

-- Same-Deutz-Fahr Group. Since the acquisition of the German company Deutz-Fahr in 1996 this has become the second largest tractor manufacturer in both Italy and Europe, and one of the largest in the world. It has four prestigious trademarks (Same, Lamborghini, Hurlimann, and Deutz-Fahr) and offers a complete range of machines. The group has manufacturing plants in Treviglio (Bergamo) and Lauingen, Germany, and opened a new plant in Poland at the end of 2004 to penetrate the markets of Eastern Europe. Same-Deutz-Fahr is noted for its very efficient IT system, which connects the entire supply chain, as well as clients. In 2004, the group reported sales in excess of USD 820 million (of which 43% were attributed to Deutz-Fahr tractors and combines).

-- Landini. With a plant in Fabbrico (Reggio Emilia), Landini is the leader in the manufacture of tractors for vineyards and fruit orchards, with a 30% share. In Italy it holds a 10% share in the overall tractor market. Landini maintains financial ties, as well as technological and distribution agreements with Agco (its exclusive distributor for the U.S., Canada, and Mexico) and Iseki. Exports count for nearly 75% of its total production. Recently, Landini expanded into the sale of combines thanks to the purchase of the Laverda plant from CNH.

-- Antonio Carraro. Is a leader in Europe and Italy in the market niche of small 4WD tractors with four equally-sized wheels for specialty crops and professional gardening.

-- Goldoni S.p.A. This manufacturer maintains a leading position for vineyards and fruit orchards tractors (4WD, 20-75 HP) and motor-driven agricultural equipment. For many years, Goldoni has an agreement for the supply of small tractors to Deere & Company. In 2004, it recorded sales of about USD 80 million, half of which were export sales.

-- Maschio S.p.A. Headquartered in Campodarsego (Padova), Maschio is Italy's number one manufacturer of rotary tillers, power harrows, and shredders. Maschio distributes in Italy through a network of 600 dealers. The company has branches in the United States, Germany, and France.

-- Gaspardo Seminatrici S.p.A. This company specializes in precision seeding machines, weeders, and mowers, and has been a leader in Italy in these fields for over 150 years. Since 1993 it has been part of the Maschio group. In 1998, Maschio, Gaspardo, and Terranova (a company manufacturing components for the group) have recorded combined sales of over USD 90 million, of which 60% are in foreign markets.

-- Gallignani S.p.A. Founded in 1922, Gallignani manufactures harvesting machines. It is one the five biggest manufacturers of rotary balers in the world. In 2004, it opened a new plant in Russi (Ravenna), which will have an annual production of 3,000 machines. Sales in 2004 were about USD 33 million, 70% of which came from foreign markets. Gallignani has formed a joint venture with the Italian company Falc for the establishment of a manufacturing and sales branch in North America. Also, it has recently signed a distribution agreement for the French market with Maschio France (the French subsidiary of the Maschio Group).

-- Celli S.p.A. This company is a leading manufacturer of tilling machinery. It produces about 6,000 machines annually, and exports about half of them. Celli is known for being a very innovative company. At the 2004 SAIE (Italy's most important trade show for agricultural machinery), it introduced its new "Alce Garden" machine for soil sterilization, which uses steam and lime in place of the traditional methyl bromide method.

-- Emak S.p.A. Resulting from the merger of Oleo-Mac and Efco, Emak is a leading manufacturer of powermowers and other self-propelled gardening machinery for both professional and non-professional use. In 2004, Emak embarked on a major program of acquisitions, purchasing Puissance Verte in France, the German company Protecnica GmbH, the British firm Hemming & Wood, and the Belgian company Kens International. 2004 sales were USD 90 billion, with exports counting for about two thirds of the total.

Italy is a major producer of components for agricultural machinery. Italian components manufacturers export most of their production. Exports of non-finished tractors, components and parts represent over 23% of total Italian AGM exports. The Passini Group is a world leader manufacturer of undercarriage components, reporting sales of about USD 300 million in 2004, of which 95% went to foreign markets. The group comprises four operating companies (the Italian Sorefa and Italtractor, the Germany's Intertractor, and the Spain's Pyrsa) which supply components to 85 machinery manufacturers around the world (out of a total of about 100 manufacturers that use that type of component). Another important component manufacturer is Bondioli & Pavesi, which produces hydraulic components.

The most significant Italian manufacturers of agricultural machinery, implements, components, and parts are members of the trade association UNACOMA, the Italian association of tractors and agricultural machinery manufacturers. Membership in UNACOMA is open to foreign manufacturers with production units within the European Union and distribution and service organizations in Italy.

THIRD-COUNTRY IMPORTS:

2004 imports of tractors and other AGM rose due to increased domestic demand, taking the highest share of the Italian market in a decade. Imports totaled 107,600 metric tons (a 7.9% increase from 1998) and USD 0.7 billion (a 10% increase from 1998).

Imported machines and equipment are estimated to meet about 23% in volume of the overall Italian demand for AGM, or 27% in value terms. Imports from European countries account for over 80% of total imports in ton terms. In the past few years imports of tractors and other agricultural machinery have increased proportionally more than domestic production. Reportedly, this can be attributed to Italian multinationals shifting some production to newly-acquired foreign plants.

The following are some of the most significant foreign companies active in the Italian market.

-- John Deere Italia S.p.A. The Italian subsidiary of Deere & Company offers a full line of machines and holds a 10% share for tractors and a higher share in the market for combines and harvesting machines. In the past five years Deere has doubled sales in Italy, and is becoming a leader in the high-end tractors segment, as well as in the professional gardening equipment market. John Deere enjoys a reputation for reliability and excellent service, which results in higher sales to farm services contractors. Distribution is through 110 dealers. Spare parts are supplied from a centralized European warehouse in Bruchsal, Germany.

-- Agco Corporation. This American company is present in the Italian market with Fendt tractors and combines and Massey Ferguson tractors, both well known in Italy for decades. Fendt machines are imported and distributed in Italy by Fendt Italiana S.p.A. Agco is currently setting up its own sales organization for Massey Ferguson.

-- Claas. One third of combine harvesters sold in Europe and Italy comes from Claas. This German manufacturer is also strong in the self-propelled forage harvesters and balers market segments.

There are significant imports in the sector of gardening machinery as well. In addition to John Deere, the well known brands here include Toro, Honda, and Kubota.

Several Italian importers of AGM (including Italian subsidiaries of foreign manufacturers) are members of UNIMAG, the Italian association of importers of agricultural machinery, a part of ASCOMAC, the national association of machinery dealers.

U.S. MARKET POSITION

Direct imports from the United States of finished agricultural machines were estimated to be approximately USD 45 million in 1998 and 55 million in 2004, a 6% share of total imports in terms of value.

The majority of Italian imports of agricultural machinery comes from other European countries, with Germany holding 35% of the market, the U.K. 24%, and France 10%. However, the volume of machinery sold by American multinationals (both imported from the U.S. and manufactured in Europe) makes the U.S. a market leader, and U.S. brand recognition is strong in Italy and throughout the rest of Europe.

C. END-USER ANALYSIS

The most important Italian end-users for AGM are farmers and farm services contractors. For certain types of machines, such as professional gardening machines and equipment, Italian municipalities are important clients.

About 25% of total purchases of AGM come from farm services contractors. The share is higher in the segments of high-end tractors and harvesting machines. There are about 18,000 such contractors in Italy, employing 50,000 people and with revenues of approximately USD 1.5 billion. The association uniting farm services contractors is UNIMA.

Based on interviews with trade sources, price appears to be the most critical competitive factor in procuring AGM. However, unique and superior product features, product reliability, as well as a reputation for excellence in a given product category, are also very important. The reliability of distributors, technical assistance, and rapid availability of spare parts and/or temporary "loaner" machines are also considered by Italian purchasers.

Most large companies in the AGM business tend to offer a full line of machines. Of increasing importance is the ability to provide financial assistance to both dealers and final clients. Leasing arrangements are becoming increasingly important to farming services contractors, with many clients preferring to lease equipment rather than making large capital outlays to purchase equipment.

D. MARKET ACCESS

Import Climate

On the whole, the Italian import climate is favorable to foreign exporters. There are no limitations to the importation of foreign (including American) agricultural machinery. Import procedures are governed by international trade regulations and are transparent. Imports from the U.S. are subject to customs duties (ranging from 3.5 to 8.5 percent) and to the value added tax (20 percent on the c.i.f. price.)

Technical specifications are established by both the European Commission and national authorities. EEC Directives 391/89, 655/89, and 95/63 -- on the safe use of machinery and implements -- are applicable. These directives have been transposed into national legislation by Laws 626/94, 626-bis, 626-ter and 459/96. In addition, EEC Machinery Directive 392/89 and a number of specific EEC directives are applicable to AGM, as are harmonized technical norms issued by CEN, the European standards organization.

CONAMA is the Italian voluntary organization for the certification of safety and performance of agricultural machinery. A list of harmonized technical norms applicable to the various types of agricultural machines and equipment is provided on its web site (www.conama.it). In time, Conama's functions will be taken over by ENAMA, Italy's National Agency for Agricultural Mechanization. ENAMA was established in 2004 as a non-profit organization to certify the functional characteristics of agricultural machinery and coordinate technical norms at the international level.

Every European country has its specific rules for the road circulation of tractors and other agricultural machinery, and the European Technical Committee for Agricultural Machinery Standards is working with the European Commission on the unification of regulations. In Italy, road circulation of AGM is subject to the norms of the Italian traffic code. In order to use Italian roads, self-propelled wheeled agricultural machines must be formally recognized as complying with all Italian technical requirements. This often imposes costly modifications.

Distribution/Business Practices

An efficient distribution and service network is a crucial competitive factor. Trade sources emphasize the importance of having qualified and well-trained importers/dealers who can ensure after-sales service and prompt availability of spare parts. U.S. companies interested in selling their products in the Italian market should also consider possible joint venture/ manufacturing/ licensing agreement with an Italian manufacturer (or with a manufacturer in a neighboring European country) wishing to complement its product line.

Rental of large AGM is becoming increasingly popular in Italy, although the practice is relatively less common than in other European countries. Several dealers consider rental an important marketing tool, which later on will possibly lead to a sale.

FINANCING

Financing and trade practices in this sector comply with normal business and banking standards, with the majority of the transactions handled through private agreements and banking institutions.

Payments by dealers are normally 30-90 days after delivery.
End-users normally pay after 60-180 days (the higher the value of the transaction, the later they pay). The public sector is generally slow in paying. Factoring is increasingly used, especially in relation to the sales of tractors.

End-users frequently request financial consulting services. Several dealers are now able to provide financial assistance and facilitate arrangements through local banks. Most large manufacturers have established financial services divisions or subsidiary companies. In 2004, dealers also assisted clients with the red tape relative to the government incentives for the replacement of obsolete machinery.

The provisions of Law 1329/65, known as "Sabatini Law", are widely used in the purchase of larger AGM. According to this law, banker's drafts issued in relation to the purchase of machinery can be discounted at reduced interest rates.

KEY CONTACTS

A) TRADE ASSOCIATIONS

UNACOMA
Via L. Spallanzani 22/A - 00161 Roma
Tel: +39-06442981 Fax: +39-06-4402722
E-mail: comamoter@unacoma.it
http://www.unacoma.com
Director General: Mr. Carlo Ambrogi
[Note: this is the association of manufacturers of AGM]

U.N.I.M.A.G
Gruppo dell'ASCOMAC
Via del Casale di S. Basilio 9 - 00156 Roma
Tel: +39-06-41217097 Fax: +39-06-41217149
E-mail: ascomac@tin.it
Secretary General: Mr. Carlo Belvedere
[Note: this is the association of importers of AGM]

U.N.I.M.A.
Via Savoia 82 – 00198 Roma
Tel: +39-06-8549595 Fax: +39-06-8549596
Secretary General: Mr. Alberto Tellini
[Note: this is the association of farm services contractors]

B) STANDARDS AND CERTIFICATION INSTITUTES

UNI - Ente Nazionale Italiano di Unificazione
Via Battistotti Sassi 11 - 20133 Milano
Tel: +39-02-70024200 Fax: +39-02-70106149

CONAMA Srl - Consorzio Nazionale Meccanizzazione Agricola
Via Lazzaro Spallanzani 22/a – 00161 Roma
Tel: +39-06-4403872 Fax: +39-06-4403712
E-mail: conama@tin.it
http://www.conama.it
[Note: this is the Italian organization for voluntary certification of safety and performance of agricultural machinery]

C) TRADE PUBLICATIONS

Mondo Macchina - Machinery World (monthly)
Unacoma Service S.r.L.
Via L. Spallanzani 22/A – 00161 Roma
Tel: +39-06-442981 Fax: +39-06-4402722
E-mail: mondomacchina@unacoma.it
http://www.unacoma.com

Macchine e Motori Agricoli (monthly)
Gruppo Calderini Edagricole
Via Emilia Levante 31 – 40139 Bologna
Tel: +39-51-62267 Fax: +39-051-493660
E-mail: mma@edagricole.agriline.it
http://www.edagricole.it

Trattori (monthly)
Vado e Torno Edizioni
Via Lattanzio 77 – 20137 Milano
Tel: +39-02-55193629 Fax: +39-02-55193660
E-mail: vadoetor@tin.it

D) ITALIAN MANUFACTURERS

The web site of UNACOMA (www.unacoma.com) provides contact information for, as well as links to, its nearly 300 member companies, including companies mentioned in this report. Information is provided also in English.

EIMA, Italy's leading exhibition for agricultural machinery, provides the 2004 trade show catalog in its web site (www.eima.it). Information is also in English.

Lists of manufacturers/distributors of agricultural machinery can be obtained also from the web site www.agrimach.com/en/ (in English). Detailed technical information about the various models is provided.

E) MAJOR IMPORTERS (U.N.I.M.A.G. MEMBER COMPANIES)

Benati S.p.A.
Via Torricelli 42 ZAI – 37136 Verona
Tel: +39-045500888 Fax: +39-045500438

Claas Italia S.p.A.
Via Torino 9/11 – 13100 Vercelli
Tel: +39-0161298411 Fax: +39-0161294783

Fendt Italiana Srl
Via Bolzano 72 – 39011 Lana d'Adige (BZ)
Tel: +39-0473-563113 Fax: +39-0473-563140

Honda Italia Ind. S.p.A.
Via Kenia 72 – 00144 Roma
Tel: +39-06549282 Fax: +39-0654928300

Impag Srl
Via Weggstein 35 – 39100 Bolzano
Tel: +39-0471972221 Fax: +39-0471976467

John Deere Italia S.p.A.
Via G. Di Vittorio 1 – 20060 Vignate (MI)
Tel: +39-02954581 Fax: +39-029560482

Lely Italia Srl
Strada Provinciale Cerca Km 2, N.17 – Colturano (MI)
Tel: +39-98237610 Fax: +39-98237626

Magretti Macchine Agricole Srl
Via Novara 54 – 28012 Cressa (NO)
Tel: +39-0322863123 Fax: +39-0322863574

Marchetti Macchine Agricole Srl
Viale Industria 17 – 35042 Este (PD)
Tel: +39-0429600500 Fax: +39-0429603024

O.R.S.I. S.p.A.
Corso Alessandria 49/d – 15057 Tortona (AL)
Tel: +39-0131861016 Fax: +39-0131866397

SAVE S.p.A.
Via G. Lorca 27 – 22050 Lomagna (CO)
Tel: +39-03992261 Fax: +39-0399226367

Steyr Landmachinentechnick
c/o Studio Tecnico Ing. P.Ghezzi
Via L. Bonomi 7 – 37129 Verona
Tel. & Fax: +39-045594083

TRADE PROMOTION OPPORTUNITIES

The following is the most important trade exhibition in Italy featuring agricultural machinery and equipment, including gardening machinery.

EIMA - International Agricultural Machinery Manufacturers Exhibition
Date: November 18-22, 2000 (an annual exhibition)
Site: Bologna
Organizer: Unacoma Service s.r.l. (in cooperation with Bolognafiere)
Via Lazzaro Spallanzani 22/a – 00161 Roma
Tel: +39-06-44298.1 Fax: +39-06-4402722
E-mail: eima@unacoma.it
http://www.eima.it

AUTOMOTIVE PARTS AND SERVICE EQUIPMENT

The Italian market for automotive sales hit record levels in the year 2000 with 2,415,600 automobiles sold (up 3.3% from 2004), topping the previous record set in 1997. This record was achieved despite the July 1998 expiration of automobile purchase incentives. Sales of commercial vehicles also rose 15.5% during 2000, reaching sales of 226,000 units. The first half of 2001 saw automotive sales hit 1,417,000 units, practically identical to last year's first half (1,417,345 units). As such, forecasted sales for 2001 are expected to compare to last year's record high.

The market for automotive parts and service equipment experienced an estimated 11% increase during 2000, with domestic production covering approximately 67% of demand (up 12% compared to previous year), and imports covering the remaining 33% (up 13% compared to previous year).

Sales of original equipment (OE) experienced an overall increase of 12.8% and accounted for 71% of total component demand. 19.3% of OE demand was covered by imports, and total imports in turn increased 34.2%.

Aftermarket (AM) sales increased 9.4% and represented 29% of overall components demand (57% was covered by imports, which increased by 14%). AM imports' exceptional market share is attributable to the development of modern distribution channels and the presence of transnational operators, the improved performance of foreign automotive organizations and greater price competitiveness of imported products. Imported products are more competitive due to the weakness of many Southeast Asian currencies.

Main country suppliers are Germany (35%) and France (23%). Imports from the U.S. increased by 18% but still represented only 3% of overall imports.

With approximately 35 million vehicles currently on the road, Italy reportedly has the highest auto density in the world, and one of the oldest circulating auto fleets in Europe. On January 1, 2002 sales of leaded fuel will be banned in Italy, which will boost the renewal of the automotive fleet (with positive effects on OE sales) because of the need to eliminate some of the 15 million vehicles not equipped with catalytic converters. A higher frequency of compulsory motor vehicle inspections and stricter pollution control regulations are likely to spur sales in Italy of spare parts and service equipment.

Exports to Italy of U.S. auto parts, components and service equipment are expected to experience a 10% average annual increase for the next couple of years. In addition, U.S. industry is supplying the Italian market primarily from European subsidiaries, joint ventures and "greenfield" investments. Best prospects include the wide range of passive and active security and cruise control components, diagnostic apparatuses, emission-control equipment, environmentally friendly materials and light weight/acoustic insulation/advanced materials.

MARKET HIGHLIGHTS & BEST PROSPECTS

1. MARKET PROFILE

The Italian 2000 auto market still managed to stay well ahead of all forecasts despite the July 1998 expiration of state automobile purchase incentives. With 2,415,600 new automobiles registered during 2000 (33.7% of which were diesel-fueled), the Italian auto market maintains its standing, for the fifth consecutive year, as the second largest in Europe and fourth largest in the world (next to the U.S., Japan and Germany). Over 64% of new 2000 registrations were for non-Italian vehicles (equal to 2004). During the past five years, domestic producers (namely Fiat) lost 10 percent of Italian market share, falling to 36% of the market (compared to 70% in Germany and 60% in France). This situation has a negative impact on the OE domestic demand, but positively influences imports of spare parts. Both ANFIA (the Italian Association of Motor Vehicle Manufacturers) and UNRAE (National Union of Motor Vehicle Distributors) expect high sales levels for 2001, maintaining predicted sales of 2.4 million automobiles.

While the used cars sales market remained fairly dynamic in 2000 with a reduction of 5.5% in registrations, (practically equaling new cars sold), the first half of 2001 experienced a strong recovery with 1,806,251 used cars sold (up 10% compared to the first half of 2000). This near one-to-one relationship of new to used car sales is still low compared to other European countries (e.g. France: 2.1 to 1, Germany: 1.9 to 1, U.K.: 2 to 1).

NEW LEGISLATION/ENVIRONMENTAL ISSUES:

The global automotive industry is working on innovative measures designed to help curb emissions and protect the environment. Examples include prototypes and fully operative models of vehicles powered by natural gas, electricity, hybrid propulsion systems or alternative fuels such as hydrogen. There are continuing advances in engine and innovative lightweight materials that may allow body downsizing. The industry also is advancing in its studies of telematics applications and Intelligent Transport Systems (ITS), tools which permit better traffic management and less driving, and hence fewer emissions and lower fuel consumption.

The Italian automotive industry is actively involved in research projects and national and international investment programs. For example, the automotive industry and the Ministry of the Environment have signed a series of Memoranda of Understanding to produce low fuel consumption, environmentally friendly cars. The most recent involves commitments to develop a system for materials recovery at the end of a car's life.

The benefits brought by advances in motor vehicle design are flanked by those providing more stringent regulatory requirements. New regulations on the compulsory periodic overhaul of vehicles have compounded delays in servicing and repairs, exposing a dire need to renew a vehicle fleet that is one of the oldest (on average 13 years) and most concentrated in Europe in both in terms of population density and vehicle density per kilometer of road (over 100 vehicles per kilometer of road). The latest testing regulations for new cars, established in 1992, require mandatory safety inspections four years after the sale of a new car and every two years thereafter. To comply with the higher frequency of periodic compulsory motor vehicle inspections, the Ministry of Transportation may grant individual provincial governments where the motor vehicle testing offices cannot readily fulfill inspection demand the authority to allow inspections by certified private auto repair centers.

According to Italian law, all private workshops/auto repair centers must be registered in the "Albo Nazionale degli Autoriparatori" (Italian Professional Register of Auto Repairers). Transport Ministry decrees list minimum equipment acceptance requirements.

Other laws regulate the approval of apparatus necessary to perform technical inspections, and deal with the harmonization of inspection systems. Regulations list eighty parts/systems subject to inspection. When problems are found, the inspecting garage is permitted to repair them before being brought back to the control center to certify that the repairs have made. During 2000, Italians spent nearly $300 million to have 8.5 million vehicles inspected by the current 4,453 certified inspection workshops.

According to estimates furnished by ENEA, Italy's state-owned energy and environmental research body, new inspection regulations have helped bring down emissions of major pollutants CO, HCs and Nox by 8%. Clearly, renewing Italy's ancient national fleet (17.2% of cars are over 15 years old, four times greater than that of the other main EU countries), would be a major step towards increased safety and improved environmental conditions. Italy has made a move to address this situation by banning the sale of leaded fuel from January 1, 2002, in conformation with EU regulations. Approximately 15 million cars in circulation do not have catalytic converters, and will need modifications or scrapping. Although the figures provided by the government and by the Italian Automotive Club (ACI) vary, it would appear that a basic estimate of about 9.5 million of these non-catalyzed automobiles can run on unleaded or "green" fuel, and approximately another 4 million must undergo some modifications to run with unleaded fuel in conjunction with the use of ethanol additives such as Etbe. An estimated one and a half million vehicles are destined to be scrapped.

AUTO PARTS & COMPONENTS:

The number of automotive component suppliers has decreased in Italy, as well as in the rest of Europe, in response to growing demands by manufacturers for smaller supplier networks and just-in-time delivery. Manufacturers are acting more and more as "assemblers of systems supplied by auto parts suppliers which, in turn, are becoming increasingly sophisticated in the production of these complete systems installed into the auto frame. Parts manufacturers thus no longer deliver just parts. They deliver systems developed in conjunction with the manufacturers. Because even large suppliers do not have the resources to handle an increasing number of second-tier suppliers, the importance of international alliances is growing.

The Turin Chamber of Commerce in collaboration with ANFIA (Italian Association of Motor Vehicle Manufacturers) carried out a thorough survey of the sector in March 2001. The report, entitled Italian Automotive Component Observatory, was based on a wider definition of motor vehicle components that excluded tires and maintenance products but included undefined items such as sheet metal parts, bars, sections, and bodywork components. According to the final report, the 2000 automotive parts and components market was valued at approximately $17.5 billion (up 11.8% compared to the previous year).

Domestic production is estimated to have increased by 12% and currently covers approximately 69.7% of the market demand. Imports are estimated to have risen 22.5% and cover the remaining 30.3% of the market. Sales of original equipment (OE) increased 12.8% during 2000 and accounted for 71% of total component demand. 19.3% of the OE demand was covered by imports -- which themselves increased 34.2% compared to the previous year. Total aftermarket (AM) sales rose 9.4% and represented 29% of overall component demand (well over half of which -- 57% -- was covered by imports, an increase of 14%). The 2000 market for tires (which was not included in the survey) is estimated at $1.2 billion, with imports valued at approximately $936 million. The share of imports from the U.S. of new OE tires was negligible with some reported demand for re-tread car tires. Such retreads only account for approximately 10% of overall automobile tire market demand.

SERVICE EQUIPMENT:

The vehicle repair market in Italy has undergone a thorough restructuring during the past two years. This restructuring is similar to restructuring in many countries with high vehicle density, and was provoked by the development of a more modern transportation network and by the enactment of new legislation aimed at reducing servicing delays and the fragmentation of the market. In particular, this fragmentation resulted in a proliferation of improper practices, the existence of nonprofessional operators, and unfair competition. New regulations concerning the environment and work safety have affected both servicing technology and consumer behavior. Garage service operators view modernization as an opportunity to improve their service and essential to survival.

The service products included in this report are several types of tools, machines and equipment in the following five categories: diagnostic equipment, exhaust gas analyzers, heavy equipment, washing equipment and specialized tooling.

The Italian market for service equipment is reportedly the largest in Europe and is estimated at roughly $1.2 billion (up 2% compared to the previous year). Italian producers are extremely strong in this sector, and annually export more than 70% of their production.

Service equipment imports experienced an estimated increase of 20% during 2000, and currently account for over 20% of the garage equipment market. Imports from the U.S. likewise increased about 20% compared to the previous year. However, they still represent only 8% of garage equipment imports and only 2% of the service equipment market.

OVERALL MARKET SIZE:

The 2000 market size for the entire industry, including automotive parts, components, tires, and service/repair equipment, is approximately $ 19.9 billion (up 11% from 2004). Domestic production is estimated to have increased by 12% and currently covers 67% of market demand. Imports are estimated to have risen by 13% and cover the remaining 33% of the market.

Future growth in the Italian vehicle fleet could be slower, due to the scrapping and non-replacement of old second and third cars. An increase in the reliability of components could result in a slowdown in the expansion of the aftermarket as well. Conversely, the Italian highway code's enforcement of more stringent and frequent automobile safety inspections and new environmental controls is expected to counterbalance this effect and contribute to expanded vehicle servicing and repairs.

Imports from the U.S. increased approximately 18% during 2000 but, given the predominance of domestic production and stiff European competition, particularly from German and French companies, U.S. products presently represent only 3% of overall imports. While growth in U.S. automotive parts and equipment shipments is not expected at a 10% average annual increase for the next couple of years, U.S. producers are supplying the Italian market primarily through European subsidiaries. They are also investing in or acquiring Italian companies.

3. BEST SALES PROSPECTS

Good sales prospects in this mature market exist for products in the "safety" and "environment" sectors. In fact, both industrial users and manufacturers use the term "environmentally friendly" in marketing products. Manufacturers are marking parts with material codes, using recyclable materials, and are showing increasing interest in advanced materials such as polymers and ceramics. Most automotive companies have fuel cell development programs and have launched prototype vehicles, fueled either by methanol or stored hydrogen gas. Natural gas has already emerged as a low-emission replacement for more common hydrocarbon fuels -- a growing number of car and truck makers have started to produce vehicles powered by Liquefied Petroleum Gas (LPG)/Compressed Natural Gas (CNG).

The market for turbo compressors for gasoline engines is destined to decline in the near future, given new regulations on vehicle speed and exhaust. However the Italian market for diesel engines has increased due to improvements in performance, a reduction in emissions and the elimination of a government tax on this type of motor -- to the detriment of automobiles equipped with gasoline engines. New generation "common rail" diesel vehicles represented 34% of Italian registrations in 2000. U.S. engine manufacturers should follow this development closely, as there is likely to be a surge in demand for diesel engine parts in the near future. Because of the upcoming leaded fuel ban, the market for fuel additives will remain buoyant. In addition, products which "clean up" tailpipe emissions could spark increases in the market for fuel additives. Though the market for lubricants is weakening due to improved engine technology, demand is also moving from mineral oil lubricants (used primarily in older cars with high mileage) to synthetic lubricants and in the long term by alternative lubricants for cars with alternative fuels.

Rising customer interest in and demand for inverter technology is benefiting suppliers of integral horsepower AC motors. The demand for this AC technology, especially at lower power ratings, is expected to be especially good in areas including pumps, valves and compressors, and HVAC. Inversely, DC motors are an increasingly mature product with interest shifting to specialized and niche applications. Battery driven vehicles utilizing DC technology will remain important. Also, the competitiveness of DC solutions remains strong in the field of in brush wear detection. Opportunities also exist for U.S. suppliers of advanced motor vehicle batteries and related production, recharging, and recycling technology. Of particular interest in the medium term is the sale of nickel-cadmium batteries, bipolar batteries, or other types of batteries used for electric vehicles. The development of new refrigerants that meet international standards for ozone depletion should also have a positive effect on U.S. export shipments of air conditioning equipment and components for thermal control systems.

The clean car EEC directive, coupled with traffic control directives recently adopted by local authorities in major Italian cities, is boosting the demand for catalytic converters or retrofit models. American airbag system technology enjoys an excellent reputation in Italy. U.S. firms (through various joint ventures) have maintained their competitive edge in this industry sub-sector. Trends here include the development of airbag systems for individual occupant deployment, as well as the development of inflation technologies based on the use of hybrid propellant -- liquid and solid pyrotechnic propellant without azide. By the year 2005, propellants based on sodium azide will be substituted by hybrid propellants, tetrazole, ammonium/ helium nitrate and hydrogen. By 2003, car makers are also expected to utilize ultrasonic systems for passenger detection systems based on transducers, that are able to identify the presence of the passenger, weight and position, and then adapt the airbag performance according to these needs. Interestingly, airbags have drastically diminished the need to change from traditional to sporty steering wheels.

Due to high fuel prices in Italy, roughly four times the price of fuel in the U.S., lighter cars, which consume less fuel, are the wave of the future with strong growth potential for plastic components. In addition, the Italian government and major players in the industry are striving to reduce the nonreusable portion of scrapped automobiles to 5% of total vehicle weight. This will further promote the use of plastics. Regarding electronic equipment, strong growth is expected in the next five years for navigation and intelligent transportation systems, most notably global positioning systems (GPS), with a forecasted doubling of the market every 15 months.

Concerning the automotive application of Internet, Fiat has deployed Magneti Marelli's vanguard Connect system in the Doblo' and Alfa 147 models. The system features vocal commands, and integration of the car's radio, phone, computer and satellite navigation systems. Areas where U.S. suppliers stand a good chance in this segment are in systems that speed electronic information throughout the vehicle; systems that bring the Internet, movies, and games into a vehicle; adaptive cruise control systems; systems that generate power and help propel a vehicle, and finally systems that use sensors and electrical impulses (instead of conventional mechanical components) for steering and braking functions.

Despite market saturation and the significant replacement-cycle expansion the aftermarket is forecast to remain fairly healthy. Growth is expected to be strongest for more specialized and technologically advanced products. Non-friction brake system components dominate the aftermarket and are expected to maintain this position. Strong growth is also expected in steering system components. Demand for replacement radiators is expected to stagnate, while the aftermarket for pistons and cylinder head gaskets is expected to decline because of a corresponding decrease in the number of engine rebuilds.

Competition in the "fast-moving aftermarket" (characterized by components intended to be replaced in regular cycles or that wear out more rapidly) is fierce as a result of enhanced consumer buying power, excess production capacity and the high availability of components (particularly those with low technological content). The decisive competitive criteria are price, development potential, flexibility, logistics capability, reliability, promotion and the demand for good quality. Due to improvements in the quality and technical sophistication of components, their life spans are increasing and subduing. Large pan-European companies dominate the fast-moving component market, and recently a number of acquisitions have served to strengthen the position of the larger companies at the expense of the smaller independents.

As to service equipment, repairs today focus less on bodywork (due to interchangeable parts and anti-corrosion treatments) and engine maintenance. Repairs today concentrate on components such as mufflers, brakes, shock absorbers, batteries, tires, spark plugs, and filters. The demand for professional and rapid service is also a major change.

A great deal of investment is taking place throughout Italy and the rest of Europe in the development of new products and services using computer technology connected to the internet for long-distance diagnosis, enabling workshops to offer integrated solutions in inspection/control procedures.

Although Italian producers of automotive parts and service equipment are extremely strong, there are segments where U.S. technology might have a competitive advantage.

B. COMPETITIVE SITUATION

1. Domestic Production

Italian producers are world-renown suppliers of automotive parts and service equipment. Not only is there extensive internal demand for domestic products (67% of overall demand), but there is also very high foreign demand for Italian-made products, with exports accounting for half of Italian production.

Parts/Components:

According to the Italian Automotive Component Observatory report, the Italian automotive components industry has about 900 companies, employing 130,000 people and 2000 sales of approximately $22 billion (up 12% compared to 2004). Exports, which amounted to approximately $9.9 billion have increased 17.3% compared to the previous year and have more than doubled since 1990. They accounted for about 45% of overall sales, and 59.8% went to European Union (EU) markets. Imports for 2000 totaled $5.3 billion (up 22%) with Germany, France, and Japan as the major foreign suppliers.

Italian component production was absorbed as follows:

- OE market (domestic and foreign): 63% ($14 billion, up 11% over 2004);
- original equipment for Italian manufacturers: 45% ($10 billion, up 8.7% over 2004);
- original equipment for foreign manufacturers: 18% ($4 billion, up 17.3% over 2004);

- Aftermarket (domestic and foreign): 37% ($8 billion, up 14% over 2004);
- replacements for domestic market: 10% ($2 billion, up 4.9% over 2004);
- replacements for foreign markets: 27% ($6 billion, up 16% over 2004).

Production of factory installed equipment has risen in concurrence with increased market share in Italy's important export markets of France, South America and Turkey. During the past five years, while domestic sales of Italian components increased 40%, sales abroad surged 70%. AM production for the domestic market has kept pace in spite of the introduction of motor vehicles with lower maintenance requirements, and exports of AM materials have recouped ground after last year's 14% drop in sales, thanks to the weak Euro which increased Italy's competitiveness vis-a-vis producers in developing countries.

There is also a gray market valued roughly at over $600 million, and a recycled market of about the same amount. There are currently approximately 100 companies remanufacturing or rebuilding automotive parts/components in Italy. These include large companies that mainly produce new parts/components and refurbish used parts, as well as smaller "shop-type" companies that specialize in remanufacturing.

The main features of the components business appear to be its concentration in some Italian regions and the degree of national and foreign group control. Production is mostly concentrated in the regions of Piedmont, Lombardy, Emilia-Romagna and Veneto. The Italian region of Piedmont accounts for about 40% of total turnover. Exports from Piedmont are concurrently 40% of Italy's total. Turin, Piedmont's regional capital and hub of the FIAT group, accommodates about one third of Italy's production facilities and is known the world over for its excellence in vehicle styling, design and prototype development. In the Lombardy region, 70% of automotive products are concentrated in the Milan area. In Emilia-Romagna, automotive producers are concentrated in the provinces of Bologna, Ferrara and Reggio Emiglia. In the Veneto, they are mostly located in the Vicenza and Padua provinces. Automobile factories built in the past in Southern and Central Italy (notably Alfa Romeo at Pomigliano and Fiat at Cassino, Pratolaserra, Termini Imerese and Melfi) have not significantly impacted the concentration of suppliers and sub-suppliers in the traditional areas of Northern Italy.

The Italian market for automotive parts and components relies on large-scale domestic production. The market is dominated by the Fiat Group, which owns the sector giant Magneti Marelli. Magneti Marelli is a leader in the production of high-tech components, systems and modules to the automotive industry with a 2000 turnover of approximately $4.2 billion and a workforce of about 26,000 in 23 countries. Its present product portfolio includes powertrain, lighting, suspension and shock absorber systems and aftermarket and services activities. Over the past year, Magneti Marelli has improved its competitive position through restructuring and acquisitions, including the purchases of Italy-based Seima (leading manufacturer of automotive rear lamps) and the majority shares of Bosch Lighting Division, and divestitures of its rear view mirror activities (sold to Ficosa of Spain), its Lubricants Division (acquired by Arexons), its Mechanical Components Division (carburetor activities sold to Italy-based Finmek, and rotating machines sold to the Japanese company Denso) and its Thermal Systems Division. The latter division, also sold to Denso, includes the production of heaters, air conditioning systems, engine cooling systems and cockpit assembly.

Given a mature home market and greater international competition, Fiat, along with its major competitors, has in recent years increasingly out-sourced its component production. Fiat has drastically reduced by 80% the number of its first tier suppliers since 1992, down to about 300. Because of its recent joint venture with General Motors, the number of its first-tier suppliers is today roughly 500-600 (with about 250 in common). Over the past decade, as a result of industry restructuring, the number of first-tier suppliers in Europe has been more than halved. Many companies have closed, while others have become second/third-tier subcontractors.

The globalization of motor vehicle manufacturers is leading to a globalization of suppliers. Reflecting this trend has been the reduction of Italian direct suppliers with many mergers or other consolidations in the components industry. First-tier suppliers have thus assumed more responsibility, with particular attention towards product quality. In many cases, they had to radically transform all company departments in terms of size, structure, technology and efficiency, in order to be competitive internationally.

Here are some examples, in addition to Magneti Marelli's operations, of significant developments in the Italian auto components/accessories sector:

--Carlo Gnutti has recently acquired for $18 million the Canadian company Kendar Manufacturing, thus becoming a world leader in the production of rocker arms for diesel engines;

--Brembo, a world leader in the production of brake disks, has set up two joint ventures in Mexico, and is collaborating with the German firm Continental to develop electronic braking systems;

-- C.F. Gomme acquired at the end of 2004 the French RBT (Vibration-Damping Division of PSA(Citroen-Peugeot). The PSA Group currently absorbs 45% of company's production, ousting Fiat, which absorbs a 30%. Through these acquisitions the company strengthened its position as world leader in the field of brake piping and as the fourth biggest manufacturer of air springs;

--Fiamm recently acquired the Italy-based, Belgian-controlled Uranio and the Belgian company United Energy, thereby becoming the third largest European manufacturer of vehicle batteries (over 14% of European market share). In recent years, the Fiamm group, which is also a world leader in horn production, has purchased the companies Clacson and Mecaniplant in France, the horn division of Magneti Marelli in Italy, Baeren in Austria, Oakdale in Ireland and Akuma in the Czech Republic, and is setting up new subsidiaries in Australia, China, France and the U.S.;

--Manuli Rubber, European leader in the field of piping and rubber parts for air conditioning systems, acquired during 2004 the French company Otim, the Korean company Keasan Manuli and the total control of Murray Europe, now Manuli Automotive;

--Momo, a manufacturer of steering wheels acquired by the U.S. firm Breed Technologies, has built two new production facilities in Hungary and Mexico;

--Saiag (rubber components/extruded products/floor panels) has set up a joint venture with U.S.-based Gen Corp. to produce parts in Argentina;

--Sata, the leader of a group including seven other companies, and specialized in mechanical processes, with a plant in the province of Isernia and another two in the Turin area, is building a factory in Argentina and establishing another factory in India;

--Turinauto, a joint venture created last year between Stola and Itca for the acquisition of Fiat's presses department of Rivalta, has recently acquired a new German partner, the steel company Voest Alpine;

--VM Motori, a manufacturer of diesel engines which has been acquired by the U.S. firm Detroit Diesel, is operating a plant in Curitiba, Mexico.

In addition, according to a plan of collaboration launched by Fiat and Renault, Teksid has acquired their cast-iron, aluminum and magnesium foundry activities for the automotive industry. The current turnover of the new Teksid group comes to approximately $1.8 billion and is expected to increase to $2.3 billion by 2003. The new group is owned 65.5% by Fiat and 33.5% by Renault. This acquisition followed the transfer of Teksid's steel components division (which accounted for 12% of the company's turnover) to the German company Neumayer.

SERVICE/REPAIR EQUIPMENT:

The largest concentration of garage equipment manufacturers is in Italy, and exports over 70% of its production worldwide. For instance, well over 30% of the turnover of Italian companies such as Beta Utensili (with 60 sales agencies worldwide),Usag and Pastorino is sent abroad. In countries with more sophisticated automobiles and where technology is more important, Italian products are particularly competitive, both in terms of such factors as "price vs. quality" and product versatility.

According to the "Osservatorio Autopromotec" (Market Analysis Division of major Italian service equipment show organizer Promotec S.r.l.), there are approximately 380 Italian producers of workshop equipment with a total workforce of about 18,000, and an estimated sales volume of about $3.3 billion. These are concentrated in the regions of Emilia-Romagna, Veneto, Lombardy and Piedmont. This highly specialized sector consists of small and medium-sized metallurgical and mechanical companies.

Italian producers of diagnostic instruments are world-renowned for the quality of their products. The components used in the production of these instruments are mainly Italian. Imported components in this category are those with a high technological content not yet available in Italy. The large automotive concern Magneti Marelli both produces the most complete array of components and electronic devices and supplies diagnostic equipment to its network of over 4,000 workshops throughout Italy. About three years ago, Magneti Marelli acquired from the U.S. firm Wellcar the "Midas" brand for fast-fit centers. There are presently 21 Midas fast-fits in Italy and their number is expected to increase to 50.

Exhaust fume analyzers are quite popular as a diagnostic instrument for catalyzers and lambda probes, to determine sealing problems of cylinder heads, to verify the integrity of injection systems and emission lines, and to check the percentage of carbon monoxide and opacity in gasoline engine and diesel engine emissions. This check is needed to adhere to the emission control directives recently adopted by local authorities in major Italian cities. In fact, according to a Ministerial decree in force as of June 2004, all cars and trucks (gas/diesel run) registered over 4 years ago, even though equipped with a catalytic converter, have to undergo a certified workshop check-up annually to obtain a special certificate, called "Bollino Blu", in order to circulate in urban areas.

Italian producers of systems and materials for tire retreading are also world leaders. Industry sources report that tire changers are made almost exclusively at Corregio, Italy.

2. Third-Country Imports

The EU accounts for about 82% of Italian auto parts and equipment imports. However, imports have significantly risen from Mexico, China, India, South Korea, Brasil, Argentina, Poland, Taiwan and Japan, although the amounts remain relatively small. Italy continues to enjoy a positive balance in the sector with all countries, except for Japan, Taiwan and, as of 2000 year end, the Netherlands.

Germany is by far the largest foreign supplier to Italy with a 35% share of the import market.
The close, long-lasting commercial relationships between German and Italian companies is a major factor in Germany's strong market share. Both the Common Market and product innovation also contributed to Germany's success. Such flagship German companies as Bosch, Siemens, Thyssen Krupp Automotive and Mannesmann are major players in the Italian market and are leading the components industry in advanced engineering and product durability. In addition, over 50 German companies sell service equipment in Italy either through subsidiaries and/or representatives Other important country suppliers are the U.K., Sweden, the Netherlands , Spain and Japan.

During the past few years, several companies totally or partly owned by foreign investors have built up new plants or improved existing ones, such as the Siemens factory in Fauglia, which brings together all Siemens activities in Europe in the field of injection systems, and the German company Getrag's plant in the province of Bari for the production of transmission systems. However, the most dynamic type of foreign investment in Italy in the automotive sector has been the acquisition of interests in existing companies. This type of investment has involved more than twenty companies of different sizes, belonging to a variety of commodity sectors (mostly OE suppliers, but also "spare part" and equipment and die manufacturers). There are about 120 companies whose share capital is owned partly or fully by foreign investors, accounting for a 40% share of total production sales in the Italian component sector. North American investments account for 23%, followed by German (7%), French (4%), and British investments (2%). Another 3% is due to Swedish, Swiss, Belgian and Japanese companies. Most recent examples illustrating Italy's appeal for foreign investments include the Japanese giant Sumitomo's February 2001 acquisition of Turin-based Cabind Automotive, for the manufacture of wiring harnesses for the automotive and truck markets and the Swiss holding Rieter's control of Turin-based I.DE.A. for internal thermal and acoustic insulation materials.

It is apparent that the components and accessories industry is reorganizing under the thrust of thirty or forty "global players". Though Italy has a highly qualified production and strong points in terms of individual or niche products, it is not as strong in system production, as this is mainly in the hands of companies under the control of foreign investors. Hence, it is natural that the leaders in the acquisition process are the transnational groups. This is especially so when one considers that the "skills" attracting their interest often belong to small size companies which can be taken over with greater ease.

3. U.S. Market Position

Imports of U.S. automotive parts and service equipment are estimated to have risen 18% in 2000 compared to 2004. The U.S. import market share of 3%, however, remains quite small, accounting for only 1% of total Italian market demand. There is indeed a tremendous difference between US and European cars in terms of design and engines, thus many American parts are not imported. The main opportunities for U.S. suppliers of parts stem from technology, while forged or cast parts face much larger competition from European suppliers who are most likely better set up for the European market. However, as a result of the recently concluded Fiat/GM joint venture -- which involves technical collaboration, component acquisitions and presumed joint servicing, the U.S. import market share is expected to reach 4% during the next couple of years, with growth in U.S. shipments averaging annual increases of 10%. The potential for sales of U.S.-manufactured parts to Fiat is also expected to grow because Fiat may be inclined to include more U.S. content in view of possible future car sales in the U.S.

The U.S. industry is mainly supplying the Italian market from European subsidiaries and joint ventures, a practice that should further expand its presence in Italy. During the past decade, a considerable number of agreements have been concluded in Italy increasingly involving U.S. companies producing automotive parts and components. Worthy of note is the Fiat-GM collaboration in the area of engines and transmissions which have given way to the creation in Turin of "Fiat-General Motors Powertrain Co.", which will manage the entire European production of both Groups' transmissions and engines, with a forecast workforce of 13,000 employees (half of which in Italy) and an annual output of 5 million units.

In the service equipment area, Snap-On, SPX and Sunnen Products have established U.S. subsidiaries in Italy. About twenty U.S. service equipment companies are present in the market through Italian distributors.

C. END-USER ANALYSIS

The market for end-users of automotive components and accessories consists of two segments: original parts (OE) and replacement parts and accessories. Original parts are purchased directly by Italian automobile manufacturers or by their systems suppliers. Fiat [which includes Alfa Romeo, Autobianchi, Lancia, Innocenti, Iveco, Ferrari (90%-owned), and Maserati (49%-owned)] is by far the largest Italian motor vehicle producer. Other motor vehicle manufacturers include Automobili Lamborghini (acquired by Audi in June 1998), Bugatti Automobili and De Tomaso Modena (sports cars), Altra, Boxel and Micro-vett (electric vehicles), Bredamarinibus (buses) and Piaggio Veicoli Europei (minivans).

While automotive parts and equipment suppliers purchase directly from manufacturers and distributors, the procurement procedure for Italian motor vehicle manufacturers is to turn to their list of qualified suppliers. As a result of the recent Fiat-General Motors (GM) agreement, a joint venture operation called "General Motors-Fiat Worldwide Purchasing Co." has been set up at Russelsheim Germany to manage the acquisitions of both car manufacturers, except for the U.S. and the Asia-Pacific markets. This company, in turn, has delegated to approximately 70 Fiat/GM "creativity teams" (the previous acquisition departments) the bids and purchases of OE products. In order to select the supplier for a certain product, the appropriate "creativity team" calls for bids among Fiat/GM panel suppliers (approximately 600, of which 250 are in common) which handle the given product. In theory, if none of the company's usual suppliers tendering for the contract offers a satisfactory solution, then "creativity team" may turn elsewhere.

A difference between the various vehicle manufacturers may exist in their approach towards the non-European supplier. While Ferrari, Lamborghini, Maserati, Audi, BMW or Mercedes may be drawn to high tech products, Fiat, Opel or Ford may still be looking on a more practical level because their average target customer does not pay premium prices. U.S. suppliers wishing to talk to the vehicle manufacturers need to be fully prepared and follow the correct procedure in the bidding process.

EVOLUTION IN PROCUREMENT PROCEDURES:

Worthy of note is that both the massive car manufacturers' outsourcing of entire systems and "Business to Business" (B2B) internet sales are transforming the overall structure of component procurement. Today's classic top to bottom system has car manufacturers acting as "assemblers" of component systems, followed by 1st tier suppliers (JIT system integrators), 2nd tier suppliers (system specialists) and 3rd tier suppliers (suppliers of parts and components). However, in the near term, the present structure is expected to flatten and thin out with the integration of 1st and 2nd tier suppliers which will give way to a limited group of highly standardized "mega-suppliers".

The 3rd tier will be composed of a reduced number of highly standardized and specialized suppliers of parts and components. In the long term, the present pyramid is prospected to give way to a box-like structure, with vehicle assembling at the top level carried out in collaboration between car manufacturers and mega-suppliers. The inside of this structure will host a network of independent, specialized and flexible suppliers, which will refurbish the operators of the top level. The bottom level will be composed of component and system specialists who will mainly supply the network but also deliver directly to top-level operators. This scenario depicts a highly integrated system, whereby both the assemblers (vehicle manufacturers and system suppliers) and the suppliers (small, medium and large) interact and collaborate in a joint effort.

Increased integration should continue to ensure differentiation in the characteristics of the vehicles sold by car manufacturers. This differentiation entails an involvement of a variety of intermediate suppliers able to incorporate know-how and innovation for different yet flexible deliveries. Collaboration, both horizontal and vertical, becomes a determining factor for the success of intermediate suppliers. It could well be up to the same mega-suppliers to create smaller and more flexible production units. In sum, the even increased presence of mega-suppliers will not prevent intermediate suppliers to remain competitive, also as direct suppliers.

INTERNET AND E-BUSINESS:

To crease the competitiveness of their suppliers, the big three -- DaimlerChrysler, GM and Ford -- recently launched the Covisint portal, presenting the first grand operation of "digital marketing" (B2B) which concerns online contract/bid negotiations with their suppliers and purchases for an estimated 240 billion dollars annually. This could reduce the final cost of a car by 6%. Nissan, Renault and Fiat also recently joined Covisint. Car manufacturers are also pushing for their mega-suppliers to use the portal and ultimately have included in Covisint's board of directors managers of five large component suppliers: Delphi, Johnson Controls, Siemens, Lear and Magna. The component suppliers, however, appear to prefer portals that do not depend on the car manufacturers. The Free Markets portal, for example, has held bids online for almost $11 billion and is the preferred portal by component suppliers such as Visteon, Delphi, Pilkington, Dana and Eaton.

B2B is, nonetheless, viewed mostly as an instrument to increase the efficiency of network suppliers and to improve relationships between car manufacturers and suppliers rather than as a means to select best prices. In the aftermarket and after-sales area, B2B will play an important role especially between wholesalers and retailers for stock management, and between equipment producers and workshops for online repair and maintenance instructions. "Business to Consumer" (B2C) is viewed mostly as a tool to interact with the consumer, sending messages on recalls or vehicle maintenance rather than for direct sale purposes.

In the aftermarket sector, small and medium sized U.S. exporters interested in selling in the Italian market may contact several consortia and associations such as the recently formed Italian AERO (European Association of Spare Parts Distributors - www.aeroass@infinito.it), A.DI.R. (Spare Parts Distributors Association - www.aps-service.com, AICARR (Italian Association of Air Conditioning, Heating and Refrigeration - www.aircarr.it), ASSORICAMBI (Consortium of Automotive Parts and Accessories Suppliers - www.assoricambi.it), and I.DI.A. (Independent Distributors Automotive - www.idia.it). Companies wishing to contact importers or locate distributors for their individual product lines can also consult an annual directory of the Italian automotive spare parts and accessories industry, called Catalogo Motoristico". The directory also carries a special "worldwide offers and requests" section, which is published in monthly issues of a related magazine called Notiziario Motoristico (www.netcollins.com).

Regarding the ultimate end-user -- the consumer -- in Italy vehicle ownership is a little over half a vehicle per capita. Seventy-six percent of Italian families own at least one car; fifty-six percent have two cars (the highest level in Europe), with the second car usually small and equipped with minimal accessories. Due to the aging Italian population, some 24% of Italian families do not own a car. Over 17% of cars circulating in Italy are over 15 years old, compared to a 4.3% average of major European country competitors (Germany, France, and the U.K.). The general aging of Italian cars is also due to improved durability of modern cars, the termination of government scrappage schemes, and relatively high new car prices. The average annual mileage for a car in Italy is only 13,900 km, lower than the European average of 14,600 km. On average, the Italian car owner will not change his car until it reaches 78,800 km (compared to Europe's average of 90,600 km). Italy currently supports 1,200,000 LPG-run vehicles, equal to half of the total European LPG vehicle fleet. With increasing concern over vehicle emissions, LPG is indeed seen by many Italians (especially in the South) as a key alternative fuel option, being not only cleaner but also significantly cheaper than gasoline or diesel and more convenient than CNG or electricity. As such, Italy (along with the Netherlands) has the most developed auto LPG service station network in Europe with approximately 2,000 sites. However, the cost of converting vehicles to use LPG remains a key factor limiting its uptake.

Italy's increase in fuel prices and automotive insurance in addition to the current fiscal pressure could influence future demand for automobile ownership and spin-offs. A car-owner with a medium-size car spends approximately $1,000 annually just to possess a car. In the past five years, inflation and vehicle prices (up roughly 7.5%) have remained low; however, fuel prices (up 15%) and transfer of car ownership costs (up 25%) have soared, not to mention skyrocketing car insurance costs.

Italians place the automobile at the top of their wish list and consider it a status symbol, but strangely enough still spend less compared to other European car owners in car-care and maintenance. However, Italian legislation is compelling car owners to consider safety and the adoption of quality components in order to pass the biennial car inspections. Today, the car has to be repaired fast, at an affordable price, and with quality spare parts. It should be noted, however, that the farther south one goes in Italy, the lesser the interest in safety. According to the "Osservatorio Autopromotec", each Italian family spent an average of $600 in 2000 on car maintenance, resulting in a turnover of $19 billion (up 4.6% compared to the previous year).

There are an estimated 80,000 auto repair and service shops operating in Italy. The majority of these are independent car repair shops (27,000) and body repair shops (19,500). Car dealers run approximately 12,200 workshops. Other types include workshops run by gas stations (approximately 5,500) and companies specializing in electrical repair (8,500), tire service (6,500), tire re-tread services (200) and engine rebuilding (600). Fast-fit franchise centers (e.g. Magneti Marelli's "Midas") are seeking to compete with the traditional suppliers of vehicle repairs. However, according to the "Osservatorio Autopromotec", only 34% of car owners turn to automobile dealer service facilities after the warranty period expires. The majority of car owners then prefer other smaller types of repair shops, not only for their lower cost and more accessible locations, but also for the personal rapport.

U.S. exporters interested in selling service equipment in Italy may contact the various automotive service and repair associations such as AICA (Italian Automotive Service Equipment Manufacturers Association - www.asso-aica.it), AIRA/CNA (Italian Association of Car Repairers/Federation of Craftsmen and Small Enterprises), AIRP (Italian Tire Retreaders Association - www.asso-airp.it), and CONFAUTO (Association of Professional Automotive Repairers).

D. MARKET ACCESS

1. Import Climate

Import Taxes:

As a member of the European Union (EU), Italy applies EU common external tariffs to goods imported from non-EU countries. Customs duties for automotive parts and equipment range from 3.4 percent to 6 percent. Import duty is charged on the C.I.F. value (cost, insurance, freight). In addition, a 20 percent value added tax (VAT) is charged on the C.I.F. value plus duty. VAT applies to both imports and domestically produced goods. Trade restrictions or other non-tariff barriers (such as quotas) do not exist, but all equipment has to comply with Italian (and/or European) safety regulations and technical standards. The metric system of weights and measures is standard in Italy. With regard to batteries, in accordance with EU Directive 91/156, Italy has established the COBAT Consortium, which undertakes the compulsory disposal and recycling of used batteries. Each domestic producer and importer of motor vehicle batteries pays the Consortium a tax -- amounting to approximately $1.00 per battery sold. The revenues helps finance COBAT's activities, thus guaranteeing collection and recycling of used and discarded batteries, irrespective of the price of lead.

Technical Standards:

Technical standards, including marking and labeling for automotive parts and equipment are issued and maintained by various Italian public and private agencies, such as UNI -- Ente Nazionale Italiano di

Unificazione (Italian Institute for Standards), and CUNA -- Commissione Tecnica di Unificazione nell'Autoveicolo" (Technical Committee for Motor Vehicle Harmonization). These agencies adhere totally to EU regulations.

With a decree issued on May 8, 1995, Italy officially conformed to EU directives concerning the sale of motor vehicle spare parts. The document specifies that all spare parts for motor vehicles consisting of independent safety units must comply with current regulations and be stamped with the E-mark of the specific country.

LPG/CNG retrofit systems must abide by regulations set forth by the ECE-ONU Working Party on Pollution and Energy which concern the homogenization of LPG/CNG components and their retrofit installation.

Workshop equipment producers have had to comply with the most recent laws concerning safety at work for end-users. Italian law does not only regulate the production of some equipment, but also deals with the nature of all manual instruments. In Italy, verification and homologation tests for workshop equipment are handled by the "Centro Superiore Ricerche e Prove Autoveicoli e Dispositivi" of the "Direzione Generale della Motorizzazione Civile e dei Trasporti in Concessione" of the Italian Ministry of Transportation. The Ministry has recently authorized CUNA to be a certification body for initial tests on equipment in workshops performing biennial vehicle inspections. Tests on general workshop equipment (and especially on vehicle lifts) are also carried out by ISPESL (National Institute for Health and Safety in the Workplace).

A certificate for electromagnetic compatibility can be issued in Italy by the Istituto Marchio di Qualita'(IMQ). Electrical requirements are 220 volts, 50 Hz.

IMQ -- ISTITUTO MARCHIO DI QUALITA'
Via Quintiliano 43
20100 Milan, Italy
Tel: 39/02/5073-220
Fax: 39/02/5073-271.

Since over 70% of a car's value is currently provided by outside suppliers, it has become important for motor vehicle manufacturers to guarantee the best quality for their components, starting with the design. Therefore, vehicle manufacturers have sought to set common criteria for quality standards, to which the component suppliers must adhere, developed on the basis of ISO 9000 standards. An International Automotive Task Force (IATF) was created in 1995 with the ultimate goal of establishing a standard conformity assessment system applying to both Europe and the United States. In April 1998, IATF finally set its seal to the final agreement establishing standard guidelines. Published in July 2004 as ISO/TS 16949, these guidelines crowned a joint endeavor that had lasted over three years. Today, the ISO/TS global certificate is fully operative.

CE MARK:

Product compliance with recent regulations and standards required by the EU market is guaranteed by the "CE" mark. The CE (from the French "conformite europeenne") mark is a "passport" that allows manufacturers to move industrial products freely within the internal market of the EU. The CE mark attests as to the conformity to certain safety performance, compatibility, and other requirements. These requirements are determined by EU authorities through EC directives for certain product categories or for certain horizontal risks (such as electromagnetic compatibility). In other words, the CE mark indicates that the manufacturer has followed all procedures to conform to requirements established for a particular product or risk. Some products may be governed by more than one directive because different risks may be dealt with under separate directives. The manufacturer is responsible for ensuring that products meet the requirements for all applicable directives. U.S. manufacturers that comply with these EU directive requirements may affix the CE mark.

In order to be able to affix the CE mark the manufacturer must:

-- prepare a declaration of conformity [to the relevant directive(s)];

-- compile a technical file that allows a verification of the declared conformity;

-- keep the technical file available for eventual verification from the notified control bodies (It is important to note that in the case of a product imported from a non-EU country, the importer is responsible for the conformity of the product, and therefore must have a copy of the product technical file);

-- undertake the necessary measures to certify both the production process and the final product (Companies that are certified under ISO 9000 quality certification need only to refer to the different production phases contained in the quality manual already developed for the ISO 9000 certification).

In the case of electromagnetic compatibility (EMC) (directives 89/336 and 93/68), the manufacturing firm can affix the CE mark itself, using the same procedures and adhering to the requirements stated in the Official Gazette of the European Union for the EMC standard.

If the manufacturer has not followed these standards completely, because no standard has been issued for this product or risk, or the standard is only partially applicable, the manufacturer must prepare the technical file for the product and obtain a technical certification from a notified body before affixing the CE mark.

ASSISTANCE IN THE UNITED STATES ON STANDARDS ISSUES:

The National Center for Standards and Certification Information (NCSCI), a U.S. Government agency, which is part of the Department of Commerce's National Institute of Standards and Technology (NIST), in Gaithersburg, Maryland, should be a first point of contact for U.S. companies attempting to determine which Italian standard or EU directive may be applicable to their products. NIST maintains standard information for all ISO (International Organization for Standardization) countries, including Italy. Its address is:

National Center for Standards and Certification Information (NCSCI)
National Institute for Standards and Technology (NIST)
TRF Room A 163
Gaithersburg, MD 20899
Tel: (301) 975-4040
Fax: 301) 975-2128 or 926-1559
e-mail: ncsci@nist.gov

General information on the EU directives and CE mark regulations can be obtained from:

U.S. Mission to the EU
40 Boulevard du Regent
B-1060 Brussels, Belgium
Tel: 32/2/508-2746
Fax: 32/2/513-1228
e-mail: sylvia.mohr@mail.doc.gov

Office of European Union and Regional Affairs - OEURA
U.S. Department of Commerce
14th & Constitution Avenue, NW Room 3036
Washington, DC 20230
Tel: 202/482-5276
Fax: 202/482-2155

OEURA staff can provide the latest information on CE mark requirements, including the so-called new approach to CE mark conformity, copies of directives, availability of standards, lists of notified bodies, interpretive guides and other commercial information.

Another source of information is the American National Standards Institute (ANSI) in New York. ANSI is the official U.S. depository for all ISO member-countries and has English translations of foreign standards. U.S. firms may request a standard search for a fee.

American National Standards Institute
11 West 42nd Street, 13th floor
New York, NY 10036
Phone: (212) 642-4900
Fax: (212) 302-1286

ANSI has also an office in Brussels:

American National Standards Institute
c/o American Chamber of Commerce
Ave. des Arts 50
B-1040 Brussels, Belgium
Phone: (32) 2-5136892
Fax: (32) 2-5137928.

In some cases, Underwriters Laboratories Inc. (UL) in the United States can assist U.S. manufacturers and exporters in understanding and complying with foreign national and international standards and certification requirements and procedures. UL's TATE (Technical Assistance To Exporters) program can provide technical information about standards in many foreign countries. UL has agreements with a number of foreign agencies, including Italy's IMQ, for conducting product testing and factory evaluations. U.S. firms wishing to avail themselves of UL's TATE program may contact the TATE coordinator at one of the following facilities:

Underwriters Laboratories - UL
International Compliance Services Department
333 Pfingsten Road
Northbrook, IL
Tel: (708) 272-8800
Fax: (708) 272-9562

Underwriters Laboratories - UL
International Compliance Services Department
1285 Walt Whitman Road
Melville, NY 11747
Tel: (516) 271-6200
Fax: (516) 271-8265

Underwriters Laboratories - UL
International Compliance Services Department
1655 Scott Boulevard
Santa Clara, CA 95050
Tel: (408) 985-2400
Fax: (408) 296-3256

Underwriters Laboratories - UL
International Compliance Services Department
12 Laboratory Drive
Research Triangle Park, NC 27709-3995
Tel: (919) 549-1400
Fax: (919) 549-1842.

For further information on trade regulations, U.S. interested companies should consult the U.S. Embassy to Italy's Country Commercial Guide for Italy, which can be accessed through the National Trade Data Bank (NTDB) of the U.S. Department of Commerce or via its website: www.usembassy.it/fcs.

2. DISTRIBUTION/BUSINESS PRACTICES

Italian manufacturers as well as foreign companies with subsidiary operations in Italy use their own distribution networks. There are also numerous independent distributors covering the entire aftermarket territory through a network of representative agents in the major cities. Most of the distributors are well entrenched in the independent repair market, as well as in the technical inspection center chains. For some years the Association of Spare Parts Distributors (A.DI.R. - APS) has been setting up a network of independent spare parts distributors and vehicle repairers. This is a vertical organization with a limited number of distributors and spare parts dealers, which in turn serve numerous repair shops. Products sold to members of ADIR-APS are discounted. There are approximately 100 spare part dealers belonging to this association, serving 700 workshops.

Foreign companies operate through locally appointed distributors or agents, usually on an exclusive basis, that are well established throughout the country, experienced, and able to offer good technical and after-sales service. The distribution of hand tools, for example, is carried out by about 1,000 qualified distributors throughout Italy, that are able to offer both user-friendly products and technical advice to their clients. Workshop operators normally turn to these qualified dealers for entire sets of tools, or when in need of single pieces for integration or replacement. The number of different tool brands in Italian workshops is not high, which means that operators tend to turn to companies that offer a complete range of high quality tools. The price ratio between good quality tools and lower quality ones is 9 to 1. In order to ensure satisfied clients, in addition to manuals of instructions, many service equipment manufacturers offer annual training seminars or refresher courses for the Italian and/or foreign agents or distributors, who in turn will train workshop operators. Other marketing channels include cooperation, joint venture, or licensing agreements with carmaker's suppliers.

The distribution channels to the end-user for after-market automotive parts and service equipment, by percentage of sales, are as follows:

Accessories and parts dealers 24%
Ricambisti (wholesale distributors) 19%
Car workshops approved by auto manufacturers: 18%
Independent workshops: 10%
Tire specialist operations: 9%
Gas stations: 8%
Body part specialist operations: 5%
Electrical specialist operations: 3%
Hypermarkets: 2%
Auto centers/fast-fits: 1%
Demolition centers: 1%

ITALIAN AFTERMARKET COMPLEXITIES:

Due to extreme complexity and the large number of distribution stages, the Italian aftermarket has not reflected the changes experienced in the rest of the European aftermarket, with higher prices resulting from its numerous differences and intricacies.

Distribution of auto parts in French-style hypermarkets and auto centers has reached Italy, mainly in the north, while the south of Italy keeping to traditional distribution methods. Two large French auto parts chains, Norauto and Maxauto, have entered the Italian market. This new form of distribution is mainly controlled by large foreign groups, which cover 45% of hypermarket sales and 16% of supermarket sales of automotive products. However, mass distribution in Italy is still generally viewed as synonymous to mass de-specialization. High quality products sold in hypermarkets risk to be identified as mediocre. The spread of Internet access has made consumers even more aware of price differences. While 30% of sector companies have a website, only 5% have e-commerce operations.

Though some Italian regions may slowly be adopting these new distribution trends, most of the aftermarket continues to follow past distribution methods. There are about 150-200 traditional distributors and around 100 manufacturers' and importers' agents. These distributors sell to around 5,500 "ricambisti" or resellers, who may have retail outlets in their own right, but are generally similar to traditional wholesale distributors. The ricambistis then sell to the retail outlets and to smaller ricambisti. The smaller ricambistis in turn sell to workshops. Though Italian drivers traditionally do not use franchise repair shops and prefer instead to use small local shops, both the numbers of repair outlets and ricambistis are declining. Approximately 45,000 repair outlets remain in Italy far too many for its car fleet.

In addition to the complex stages of distribution in the Italian market, there are traditionally four distinct specialized types of repair shops with further degrees of sub-specialization within each sector. First, there are electrical, mechanical, body parts and tire specialists. Recently, however, the electrical and mechanical operations are merging because there is not enough work to sustain such a specialized area of activity. The tire specialists, body parts and even exhaust specialists remain exceptions, and have tended to remain specialized.

Not many buying groups operate in Italy. Although Euro CME -- consisting of more than 30 members and specializing in electrical parts -- is one example of a buying group, these groups have not traditionally been strong in the Italian market. Euro CME also represents the Italian market in the Europe-wide Group Auto Union (GAU). In addition, though MEMA and SEMA are associate members of the International Federation of Independent Distributors (FIGIEFA), until recently there was no Italian association participating in this important organization. The Italian organization, Assodispart, joined FIGIEFA in 1998 but was dissolved in 2000 with the majority of its members creating a new association called Aero.

The Italian group Tuttemarche, a consortium comprising 50 warehouse distributors with 60 points of sale throughout Italy, became the 16th partner of ADI in January 2004. ADI is the oldest international group of warehouse distributors, present in 15 European countries.

Noteworthy is also the recent agreement between Delphi-Diavia and Rhiag, national leaders in the distribution of spare parts in the independent market, for the distribution of automotive HVAC spare parts and equipment. Also remarkable is the presence of the Cecauto-APS group, with 70 resellers with 103 points of sale and 850 workshops throughout Italy.

ADVICE TO U.S. SUPPLIERS:

U.S. companies should not expect Italian representatives to take high numbers of product right away in return for exclusive distribution. If exclusive distribution rights are offered, the appointed representative should indeed be able to sell throughout Italy and possibly Europe. A company may be very strong domestically in Italy, or in certain regions, but know nothing about other markets. The Euro is going to make prices more transparent in the EU market, but there is still a long way to go before Europe really becomes one market like the U.S. In their approach to the European and Italian market, U.S. companies can improve by taking time gradually to introduce and sell a product. An U.S. company should not try to push hard and should use more of a "hands off" approach.

Challenges for U.S. companies wishing to enter the European and Italian market are that U.S. culture and vehicles are very different from those in Europe. The U.S. is large with long driving distances and Italy is much smaller. The best way for U.S. companies to do serious business in the European and Italian markets is to "bend the trend" of the recipient market.

US GOVERNMENT SERVICES AVAILABLE TO AMERICAN EXPORTERS IN ITALY:

The services available through the U.S. Commercial Service in Italy offer an excellent way for U.S. exporters to enter the Italian automotive parts and equipment market. In particular, the Gold Key Service, for a nominal fee, provides scheduled appointments with qualified and pre-selected potential agents, distributors, joint venture partners and other Italian firms that can help ensure the success of U.S. companies in Italy. For details on this and other CS programs that can help U.S. firms better understand and enter this market, contact the Commercial Service in Genoa or the nearest U.S. Department of Commerce Export Assistance Center in the United States or consult www.usis.it/fcs.

U.S. exporters wishing to test the market or find agents/distributors may wish to participate in the U.S. Commercial Service Catalog Exhibits at AUTOMOTOR and AUTOPROMOTEC. AUTOMOTOR, scheduled in March 2003, is the most important show in Italy and one of the largest in Europe devoted to automotive components, spare parts and accessories, while AUTOPROMOTEC, scheduled in May 2003, is Europe's premier International Exhibition specifically devoted to Machinery, Tools and Products for Auto Repair Centers, Service Stations, Body Repair Shops, Tire Retreading and Servicing. (More information is contained in the Trade Promotion Opportunities section of this report).

3. FINANCING

Financing practices in the automotive parts and equipment sector adhere to normal business standards used in Italy and are usually handled by banks. While importers/distributors tend to make payments in an average 60 - 90 days, Italian auto manufacturer turnaround times range from 60 to 180 days.

4. TRADE PROMOTION OPPORTUNITIES

Following are the most important motor vehicle and related parts and accessories exhibits in Italy:

MOTOR SHOW (International Car, Motorcycle and Bicycle Exhibit)
December 7 - 16, 2001
Bologna, International Expo Fairgrounds
Annual - 850 exhibitors; 1,300,000 visitors
Organizer: Promotor S.r.l.
Via Milazzo 30
40121 Bologna (BO)
Tel: 39/051/645-1011
fax: 39/051/645-1099
e-mail: salone@motorshow.it
website: www.motorshow.it
Contact: Dr. Umberto Bassi, Director

INTERNATIONAL MOTOR VEHICLE SHOW (Cars, Car Bodies, Components, Tires and Wheels)
April 24 – May 5, 2002
Turin, Lingotto International Fairgrounds
Biennial - 150 exhibitors; 550,000 visitors
Organizer: Promotor S.r.l.
Via Milazzo 30
40121 Bologna (BO)
tel: 39/051/645-1011
fax: 39/051/645-1099
e-mail: info@saloneautotorino.it
website: www.saloneautotorino.it
Contact: Dr. Umberto Bassi, Director

TRANSPOTEC & LOGITEC 2002 (Industrial and Commercial Vehicles)
April 25 - 28, 2002
Verona, International Expo Fairgrounds
Biennial - 400 exhibitors; 50,000 visitors.
Organizer: Transpotec S.r.l.
Via Cadorna 12
35123 Padova (PD)
tel: 39/049/875-7988
fax: 39/049/875-3162

e-mail: info@transpotec.it
website: www.transpotec.it
Contact: Mr. Giampaolo Pinton, Director

AUTOMOTOR 2003 (22nd International Exhibition of Components, Spare Parts and Accessories for the Motor Vehicle)
March 2003
Turin, Lingotto Int'l Fairgrounds
Biennial - 480 exhibitors; 35,000 visitors
Organizer: Lingotto Fiere S.p.A.
Via Nizza 294
10126 Turin (TO)
Tel: 39/011/664-4111
fax: 39/011/664-7847
e-mail address: info@lingottofiere.it
website: www.lingottofiere.it
Contact: Mr. Andrea Ferrari, Manager

AUTOPROMOTEC (International Exhibition of Machinery, Tools and Products for Auto Repair Centers, Service Stations, Body Repair Shops, Tire Retreading and Servicing)
May 2003
Bologna, Int'l Expo Fairgrounds
Biennial - 850 exhibitors; 90,000 visitors
Organizer: Promotec S.r.l.
Via A.G. Ragazzi 9
40011 Anzola Emilia (BO)
Tel: 39/051/733-000
fax: 39/051/731-886
e-mail: info@autopromotec.it
website: www.autopromotec.it
Contact: Dr. Gabriele Giorgi, Marketing Manager

EARTHMOVING MACHINERY

The earthmoving machinery (EMM) market in Italy was estimated to be about USD 1.3 billion in 1998. In that year, sales in units of earthmoving machinery increased by 15 percent over the previous year, following a 12 percent increase in 1997. Trade sources have forecast increases of the same magnitude also in 2004 and 2000. The development of the EMM market is closely tied to that of the construction industry, especially public works. The good results seen in the EMM sector in the past two years are largely due to the resumption in investments in civil engineering and non-residential public buildings. Moreover, the optimistic forecasts for the years 2004 and 2000 stem from the substantial increase, in 1997 and 1998, of tenders for public works, which are expected to be reflected in increased activity over the next two years.

The crises that beset the EMM sector in the early nineties drove several medium-sized Italian manufacturers and distributors out of the market. Fiat-Hitachi Excavators and Fai Komatsu Industries are by far the two leading domestic manufacturers of finished machinery. At the same time, imports play a major role in this market. Approximately 50 percent of nontraditional earthmoving machines and 60 percent of compact machines are imported. Imports include several hundred units of used machines. Among the leading imported brands are Caterpillar, Case, Bobcat, JCB, Volvo. U.S. brands enjoy an excellent reputation and continue to be market leaders.

In the past few years, the composition of the EMM market has changed significantly. The shift of the construction industry towards renovation activities favors the use of multi-function and compact machinery. In fact, demand for compact machinery is likely to grow at a rate higher than the market average in the next few years. In order to be marketed in Italy, earthmoving
machinery must conform to the European Union Machinery Directive and carry the EC mark.

A. MARKET HIGHLIGHTS & BEST PROSPECTS

MARKET PROFILE

In value, the EMM market is estimated to be about USD 1.3 billion in 1998. Approximately 50 percent of ôtraditionalô machines and 60 percent of compact machines are imported. Imports include several hundred units of used machines.

Trends in the EMM market are directly tied to those in the construction industry, especially in public works. According to research organizations and sector experts, 1998 -- with an estimated 2 percent real increase -- marked the end of the recession that had characterized the Italian construction industry since 1993. A more significant increase of at least 3.2 percent in real terms is expected in 2004.

Investment in the Italian construction industry totaled USD 108.7 billion in 1997 (the last year for which complete data is available), broken down as follows:

Market Segments:		USD (billions)	%
New Construction of which:		54.2 49.9	
Residential Construction	23.6 21.7		
Private Non-Residential Construction		16.1 14.8	
Public Non-Residential Construction	3.5	3.3	
Civil Engineering	11.0 1	0.1	
Renovation of which:		54.5	50.1
Residential Construction	28.1	25.8	
Private Non-Residential Construction	15.1	13.9	
Public Non-Residential Construction	3.6	3.3	
Civil Engineering	7.7	7.1	
Total Investment	108.7 100.0		

As this table shows, investment in renovation activities exceeds slightly that in new construction. Renovation activities are especially important in the residential building market segment, where -- since 1993 -- investments have consistently exceeded those in new residential buildings. This is not surprising in light of the fact that the existing stock of homes (26 million) meets the needs of Italy=s 21 million Italian families. Owing to the rapid aging of the existing stock of homes, renovation activities of residential buildings are predicted to be even more important in the next few years. At the same time, there is likely to be a decline in new residential construction.

Combined investment in public non-residential construction and civil engineering (that is, investment in public works) increased from USD 25.8 billion in 1997 to 28.6 billion in 1998 (an increase of 11 percent). A significant increase is expected in 2004, considering the increased number of tenders issued in 1997 and 1998, which will be reflected in actual investments in public works in the next two years. In particular, major investments are planned for the construction or renovation of important highways (Salerno-Reggio Calabria, Bologna-Florence), the construction of the new high-speed rail system, and the year 2000 Jubilee.

After an all-time high of 210,000 metric tons of equipment sold in 1989, the EMM market underwent a major decline beginning in 1991, reaching its lowest level in 1993 (with 98,000 metric tons sold). Following the ôclean handsö (anti-corruption) judicial investigations, 1993 saw a 5.9 percent decrease in overall construction activity, and an almost complete collapse of public works projects. As a consequence, the EMM market also collapsed, registering a 42.5 percent decrease (in tons) over the previous year. Since then, the EMM market has been gradually recovering. However, it should be noted that in 1998, with approximately 166,400 tons of equipment sold, the market was still 21 percent lower -- in weight terms -- than it was in 1989.

The recovery is to be attributed, in part, to the replacement of obsolete machinery, after years of cutbacks in investment. This trend was largely due, in 1995 and 1996, to the ôTremonti Lawö, which exempted incremental investment in capital goods from income taxes. In the near future, the renewal of the Italian EMM fleet -- currently one of the most obsolete in Europe -- could be enhanced by the issuance of specific incentive schemes, similar to those approved in 1998 in the agricultural machinery sector. However, the recovery in the EMM sector will come primarily from the resumption of investment in public works, which rose significantly in 1997 and 1998 and which will continue in 2004. The approval of the ôMerloni-ter Lawö on public works at the end of 1998 should streamline bidding procedures and accelerate investment.

In the past few years, the composition of the EMM market had drastically changed. The increasing shift of the construction industry towards renovation activities favors the use of multi-function and compact machinery

Northern Italy absorbs 59 percent of total sales of earthmoving machinery, central Italy 23 percent, and southern Italy 18 percent. Sales in southern Italy are increasing at a slower rate than in the rest of Italy.

BEST SALES PROSPECTS

American products enjoy an excellent reputation in the marketplace. Italy offers distinct opportunities for U.S. advanced EMM machinery. Trade sources indicate that demand for compact machinery is likely to grow at a rate higher than the market average over the next few years. Price-competitive machines equipped with devices which control vibrations, noise and dust, and with advanced safety features have the best chance. In order to be marketed in Italy, machines must conform with the European Union Machinery Directive and carry the EC mark.

B. COMPETITIVE ANALYSIS

DOMESTIC PRODUCTION

The domestic production of EMM reached nearly USD 2.3 billion in 1998. In 1997 (the last year for which data is available), Italian production totaled USD 2 billion, or about 480,000 metric tons. These included 226,100 tons of finished machines and 253,900 tons of non-finished machines for export and final assembly in the country of destination, trucks, and other components, primarily axles.

Italian finished machines and components are of high quality. Exports in 1998 were estimated at about USD 1.6 billion. In 1997, they totaled USD 1.5 billion, of which 47 percent were components (in weight, 417,000 tons, inclusive of 242,000 tons in components). The U.S. is the principal export destination for Italian finished machinery, with a 21 percent share in value.

ôTwo Goliathes and a number of Davidsö is how experts describe the structure of the domestic EMM industry. Fiat-Hitachi Excavators and Fai Komatsu Industries hold over 40 percent of total domestic production. They are followed by some 100 manufacturers of finished machines with sales volumes that rarely exceed USD 10 million each. The crisis which beset the sector in the early nineties drove a number of producers (and distributors) out of the market. Most manufacturers are in the Piedmont, Emilia-Romagna, Veneto, and Lombardy regions.

The most important manufacturers of complete earthmoving machines in Italy are the following:

-- Fiat-Hitachi Excavators, This is a joint venture established in 1986 between New Holland -- which is part of the Fiat group-- and Hitachi Construction Machinery. It is a ôfull-linerö, with 11 different product lines

totaling 52 models offered in over 250 different variations. In its modern plants in Lecce and San Mauro Torinese, Fiat-Hitachi produces crawler bulldozers,
wheel and crawler loaders, motor-scrapers, motor-graders, crawler and wheel excavators. Furthermore, its Light Equipment Division produces mini-excavators, compact hydraulic excavators, skid-steer loaders, mini wheel loaders, and backhoe loaders.

In 1998, Fiat-Hitachi reached a sales volume of approximately USD 635 million, of which 70 percent was exported. In Italy, it employs approximately 1,700 people and produces about 7,500 units per year. Fiat-Hitachi holds 50 percent share in the ôtraditionalö machinery market segment in Italy. In the past two years, 80 percent of its products have been re-designed. This process was initiated in 1996, when Fiat-Hitachi launched a new line of compact machines designed to work in limited spaces, such as urban areas. After establishing a joint venture in 1997 for the distribution of machinery in America, New Holland recently signed an agreement for the acquisition of 75.1 percent of the German EEM manufacturer Orenstein and Koppel. In Italy, Fiat-Hitachi machines are distributed and serviced by 15 dealers.

-- Fai Komatsu Industries (FKI). After the acquisition in 1996 of 63 percent of the shares then still in the hand of the original Fai owners, FKI is now totally owned by Komatsu. In Italy, FKI manufactures utility machines and distributes the full range of Komatsu machines through approximately 45 dealers.

The FKI Utility Division headquartered in Este, near Padua, is an autonomous business unit of Komatsu that develops and produces machines of up to 11 tons (compact excavators, mini-excavators, rigid, articulated and four steering wheels backhoe loaders, skid-steer loaders), of which 70 percent are exported. FKI plans to launch 24 new models by the year 2000. The factory in Este (700 employees; production of 7,000 units per year) is implementing a ôflexible manufacturing systemö (FMS) based on the extensive use of robots. In 1998, FKI=s sales volume was approximately USD 290 million, including about USD 115 million in imported Komatsu machinery.

-- VF Venieri SpA. This is the only medium-sized manufacturer of finished EMM still in Italian hands. It produces articulated loaders and articulated and rigid backhoe loaders. It 1998, it recorded sales of approximately USD 30 million, of which 50 percent was exported.

Italy is a major producer of components. Italian components manufacturers export most of their production. Well known companies in this sector are Berco, Italtractor, and Sorefa, which produce tracks for excavators and bulldozers, and Bondioli & Pavesi, which produces hydraulic components.

Most Italian manufacturers of earthmoving machinery, implements, components, and parts are members of the association Comamoter (association of manufacturers of earthmoving machinery). Comamoter is part of UNACOMA, the national association of tractors and agricultural machinery manufacturers. Membership in Comamoter is open to foreign manufacturers having production units within the European Union and distribution and service
organizations in Italy.

THIRD-COUNTRY IMPORTS:

Imports of EMM were estimated at about USD 950 million in 1998. Imports of parts are negligible. Imported machines are estimated to meet more than 50 percent of the overall demand for EEM. Imports from countries belonging to the European Union account for over 80 percent of total imports in ton terms. The following are some of the most significant foreign companies active in the Italian market. Sales estimates are based on interviews with the trade and press reports.

-- Caterpillar (USA). Trade sources indicate that Caterpillar and Fiat-Hitachi Excavators together cover nearly 75 percent of the ôtraditionalö EEM market. At the 1998 Bauma trade show in Munich, Germany, Caterpillar introduced a new line of compact machines, thereby completing its range of products. In Italy, Cat machines are imported by MAIA -- which had total sales of over USD 210 million in 1997 and covers central and southern Italy -- and CGT -- Compagnia Generale Trattori -- which had total sales of USD 290 million in 1998 (inclusive of Cat engines and other machinery) and covers northern Italy, plus the Tuscany and Marche regions.

Caterpillar and its Italian dealers are placing increasing emphasis on service. CGT (800 employees, three divisions, and 23 branches and service centers) successfully introduced a new type of service contract, which provides for temporary replacement of machines to be serviced. Furthermore, CCT established a separate company to provide rental services, which are expected to make up 50 percent of its sales volume within a few years.

-- JCB (U.K.) competes in eight market segments, which include the machines most in demand in Europe -- backhoe loaders, telescopic handlers, mini-excavators, skid-steer loaders, crawler excavators, wheel excavators, wheeled loaders, lift trucks. After terminating an agreement with Sumitomo, JCB maintained proprietary rights to manufacture and market excavators with widths of 2.5 and 3 meters, which had been especially adapted for the European markets. JCB has a subsidiary in Assago, near Milan, and about 30 dealers. In 1997, it had sales of approximately USD 95 million.

-- Case (USA) is a ôfull linerö, selling excavators, wheel loaders, mini-excavators, skid-steer loaders. At the end of 1998 -- following a similar agreement made in 1992 for the U.S. market -- Case made a global agreement with Sumitomo for the production and distribution of excavators. In Europe, it will distribute five types of Sumitomo excavators (from 7 to 46 tons), which will complete its product range. Furthermore, Case will market a new line of compact machines (mini-excavators and backhoe loaders) manufactured at its Manchester (U.K.) plant. Case -- which reported sales of approximately USD 50 million in 1998 -- has a subsidiary in Rozzano, near Milan, and approximately 30 dealers. In addition, Fermec -- a company acquired by Case in 1996 -- imports and distributes EMM produced in Manchester in Italy.

-- Bobcat Melroe-Ingersoll Rand (USA) sells over 3,000 machines a year with a sales volume of approximately USD 40 million. It is reportedly the most important player in the market segment of compact machinery (e.g., skid-steer loaders and compact excavators). Its machines are imported from Belgium through MAIE, a dealer which also distributes Fiat-Hitachi products, and by MIDEC, a dealer which also imports Volvo=s earthmoving machinery, and by about 25 other, smaller regional importers.

-- Volvo Construction Equipment (Sweden) has, thus far, been especially active in the market for compact machinery. However, after its acquisition of Samsung, it has also been successful in marketing heavy machinery. As a consequence, it is developing plans to establish a subsidiary in Italy. Currently, Volvo equipment is imported by MIDEC. Volvo's controlled companies, Pel Job (which has a subsidiary in Italy) and Mecalac, are also active in Italy.

Other companies with a significant presence in the Italian market are Liebherr (which has a subsidiary in Italy) and Furukawa.

Several Italian importers of EMM (including Italian subsidiaries of foreign manufacturers) are members of Cantiermacchine, (association of importers of earthmoving machinery, a part of ASCOMAC (the national association of machinery dealers).

U.S. MARKET POSITION

Direct imports from the United States of finished earthmoving machines were estimated to be approximately USD 32 million in 1998, a 5.5 percent share of the total imports in terms of value.

The countries from which EMM is mostly imported are the U.K. (27 percent of total imports), Belgium (24 percent, including significant amounts of used machinery), France (16 percent), and Germany (9 percent).

However, the volume of machinery sold by American multinationals (both imported from the U.S. and manufactured in Europe) make the U.S. a market leader in this sector, while U.S. brand recognition is strong in Italy and throughout the rest of Europe.

C. END-USER ANALYSIS

The most important Italian end-users groups for EMM are construction companies, especially those engaged in public works (e.g., railways, roads, water works, airports, ports, land reclamation), the state-controlled agency for roads and highways û ANAS --, and some utility companies. Significant users are also the Italian agency for civil protection and the quarry and mining sectors.

In Italy, there are about 50,000 construction firms registered with the National Register of Building Contractors (Albo dei Costruttori). The market for construction services is very fragmented. Only 107 Italian construction firms recorded sales of over USD 11.7 million in 1997. Approximately thirty leading contractors, including most of those engaged in major civil engineering works in Italy and overseas, are associated with AGI (association of general contractors). Other contractors (including some large contractors) are associated with ANCE (national association of building contractors).

In 1998, the most important players in the public works sector were the Italian provinces and municipalities (43 percent), followed by the central government (11 percent), the regions (10 percent), the Italian Railways (10 percent), ANAS (7 percent), and ENEL, the state-controlled electric utility (7 percent). In most cases, government agencies do not undertake construction projects directly. These are normally contracted out through open bidding procedures.

In interviews with trade sources, price appears to be the most critical competitive factor in procuring EMM. However, unique and superior product features and a reputation for excellence in a given product category are also very important, as are the reliability of distributors, technical assistance, and the ability to provide spare parts quickly or machinery for temporary replacement purposes. Most companies in the EMM business tend to offer a full line of machines. Of increasing importance is the ability to provide financial assistance to both dealers and final clients. Leasing arrangements are becoming increasingly important, with many clients preferring to lease equipment rather than making large outlays to purchase equipment.

D. MARKET ACCESS

Import Climate

On the whole, the Italian import climate is favorable to foreign exporters. There are no limitations to the importation of foreign (including American) earthmoving machinery. Import procedures are governed by international trade regulations. Imports from the U.S. are subject to customs duties (ranging from 4.1 to 6.5 percent) and to the value added tax (20 percent on the c.i.f. price.)

Technical specifications are established by both the European Union and national authorities. EEC Directives 391/89, 655/89, and 95/63 -- on the safe use of machinery and implements -- are applicable. These directives have been transposed into national legislation by Laws 626/94, 626-bis, and 626-ter. EEC Directive 89/662 regulates noise testing methods.

In addition, EEC Machinery Directive 392/89 is applicable to EMM, as are the harmonized technical norms CEN, series EN 474, 1 to 12. The EEC Machinery Directive does not cover road circulation of EMM. In fact, every European country has its specific rules on road circulation, and the Committee for European Construction Equipment (CECE) is working on the unification of regulations with the co-operation of the European Commission. In Italy, road circulation of EMM is subject to the norms of the Italian traffic code. In order to be authorized to circulate, self-propelling wheeled earthmoving machines must be homologated, that is, formally recognized as complying with all Italian technical requirements. This often imposes costly modifications. Special permits are required for driving machines with a width of between 2.5 and 3 meters, while police escorts are required for machines over 3 meters in width.

DISTRIBUTION/BUSINESS PRACTICES

An efficient distribution and service network is a crucial competitive factor. Trade sources emphasize the importance of having one or more qualified and well-trained dealers who can ensure after-sales service and prompt availability of spare parts. U.S. companies interested in selling their products in the Italian market should also consider possible joint venture/ manufacturing/ licensing agreement with an Italian manufacturer (or with a manufacturer in a neighboring European country) wishing to complement its product line.

Rental of EMM is becoming increasingly popular in Italy, although the practice is relatively less common than in other European countries. In 1997, there were approximately 600 rental agencies, with total sales of nearly USD 200 million (and increase of 430 percent over 1992.) Most EMM rental firms are members of ASSO.DIMI, the association of distributors of industrial machinery.

FINANCING

Financing and trade practices in this sector comply with normal business and banking standards, with the majority of the transactions handled through private agreements and banking institutions.

Payments by local distributors are normally 120 days after delivery, while end-users normally pay after 180 days. The public sector is generally slow in paying.

End-users frequently request financial consulting services. Several distributors are now able to provide financial assistance, including leasing and facilitating arrangements through local banks. Leasing -- through specialized firms, often associated with the manufacturer -- is also quite extensive, particularly in Northern Italy. Leasing contracts normally extend over a three-year period.

KEY CONTACTS

A) TRADE ASSOCIATIONS

CO.MA.MO.TER - Costruttori Macchine Movimento Terra
Gruppo dell=UNACOMA
Via L. Spallanzani 22/A - 00161 Roma
Tel: +39-06442981 Fax: +39-06-4402722
E-mail: comamoter@unacoma.it
http://www.unacoma.com
Director General: Mr. Carlo Ambrogi

Cantiermacchine
Gruppo dell=ASCOMAC
Via del Casale di S. Basilio 9 - 00156 Roma
Tel: +39-06-41217097 Fax: +39-06-41217149
E-mail: ascomac@tin.it
Secretary General: Mr. Carlo Belvedere

ASSO.DIMI û Associazione Distributori Macchine Industriali
Via de= Tornabuoni 1 - 50123 Firenze
Tel: +39-055-294206 Fax: +39-055-217760
E-mail: assodimi@tirreno.it
http://www.assodimi.it
Secretary General: Ing. Franco De Michelis

A.G.I. Associazione Imprese Generali
Via Crescenzio 38 - 00193 Roma
Tel: +39-06-68281500 Fax: +39-06-68891503

A.N.C.E. Associazione Nazionale Costruttori Edili
Via G.A. Guattani 18 - 00161 Roma
Tel: +39-06-84881 Fax: +39-06-44232832
E-mail: ancere@ance.it

B) STANDARDS INSTITUTES

UNI Ente Nazionale Italiano di Unificazione
Via Battistotti Sassi 11 - 20133 Milano
Tel: +39-02-70024200 Fax: +39-02-70106149

C) TRADE PUBLICATIONS

Costruire (monthly)
Editrice Abitare Segesta SpA
Corso Monforte 15 - 20122 Milano
Tel: +39-02-760901 Fax: +39-02-76021904

Quarry and Construction (monthly)
Edizioni PEI S.r.L.
Strada Naviglio Alto 46 - 43100 Parma
Tel: +39-0521-771818 Fax: +39-0521-773572
E-mail: ed.pei@rsadvnet.it
http://www.rsadvnet.it/edizioni.pei

Mondo Macchina-Machinery World (monthly)
Unacoma Service S.r.L.
Via L. Spallanzani 22/A û 00161 Roma
Tel: +39-06-442981 Fax: +39-06-4402722
E-mail: mondomacchina@unacoma.it
http://www.unacoma.com

D) MAJOR IMPORTERS

MAIE S.p.A.
Via Faentina 258 û 48010 Fornace Zarattini (RA)
Tel: +39-0544-462666 Fax: +39-0544-461433

MIDEC S.p.A.
Via Fratelli Cervi 2 û 20090 Trezzano sul Naviglio (MI)
Tel: +39-02-484391 Fax: +39-02-48402286

AMCA S.r.L.
Centergros, Via dei Notai Blocco 22 - 40050 Funo di Argelato (BO)
Tel: +39-051-6647024 Fax: +39-051-6646784

Case Italy S.p.A.
Via Boccaccio 5, Ponte Sesto û 20089 Rozzano (MI)
Tel: +02-8228301 Fax: +39-02-8258954

C.G.T. S.p.A.
S.S. Padana Superiore 19 û 20090 Vimodrone (MI)
Tel: +39-02-274271 Fax: +39-02-27427554

Imer International S.p.A.
Localita= Salceto 55 û 53036 Poggibonsi (SI)
Tel: +39-0577-983300 Fax: +39-0577-983304

JCB S.p.A.
Via E. Fermi 16 û 20090 Assago (MI)
Tel: +39-02-4880374 Fax: +39-02-4880378

Liebherr Italia S.p.A.
Via Schiavetti 11 û 34074 Monfalcone (GO)
Tel: +39-0481-710901 Fax: +39-0481-484871

M.A.I.A. S.p.A.
Via Nomentana 995 û 00137 Roma
Tel: +39-06-82601 Fax: +39-06-927654

Manitou Costr. G. S.r.L.
Via E. Fermi 5, Villaggio Venturina û 41013 Castelfranco E. (MO)
Tel: +39-059-950511 Fax: +39-051-927654

O & K S.p.A.
Via F. da Desio 56 û 20083 Desio (MI)
Tel: +39-0362-624741 Fax: +39-0362-627768

Pel Job Italia
Via Giovanni da Udine 34 û 20156 Milano
Tel: +39-02-38093222 Fax: +39-02-38003305

Rammit S.r.L.
Via Cancelliera 33 û 00040 Ariccia (Roma)
Tel: +39-06-9344029 Fax: +39-06-9344315

Vermeer Italia S.r.L.
Via E. Natta 21 û 37026 Settimo di Pescantina (VR)
Tel: +39-045-6702625 Fax: +39-045-6702220

TRADE PROMOTION OPPORTUNITIES

The following trade exhibitions in Italy feature earthmoving machinery:

SAIE - International Building Exhibition
Date: October 13-17, 2004 (an annual exhibition)
Site: Bologna
Organizer: Bolognafiere
Viale della Fiera 20 - 40128 Bologna
Tel: +39-051-282111 Fax: +39-051-282332
E-mail: dir.gen@bolognafiere.it
http://www.Bolognafiere.it

The Commercial Service Office at the U.S. Consulate in Florence organizes a U.S. Pavilion at SAIE every year. To obtain additional information, please contact Barbara Lapini at U.S. Consulate, Lungarno Amerigo Vespucci 38, 50123 Firenze, Italy (tel: +39-055-211-676; fax: +39-055-283-780; e-mail: Florence.Office.Box@mail.doc.gov).

SAMOTER - International Earthmoving and Building Machinery Exhibition
Date: March 3-7, 2004 (held every three years)
Site: Verona
Organizer: Veronafiere
Viale del Lavoro 8 - C.P. 525 - 37135 Verona
Tel: +39-045-8298201 Fax: +39-045-8298237
E-mail: info@veronafiere.it
http://www.veronafiere.it

E-COMMERCE

Italy is the world's sixth largest industrialized economy and Europe's fourth largest market for the information and communications technology (ICT) industry. Although some structural problems still hinder the full evolution of the Italian ICT market, the growth of the ICT sector there is accelerating, following the pattern of other countries in Europe.

The convergence between information technology and telecommunications, and the availability of new technologies underpin the great potential of the Italian ICT market.

The market for Internet and related services boomed in 2004, and both Business-to-Business and Business-to-Consumer e-commerce applications took off. E-commerce is expected to become one of the most dynamic and fastest growing segments in the next three years, thanks to improved access infrastructure and to new Italian government plans for accelerating ICT acceptance and e-commerce adoption.

The need for specialized skills to implement e-business strategies is leading Italian companies to resort to external consulting, and excellent opportunities exist for American e-commerce integrators and service providers offering the strategy, marketing, design, and technical services associated with building advanced e-commerce sites.

The domestic market relies heavily on the expertise of foreign companies, and U.S. firms account for 80 percent of the revenues of foreign-owned establishments. As U.S. technological expertise is highly regarded, and U.S. advancements in the e-commerce sector are widely recognized, excellent opportunities exist for specialized U.S. computer services companies. The greatest opportunities for success are for American companies offering innovative and sophisticated services, and willing to team up in cooperative agreements with well-established local firms.

Sources utilized: No official statistics are available in Italy on the Internet and e-business/e-commerce applications. The estimates and forecasts indicated are based on interviews, information from trade sources, and reports from the trade associations ASSINFORM, ASSINTEL, AIIP and EITO, and from the market research organizations Net Consulting, Gartner Group, Databank Consulting, IDC, SIRMI, MATE, and Osservatorio Bocconi.

A. MARKET HIGHLIGHTS AND BEST PROSPECTS

1. MARKET PROFILE
The Italian ICT market is still lagging behind other European countries, but it is rapidly catching up, with Italian companies increasingly investing in ICT technologies.

2004 represented a turning point for the Italian Internet market. The number of business and domestic Internet users showed explosive growth, pushed by the availability of improved access technologies, new subscription options, free Internet access and strong advertising campaigns by all the main providers.

As a result, a market for e-business services and e-commerce applications is rapidly developing and all trade sources concur that it will boom in the next two years.

In 2004, the total Italian market for computer software was estimated at $3.2 billion, an increase of 10.9 percent over 1998, while the market for computer services was estimated at $7.7 billion, an increase of 13.7 percent over 1998. Although there are no official statistics, trade sources estimate that expenditures for e-business/ e-commerce related software and consulting services might have reached $500 million in 2004. These expenditures could double in value in the year 2000, reaching $1 billion. The relative weight of professional services will continue to grow and is expected to represent over 50 percent of the market value by the year 2001.

The total market value for both Business-to-Business (B2B) and Business-to-Consumer (B2C) e-commerce transactions in Italy was estimated at approximately $360 million in 1998, and soared to over $1.1 billion in 2004. It is expected to reach $4.3 billion in the year 2000, and close to $8 billion in 2001.

The main factors fueling the development of e-commerce in Italy are expected to be: 1) increasing recognition of e-commerce as a means to provide better support to customers and suppliers; 2) improved consumer protection legislation; 3) Italian legislation which recognizes the legal validity of digital signatures and digital contracts; 4) agreements between Italian banks and credit card operators to introduce Secure Electronic Transaction (SET) protocol; 5) Italian government programs to accelerate the development of a New Economy culture, especially among Small-and Medium-sized Enterprises (SMEs); 6) a mobile phone diffusion among the highest in the world, which will enable both the business and consumer segments to take advantage of WAP technologies for e-commerce transactions.

INTERNET PENETRATION IN THE BUSINESS COMMUNITY

1.5 million Italian businesses were estimated to be connected to the Internet at the end of 2004 -- out of a total of 3.4 million. They are expected to surpass 2 million by the end of 2001. All businesses are forecasted to be connected by the year 2003. Recent market surveys indicate that over 90 percent of Italian companies having more than 100 employees are connected to the Internet, while this rate decreases to 70 percent for SMEs with between 10 and 100 employees.

Within the framework of the European Union eEurope 2002 Initiative, the Italian government has recently approved an Action Plan to accelerate the diffusion of the New Information and Communication Technology (NICT) in the Italian economy. $650 million was allocated for the year 2000 to promote NICT in private companies and schools, and over $165 million was allocated to promote electronic commerce and new technologies in the textile, apparel, and shoe-making sectors. Trade associations, major organizations and local governments are also actively promoting initiatives to foster innovation and to promote e-commerce among SMEs by offering them hosting solutions for both B2B and B2C e-commerce applications (malls, virtual marketplaces, portals, etc.).

Many of the approximately 180,000 Italian companies with a web site still utilize it only to create brand awareness, offer product information, and generate leads, but this is rapidly changing. The evolution of organizational business models and strategies has created the need for increased interaction with suppliers and customers. A growing number of large and medium sized companies are investing heavily in Intranet/Extranet infrastructure and are implementing web sales and purchasing applications.

The growing complexity of network technologies and the need for specialized skills to implement e-business strategies is leading large and medium-sized businesses increasingly to resort to outsourcing services to supplement their in-house capabilities. It is expected that American e-commerce integrators and service providers will play a key role in providing the strategy, marketing, design, and technical services associated with building advanced e-commerce sites.

BUSINESS-TO-BUSINESS TRANSACTIONS

Business-to-business transactions are expected to produce a dramatic impact on the Italian economy, similarly to what is happening in other countries. According to IDC, the total market value for B2B e-commerce transactions in Italy passed from approximately $290 million in 1998 to over $970 million in 2004. It is expected to reach $4 billion in the year 2000, and $7 billion in 2001.

The most active players focusing on the implementation of B2B solutions are the telecommunications sector, the financial sector and the manufacturing sector.

Virtually all major Italian industrial groups are organizing for e-procurement, and it is predicted that in three years time at least half of all company purchases will be via e-procurement. The giant automotive manufacturer Fiat has made major investments in Fast Buyer - - an e-procurement company formed jointly with General Motors - - and it is also discussing joining the mega-portal Covisint, together with GM, Ford and Daimler-Chrysler. Other major cases of e-procurement are represented by ENEL, the recently privatized power utility, which has joined forces with 12 European power and water utilities, and by the giant tire manufacturer Pirelli, which will be part of the marketplace RubberNetwork.com together with 5 other major international tire manufacturers.

Other B2B portals and marketplaces becoming increasingly important include the sites for the Italian design furniture sector (www.arenafurniture.com), for the transportation and logistics sector (www.infologistic@.it), for the pharmaceutical sector (www.pharmaidea.com), and for the packaging/plastics/printing sector (www.trhubnet.com). Some relevant B2B programs are also being developed by a few major apparel manufacturers for on-line stock control and on-line ordering. Good examples of industry-to-industry trading communities for SMEs are found at www.i2i.com, www.consorzioprisma.it, www.biztob.it, and www.cooplink.it.

INTERNET PENETRATION IN THE CONSUMER MARKET
Internet subscriptions in the consumer segment grew from 540,000 in 1998 to over 3.7 million in 2004, mainly thanks to the availability of free internet access. The relatively low diffusion of personal computers (approximately 25 percent of Italian families now have one) has represented one of the major obstacles to the development of the Internet consumer market and of business-to-consumer e-commerce transactions. High telephone tariffs and cultural factors have also hindered faster development of this market segment.

Free Internet access, new Italian government investments to foster ICT and have all Italian schools connected to the Internet by 2001, the increasing availability of inexpensive personal computers and set-top-boxes, and the decreasing costs of Internet-related telephone calls are all acting as a strong driving force for the development of the sector. More importantly, as mobile phone diffusion in Italy is among the highest in the world, the Internet consumer market is expected to be driven by the availability of web-enabled WAP mobile phones, which should allow Italy to catch up quickly.

BUSINESS-TO-CONSUMER TRANSACTIONS
Business-to-consumer transactions via the Internet have been marginal in Italy, but are forecasted to grow at a very high rate in the next two years. They were estimated at $70 million in 1998, and at $195 million in 2004, but are expected to reach $350 million in 2000, $890 million in 2001 and $3.8 billion in 2002.

The most promising sectors for B2C in Italy are computers and software, publishing, internet music and videos, and bookings for entertainment events, vacation and travel. The media and publishing sector is increasing IT outlays to develop B2C solutions. Some of the most successful sites in Italy are www.Zivago.com for the purchase of books and records, www.chl.it for the purchase of computers, www.lastminutetours.it for the purchase of tickets and vacation packages, and the general portals www.goitaly.com, www.ciaoweb.it, www.kataweb.it, and www.jumpy.it. Successful sites aimed at the sale of Italian consumer goods abroad are www.best-of-italy.com, www.dolcevita.com, www.TheBestRaffaello.com.

FINANCIAL SERVICES

On-line trading of financial services took off in 2004, totaling 4 percent of all traded securities, a share that is forecast to increase to 20 or 30 percent in the next two to three years. It is expected that the number of clients utilizing on-line trading services will grow from 200,000 in the year 2000, to 450,000 in 2001, and to 700,000 in 2002. Total investments in stocks and bonds are expected to increase from $4 million in the year 2000, to $11.5 million in 2001 and to $19 million in 2002. The possibility of accessing financial markets through new generation WAP cellular phones is considered the major driving force. Banks are investing considerable resources in e-commerce applications both to sell their own home and corporate banking services, and to support the e-business strategies of their clients by developing virtual malls and vertical portals and by supporting them with secure transactions.

E-GOVERNMENT

A very important E-Government Action Plan, calling for an investment of $1.3 billion, was presented by the Italian government in June 2000. Its goal is to offer higher levels of efficiency, integrated and higher quality public services, and Internet access to information and services to all citizens. Following are the actions which will be taken: a nation-wide Extranet will connect all central and local government networks; specific portals will be created for accessing to the different services; one million electronic cards will be issued to allow easier access to public services; digital signature acceptance will be widely promoted and utilized; and e-procurement at central and local government levels will become a priority.

ICT PROFILE

Although Italy is still lagging behind other European countries in the ICT sector, it is rapidly closing the gap. Italian companies are increasingly investing in ICT technologies, now recognized as a means for strategic innovation to implement business process re-engineering, improve communications and expand the company's client base. The increasing convergence between information technology and telecommunications and the availability of new technologies increase the potential of the Italian ICT market.

According to ASSINFORM, the Italian Association of Computer and Office Machine Manufacturers, the total Italian market for information technology in 2004 reached sales of $17.9 billion, a 10.6 percent increase over 1998, while sales in the telecommunications sector – including equipment and services -were over $34.8 billion, a 14.6 percent increase over 1998.

The installed base of computer hardware in Italy at the end of 2004 was estimated at 3,970 mainframes, 247,000 mini-computers, 111,000 workstations, and 7.7 million Personal Computers. Approximately 6.2 million PCs were connected on-line. PCs sold in 2004 were 2,365,000 (an increase of 21.3 percent in units), of which 115,500 were PC servers (an increase of 31.3 percent over 1998, due to their extensive use for Internet and e-mail applications), 1,840,000 were desktops (an increase of 18.4 percent), and 409,500 were portables (an increase of 33 percent.). 640,000 units were sold to consumers, which represented 27.1 percent of the total market.

TELECOM INFRASTRUCTURE

Italy is the world's sixth largest market for basic telecommunications services and the fifth largest market for telecommunications equipment. The recent liberalization of the Italian telecommunications sector, with the end of the monopoly on fixed network voice transmission on January 1, 1998, has had a profound impact on both demand and supply, attracting new operators and increasing the client base.

There are now approximately 50 fixed telephony operators in Italy. The major ones are Telecom Italia, Infostrada, Albacom, Wind, Tiscali, MCI-WorldCom, COLT, and Cable & Wireless. Telecom Italia (TI) owns and operates the only existing publicly available fixed telecom network, consisting of approximately 27 million digital lines. In addition, there are three other private networks, owned by major industrial and utility companies and leased to telecom carriers as an alternative to Telecom Italia.

The arrival in Italy of new telecom service providers and the exponential growth of the Internet are resulting in major investments to upgrade and expand telecommunications infrastructure. The adoption of ISDN and Frame Relay technologies is becoming more prevalent, and major ISPs are investing heavily in ATM technologies. At the end of 2004, TI and other telecom operators started to provide Internet access through ADSL technology, and TI expects to sign 100,000 subscriber contracts over the next twelve months.

There are four mobile phone operators, which are TIM (TI group), Omnitel, Wind and Blu. Five licenses to operate the new generation UMTS mobile telephones will soon be awarded. Internet access providers and content/service providers number about 900, with over 3,000 Points of Presence (POP). The major operators are TIN, I.Net, Tiscali, Infostrada, Albacom, and Galactica.

At the end of 2004 there were 30 million active users of cellular telephones in Italy, equal to a penetration rate of 53 percent of the population, compared with an average of 40 percent for the rest of Europe. The number of mobile phones in Italy is expected to grow to 35 million in the year 2000, and to 40 million in 2001.

SECURITY AND PAYMENT TECHNOLOGIES

Security is one of the major concerns of Italian companies and consumers for e-commerce transactions. Presently, e-commerce security is not regulated by specific laws, and companies resort to firewalls and secure protocols, such as Secure Sockets Layer (SSL), digital certificates, and Secure Electronic Transaction (SET). Italian legislation recognizes the legal validity of digital signatures and digital contracts. The extended use of digital signatures is expected to reinforce the level of trust in e-commerce transactions and to accelerate the diffusion of e-business in the Italian economic system. Italian legislation fully complies with EU consumer protection directives with regard to specific information that an e-commerce site must provide, and sets rigid privacy protection requirements for the opening of an e-commerce site.

BEST SALES PROSPECTS

The development of E-business in Italy will create superb opportunities for companies specializing in this sector. Consulting services to assist the customer in developing an e-business strategy and custom development services for e-commerce applications in the areas of marketing, sales, post-sales, and purchasing are expected to boom in the next two years.

The need for customized vertically-oriented business solutions is also expected to create new opportunities for service companies. In particular, most promising application areas include on-line financial services, on-line trading services, on-line centralized and local administration services, on-line health care services, tax services, insurance services, and multimedia publishing.

Forecasts indicate that outsourcing services will represent one of the fastest growing market segments. Hosting services, transaction and purchasing processing, management of sales orders and distribution, customer service and security are expected to register the highest growth.

B. COMPETITIVE ANALYSIS

1. Market position of locally-owned establishments

It is estimated that locally-owned companies hold approximately 50 percent of the e-business/e-commerce related market for software and consulting services, amounting to approximately $250M in 2004, and $500M in the year 2000.

Some of the most important Italian companies offering e-commerce solutions include:
InterBusiness and Telecom Italia Net (TIN), offering Internet access and e-commerce services respectively to the business and to the consumer markets, both controlled by Telecom Italia;
I.Net, exclusively oriented to the business market, controlled by the information services company Etnoteam and by British Telecom;
Tiscali, the second largest ISP in Europe, which has just acquired the Dutch company World Online.
IT.Net, specialized in Internet access and services to the business market, recently acquired by the fixed and mobile telecom operator Wind (controlled by the Italian electric utility company ENEL, Deutsche Telecom and France Telecom).

Several new telecom operators offering Internet access also provide e-commerce related services directly. Among the most important are Albacom, a joint venture between the major Italian bank Banca Nazionale del Lavoro (BNL), British Telecom, the giant oil and gas conglomerate ENI and the Italian entertainment conglomerate Mediaset; and Wind, which is a partner of Nokia and of the on-line bank ImiWebTrader providing Italy's first on-line trading service from WAP phones.

All the most important Italian software and service companies offer e-commerce related services. They include: Gruppo Finsiel, the large software and services group controlled by Telecom Italia; Elsag Bailey (part of the Finmeccanica group); Datamat Ingegneria dei Sistemi; Gruppo Formula; Etnoteam, which controls the ISP I.Net; Gruppo Engineering; Datitalia Processing; Zucchetti, and several others.

Among the most important Italian companies specialized in Web site development with e-commerce capabilities there are Matrix, controlled by Seat, the Yellow Pages company of Telecom Italy, and by the publishing company DeAgostini; GLAMM and Inferentia.

THIRD COUNTRY COMPETITORS

E-Business/e-commerce related software and services offered by foreign-owned establishments represent about 50 percent of the total Italian market. Sales of non-U.S. companies were estimated at approximately $75 million in 2004 and are expected to hit $150 million in the year 2000.

The importance of foreign companies in this sector is forecast to remain high in the next three years. Many foreign computer hardware and software vendors and service companies are already present in the Italian market through subsidiaries. They include the French companies Bull, Atos, and Sema, the German firm SAP and Siemens, and the Dutch firm Getronics.

Major foreign ISPs and telecom operators offering Internet access and e-commerce services include:

Infostrada, formerly a joint venture between Olivetti and the German Mannesman, and now totally controlled by the British firm Vodafone;
IUNet, specialized in the business market, also controlled by Infostrada;
Flashnet, recently acquired by the multinational Cybernet Internet Services International, Inc.
City of London Telecommunications (COLT Telecom), focusing on the financial sector in the Milan area;
Cable & Wireless (U.K.);
Global One, controlled by Sprint, Deutsche Telecom and France Telecom;
Unisource Italia;
Swisscom (Switzerland).

U.S. MARKET POSITION

U.S. services companies dominate the market, holding approximately 70 percent of the total revenues of foreign- owned establishments. U.S. sales were estimated at $175 million in 2004. They are expected to reach $350 million in the year 2000.

Several U.S. consulting and services companies are already strongly positioned in the Italian market. They include the giant EDS group; Andersen Consulting; GE Information Services; Cap Gemini Ernst & Young; KPMG; and Price Waterhouse Coopers.

All the leading U.S. information and communications technology firms - IBM, Compaq, Hewlett Packard, Sun Microsystems, Microsoft, Novell, Lucent Technologies, Cisco Systems, 3COM, etc. - are directly present in Italy through subsidiaries or branch offices.

WorldCom Italia, together with UUNet/MCI and Sprint, is the major U.S. telecom company offering Internet services in Italy.

Good opportunities exist for other highly specialized U.S. computer services companies with specific vertical market experience. They should be willing to partner with well- established Italian firms for cooperative agreements. As U.S. technological expertise is highly regarded, and U.S. advancements in the Internet sector are also widely recognized, the United States is expected to increase its already excellent market position over the next three years.

Competitive Factors

Solid financial and organizational structure, a high degree of professionalism, proven knowledge of innovative technologies, business reputation, and business references are key factors for a supplier's success in Italy. Availability and integrability of high- quality solutions, adherence to industry standards, vertical market experience, reliable pre-sales and after-sales service, training and timely delivery have also become crucial to ensuring customer satisfaction.

A crucial factor for new-to-market U.S. firms is also the ability to understand the structure of the Italian market and the user culture, and to communicate constantly with clients. It is essential for suppliers to understand and analyze customer needs fully and possess the necessary skills and flexibility to offer new value-added, integrated solutions.

END-USER ANALYSIS

The industrial sector is the most important end-user for e-business/e-commerce related services. Larger companies are investing in e-business projects and require the assistance of specialized consulting firms that can supplement their own internal resources.

The media and publishing sector (newspapers, magazines, and television) is highly interested in e-business solutions and has a relatively strong presence on the Internet. This sector is expected to become one of the most important clients/providers of Internet services over the medium term. Major Italian publishers aim at managing important portal sites, which should bring growing advertising revenues in the medium term.

The banking/financing and insurance sectors have started to invest in Internet solutions and e-commerce projects. As applications such as home banking and on-line financial and insurance services develop, Internet- and Intranet-related computer and network services are expected to be in great demand. Information technology and telecommunications will continue to play a key role in supporting the strategies of banks, financial institutions, and insurance companies to improve productivity and profitability.

The public administration sector (at both the national and local government levels) is also an important prospective client for the services market. As mentioned, the perceived need to reach higher levels of efficiency and to offer higher quality public services will play a key role in the growth of the e-business/e-commerce sector. In particular, significant developments are expected in the fields of e-procurement, health care management and fiscal services.

By the year 2002 the Italian government aims to have all schools connected to the Internet, as provided for in the eEurope 2002 Initiative. Over 30 percent of all Italian schools currently have access to the Internet, including 60 percent of secondary schools nationwide and 85 percent of all schools in the Emilia-Romagna region. The city of Bologna (Emilia-Romagna's capital) has received international recognition for its innovative approach to encouraging Internet use. In 1995, the city began its "Iperbole" network and became the first city in the world to offer free access to the Internet to residents and institutions. In Italy, more than 1,100 Italian cities and towns now offer community interactive sites.

The retail and wholesale distribution systems are starting to invest in e-commerce applications and in intranet applications, and should represent a good potential market for service companies in the short to medium term.

MARKET ACCESS

1. Import Climate

The Italian climate for cooperative agreements and investment from U.S. companies is favorable. There are no trade barriers limiting the presence of foreign computer services companies in Italy. In fact, many multinational companies have established an office in Italy. In some cases, foreign computer services companies, usually specialized in vertical market niches, have reached agreements with well-established local companies or major end-users and have relocated personnel to Italy.

The main laws affecting the Internet in Italy are the "Bassanini" law, which recognizes the legal validity of digital signatures and digital contracts in electronic commerce applications; and the Legislative Decree on Commerce of March 1998, which improves consumer protection and identifies the responsibilities of Internet Service Providers, System Operators, and Content Providers. National legislation is basically in-line with EU directives, although several aspects are still considered "gray areas" and will be solved as the situation evolves.

A special Committee of the Italian Ministry of Industry is presently in charge of certifying electronic commerce sites.

The ISO-9000 certification for quality assurance is not mandatory in Italy. However, major Italian clients increasingly require that their suppliers be certified as a prerequisite for doing business with them. The Italian institute IMQ (Istituto Italiano Marchio Qualita'), which is part of EQNet (European Quality Systems Assessment and Certification Network), is the official local certifying agency for ISO-9000 in the information technology and software sectors.

2. Distribution/Business Practices

Major multinationals and large companies use their own direct networks and sales organizations.

U.S. firms which do not have a direct presence in Italy usually operate through locally appointed partners. These are well-established throughout the country, offer good pre-sales assistance and after-sales technical services, have experience in the different market sectors, and maintain person-to-person contact with customers. American companies interested in entering the Italian market should consider cooperative arrangements or joint ventures with carefully selected Italian partners.

3. Financing

Financing practices in this sector adhere to normal business and banking standards, with the majority of the transactions arranged through private agreements and banking institutions. U.S. companies should be aware that the turnaround time for paying invoices is almost always 90 days in Italy, but in many cases it may be as many as 120-180 days. The Italian public sector is very slow in paying its debts, sometimes taking more than a year. A certain degree of flexibility is considered normal in the establishment of terms and conditions.

KEY CONTACTS FOR THE INDUSTRY

1) Trade Associations

AIIP - ASSOCIAZIONE ITALIANA INTERNET PROVIDERS
Attn. Mr. Stefano Lamborghini, Secretary General
Via Bono Cairoli 34
20127 Milano
tel. 39/0347/4192974 - fax 39/02/48365460
segre@aiip.it, www.aiip.it

ASSINFORM - Association of Information and Communication Technology Companies
Attn. Mr. Paolo Gregotti, Secretary
Via Larga 23
20122 Milano
Tel. 39/02/58304141 Fax 39/02/58304457
www.assinform.it
Assinform@assinform.it

ANASIN - Italian Software Association
Attn. Mr. Franco Patini, Secretary General
Via Santa Tecla 4
20122 Milano
Phone: 39/02/862134 Fax 39/02/874259
www.anasin.it
(f.patini@anasin.it)

ASSINTEL - Italian Software Association (smaller companies)
Attn. Mr. Erminio Bianchi, Secretary General
Corso Venezia 47/49
20121 Milano
Phone: 39/02/7750231 Fax 39/02/7750413
www.assintel.it
assintel@assintel.it

COMMERCENET ITALY
Attn. Ms. Anna Maggi Deputy Secretary General
Corso C. Colombo 10
20144 Milano
Tel. 39/02/58106716 Fax 39/02/8358747
www.commercenet.it
info@commercenet.it

EUROBIT - European Association of Manufacturers of Business
Machines and Information Technology Industry
Lyoner Strasse 18
D-60528 Frankfurt/Main
Tel. 49/69/66031530 Fax 49/6966031510
http://www.eurobit.org
(It publishes the annual report "European Observatory" on the ICT market in Europe. The 2004 edition has a special chapter on Electronic Commerce in Europe)

2) STANDARDS AND CERTIFICATION INSTITUTES

IMQ - ISTITUTO ITALIANO DEL MARCHIO DI QUALITA'
Attn. Mr. Mario Niccolucci, Division Manager
Via Quintiliano 43
20138 Milano
Tel. 39/02/5073220 Fax 39/02/5073271
www.imq.it

CONCIT - Commissione Nazionale Coordinamento Information Technology
(Coordinating Committee for Information Technology Standards)
Attn. Mr. Giuseppe Pellegrino,Director
Viale Monza 259
20126 Milano
Tel. 39/02/257731 Fax 39/02/25773210
concit@ceiuni.it

3) ITALIAN GOVERNMENT CONTACTS

PALAZZO CHIGI
www.palazzochigi.it/fsi/eng (the official Italian government web site for the New Economy)

MINISTERO DELL'INDUSTRIA, DEL COMMERCIO E DELL'ARTIGIANATO
Via Molise 2
00187 Roma
Tel. 39/06/47051
www.minindustria.it/Osservatorio/pol_ce_engl.index/html (for Italian legislation on electronic commerce in English)
osservatorio.ecom@minindustria.it

4) European Legislation
The following list of web sites on regulatory issues is provided by EITO:
Consumer Protection:
www.oecd.org/dsti/sti/consumer/index.htm
www.echo.lu/legal/en/internet/internet/html
Security, including digital signatures, authentication, certification and encryption:
www.ispo.cec.be/eif/policy/97503toc.html
www.oecd.org/dsti/sti/it/secur/index.htm
Taxation:
www.oecd.org/dst/sti/it/ec/index.htm
www.ottawaoecdconference.org/english/homepage.html
Domain names and trademarks:
www.ispo.cec.be/eif/policy/governance
www.oecd.org/dsti/it/index.htm
Standards:
www.cenorm.be (this provides references to all other formal or informal standardization bodies)
Privacy:
www.ispo.cec.be/ecommerce/docs/personaldirective.pdf
europa.eu.int/comm/dg15/en/media/dataprot/index.htm
Liability, contract law and commercial communications:
europa.eu.int/comm/dg15/en/media/eleccomm/999.htm

5) MAJOR ITALIAN INTERNET SERVICE PROVIDERS

ALBACOM SPA
Via Tucidide 56
20134 Milano
Tel. 39/02/752921 Fax 39/02/75292778
www.albacom.it

ATS-FINITAL
Via Galileo Ferraris 216
52100 Arezzo
Tel. 39/0575/98561
www.ats.it

COMM2000
Via Leopardi 9
20123 Milano
Tel. 39/02/48009597 Fax 39/02/48013716
www.comm2000.it

INTERBUSINESS
www.interbusiness.it

ITALIA ON LINE (IOL)
Via Caldera 21
20153 Milano
Tel. 02/48201110
www.iol.it
info@iol.it

IT.NET
Via Greto di Comigliano 6
16152 Genova
Tel. 39/010/6503641
www.it.net

IU.NET
Via Lorenteggio 257
20147 Milano
www.iunet.it

NETTUNO
www.nettuno.it
consulenza@cineca.it

TELECOM ITALIA NET (TIN)
Via S. Dalmazzo 15
10122 Torino
Tel. 39/011/55141
www.tin.it

TISCALI SPA
Piazza del Carmine 22
09124 Cagliari
Tel. 39/070/46011 Fax 39/070/4601400
www.tiscali.it

6) MAJOR ITALIAN COMPANIES PROVIDING INTERNET SERVICES (PARTIAL LIST)

DATAMAT INGEGNERIA DEI SISTEMI SPA
Via Laurentina 760
00143 Roma
Tel. 39/06/50274702 Fax 39/06/50511407
www.datamat.it

ELSAG SPA
Via Puccini 2
16154 Genova
Tel. 39/010/65821
www.elsag.it

ENGINEERING SPA
Via dei Mille 56
00185 Roma RM
www.eng.it

ETNOTEAM SPA
Via Bono Cairoli 34
20127 Milano MI
Tel. 39/02/261621 Fax 39/02/2611755
www.etnoteam.it

FINSIEL SPA
Via Collatina 385
00155 Roma
Tel. 39/06/41422144 Fax 39/06/41422081
www.finsiel.it

GLAMM INTERACTIVE
Viale Corsica 7
20133 Milano
Tel. 39/02/7481171 Fax 39/02/74811726
www.glamm.it

GRUPPO FORMULA
Corso IV Novembre 57
10192 Cascine Vica TO
Tel. 39/011/9500500 Fax 39/011/9500555
www.formula.it

INFERENTIA SPA
Via Tacito 6
20137 Milano
Tel. 39/02/599281 Fax 39/02/59928221
www.inferentia.it
info@inferentia.it

MATRIX
Via Parini 14
20121 Milano
Tel. 39/02/290471 Fax 39/02/29047560
www.matrix.it

ZUCCHETTI.COM
Corso Vittorio Emanuele 21
26900 Lodi
Tel. +39/0371/594623
Fax +39/0371/421779
dimarco@zucchetti.com
www.zucchetti.com

7) TRADE PUBLICATIONS (PARTIAL LIST)

COMPUTERWORLD ITALIA
IDG Communications
Via Malipiero 14
20138 Milano
Tel. 39/02/580381 Fax 39/02/58011670
computerworld@idg.it
Circulation: 26,000

LINEA EDP
Gruppo Editoriale Agepe - Div. Alfa Linea
Via Rosso di San Secondo 1/3
20134 Milano
Tel. 39/02/215621 Fax 39/02/70120032
ledp@alfalinea.iunet.it
Circulation: 40,000

NETWORK NEWS ITALIA
Gruppo Editoriale Jackson
Via Gorki 69
20092 Cinisello Balsamo MI
Tel. 39/02/660341 Fax 39/02/66034238
nn@jackson.it
Circulation: 22,000

NETWORKING ITALIA
IDG Communications
Via Malipiero 14
20138 Milano
Tel. 39/02/580381 Fax 39/02/58011670
networking@idg.it
Circulation: 13,500

OFFICE AUTOMATION
SOIEL International
Via Martiri Oscuri 3
20125 Milano
Tel. 39/02/26148855 Fax 39/02/26149333
soiel.int@pn.itinet.it
Circulation: 14,500

SISTEMI DI TELECOMUNICAZIONI
Edizioni IENS
Via Taramelli 19
20124 Milano
Tel. 39/02/6085837 Fax 39/02/6072078
Circulation: 11,000

ZEROUNO
Mondadori Informatica
Centro Dir. Milano Oltre, Pal. Mantegna
Via Cassanese 224
20090 Segrate (Milano)
Tel. 39/02/216221 Fax 39/02/21622275
uberti@mondadori.it
Circulation: 18,000

8) MARKET RESEARCH COMPANIES

DATABANK CONSULTING
Mr. Franco Morganti, President
Corso Italia 8
20122 Milano
Tel. 39/2/721071 Fax 39/0272107402
www.databank.it-bbc

GARTNER GROUP
Via Caldera 21
20153 Milano
Tel. 39/02625291
fax 39/02/48289389
www.gartner.com

MATE SRL
Mr. Daniele Gerundino, Managing Director
Corso C. Colombo 10
20144 Milano
Tel. 39/2/8394414 Fax 39/2/8358747
mate@mate.it

NET CONSULTING
Mr. Giancarlo Capitani , Director
Via Leopardi 14
20123 Milano
Tel. 39/02/4392901

SIRMI SPA
Mr. Maurizio Cuzari, Managing Director
Piazza Castello 4
20121 Milano
Tel. 39/2/876541 Fax 39/2/876985
maurizio.cuzari@sirmi.it

9) LAW FIRMS SPECIALIZING IN INTERNET ISSUES

BROSIO, CASATI & ASSOCIATI – ALLEN & OVERY
Via Manzoni 43
20121 Milano
Tel. 39/02/29010200 Fax 39/02/29049333
www.bc-a.it
bca.law.mi@allenovery.com

STUDIO ASSOCIATO (part of the KPMG Group)
Via Vittor Pisani 27
20124 Milano
Tel. 39/02/676441 Fax 39/02/67644758

STUDIO TABELLINI
Via Donizetti 20
20122 Milano
Tel. 39/02/76013601 Fax 0276013044

STUDIO LEGALE ASSOCIATO MUNARI & GATTI
Piazza Castello 13
20121 Milano
Tel. +39/02/860154 Fax +39/02/809447 mungat@planet.it

TRADE PROMOTION OPPORTUNITIES

SMAU
The most important Italian information technology and telecommunications show. Held in Milan every year in October. Next edition: October 19-October 23, 2000 - October 18-22, 2001. Close to 3,000 exhibitors, of which 1,100 represented foreign companies - 500,000 visitors. Organizer: SMAU-COMUFFICIO, Attn. Ms. Maura Gritti, International Marketing Manager – Via Merano 18, 20127 Milano - Tel. 39/02/28313-251, fax 39/02/28313-470, maura.gritti@smau.it, www.smau.it

For the seventh consecutive year, the Commercial Service of the U.S. Department of Commerce in Italy will organize a U.S. Pavilion at the SMAU show. For further information please contact:

U.S. Department of Commerce
Commercial Service
Attn. Ms. Maria Andrews, Principal Commercial Officer
Via Principe Amedeo 2
20121 Milan, Italy
Tel. 39/2/6592260 Fax 39/2/6596561
www.usatrade.gov
Milan Office Box@mail.doc.gov

U.S. DEPARTMENT OF COMMERCE SERVICES

The offices of the Commercial Service in Italy offer U.S. companies the Gold Key Service, a program tailored to the needs of business executives travelling to Italy and looking for distributors or partners. The CS staff identifies, selects, and sets up appointments with Italian key contacts in the specific sector of interest. For information, please contact:

American Embassy Rome
Commercial Service
Via Vittorio Veneto 119/A
00187 Roma
Tel. 39/06/4674-2382
Fax. 39/06/4674-2113

INTERNET SECURITY

The Italian information and communication technology (ICT) market is still lagging behind other European countries, but it is rapidly catching up, with Italian companies increasingly investing in ICT technologies.

The Italian market for Internet and related services boomed in 2004, and both Business-to-Business and Business-to-Consumer e-commerce applications took off. E-commerce is expected to become one of the most dynamic and fastest growing segments in the next three years, thanks to improved access infrastructure and to new Italian government plans for accelerating ICT acceptance and e-commerce adoption.

The "culture" of ICT and Internet security in Italy is still at an embryonic level, but is it expected to develop rapidly. There is still significant resistance at the managerial level to approve specific investments for ICT and Internet security plans, but the situation is changing rapidly. Companies are increasingly relying on intrusion detection systems, more secure networking equipment, firewall software and equipment, secure content control software, internet access control tools, and security authentication, authorization and administration tools. Security management policies and management support applications are also being widely implemented.

The need for specialized skills to implement internet security strategies is leading Italian companies to depend on external consulting, and excellent opportunities exist for American service providers offering the strategy, marketing, design, and technical products and services associated with building a secure internet environment.

The domestic market relies heavily on the expertise of foreign companies, and U.S. firms account for 80 percent of the revenues of foreign-owned establishments in Italy. As U.S. technological expertise is highly regarded, and U.S. advancements in the internet security sector are widely recognized, excellent opportunities exist for specialized U.S. computer services companies. The greatest opportunities for success are for American companies offering innovative and sophisticated services, and willing to team up in cooperative agreements with well-established local firms.

Sources utilized: No official statistics are available in Italy on the Internet and e-business/e-commerce applications. The estimates and forecasts indicated are based on interviews, information from trade sources, and reports from the trade associations ASSINFORM, ASSINTEL, and EITO, and from the market research organizations Net Consulting, Gartner Group, Databank Consulting, IDC, SIRMI, and Osservatorio Bocconi.

MARKET HIGHLIGHTS AND BEST PROSPECTS

1. MARKET PROFILE

THE INTERNET SECURITY MARKET

Italy is the world's sixth largest industrialized economy and Europe's fourth largest market for the information and communications technology (ICT) industry. Although some structural problems still hinder the full evolution of the Italian ICT market, the growth of the ICT sector is accelerating, following the pattern of other countries in Western Europe. Italian companies are increasingly investing in ICT solutions as a means to implement renewed business strategies and face the challenges of the new Web Economy.

The total Italian market for information technology in 2004 reached sales of $17.9 billion, a 10.6 percent increase over 1998, while sales in the telecommunications sector - including equipment and services -were more than $ 34.8 billion, a 14.6 percent increase over 1998. It is estimated that in the year 2000 ICT market revenues totaled $ 59 billion, a growth of 12.5 percent.

The "culture" of ICT and Internet security in Italy is still at an embryonic level, but is it expected to develop rapidly. Many Italian companies still lack a systematic approach to security issues in terms of prevention, identification and monitoring the existing security measures. There is still a significant resistance at the managerial level to approve specific investments for ICT and Internet security plans, especially if the company has not suffered from, or has not become aware of, direct security attacks. In many companies the top management has started to develop some security awareness and to perceive security as a core business requirement, but only after the latest worldwide cyber attacks and e-mail diffusion of viruses were widely publicized. Security, however, becomes one of the major concerns of Italian companies and consumers when it comes to e-commerce transactions and possible payment fraud.

According to the 2nd Report on ICT Crimes from the Italian Sicurforum Association, a sample of 200 Italian companies and public organizations in 2004 revealed number of attacks to ICT systems grew by 242 percent from 1998. Virus attacks represented 32.8 percent of the total, followed by theft of machines with data (15.6 percent), unauthorized data access (11.6 percent), unauthorized use (11.6 percent), unauthorized changes (8.9 percent), unauthorized access to telecom services (8.6 percent), and denial of service attacks (8.3 percent). Two thirds of the attacks were attributed to external sources, and the remaining third to internal staff. The number of attacks is projected to increase as internet usage develops.

No specific statistics are available on the Italian Internet security market, but trade sources estimate that Internet related expenditures to support intranet/extranet and electronic commerce solutions in Italy were $ 1.6 billion in 2004 and reached $ 2.7 billion in the year 2000.

The diffusion of IP based network platforms is fueling an increased demand for internet security services and solutions from Italian companies. A growing number of large and medium sized Italian businesses are investing heavily in Intranet/Extranet infrastructure and are implementing web sales and purchasing applications to meet their needs for improved interaction with suppliers and customers. All major industrial groups are also organizing for e-procurement. Companies are increasingly resorting to intrusion detection systems, more secure networking equipment, firewall software and equipment, secure content control software (anti-virus and malicious code detection), internet access control tools, and security authentication, authorization and administration tools. Security management policies and management support applications are also being widely implemented. The adoption of Virtual Private Networks is still at an early stage, and the use of biometrics has not started yet.

Telecom security will represent a special market driver, as a result of the extraordinary development of the Italian telecom infrastructure market and of the increased demand for network management systems. Telecom security encompasses software solutions that allow network monitoring and fraud detection. IDC estimates that telecom security expenditures in Italy grew from $ 2.5 million in 1998, to $ 7.5 in 2004, to $ 11.3 in the year 2000. They are expected to reach $ 15 million in 2001, $ 19.3 million in 2002, $ 21.7 million in 2003, and $ 24.3 million in 2004.

Another major market driver for the internet security sector will be increased investments of the Italian government in ICT technologies, and the related demand for security technologies, especially certification authority services and digital signature related services. An important e-government action plan, calling for an investment of $1.3 billion, has recently been approved by the Italian government within the framework of the European Union's E-Europe program. It aims to offer higher levels of efficiency, integrated and higher quality public services, and Internet access to information and services for all citizens. Among the actions being taken are the creation of a nation-wide extranet, which will connect and integrate all central and local government networks; the creation of specific portals for accessing different government services; issuance of one million electronic ID cards/smart cards to allow easier access to public services; adoption of e-procurement at the central and local government levels; and countrywide promotion and use of digital signatures.

These actions will be made possible by the final implementation of the so-called "Bassanini" law of 1997 and subsequent related decrees and notes, that recognize and set the standards for the legal validity of digital contracts and digital signatures based on the public key infrastructure system. Digital signatures will be utilized as an important support tool to simplify bureaucratic procedures, and their extended use is expected to reinforce the level of trust in e-commerce transactions and to accelerate the diffusion of e-business in the Italian economy.

Internet security products and solutions will also be in high demand in on-line banking and on-line trading of financial services. Banks are investing considerable resources in e-commerce applications both to sell their own home and corporate banking services, and to support the e-business strategies of their clients by developing virtual malls and portals and by supporting secure transactions. The on-line trading market took off in 2004, totaling 4 percent of all traded securities, a share that is forecast to increase to 20 or 30 percent in the next two to three years. It is expected that the number of clients utilizing on-line trading services will grow from 200,000 in the year 2000, to 450,000 in 2001, and to 700,000 in 2002. Total investments in stocks and bonds are expected to increase from $4 million in the year 2000, to $11.5 million in 2001 and to $19 million in 2002. The possibility of accessing financial markets through new generation cellular phones will contribute greatly to the development of this market, and demand for specially developed smart cards should increase.

As the use of the internet becomes pervasive, the Internet security market will develop immensely, and will offer excellent opportunities to American companies providing innovative security solutions and services.

The growing complexity of technologies is leading Italian companies to depend increasingly on external service providers to supplement their in-house capabilities, and to operate efficiently and cost-effectively. It is expected that U.S. firms will play a key role in providing the strategy, marketing, design, and technical products and services associated with building a secure internet environment in Italy.

INTERNET PENETRATION

After a slow start, since 2004 Internet usage is experiencing explosive growth. The number of business and domestic Internet users is booming: Internet users were estimated at approximately 12 million at the end of 2000, projected to reach 29 million by 2003. This growth is pushed by the availability of improved access infrastructure, new subscription options, free Internet access and new Italian government plans for accelerating ICT acceptance and e-commerce adoption.

According to recent surveys, 1.5 million Italian businesses were connected to the Internet at the end of the year 2000 -- out of a total of 3.4 million - and 300,000 of them had a web site. Connected companies are expected to surpass 2 million by the end of 2001, and to become the totality by the year 2003. Many small and medium sized enterprises are less inclined to innovate and have yet to invest in the Net.

In the consumer segment, Internet subscriptions grew from 540,000 in 1998 to over 3.7 million in 2004, and to an estimated 4.5 million in the year 2000. Sales of PCs for home use are expanding and approximately 32.5 percent of Italian households now have one. Mobile phone diffusion in Italy is among the highest in the world, and the Internet consumer market will be driven by the availability of web-enabled new-generation mobile phones.

E-COMMERCE

The total market value for e-commerce transactions in Italy was estimated at over $1.1 billion in 2004 and at $4.3 billion in the year 2000. It is projected to register revenues of close to $8 billion in 2001 and to reach over $ 50 billion by 2003. According to IDC, Web buyers are projected to increase from 960,000 in 2004 to 9.8 million in 2003.

B2B e-commerce transactions passed from an estimated $ 970 million in 2004 to $ 4 billion in the year 2000, while B2C transactions went from $195 million in 2004 to $350 million in 2000. They are expected to reach respectively $7 billion and $ 890 million in 2001, and $ 38.5 billion and $ 11.5 billion in 2003, with the relative weight of B2B transactions growing constantly.

The main factors fueling the development of e-commerce in Italy are expected to be: 1) increasing recognition of e-commerce as a means to provide better support to customers and suppliers; 2) improved consumer protection legislation; 3) Italian government legislation that recognizes the legal validity of digital signatures and digital contracts; 4) agreements between Italian banks and credit card operators to introduce Secure Electronic Transaction (SET) protocol; 5) Italian government programs to accelerate the development of a new economy culture, and initiatives of trade associations, major organizations and local governments to foster innovation and to promote e-commerce, especially among small-and medium-sized enterprises; 6) mobile phone diffusion among the highest in the world, which will enable both the business and consumer segments to take advantage of new technologies for e-commerce transactions.

ITALIAN LEGISLATION RELATED TO INTERNET SECURITY

Italian legislation is basically in-line with EU directives, although several aspects are still considered "gray areas" and will be solved as the situation evolves.

As mentioned, Italian legislation recognizes the legal validity of digital signatures and digital contracts through the so-called "Bassanini" law and subsequent related decrees and notes. This set of laws and decrees establishes the criteria and methodology for the development, filing, transmission, duplication, reproduction and validation of electronic documents. AIPA, the Information Technology Authority for the Public Administration, will maintain a list of Certification Authorities, which can be public or private organizations meeting specific reliability requirements. To date, AIPA has granted certification authority to the following eight companies: SIA - Societa' Interbancaria per l'Automazione/Cedborsa, SSB-Societa' per i Servizi Bancari, BNL Multiservizi, InfoCamere, Finital, Saritel, Postecom and Seceti. These companies have joined into the trade association Assocertificatori.

Italian legislation fully complies with EU consumer protection directives with regard to the specific information an e-commerce site must provide, and sets rigid privacy protection requirements for the opening of an e-commerce site. The Legislative Decree on Commerce of March 1998 improves consumer protection and identifies the responsibilities of internet service providers, system operators, and content providers. A special committee of the Italian Ministry of Industry is presently in charge of certifying electronic commerce sites.

BEST SALES PROSPECTS

Intrusion detection systems, secure networking equipment, firewall software and equipment, secure content control software (anti-virus and malicious code detection), security authentication, authorization and administration, PKI/CA, security monitoring and management services.

The development of e-business in Italy will create superb opportunities for companies specializing in Internet security. Consulting services to assist the customer in developing risk analysis and assessment and security management are expected to grow in the next two years. Forecasts indicate that outsourcing services will represent one of the fastest growing market segments.

COMPETITIVE ANALYSIS

1. Market position of locally-owned establishments
The trade association Federcomin and the market research company Net Consulting estimate that the number of Italian companies active in the Internet economy grew from approximately 3,330 in 2004 to more than 4,800 in the year 2000. Although no statistics exist for the Internet security market, trade sources estimate that locally owned companies hold approximately 40 percent of the Internet security market.

Some of the most important Italian companies offering internet security products and solutions include:

- Telecom Italia, the most important telephone operator which also offers internet access and e-commerce services;

- I.Net, exclusively oriented to the business market, controlled by the information services company Etnoteam and by British Telecom;

- IT.Net, specialized in Internet access and services to the business market, recently acquired by the fixed and mobile telecom operator Wind.

Several new telecom operators offering Internet access also provide internet security related services directly. Among the most important are 1)Albacom, a joint venture between the Italian bank Banca Nazionale del Lavoro (BNL), British Telecom, the giant oil and gas conglomerate ENI, and the Italian entertainment conglomerate Mediaset; 2) Wind, a partner of Nokia and the on-line bank ImiWebTrader to provide Italy's first on-line trading service from WAP phones; and 3) Infostrada, previously owned by Olivetti/Mannesman and then by Vodafone, and recently acquired by Wind.

All the most important Italian software and service companies offer security related products and services. They include: Gruppo Finsiel, the large software and services group controlled by Telecom Italia; Elsag (part of the Finmeccanica group); Datamat Ingegneria dei Sistemi; Gruppo Formula; Etnoteam, which controls the ISP I.Net; Engiweb.com of Gruppo Engineering; Intesis of the Finmatica Group; Mover, Siosistemi, Zucchetti, and several others.

2. Third Country Competitors

Internet security products and services offered by foreign-owned establishments represent about 60 percent of the total Italian market.

The importance of foreign companies in this sector is forecast to remain high in the next three years. Many foreign computer hardware and software vendors and service companies are already present in the Italian market through subsidiaries. They include the French companies Bull, Atos, Sema, and GFI, the German firm SAP and Siemens, the Belgian Ubizen, the British Marconi, and the Spanish Panda Software.

3. U.S. Market Position

U.S. companies dominate the Internet security market, and they are estimated to hold approximately 80 percent of the import market.

All the leading U.S. information and communications technology firms - Cisco Systems, Compaq, Computer Associates, Hewlett Packard, IBM, iPlanet, Lucent Technologies, Microsoft, Novell,, 3COM, etc. - are directly present in Italy through subsidiaries or branch offices. Specialized companies such as BMC Software, Check Point Software Technologies, ISS-Internet Security Systems, Network Associates, RSA Security, Symantec, and Verisign also have subsidiaries in Italy, and others such as Cyber IQ Systems, Entrust Technologies, and Rainbow Technologies are represented through Italian companies.

Several U.S. consulting and services companies are already strongly positioned in the Italian market. They include the EDS group; Accenture; GE Information Services; Cap Gemini Ernst & Young; KPMG; and Price Waterhouse Coopers.

Good opportunities exist for other highly specialized U.S. computer services companies with specific vertical market experience. They should be willing to partner with well-established Italian firms for cooperative agreements. As U.S. technological expertise is highly regarded, and U.S. advancements in the Internet security sector are also widely recognized, the United States is expected to increase its already excellent market position over the next three years.

4. Competitive Factors

Solid financial and organizational structure, a high degree of professionalism, proven knowledge of innovative technologies, business reputation, and business references are key factors for a supplier's success in Italy. Availability and integration of high-quality solutions, adherence to industry standards, vertical market experience, reliable pre-sales and after-sales service, training and timely delivery have also become crucial to ensuring customer satisfaction.

A crucial factor for new-to-market U.S. firms is to understand the structure of the Italian market and the user culture, and to communicate constantly with clients. It is essential for suppliers to understand and analyze customer needs fully and possess the necessary skills and flexibility to offer new value-added, integrated solutions.

END-USER ANALYSIS

The telecom sector is one of the most important end-users for internet security solutions and products. The arrival in Italy of new telecom service providers and the rapid growth of the Internet are resulting in major investments to upgrade and expand telecommunications infrastructure and to guarantee telecom security.

The manufacturing sector is also an excellent end-user. Larger companies are investing in Intranet/Extranet and e-business projects and require the assistance of specialized consulting firms that can supplement their own internal resources.

The banking/financing and insurance sectors have started to invest in Internet solutions and e-commerce projects. As applications such as home banking and on-line financial and insurance services develop, Internet- and Intranet-related computer and network services are expected to be in great demand. Information technology and telecommunications will continue to play a key role in supporting the strategies of banks, financial institutions, and insurance companies to improve productivity and profitability.

The public administration sector (at both the national and local government levels) is also an important prospective client for the services market. As mentioned, the need for higher levels of efficiency and to offer higher quality public services will play a key role in the growth of PKI/CA. Significant developments are expected in the fields of e-procurement, health care management and fiscal services.

MARKET ACCESS

1. Import Climate

The Italian climate for cooperative agreements and investment from U.S. companies is favorable. There are no trade barriers limiting the presence of foreign computer services companies in Italy. In fact, many multinational companies have established an office in Italy. In some cases, foreign computer services companies, usually specialized in vertical market niches, have reached agreements with well-established local companies or major end-users and have relocated personnel to Italy.

ISO-9000 certification for quality assurance is not mandatory in Italy. However, major Italian clients increasingly require that their suppliers be certified as a prerequisite for doing business with them. The Italian institute IMQ (Istituto Italiano Marchio Qualita'), which is part of EQNet (European Quality Systems Assessment and Certification Network), is the official local certifying agency for ISO-9000 in the information technology and software sectors.

2. Distribution/Business Practices

Major multinationals and large companies use their own direct networks and sales organizations. U.S. firms with no direct presence in Italy usually operate through locally appointed partners. These are well-established throughout the country, offer good pre-sales assistance and after-sales technical services, have experience in the different market sectors, and maintain person-to-person contact with customers. American companies interested in entering the Italian market should consider cooperative arrangements or joint ventures with carefully selected Italian partners.

3. Financing

Financing practices in this sector adhere to normal business and banking standards, with the majority of the transactions arranged through private agreements and banking institutions. U.S. companies should be aware that the turnaround time for paying invoices is almost always 90 days in Italy, but in many cases it may be as many as 120-180 days. The Italian public sector is very slow in paying its debts, sometimes taking more than a year. A certain degree of flexibility is considered normal in the establishment of terms and conditions.

4. Trade Promotion Opportunities

SMAU
The most important Italian information technology and telecommunications show. Held in Milan every year in October. Next edition: October 18-22, 2001. Over 3,000 exhibitors, of which 1,100 represented foreign companies - 500,000 visitors. Organizer: SMAU-COMUFFICIO, Attn. Ms. Maura Gritti, International Marketing Manager - Via Merano 18, 20127 Milano - Tel. 39/02/28313-251, fax 39/02/28313-470, maura.gritti@smau.it, www.smau.it

For the eighth consecutive year, the Commercial Service of the U.S. Department of Commerce in Italy will organize a U.S. Pavilion at the SMAU show. For further information please contact:

U.S. Department of Commerce
Commercial Service
Attn. Ms. Maria Andrews, Principal Commercial Officer
Via Principe Amedeo 2
20121 Milan, Italy

Tel. 39/2/6592260 Fax 39/2/6596561
www.usatrade.gov
Milan Office Box@mail.doc.gov

INTERNET SERVICES

Italy is the world's sixth largest industrialized economy and Europe's fourth largest market for the information and communications technology (ICT) industry. Although some structural problems still hinder the full evolution of the Italian ICT market, the growth of the ICT sector there is accelerating, following the pattern of other countries in Europe.

It is estimated that the total Italian market for information technology in 1998 reached sales of $15.3 billion, an 8.5 percent increase over 1997, while sales in the telecommunications sector were over $31 billion, an 11 percent increase over 1997.

The convergence between information technology and telecommunications and the availability of new technologies are underpinning the great potential of the Italian ICT market.

The market for Internet services is expected to become one of the most dynamic and fastest growing segments in the next three years. In 1998 it was estimated at $230 million. It is forecast to more than double to $520 million in 2004 and to reach $850 in the year 2000.

The complexity of technologies and the need for specialized skills is leading companies to resort to external consulting in order to plan, design, and implement their Internet-related strategies. Excellent opportunities are therefore anticipated for companies offering not only Internet access services, but also other specialized Internet services, such as Intranet/ Extranet related services, E-business services, outsourcing services and financial services.

The domestic market relies heavily on the expertise of foreign companies, and U.S. firms account for 80 percent of the revenues of foreign-owned establishments. As U.S. technological expertise is highly regarded, and U.S. advancements in the Internet sector are widely recognized, excellent opportunities exist for specialized U.S. computer services companies. The greatest opportunities for success are for American companies offering innovative and sophisticated services, and willing to team up in cooperative agreements with well-established local firms.

The Internet services covered in this report include Internet access, Web site design, hosting, housing; Internet/ intranet/extranet related design and consulting services (including capacity planning, network design, IP Virtual Private Networks, IP telephony, development of customized software and software maintenance); Internet and E-commerce application and integration services, and operations and outsourcing services; Internet-related network installation and management services; outsourcing services; and training services.

Sources utilized: No official statistics are available in Italy on Internet- and Intranet-related computer and network services. The estimates and forecasts indicated are based on interviews, information from trade sources, and reports from the trade associations ASSINFORM, ASSINTEL, AIIP and EITO, and from the market research organizations Gartner Group, Databank Consulting, IDC, SIRMI, MATE, and Osservatorio Bocconi.

MARKET HIGHLIGHTS AND BEST PROSPECTS

1. MARKET PROFILE

As in the rest of the world, the Internet has experienced exceptional growth also in Italy, albeit from a low base. As a result, a market for Internet services has developed, which is expected to become one of the most dynamic and fastest growing markets in the next three years. In 1998, the market was estimated at approximately $230 million, of which approximately $116 million represented Internet access services, $58 million web housing and hosting services, and $56 million professional services, such as consulting, design, and training.

Forecasts indicate that the market for services will more than double in 2004, reaching $520 million, and will then increase by over 60 percent in the year 2000, reaching $850 million. The relative weight of professional services will continue to grow and is expected to represent over 50 percent of the market value by the year 2000.

The complexity of technologies and the need for specialized skills is leading companies to resort to external consulting in order to plan, design, and implement their Internet-related strategies.

Excellent opportunities are therefore anticipated for companies offering not only Internet access services, but also specialized Internet services. In particular, the areas of major development are expected to be Intranet/Extranet related services, E-business services, outsourcing services and financial services.

ICT PROFILE

Although Italy is still lagging behind other European countries in the ICT sector, it is rapidly catching up. Italian companies are increasingly investing in ICT technologies, recognized as a means for strategic innovation to implement business process re-engineering, improve communications and expand the company's clients' base. The increasing convergence between information technology and telecommunications and the availability of new technologies are underpinning the potential of the Italian ICT market.

According to ASSINFORM, the Italian Association of Computer and Office Machine Manufacturers, which conducts an annual study in cooperation with Gartner Consulting, in 1998 the total Italian market for information technology reached sales of $15.3 billion, an 8.5 percent increase over 1997, while sales in the telecommunications sector were over $31 billion, an 11 percent increase over 1997.

Investments in the ICT sector in 1998 were heavily affected by Year 2000 projects, and represented 15.5 percent of total investments for machinery and equipment.

The installed base of computer hardware in Italy at the end of 1998 was estimated at 4,030 mainframes, 237,000 mini-computers, 104,000 workstations, and 6.6 million Personal Computers. PCs sold in 1998 were 1,950,000 (an increase of 22.3 percent in units), of which 85,000 were PC servers (an increase of 44.1 percent over 1997, due to their extensive use for Internet and e-mail applications), 1,570,000 were desktops (an increase of 23.5 percent), and 295,000 were portables (an increase of 22.3 percent.) PC penetration is estimated at 33 PCs every 100 employees, 11 PCs every 100 inhabitants, and 1 PC every 5 households.

Major hardware suppliers in Italy are AST, Compaq, Dell, Hewlett Packard, IBM, Sun Microsystems, Unisys, Siemens Nixdorf, and Bull. In the networking sector, among the leaders are Ascend, Cisco Systems, Lucent Technologies, Newbridge Networks, Novell and 3COM. In the software sector leaders are Microsoft, Oracle, IBM, Computer Associates, Hewlett Packard, Olivetti Wang Global and the local Elsag Bailey, Telesoft, Gruppo Engineering and Gruppo Datamat.

With regard to the telecommunications sector, Italy is the world's sixth largest market for basic telecommunications services and the fifth largest market for telecommunications equipment. The recent liberalization of the Italian telecommunications sector, with the end of the monopoly on fixed network voice transmission on January 1, 1998, has had a profound impact on both the demand and supply sides, attracting new operators and gaining new clients.

Telecom Italia, the former monopoly operator, was privatized in October 1997. In May 2004, the Italian Olivetti company acquired over 50 percent of its shares through a Public Purchase Offer. Over 40 companies, many of which are foreign, have obtained authorization from the Italian Ministry of Communications to
install and manage publicly accessible telecommunication networks and/or provide fixed voice telephony and data/image communications services, both at a national or local level. Most of the new entrants have

reached agreements on interconnections fees with Telecom Italia, which will enable them to be competitive and offer increasingly lower tariffs. Higher competition is already leading to lower prices and better quality of infrastructure and services and, as a result, to stronger demand.

There are presently four operators of mobile services in Italy. With a population of 58 million people, Italy has a penetration of mobile phones of over 43 percent, one of the highest in the world. Subscriptions to mobile services grew from 13 million in 1997 to 20.5 million at the end of 1998 (with 9 million new obile phones sold), to 25 million in July 2004.

The advent of new fixed and mobile telecom service providers is resulting in large investments for upgrading and expanding the Italian telecommunications infrastructure to meet the growing needs of the business and consumer community.

INTERNET PENETRATION

The use of the Internet in the Italian marketplace has evolved rapidly. In 1998, according to the Computer Industry Almanac, Italy ranked 9th in the world and 5th in Europe -- after the U.K., Germany, France and Sweden -- in terms of Internet utilization (it was 14th in the world in 1997). Independent market research sources estimate that Internet subscriptions in Italy in 1998 were 1.5 million, with 3 million users.

Recent market surveys indicate that close to 90 percent of Italian companies with more than 500 employees are connected to the Internet. This rate decreases to 73 percent for companies having between 100 and 500 employees, to 68 percent for companies having 51 to 100 employees, and to 60 percent for companies having 10 to 50 employees. By the year 2003, it is expected that all Italian firms will be connected to the Internet.

There are different estimates as to the number of Italian households connected to the Internet. The most conservative figure is 500,000 households, out of a total of 20.4 million, while other estimates indicate at least 1 million households. High telephone tariffs and cultural factors have hindered a faster development of this market segment. The Internet consumer market is expected to be driven by the increasing availability of inexpensive personal computers, set-top-boxes and eventually web-enabled mobile phones, by the possibility of accessing the Internet free-of-charge, and by the expected fall in the prices of Internet-related telephone calls.

The number of Internet access providers and Internet content and service providers has increased from about 150 in 1996 to about 900 in 2004, with over 3,000 Points of Presence (POP).

Registration of domain names in Italy has grown from 45 domains per day in 1997 to 120 in July 2004. The total number of domains under ".it" is close to 67,000. The number of hosts in ".it" is estimated at 500,000 units, while the number of Italian web servers is estimated at 75,000, of which one third is registered as ".com" or other international domains.

MOST PROMISING INTERNET SERVICES

INTRANET/EXTRANET SERVICES

In the next three years, demand for Internet services is forecast to be particularly driven by the increasing use of the Internet and of IP-based solutions to support Intranet and Extranet architectures.

The growing importance of computer networks, which have become the fundamental business infrastructure for most enterprises in Italy, is giving strong momentum to the use of Intranets. It is estimated that over 40% of the larger Italian companies utilize Internet as an Intranet company network. The evolution of organizational business models has created the need for upgrading intra- and inter-company communications and optimizing group work activities. Larger Italian companies are using Intranets as a means to connect branch offices, cross-functional teams and mobile workers spread throughout the country to their headquarters. Eventually, all of them will need to connect with their suppliers and with their clients, providing on-line customer support.

Market surveys estimate that over 50 percent of all Italian companies will have Intranets developed in the next three years, while Extranets are expected to develop at a slower pace. The adoption of ISDN and Frame Relay technologies is growing rapidly, while the full utilization of ATM technologies by Italian corporate users is expected to occur in the medium term.

The liberalization of the Italian telecommunications market is also causing a major increase in demand for internetworking IP-based solutions by telecommunications service providers and Internet Service Providers. New telecommunications entrants and over 100 major ISPs have heavily invested in ATM technologies, and growth prospects for the next three years are excellent.

The increasing availability of products and services to develop secure IP Virtual Private Networks (VPNs) should also represent another growth factor for internetworking over the Internet. The rapid growth of mobile communications and the availability of Web-enabled mobile phones, together with the growing need for voice/data integration, and, prospectively, for satellite communications is also anticipated to have a significant impact on this market segment.

High speed networks, together with the development of standards and protocols and other mechanisms to address security problems, are expected to play a key role in the expansion of IP-based internetworking in all sectors of Italian industry. This situation will create excellent opportunities for specialized Internet services companies.

The growing complexity of network technology and the need for specialized skills to implement an Internet/Intranet company strategy is leading large and medium-sized businesses increasingly to use external service providers to supplement their in-house capabilities. Outside services companies are forecast to play a key role in planning, designing, and implementing company-wide Internet/Intranet strategies, offering their analytical and programming skills related to Web-to-host integration, communications, addressing, and security issues. They are also expected to become key players in producing sophisticated Web sites, offering integrated graphic design, database knowledge, and marketing and advertising skills.

Internet related network management, technical assistance, and end-user training are other distinctive growing areas for firms specializing in Internet services.

ELECTRONIC BUSINESS SERVICES

Electronic commerce applications in Italy are still in their early stages. Most Italian companies still utilize their Web home pages to create brand awareness, offer product information and generate leads. It is estimated that only 15 percent of the companies have implemented web sales applications, and less than 10 percent have implemented web purchasing applications.

According to market sources, in 1998 only 300 Italian firms sold products and services through the net. The volume of transactions was estimated at $230 million, of which 75 percent was business-to-business. Approximately 40 percent of total sales through the net were made by Italian firms, and the balance by foreign suppliers.

All trade sources, however, concur that electronic commerce in Italy will boom in the next two years. The volume of transactions is expected to reach over $1 billion in 2004, quadrupling to close to $4 billion in the year 2000.

The main factors fueling this development are: 1) the increasing recognition of e-commerce as a means to provide better support to customers/suppliers; 2) recent Italian legislation which recognizes the legal validity of digital signatures and digital contracts; 3) improved consumer protection legislation; 4) and recent agreements between Italian banks and credit card operators to introduce the SET-Secure Electronic Transaction protocol.

In business-to-business e-commerce, the most successful sectors are expected to be computers and software, financial and banking services, and general procurement services by larger companies. In the business-to-consumer e-commerce, the most promising sectors are publishing, Internet music and videos, and bookings for entertainment events, vacation and travel.

The development of E-business in Italy will create superb opportunities for companies specializing in this sector. Consulting services to assist the customer in developing an e-business strategy and custom development services for e-commerce applications in the areas of marketing, sales, post-sales, and purchasing are expected to boom in the next two years.

OUTSOURCING SERVICES

Outsourcing services are also forecast to represent one of the fastest growing market segments. Hosting services, transaction and purchasing processing, management of sales orders and distribution, customer service and security are expected to register the highest growth.

OTHER INTERNET SERVICES

The need for customized vertically-oriented business solutions is also expected to create new opportunities for service companies. In particular, most promising application areas include home banking, on-line financial services, on-line trading services, on-line centralized and local administration services, on-line health care services, tax services, insurance services, and multimedia publishing. General information services to the residential and business markets, as well as employment information, are also expected to develop over the medium term.

BEST SALES PROSPECTS

- Integrated computer and network services for planning, designing, and implementing company-wide Internet/Intranet strategies
- Services integrating graphic design, database knowledge and marketing and advertising skills for the creation of sophisticated interactive Web sites
- E-business services
- Services for Internet-based applications of home banking, on-line financial services, on-line trading services, on-line centralized and local administration services, on-line health care services, fiscal services, insurance services, and multimedia publishing
- Outsourcing services
- Network management services
- Technical assistance services
- End-user training

KEY CONTACTS FOR THE INDUSTRY

1) Trade Associations

AIIP - ASSOCIAZIONE ITALIANA INTERNET PROVIDERS
Attn. Mr. Marco Barbuti, Secretary General
Via Bono Cairoli 34
20127 Milano
Tel. 39/2/409061 Fax 39/2/40906262
www.aiip.it

ASSINFORM - Association of Information and Communication Technology Companies
Attn. Mr. Federico Barilli, Director
Via Larga 23
20122 Milano
Tel. 39/02/58304141 Fax 39/02/58304457
http://www.assinform.it
mailto:Assinform@assinform.it

ANASIN - Italian Software Association
Attn. Mr. Alberto Tripi, Secretary General
Via Santa Tecla 4
20122 Milano
Phone: 39/02/862134 Fax 39/02/874259
www.anasin.it

ASSINTEL - Italian Software Association (smaller size companies)
Attn. Mr. Erminio Bianchi, Secretary General
Corso Venezia 47/49
20121 Milano
Phone: 39/02/7750231 Fax 39/02/7750413
http://www.assintel.it
mailto:assintel@assintel.it

COMMERCENET ITALY
Corso C. Colombo 10
20144 Milano
Tel. 39/02/58106716 Fax 39/02/8358747
http://www.commercenet.it
info@commercenet.it

EUROBIT - European Association of Manufacturers of Business
Machines and Information Technology Industry
Lyoner Strasse 18
D-60528 Frankfurt/Main
Tel. 49/69/66031530 Fax 49/6966031510
http://www.eurobit.org
(It publishes the annual report "European Observatory" on the ICT
market in Europe. The 2004 edition has a special chapter on
Electronic Commerce in Europe)

2) Standards and Certification Institutes

IMQ - ISTITUTO ITALIANO DEL MARCHIO DI QUALITA'
Attn. Mr. Mario Niccolucci, Division Manager
Via Quintiliano 43
20138 Milano
Tel. 39/02/5073220 Fax 39/02/5073271
http://www.imq.it

CONCIT - Commissione Nazionale Coordinamento Information Technology
(Coordinating Committee for Information Technology Standards)
Attn. Mr. Giuseppe Pellegrino,Director
Viale Monza 259
20126 Milano
Tel. 39/02/257731 Fax 39/02/25773210
mailto:Concit@ceiuni.it

3) Italian Government contacts

MINISTERO DELL'INDUSTRIA, DEL COMMERCIO E DELL'ARTIGIANATO
Via Molise 2
00187 Roma
Tel. 39/06/47051
http://www.minindustria.it/Osservatorio/pol_ce_engl/html
(for Italian legislation on electronic commerce in English)
mailto:osservatorio.ecom@minindustria.it

4) European Legislation
The following list of web sites on regulatory issues is provided by EITO:
Consumer Protection:
http://www.oecd.org/dsti/sti/consumer/index.htm;
http://www.echo.lu/legal/en/internet/internet/html
Security, including digital signatures, authentication, certification and encryption:
http://www.ispo.cec.be/eif/policy/97503toc.html
http://www.oecd.org/dsti/sti/it/secur/index.htm
Taxation:
http://www.oecd.org/dst/sti/it/ec/index.htm

http://www.ottawaoecdconference.org/english/homepage.html
Domain names and trademarks:
http://www.ispo.cec.be/eif/policy/governance
http://www.oecd.org/dsti/it/index.htm
Standards:
http://www.cenorm.be (this provides references to all other formal or informal standardization bodies)
Privacy:
http://www.ispo.cec.be/ecommerce/docs/personaldirective.pdf
europa.eu.int/comm/dg15/en/media/dataprot/index.htm
Liability, contract law and commercial communications:
europa.eu.int/comm/dg15/en/media/eleccomm/999.htm

5) Major Italian Internet Service Providers

ALBACOM SPA
Via Tucidide 56
20134 Milano
Tel. 39/02/752921 Fax 39/02/75292778
www.albacom.it

ATS-FINITAL
Via Galileo Ferraris 216
52100 Arezzo
Tel. 39/0575/98561
www.ats.it

COMM2000
Via Leopardi 9
20123 Milano
Tel. 39/02/48009597 Fax 39/02/48013716
www.comm2000.it

INTERBUSINESS
www.interbusiness.it

ITALIA ON LINE (IOL)
Via Caldera 21
20153 Milano
Tel. 02/48201110
http://www.iol.it
info@iol.it

IT.NET
Via Greto di Comigliano 6
16152 Genova
Tel. 39/010/6503641
http://www.it.net

IU.NET
Via Lorenteggio 257
20147 Milano
www.iunet.it

NETTUNO
http://www.nettuno.it
mailto:consulenza@cineca.it

TELECOM ITALIA NET (TIN)
Via S. Dalmazzo 15
10122 Torino
Tel. 39/011/55141
http://www.tin.it

TISCALI SPA
Piazza del Carmine 22
09124 Cagliari
Tel. 39/070/46011 Fax 39/070/4601400
www.tiscali.it

6) Major Italian companies providing Internet services

DATAMAT INGEGNERIA DEI SISTEMI SPA
Via Laurentina 760
00143 Roma
Tel. 39/06/50274702 Fax 39/06/50511407
http://www.datamat.it

ELSAG BAILEY
www.elsag.it

ENGINEERING SPA
Via dei Mille 56
00185 Roma RM
Tel. 06/522431 Fax 06/52243248

ETNOTEAM SPA
Via Bono Cairoli 34
20127 Milano MI
Tel. 39/02/261621 Fax 39/02/2611755
www.etnoteam.it

FINSIEL SPA
Via Collatina 385
00155 Roma
Tel. 39/06/41422144 Fax 39/06/41422081
http://www.finsiel.it

GLAMM INTERACTIVE
Viale Corsica 7
20133 Milano

Tel. 39/02/7481171 Fax 39/02/74811726
www.glamm.it

GRUPPO FORMULA
Corso IV Novembre 57
10192 Cascine Vica TO
Tel. 39/011/9500500 Fax 39/011/9500555
http://www.formula.it

GRUPPO SOPIN
Viale Antartide 8
00144 Roma
Tel. 39/06/5929341 Fax 39/06/5912762

INFERENTIA SPA
Via Tacito 6
20137 Milano
Tel. 39/02/599281 Fax 39/02/59928221
mailto:www.@inferentia.it
info@inferentia.it

MATRIX
Via Parini 14
20121 Milano
Tel. 39/02/290471 Fax 39/02/29047560
www.matrix.it

TELESOFT
Lungotevere R. Sanzio 9
00153 Roma
Tel. 39/06/5884381
www.tlsoft.it

ZUCCHETTI.COM
Corso Vittorio Emanuele 21
26900 Lodi
Tel. +39/0371/594623
Fax +39/0371/421779
dimarco@zucchetti.com
www.zucchetti.com

7) Trade Publications

COMPUTERWORLD ITALIA
IDG Communications
Via Malipiero 14
20138 Milano
Tel. 39/02/580381 Fax 39/02/58011670
computerworld@idg.it
Circulation: 26,000

LINEA EDP
Gruppo Editoriale Agepe - Div. Alfa Linea
Via Rosso di San Secondo 1/3
20134 Milano
Tel. 39/02/215621 Fax 39/02/70120032
ledp@alfalinea.iunet.it
Circulation: 40,000

NETWORK NEWS ITALIA
Gruppo Editoriale Jackson
Via Gorki 69
20092 Cinisello Balsamo MI
Tel. 39/02/660341 Fax 39/02/66034238
nn@jackson.it
Circulation: 22,000

NETWORKING ITALIA
IDG Communications
Via Malipiero 14
20138 Milano
Tel. 39/02/580381 Fax 39/02/58011670
networking@idg.it
Circulation: 13,500

OFFICE AUTOMATION
SOIEL International
Via Martiri Oscuri 3
20125 Milano
Tel. 39/02/26148855 Fax 39/02/26149333
soiel.int@pn.itinet.it
Circulation: 14,500

SISTEMI DI TELECOMUNICAZIONI
Edizioni IENS
Via Taramelli 19
20124 Milano
Tel. 39/02/6085837 Fax 39/02/6072078
Circulation: 11,000

ZEROUNO
Mondadori Informatica
Centro Dir. Milano Oltre, Pal. Mantegna
Via Cassanese 224
20090 Segrate (Milano)
Tel. 39/02/216221 Fax 39/02/21622275
uberti@mondadori.it
Circulation: 18,000

8) Market Research Companies

DATABANK CONSULTING
Mr. Franco Morganti, President
Corso Italia 8
20122 Milano
Tel. 39/2/721071 Fax 39/0272107402
http://www.databank.it-bbc

GARTNER CONSULTING
Mr. Giancarlo Capitani, Director
Via Caldera 21
20153 Milano
Tel. 39/02625291
fax 39/02/48289389
http://www.gartner.com

MATE SRL
Mr. Daniele Gerundino, Managing Director
Corso C. Colombo
20144 Milano
Tel. 39/2/8394414 Fax 39/2/8358747
mate@mate.it

SIRMI SPA
Mr. Maurizio Cuzari, Managing Director
Piazza Castello 4
20121 Milano
Tel. 39/2/876541 Fax 39/2/876985
mailto:maurizio.cuzari@sirmi.it

9) Law firms specializing in Internet issues (partial list)

BROSIO, CASATI & ASSOCIATI - ALLEN & OVERY
Via Manzoni 43
20121 Milano
Tel. 39/02/29010200 Fax 39/02/29049333
mailto:bca.law.mi@allenovery.com
www.bc-a.it

STUDIO ASSOCIATO (part of the KPMG Group)
Via Vittor Pisani 27
20124 Milano
Tel. 39/02/676441 Fax 39/02/67644758

STUDIO LEGALE ASSOCIATO MUNARI & GATTI
Piazza Castello 13
20121 Milano
Tel. +39/02/860154
Fax +39/02/809447
E-mail: mailto:mungat@planet.it

10) Trade Promotion Opportunities

SMAU
The most important Italian information technology and telecommunications show. Held in Milan every year in October. Next edition: September 30-October 4,2004. Over 2,200 exhibitors, of which 850 represented foreign companies - 360,000 visitors.
Organizer: SMAU-COMUFFICIO, Attn. Ms. Maura Gritti, International Marketing Manager - Via Merano 18, 20127 Milano - Tel. 39/02/28313-251, fax 39/02/28313-470,
mailto:maura.gritti@smau.it http://www.smau.it

For the sixth consecutive year, the Commercial Service of the U.S. Department of Commerce in Italy will organize a U.S. Pavilion at the SMAU show. For further information please contact:

U.S. Department of Commerce
Commercial Service
Attn. Ms. Maria Andrews, Principal Commercial Officer
Via Principe Amedeo 2 0121 Milan, Italy Tel. 39/2/6592260 Fax 39/2/6596561
www.usis.it/fcs
Milan Office Box@mail.doc.gov

THE ITALIAN DEFENSE MARKET

Italy is in the midst of a major restructuring of its armed forces, which should result in a gradual shift from the current draft system to a totally new professional volunteer Army over a five year span. The figure regarding the proposed budget for 2001 have been published by the local press. The total Ministry of Defense (MOD) funding request is 34.234 trillion Italian lira ($16.5 billion), up from 32.845 trillion lira requested in 2000, and represents 1.46 percent of Italian GDP. This overall 4.2 percent increase is higher than expected by experts who felt the current center-left government would not seek to increase the budget, or at most, would request a very modest increase to keep pace with inflation. Of this budget, approximately $12 billion is earmarked for national defense, and $ 4 billion is for domestic security.

The Italian defense industry, still partly government owned, is moving toward privatization. However the Italian Government will likely retain significant shares in this important sector. Efforts are being undertaken to streamline both management and workforce structures, increase manufacturing efficency and improve general perceptions of product quality and capabilities. Industrial and defense general staff strategies are to decrease dependence on the products of other nations for major weapons system production and to improve in-house capabilities whenever and wherever possible. Emphasis is also being placed on European partnerships for weapons system and sub-system component R&D and production, often with Italy receiving a major workshare. Expectations are that Italian defense industry will be largely privatized in the next few years. However, to achieve state-of-the-art capability in most advanced areas, Italy will continue to depend on cooperation with its allies.

The overall 2001 defense budget estimate breaks down as follows:

CATEGORY	2001 BUDGET ($ BILLION)
Defense Function	11.6
(Army)	(4.2)
(Navy)	(2.3)
(Air Force)	(3.4)
(Joint)	(1.7)
Carabinieri	3.6
External Functions	0.2
Pensions	0.9

The defense function, which includes the budget of the Army, Navy and Air Force, is the largest element of MOD funding and is further divided as follows:

CATEGORY	2001 BUDGET ($ BILLION)
Personnel	5.5
Operations	3.2
Capital	2.9

Nearly $3 billion will be appropriated for routine goods and services such as repair parts, armaments and ammunitions, quartermaster supplies, motorized vehicles, fuels, infrastructures and engineering works, health and various miscellaneous items. This capital account is further divided into the following:

CATEGORY	2001 BUDGET ($ BILLION)
R&D	0.3
Modernization/Replacement	2.4
Infrastructure	0.2

INVESTMENT PROGRAM

Investment in modernization is rather modest, especially considering the reduced buying power stemming from inflation and currency devaluation. However, this figure does not reflect the significant contribution to new weapons programs via the Ministry of Industry. To optimize resources, the Italian Government is concentrating on a few high-priority items:

-- Substituting F-104 and Tornado fighter aircraft with the new Eurofighter aircraft
-- Building the Horizon frigate with France.
-- Developing the Medium Extended Air Defense System (MEADS) cooperative program with Germany and the United States.
-- Purchasing the new C-130J transport aircraft.
-- Procuring 200 Ariete tanks and developing the Ariete 2.
-- Acquiring U-212 new generation submarines from Germany.
-- Buying FSAF anti-missile defense system, for the Army and Navy.
-- Purchasing EH-101 and NH-90 helicopters.
-- Acquiring Sicral/post Sicral satellite communication.
-- Continuing Satellite reconnaissance projects Cosmo/Skymed with France.

These projects will require an average annual investment of $ 4.5 billion up to 2010.

DEFENSE OPPORTUNITIES

Italy has worked with both U.S. and European suppliers in the past and is open to foreign manufacturers, particularly those offering Italian participation in research and new technologies. Competition from major European suppliers is getting stronger, as greater political emphasis is being given to "European solutions". It is important to note that, for the next 10 years, aerospace defense systems will dominate the Italian military acquisition budget. Most defense sector business opportunities fall within the areas of aviation, communications/electronics, command and control systems, avionics, advanced composite manufacturing, advanced electronics, advanced munitions and computer software and simulation technologies. High demand exists for improved munitions and all varieties of simulation programs. Logistics systems that increase force survivability and sustainability in remote territory are being heavily considered for future funding.

1. POTENTIAL UPGRADE, REPLACEMENT, SPARE PARTS, MAINTENANCE, LOGISTICS AND SERVICE OPPORTUNITIES

Usual budget constraints are influencing decisions on new systems production and development. Presently, plans to upgrade battle tanks, personnel carriers, artillery and howitzer systems, air defense systems, fighter aircraft, communication platforms, anti-tank systems, small arms and some rotor wings aircraft are being evaluated. In the meantime, new systems continue in development and are nearing production. There is a continuing requirement to provide spare parts for a number of existing U.S. manufactured weapon systems. Italy is developing an improved munition manufacturing capability (i.e. OTO Breda); however, some opportunities still exist for the supply of new main tank gun ammunition, artillery munitions, air defense munitions, propellants, small arms ammunitions, etc. The above mentioned need for new logistic sustainment system is an open area. Systems ranging from logistics management to heavy transports (although Fiat Iveco represents a very strong competitor) to fuels distribution are needed and are being considered as emerging requirements. Italy has long depended on a mix of U.S. and European products; however, the emphasis is shifting to European, especially Italian production. In fact, to gain approval, virtually every program must include some employment generation in Italy, and especially in Southern Italy, where the unimployment rate reaches in some areas 30%. Therefore, teaming agreements as well as licensed production are highly recommended.

2. New Systems/Major Platforms

Italy is on the verge of fielding a new main battle tank, attack helicopter, improved howitzers, personnel carrier, heavy equipment transport, jet trainer, jet fighter, and new anti-radar missiles. It is also about to deploy improved air combat maneuver instrumentation system, new anti-armor systems, an advanced command and control system, improved communication systems and the latest global positioning system (GPS) equipment. Italy has recently developed manufacturing capability in advanced composites, ceramics and electronics but is not yet self-sufficient in these areas.

3. MOD Defense Plan

The transition from a mainly conscript force to a professional volunteer force envisaged in the new defense model will hopefully result in cost savings in individual training and susteinance thus allowing greater expenditures for modernization and unit training. The MOD is said to be dedicated to promoting domestic weapons production and manufacturing, but not at the expense of modernization. Parliament reportedly is often disposed to put domestic industrial base considerations above modernization.

The logistics structure has been overhauled to improve out-of-country susteinability. Emphasis is shifting from the traditional role of national defense within borders to international security. This shift in focus is driving weapon systems evaluation and forcing changes in organizational structures. Future weapons systems must be capable of a variety of roles and functions, while being reliable and easy to maintain. In the coming years, the MOD will seek to expand communications and space-based capabilities, and improve crew protection and system survivability in more conventional systems. GPS, electro-optical and laser-related systems are in demand to improve weapons delivery and battlefield identification systems. There is also strong political will for peacekeeping and standoff precision strike capabilities.

MARKET ACCESS/PROCUREMENT

Italian MOD requirements are developed and refined in much the same manner as in the United States, including the process of obtaining funding authorizations. Once a program has been approved for acquisition, the MOD's procurement executive acts as the principal agency responsible for competition. However, actual procurements are executed by the technical procuring agencies within Segredifesa. U.S. firms looking for guidance on Italian MOD procurement procedures, should contact the office of Segretariato Generale, Via XX Settembre 123, 00100 Roma. This office will provide information on the MOD's main procurement offices and identify major Italian contractors for teaming or sub-contracting opportunities. Additionally, valuable information on bidding and contract procedures is found in the monthly publication "Bollettino del Contratto" (Contracts Bulletin), which lists all upcoming and executed procurements by procuring agency. This bulletin is published in both English and Italian and is available by subscription.

Usually, the MOD will only fund developmental costs for major weapons systems programs, while programs that involve Italian firms will receive Ministry of Industry (MOI) funding. Recently the MOD has often opted for already developed solutions and "off-the-shelf" products, capitalizing on contractor or agency funded developments, this method being more economical and timely. Quite often, a deciding factor is whether the program will involve a significant workshare for Italy, licensed production for Italy, or a teaming arrangement with an Italian firm.

Firm fixed price contracts are generally preferred by the Italian MOD, as this term fits better MOD's budget requirements; however, other contracts can be negotiated depending on the nature of the acquisition. Bid packets usually include all necessary technical specifications and contract information. Contracting procedures are generally similar to those in the United States, however, they frequently take longer to execute, sometimes two or more years from the date of bid acceptance, and the price is considered firm until the contract is finalized. Government to Government Foreign Military Sales (FMS) transactions are often preferred because of supposed economies of scale and financing by the U.S. Government.

Offset requirements can play an important role and it is useful to understand how public procurement rules are administered. Generally speaking, 100 percent offset is theoretically required for all major bids. However, this rule is not always strict and terms are at times negotiated, granting forms of co-production or reaching other ad hoc agreements.

There are sometimes considerable barriers to U.S. contractors; however, teaming with an Italian partner can help overcome such problems. It is often easier if the prime contractor or significant partner is an Italian entity.

As in the United States, the prime contractor is responsible for subcontractor selection and quality controls. The MOD normally will not interfere with the primecontractor-subcontractor relationship, but competition among subcontractors is encouraged. Contract administration is normally performed by the procuring agency, whose staffs are assisted by quality assurance and technical/financial personnel.

DOMESTIC DEFENSE SUPPLIERS

A complete listing of Italian defense suppliers can be found in the publication "Chi & dov'e' la Difesa Italiana". Copies can be obtained for approximately $70 from Gruppo Editoriale Publi & Consult SpA, Via Tagliamento 29, 00198 Roma, or from Trade Media International Corp., 1328 Broadway, New York, N.Y. 10001-2190. Another source is "Italian Defense Industry Directory" from Ritade, Viale Liegi, 44 00100 Roma.

MAJOR ITALIAN DEFENSE SUPPLIERS

Aircraft and Avionics

Aerea SpA
Via Cefalonia 18
20156 Milano
tel: 39 02 38000218
fax: 39 02 33402676
e-mail: aerea@tin.it

Aermacchi SpA
Via Ing. P. Foresio 1
21040 Venegono Superiore (VA)
tel: 39 0331 813111
fax: 39 0331 827595
e-mail: info@aermachhi.it
www.aermacchi.it

Alenia Aerospazio
Via G.V. Bona 85
00156 Roma
tel: 39 06 417231
fax: 39 06 4114439
www.aleniaerospazio.com

Alenia Difesa
Via S. Alessandro 6/10
00131 Roma
tel: 39 06 418831
fax: 39 06 41883800
www.aleniadifesa.finmeccanica.it

Calzoni SpA
Via Emilia Ponente 72
40133 Bologna
tel: 39 051 4130662
fax: 39 051 4130655
e-mail: mktdca@rivacalzoni.it
www.rivacalzoni.it

Fiat Avio SpA
Via Nizza 312
10127 Torino
tel: 39 011 6858111
fax: 39 011 6859832

Meteor Cae
Zona Industriale Soleschiano
34077
Ronchi dei Legionari (TS)
tel: 39 0481 479300

Arms, Missiles and Munitions

Alenia Difesa
Divisione Otobreda
Via Valdilocchi 15
19136 La Spezia
tel: 39 0187 581111
fax: 39 0187 582669

BPD Difesa e Spazio
Corso Garibaldi 22
00034 Colleferro (RM)
tel: 39 06 97291

Luigi Franchi SpA
Via del Serpente 12
25131 Brescia
tel: 39 030 2687311
fax: 39 030 3581554
e-mail: info@franchi.com
www.franchi.com

Oerlikon Contraves SpA
Via Affile 102
00131 Roma
tel: 39 06 43611
fax: 39 06 4130830
www.oerlikoncontraves.com

Pietro Beretta SpA
Via P. Beretta 18
25063 Gardone Val Trompia (BS)
tel: 39 030 83411
fax: 39 030 8341421
www.beretta.com

Electronics

Elettronica SpA
Via Tiburtina Km 13,700
00131 Roma
tel: 39 06 41541
fax: 39 06 4154923

GTE Telecomunicazioni SpA
Viale Europa 46
20093 Cologno Monzese (MI)
tel: 39 02 25131

Naval Vessels

Fincantieri SpA
Via Genova 1
34100 Trieste
tel: 39 040 3193111
fax: 39 040 3192305
www.fincantieri.com

Vehicles

Astra SpA
Via Caorsana
29100 Piacenza
tel: 39 0523 5431
fax: 39 0523 591773

Fiat Iveco
Via Puglia 35
10156 Torino
tel: 39 011 23911
www.iveco.com

PROGRAM MANAGERS FOR ITALIAN MOD

Food, Clothing, Field Equipment, Furniture and Fittings, Mobile Logistics, BZB Solutions

COMMISERVIZI
Piazza della Marina 4
00196 Roma
tel: 39 06 36805663

Space, Aircraft, Helicopters, Weapons Systems, Avionics, Missiles, Logistics

ARMAEREO
Viale dell'Universita' 4
00185 Roma
tel: 39 06 4958346

MEDICINES, MEDICAL ACCESSORIES, SANITARY FITTINGS

DIFESAN
Via S. Stefano Rotondo, 4
00100 Roma
tel: 39 06 7591533

CONSTRUCTION AND MAINTENANCE OF FACILITIES, BRIDGING AND BOATS, MINES, POWER GENERATION, CAMOUFLAGE, DEMOLITIONS

GENIODIFE
Palazzo Marina, Via Lungo Tevere delle Navi
00100 Roma
tel: 39 06 3603904

Armored Vehicles, Wheeled Vehicles, Petroleum, Oil & Lubricants, Ground Weapon Systems, Rockets & Missiles, Ammunitions

TERRARM
Via Marsala 104
00100 Roma
tel: 39 06 4750605

SHIPS AND NAVAL COMBAT SYSTEMS

NAVARM
Ministero della Difesa
Piazza della Marina 4
00196 Roma
tel: 39 06 36804018

RADAR SYSTEMS, TELECOMMUNICATION SYSTEMS, NAVIGATIONAL AIDS & COMPUTERS

TELEDIFE
Viale dell'Universita' 4
00185 Roma
tel: 39 06 49865258

DENTAL EQUIPMENT AND SUPPLIES

The Italian dental equipment and supplies market, valued at $680 million, has experienced sustained growth over the past ten years. Dental hygiene and prevention campaigns have exposed the younger genera tion to dental education from an early age. Regular visits to the dentist is becoming a way of life and pro-capita spending is likely to exceed that of the preceding generation. There is also increasing demand for new technologies and services from labor atories and practitioners for costly replacement work to older, and more affluent customers.

The State, through the National Health Plan, is committed to providing free health services. However, as far as dental care is concerned, this is done only nomi nally and at a level that is generally considered unsatisfactory. Largely as a consequence of this situation, recourse to the private sector for dental services is extensive.

Italy is a strong producer of dental instruments and orthodontics accessories and equipment in the low-to-medium range. France and Germany are the leading exporters of tools and instruments. American high-tech instruments and equipment, special alloys a nd amalgams have an excellent reputation and it is still possible for U.S. producers to gain a position in the market.

The industry and the distribution systems are fairly fragmented, with over 50 percent of importers employing less than 15 people and with average sales lower than $5 million. Dental equipment is channeled through highly specialized distributors (85 percent handle exclusively dental equipment and supplies) and is directed primarily to dentists (57 percent) and to dental laboratories (40 percent).

MARKET HIGHLIGHTS & BEST PROSPECTS

Italy has a population of 57.5 million (1996 data), the world=s lowest birthrate (0.2 percent), and one of the highest percentages of elderly citizens in Europe. Beginning in the sixties, the country has undergone considerable economic and
social changes. Formerly a predominantly agricultural economy, it is now the world's fifth industrial power. However, during 1998, Italy's economy grew at a l.4 percent rate, one of the lowest levels in the industrialized world.

There are uncertainties about other countries as well, motivated by the slowdown of major economic powers and especially by the lower-than-expected growth in the German economy, Italy's major trading partner. This may affect investment in capital equipment, including in dental equipment, and reduce patients' expenditure on all but the most basic and urgent treatment.

Despite the current slowdown, there remain many opportunities to expand the market. There is increasing demand for new technologies and services to assist laboratories and practitioners provide costly replacement work to older and more
affluent customers. With the younger generation exposed to dental education from an early age, regular visits to the dentist is becoming a way of life and pro-capita spending, mostly in services, is likely to exceed that of the preceding generation.

The dental market is estimated at $680 million and is the second-largest in Europe. The sector covers laboratory equipment, furniture and fixtures, instruments and tools, alloys and amalgams. (See Market Breakdown table)

Italy is a strong producer and exporter of laboratory furniture and equipment in the low to medium range. It imports hand tools and electrical and electronic instruments, dental pharmaceuticals, alloys and amalgams. Continuing growth is forecast in high -tech instruments and equipment, and in innovative chemicals, alloys and specialized pharmaceuticals. The sale of dental equipment is channeled through highly specialized distributors (85 percent handle exclusively dental equipment and supplies) and is directed primarily to dentists (57%) and dental laboratories (40%).

While Italy's dental market is the second-largest in Europe, Italy nonetheless lags behind the most sophisticated industrial countries in terms of expenditure. The National Health Servi ce provides free medical care to all residents, with varying degrees of success. State-funded dental care, from the point of view of facilities, range of treatment and quality is generally considered unsatisfactory and taken advantage by only a small percentage of citizens. Medical insurance is relatively new to Italy and insurance companies that provide dental coverage are extremely rare. The fact that dental treatment has to be paid for by the patient is a powerful deterrent: 48 percent of Italians visit their dentists once a year, and 39 admit to never doing so.

BEST SALES PROSPECTS

H.S. Codes

3006 Dental fillings, dental cements, dental hygiene preparations
3407 Dental wax, dental impression compounds
9013 Laser-fitted appliances and electrodiagnostic
equipment
9018 Dental drills, instruments and appliance

9021 Dentures, denture fixatives
9042 Dentists'chairs, dental furniture.

B.1) STATISTICAL DATA (US DOLS MILLIONS)

	Year 1998	Year 2004	Year 2000
Import Market	190	196	204
Local Production	590	619	632
Exports	100	108	117
Total Market	680	707	719
Imports from US:	23	25	28

Exchange rate: $1 equals 1737 lire in 1998; est. to equal 1760 lire in 2004; est. to equal 1760 lire in 2000
Future Inflation Rate Assumed: 1.2 percent
1998 Import Market Share (percent for USA and major competitors):
USA: 12; Germany: 52; Switzerland 13; France: 8; Great Britain 5

COMPETITIVE ANALYSIS

Italy is a strong producer of dental mechanical equipment, laboratory furniture and fixtures in the low to medium range. (It exports about 50% of its production mainly to other European countries). The sector reflects the manufacturing makeup of the country and consists for the most part of myriad small to medium size companies. Few large manufacturers specialize in dental equipment and they consider it a sideline to their surgical and medical instrumentation range. Notable exceptions are Castellini S.p.A. of Bologna and ASEG Galloni S.p.A. of Milan. A number of U.S. subsidiaries (3M and Ethicon) have been manufacturing and marketing successfully in Italy for several years.

THIRD COUNTRY IMPORTS

Italian production of dental mechanical, laboratory furniture and fixtures has reached substantial levels and foreign competitors only find favorable market conditions if their products surpass local quality. A large share of imports consists of consumables and laboratory products and specialized metal instruments. Newcomers to the market may find only small niches. Overall, x-ray apparatus, advanced chemical products, precision instruments, and those lines that reflect innovative technology find good markets. Amalgams and special alloys also have potential.

Germany leads the field in terms of ultraviolet and infrared apparatus, dental drills and instruments. Switzerland and France export small surgical equipment and supplies, Great Britain supplies electrodiagnostic instruments.

U.S. MARKET POSITION

The U.S. appears to have lost some presence in the local market to European Union competition although it is reasonable to assume that a portion of EU imports include products from European subsidiaries of U.S. companies. U.S. imports are concentrated in high-quality syringes, suture needles, catheters, electrodiagnostic apparatus and dental instruments, which together represent 88 percent of total imports from the United States.

According to Italian importers, U.S.-made equipment has a better reputation than European-made equipment but European firms offer the best and quickest after-sale service. Despite the high quality of American products, dentists are likely to turn to the European market for highly technical appliances if the importer has no repair facilities in Italy. The elimination of tariffs among European Union members has altered the market for U.S. suppliers who need to review their export prices in order to stay competitive.

END-USER ANALYSIS

According to 1996 data, Italy's population was 57.5 million, with deaths exceeding births. Italy has the lowest population growth rate (0.2 percent) and one of the highest percentages of elderly citizens in Europe: Italian senior citizens (over 65 years of age) currently represent 16.8 percent of the population. 1.5 million immigrants are estimated to reside illegally in Italy. The latter are not entitled to Social benefits but emergency treatment at no cost is available.

MARKET ACCESS

Import Climate

Italy does not impose restrictions on U.S.-origin products and import procedures are those governed by international trade regulations. While imports from EU member countries are exempt from import duties, goods from other countries are subject to duties ranging from 3 to 10 percent, according to the products. All products and services are subject to a Value Added Tax (VAT) of 20 percent. The VAT on non-EU products is applied to the total of CIF value plus the import duty.

Technical specifications for dental equipment are essentially those established by the European Union. Official technical norms are issued by UNI, the Italian Standards Institute, and electronic norms by CEI, the Italian Electrotechnical Standards Institute. Information on EU standards is available from the Commercial Service Office at the U.S. Mission to the European Union at the following address: 40 Boulevard du Regent, 1000 Brussels, Belgium. Tel. 32 2 5082746; fax 32 2 5131228. Italian institutions responsible for product standards and certification are listed under Key Contacts.

As of June 15, 1998, dental supplies (i.e. syringes, sutures, disinfectants, etc.) which are considered medical devices, must comply with the provisions of the EU directive 93/42/EEC, and carry the CE mark. For further information, contact the U.S. Mission to the European Union mentioned above or the Italian Ministry of Health listed under

KEY CONTACTS FOR THE INDUSTRY

Distribution/Business Practices

Public Sector Procurement

Italy issues special regulations governing the procurement of medical and dental equipment, products and services by public hospitals. Most purchases are made by public tenders, which are open to both domestic and foreign companies. Award criteria are normally based on the lowest price of the economically most advantageous quotation. Bidding specifications usually include a detailed technical description of the product to be purchased as well as other requirements, such as CE marking, safety standards, testing procedures, operations manuals and quality assurance. While public tenders are open to both Italian and foreign companies, it is unrealistic for a foreign firm to believe it can successfully cope with the cumbersome bureaucratic procedures of public procurement without a base in Italy. U.S. companies wishing to penetrate the Italian healthcare market should consider working through a well established, aggressive Italian representative.

There are no special procedures for selling to private dental practices or dental laboratories. Foreign companies wanting to export their products to Italy should look for and appoint a well-connected, established importer or distributor capable of offering good technical and after-sales service. Representatives working on commission are also common. U.S. sales quotations are usually given on a c.i.f. basis which is the sales price plus costs such as packing, insurance charges, and air or ocean freight at point of entry.

The c.i.f. quote is generally preferred by Italian importers since they are usually familiar with Italian customs charges and value-added taxes levied on the products at the time of importation but may not be acquainted with U.S. costs for ocean freight. American quotations, usually stated in dollars on a c.i.f. basis, are completely acceptable to Italian buyers.

The usual practice of American firms selling to a new customer is to require cash against documents on the first sale or two. After establishing credit worthiness, the importer may be allowed to pay through 30- 60- or 90-day letters of credit. The turnaround time for the settlement of commercial invoices is 60-90 days, with instances of up to 120 days. The National Health Service is a much slower payer, which can run to one year or longer.

The strong presence of foreign suppliers in the local market is signified by a special international importers' association, O.D.I. - Operatori Dentali Internazionali, with a membership of 50 Italian importers/distributors.

The network of Italian banks with branches in the U.S. (Banca Nazionale del Lavoro, Unicredito, Banca Commerciale Italiana, Monte dei Paschi di Siena, Banca di Roma, CARIPLO, etc.) will offer limited export assistance. Similarly, large U.S. banks and/or local banks located in the exporter's State can offer factoring, exchange fluctuation hedging and limited exporter's credit services. The Export-Import Bank and the FCIA consider Italy a low political risk country. Italy is classified as a "rich" country under the OECD rate classification. Small business exports may obtain assistance under the SBA\rquote s Export Revolving Line of Credit (ERLC) loan program.

KEY GOVERNMENT CONTACTS

Ministero della Sanita,
Dr. Marcella Marletta (Odontotenica)
Viale della Civilta\rquote Romana 7
00144 Rome (EUR)
tel. 39 06 5994 2423; fax 39 06 5994 2111

TRADE ASSOCIATIONS

UNIDI - Unione Nazionale Industrie Dentarie Italiane
(Italian dental manufacturers\rquote association)
Dr. Arturo Chiurazzi, Secretary General
Via Tamburini 2
20123 Milan
tel. 39 02 467510; fax 39 02 461330

O.D.I. - Operatori Dentali Internazionali
(Foreign Importers' Association)
Mr. Carlo Panichi, President
Via Aquileja 43/C
20092 Cinisello Balsamo (Milan)
tel. 39 02 6184511; fax 39 02 6184244

ANCAD - Associazione Nazionale Commercio Articoli Dentari
(Retailers' association of dental equipment and supplies)
Via delle Regioni 27 bis
53100 Siena

ANTLO - Associazione Nazionale Titolari Laboratorio Odontotecnico
(association of operators of dental laboratories)
Via Vasella 30, int. 6
00199 Rome
tel./fax 39 06 86200760

TRADE PUBLICATIONS

"Dental" - Dental Yearbook
Publisher: O.V.E.S.T. s.rl.

Via Simone d\rquote Orsenigo 22
20135 Milan

"Dental monthly"
Promunidi s.r.l.
Via Tamburini 2
20123 Milan

REGISTRATION CONSULTANTS

Dr. Maria Donowa
Via della Fonte di Fauno 22
00153 Rome
tel. 39 06 5782665; fax 39 06 5743786

IMPORTERS/DISTRIBUTORS

Adest s.a.s.
Corso F. Turati 25/4
10128 Turin
tel. 39 011 5681811; fax 39 011 5683944

Apollonia & Fama Implant s.r.l.
Via del Lazzaretto 94
50047 Prato (FI)
tel. 39 057457 2770; fax 39 0574 572777

Cabon S.p.A.
Via Melchiorre Gioia 168
20125 Milan
tel. 39 02 671621; fax 39 02 6709785

Defradental S.p.A.
Via Catania 3, Cas. Post. No. 364
37138 Verona
tel. 39 045 8101822; fax 39 045 567005

Dentalica S.p.A.
Via Rimini 22
20142 Milan
tel. 39 02 8463641-895981; fax 39 02 89504249

Heraeus S.p.A., Divisione Dentale
Via dei Chiosi 11
20040 Cavenago Brianza (MI)
tel. 39 02 957591; fax: 02 95019967

Ilic Riccardo S.p.A.
Viale Umbria 19/A 20135 Milan
tel. 39 02 55016500; fax 39 02 55016646

Krugg S.p.A.
Via dei Lavoratori 7
20090 Buccinasco (MI)
tel. 39 02 45773426; fax: 39 02 4882861

Novaxa S.p.A.
Via Aquileja 49
20092 Cinisello Balsamo (MI)
tel. 39 02 66016123 fax: 39 02 66016128

Ravelli S.p.A.
Via Valparaiso 3
20144 Milan
tel. 39 02 4984771; fax 39 02 48193359

Simit Dental s.r.l.
Via Pisacane 5/A
46100 Mantova
tel. 39 0376 267811; fax 39 0376 381261

Violi F.lli s.r.l.
Via Canalino 45
44110 Modena
tel. 39 059 218318; fax 39 059 216083

W.& H. Italia s.r.l.
Via Kuliscioff 34
20152 Milan
tel. 39 02 48300439; fax 39 02 58332310

STANDARD AND CERTIFICATION INSTITUTES

{UNI - Ente Nazionale Italiano di
Unificazione
Via Battistotti Sassi
20133 Milan
tel. 39 02 70024200; fax 39 02 270106149

CEI - Comitato Elettrotecnico Italiano (Electrical Standards)
Viale Monza 259
20126 Milan
tel. 39 02 257731; fax 39 02 25773210

IMQ - Istituto Italiano del Marchio di Qualita\rquote
Via Quintiliano 43
20183 Milan
tel. 39 02 5073220; fax 39 02 5073.

TRADE PROMOTION OPPORTUNITIES

Expodental/Tecnodental
Milan Trade Fair Showgrounds
Milan
(International exhibition of equipment and materials for
dentistry and dental technology)

This is Italy's leading dental show, held every year in Milan. The 1998 edition featured 360 Italian and foreign exhibitors and was attended by more than 29,000 professional and trade visitors, 9,000 from outside of Italy. The next edition of the show will be held October 13-16, 2004. For further information, contact UNIDI - Unione Nazionale Industrie Dentarie Italiane, Dr. Arturo Chiurazzi, Secretary General, Via Tamburini 2, 20123 Milan. Tel.39 02 467510; fax 39 02 461330.

SELECTED ITALIAN COMPANIES FOR EXPORTING AND IMPORTING

CAMERA DI COMMERCIO INDUSTRIA ARTIGIANATO E AGRICOLTURA DI AREZZO

indirizzo/address: Viale Giotto, 4 - 52100 AREZZO
Tel.: 0575/3030 - Fax: 0575/300953 Telex 575426
attività/activity:
Funzioni istituzionali: rappresentanza unitaria degli interessi economici e promozione dello sviluppo provinciale; Registro delle Imprese, Albi e Ruoli, ecc.
Chamber of Commerce; Register of Companies, professional registers, etc.; Economic Information and Promotion

CAMERA DI COMMERCIO INDUSTRIA ARTIGIANATO E AGRICOLTURA DI TORINO

indirizzo/address: Via S. Francesco da Paola, 24 - 10123 TORINO
Tel.: 011/57161 - Fax: 011/5716516 Telex 210291
attività/activity:
Funzioni istituzionali: rappresentanza unitaria degli interessi economici e promozione dello sviluppo provinciale; Registro delle Imprese, Albi e Ruoli, ecc.
Chamber of Commerce; Register of Companies, professional registers, etc.; Economic Information and Promotion

----

CAMERA DI COMMERCIO INDUSTRIA ARTIGIANATO E AGRICOLTURA DI TRIESTE

indirizzo/address: Piazza della Borsa, 14 - 34121 TRIESTE
Tel.: 040.67011 - Fax: 040.6701321 Telex 460165
attività/activity:
Funzioni istituzionali: rappresentanza unitaria degli interessi economici e promozione dello sviluppo provinciale; Registro delle Imprese, Albi e Ruoli, ecc.;Borsa Valori. Laboratorio Chimico-Merceologico
Chamber of Commerce; Register of Companies, professional registers, etc.; Economic Information and Promotion; Stock exchange; chemical and product analysis Laboratory

----

CRTRIESTE - BANCA SPA

indirizzo/address: Via Cassa di Risparmio, 10 - 34121 TRIESTE
Tel.: 040.67711 - Fax: 040.367456
attività/activity:
Capogruppo del Gruppo Creditizio CRTRIESTE; banca abilitata ad operatività piena
Leader banking Institution, in the CRTRIESTE Group; all credit services

----

CENTRO GAS SYSTEM TRIESTE

indirizzo/address: Via del Lavatoio, 2/a - 34100 TRIESTE
Tel.: 040.369693 - Fax: 040.361791
attività/activity:
Commercializzazione di apparecchi e componenti idrotermosanitari, per il condizionamento ed il trattamento dellaria e per lutilizzo dei gas.
Trade of heating, plumbing, hydraulic, air conditioning and gas appliances and components.

CHEMAPOL ITALIA

indirizzo/address: Via F. Filzi, 27 - 20124 MILANO
Tel.: 02.66987232 - Fax:
attività/activity:
Rappresentante per l'Italia della CHEMAPOL di Praga; prodotti chimici.
Representative in Italy of CHEMAPOL - Praga; chemical products

----

COLOROBBIA ITALIA SPA

indirizzo/address: Via Pietramarina, 19 - 50053 VINCI FI
Tel.: (0571) 7091 - Fax: (0571) 709853
attività/activity:
Produzione, acquisto e commercio di prodotti chimici per l'industria; ceramica conciaria e vetraria.
Production, buying and trading of chemical products for industry; vitreous and dyeing ceramics

----

COOPERATIVA AGRICOLA DI TRIESTE

indirizzo/address: Via Travnik, 10 - 34018 S. DORLIGO DELLA VALLE TS
Tel.: 040.8990111 - Fax: 040.823193
attività/activity: import/export; rappresentanze
Import/export di attrezzature e prodotti agricoli, sementi; prodotti alimentari, per il giardinaggio e hobbystica.
Import/export of agricultural products and machinery, seeds; foodstuffs products gardening and articles.

CREDITO ITALIANO

indirizzo/address: Piazza Cordusio - 20123 MILANO
Tel.: 02.88621 - Fax: 02.86465401
attività/activity:
Azienda di credito
Banking

ENTE FIERA DI TRIESTE

indirizzo/address: Piazzale De Gasperi, 1 - 34139 TRIESTE
Tel.: 040.392961 - Fax: 040.393062
attività/activity:
Organizzazione di manifestazioni fieristiche e congressuali, nazionali e internazionali.
Organization of fairs and conferences, at a national and international level

----

FERGO. IMP. EX. di M. GORUPPI

indirizzo/address: Via del Biancospino, 26 - 34016 OPICINA TS
Tel.: 040.211491 - Fax: 040.214381

attività/activity: import/export
Import/export e rappresentanze; operante con i paesi dell'est dal 1987.
Rottami (ferro, ghisa, metalli); alluminio (pani, vergella, pastiglie per estrusione, filo per metallizzazione, per uso alimentare, per saldature, fogliper uso alimentare e industriale, contenitori alimentari); PVC in granulo; acetone, toluene, metanolo; verfella acciaio; mattoni refrattari per uso civile e industriale; big bags; esche per la pesca d'acqua dolce; birra ceca e rumena.
Import/export company, dealer with east countries since 1987.
Scraps (iron, cast iron, metals); aluminium (ingots, wire, slugs, metallizing wire, for food industry wire, for welding, sheets for food and electrical industries, housecontainers); PVC granulate; acetone, toluene and methanole; steel wire; fire-proof bricks for industrial and civic uses; baits for fishing; big bags; beer from czech republic and from romania

----

FINMECCANICA SPA

indirizzo/address: Via Maresciallo Pilsudski, 92 - 00197 ROMA
Tel.: (06) 8540043 - Fax:
attività/activity:
Gruppo finanziario cui fanno capo le maggiori industrie italiane specializzate nelle alte tecnologie: produzioni aeronautiche, satelliti, sistemi missilistici, radar, centrali per la produzione di energia; materiale ferroviario; sistemi per l'automazione dei processi industriali e dei servizi. Fatturato circa 15.000 miliardi di lire annuo; oltre 60.000 dipendenti
Financial company to which the biggest italian specialized industries of high technologies are part: production of aeronautics, satellites, missile and radar system, energy production factories; railway rolling-stock; systems for industrial processes and services automation. Turnover for about italian Lire 15.00 milliards yearly; over 60.000 employees.

GORIMPEX SRL

indirizzo/address: S. Dorligo della Valle, 265 - 34018 S. DORLIGO DELLA VALLE TS
Tel.: 040.228021 - Fax: 040.228085
attività/activity: import/export
Import/export di prodotti per lilluminazione, di materie plastiche, di ricambi ed accessori per auto e veicoli industriali e di merci varie.
Import/export of ligthing items, plastic materials, car and commercial vehicle spare parts and accessories, miscellaneous merchandise.

IGOR INTERNATIONAL CONSULTANCY
Middle-Est Europe Dept.

indirizzo/address: San Polo, 1945 - 30100 VENEZIA
Tel.: 041/723216 - Fax: 041/2756466
attività/activity:
Assistenza in campo civile, fiscale, commerciale e nella cura del contenzioso nei Paesi dell'Europa Centro Orientale.
Elaborazione di ricerche su quesiti specifici - assistenza ed affiancamento del cliente nella elaborazione dei suoi programmi di investimento, nell'identificazione del quadro normativo di riferimento, nell'analisi della contrattazione in sede transnazionale, nella eventuale messa a punto di assetti societari, nelle fasi pre e post negoziale e nel coordinamento delle strutture (Istituti bancari - Compagnie di assicurazione - Agenzie Governative per gli investimenti, ect.) chiamate in causa dalla realizzazione del progetto.
Assistance in dealing with civil, fiscal, commercial and legal matters in Middle-East Europe Countries.
Research on specific subjects: the customer is assisted and supported in drawing up investment plans,

identifying reference standards, analysing negotiations with foreign third parties, setting up societes, handling the pre-negotiation phases and co-ordinating structures (such as banks, insurnce companies, government investment agencies and so on) involved in carrying the plan out.

I.L.T. SRL

indirizzo/address: P.le Legnami, 1/a - 34145 TRIESTE
Tel.: 040.383898 - Fax: 040.383938
attività/activity:
Commercio internazionale di segati (legnami di latifoglie) e prodotti affini.
International trade of broadleef of lumber (oak, ash, beech, wallnut, cherry, etc.) and other wooden products.

IMEST SRL

indirizzo/address: Via Coroneo, 5 - 34133 TRIESTE
Tel.: - Fax:
attività/activity:
Acquisto, vendita, permuta, intermediazione, locazione, programmazione e gestione di immobili
Real estate agent.

IMPREGILO SPA

indirizzo/address: Viale Italia, 1 - 20099 SESTO S. GIOVANNI MI
Tel.: 02.262481 - Fax: 02.26248293
attività/activity:
Progettazione e costruzione di: impianti idroelettrici e di produzione di energia; opere idrauliche; opere marittime; opere stradali; ferrovie e metropolitane; aeroporti; edifici per edilizia civile, ospedaliera e industriale; progettazione e realizzazione di opere per la salvaguardia ambientale ed artistica; opere di restauro. Sviluppo di attività di project financing e di ingegneria.
Planning and construction of: hydro-electric and energy production plants; hydraulic works; maritime, road, railways and underground works; airports; civil, hospitalization and industrial constructions; planning and construction of artistic, enviromental and restoring works. Project, financing and engineering developments.

INFORMEST Centro Servizi e Documentazione

indirizzo/address: Via Cadorna, 36 - 34170 GORIZIA
Tel.: 0481.597411 - Fax: 0481.537204
attività/activity:
Servizi, consulenza ed assistenza commerciale, legale, finanziaria alle P.M.I. italiane per Europa centro-orientale, ex URSS, Cina e Mongolia.
Services, commercial, legal financial consulting and assistance to italian small and medium sized companies in central-eastern Europe, former USSR, China and Mongolia.

LA FORNITRICE SRL

indirizzo/address: Via Hermet, 3/A - 34123 TRIESTE
Tel.: 040.306932 - Fax: 040.307871
attività/activity: commercio allingrosso / Wholesale trade
Commercio all'ingrosso ed import/export di prodotti industriali, chimici e delledilizia. Rappresentanze prodotti nazionali ed esteri.
Wholesale trade and import/export of industrial, chemical and building products. National and foreign products agency.

MATERIALI EDILI di MERSICH MARINO

indirizzo/address: Via Flavia, 66 - 34148 TRIESTE
Tel.: 040.812396 - Fax: 040.826963
attività/activity:
Commercio all'ingrosso e import-export di materiali edili, idraulica e sanitari.
Wholesale trade and import-export of building, plumbing materials and bathroom fixtures

----

MONTE DEI PASCHI DI SIENA SPA

indirizzo/address: Viale Toselli, 60 - 53100 SIENA
Tel.: 0577.294589 - Fax:
attività/activity: import/export
Azienda di credito.
Banking.

PARISI FRANCESCO SPA

indirizzo/address: Viale Miramare, 5 - 34135 TRIESTE
Tel.: 040.41931 - Fax: 040.44263
attività/activity:
Casa di spedizione.
Forwarding and shipping.

PRAGOTECNA SPA

indirizzo/address: Via XXX Ottobre, 19 - 34122 TRIESTE
Tel.: 040.363344 - Fax: 040.364880 Telex 460128
attività/activity: commercio / trade
Produzione, commercio, import/export e rappresentanze di articoli tecnici e materie prime per l'industria, materiali accessori e connessi per la costruzione e ristrutturazione di edifici civili e industriali, nonché attività dimportazione in genere.
Production, trade, import/export and agencies of technical supplies and raw materials for industry; accessories and other materials for the construction and restoring of houses and industrial buildings.

PRINCIPE DI SAN DANIELE SPA

indirizzo/address: Via Ressel, 1 - 34018 S. DORLIGO DELLA VALLE TS
Tel.: 040.825681 - Fax: 040.825716

attività/activity:
Produzione prosciutti cotti e würstel; produzione e stagionatura prosciutti crudi. Stabilimenti di Trieste e di San Daniele.
Production of ham and frankfurters; production and seasoning of "prosciutto". Plants in Trieste and San Daniele.

PROGRAMMA D. 1887 SRL

indirizzo/address: Largo Barriera, 5 - 34129 TRIESTE
Tel.: 040.775401 - Fax: 040.771776 - Telex 460423
attività/activity: commercio / trade
Produzione, commercio all'ingrosso e al dettaglio ed import/export di calzature. Azienda attiva da oltre un secolo, specializzata nei rapporti commerciali con i Paesi dell'Est.
Production, wholesale and retail trade and import/export of footwear. Founded over a century ago, the firm is specialized in trade relations with Eastern countries.

PROTEUS ELECTRIC SRL

indirizzo/address: Via di Noghere, 94/1 - 34015 MUGGIA TS
Tel.: 040.232188 - Fax: 040.232440
attività/activity: commercio / trade
Import/export di materiali elettrici, apparecchi e componenti elettrici ed elettronici, motori e trasformatori, parti per accumulatori elettrici, analizzatori di fumi, strumenti elettrici di processo.
Import/export of electric materials, electronic components and equipment, electronic components and equipment, electric motors and trasformers, parts for batteries, smoke analysers, process electric instruments.

SABRE

indirizzo/address: Viale R. Sanzio, 21 - 34128 TRIESTE
Tel.: 040.569904 - Fax: 040.569904
attività/activity:
Commercio all'ingrosso di articoli per fumatori, giocattoli, cartoleria e cancelleria; trasporti.
Wholesale trade of smoking products, toys, stationery; transport.

SAMER & CO. SHIPPING SRL

indirizzo/address: Via Einaudi, 3 - 34121 TRIESTE
Tel.: 040.7354 - Fax: 040.365988
attività/activity:
Trasporti marittimi e spedizioni in genere.
Maritime transport, shipping and forwarding agency.

SEMAR SRL

indirizzo/address: Via Martinelli, 12 - 34015 MUGGIA TS
Tel.: 040.232242 - Fax: 040.232490
attività/activity: industria / industry
Import/export di prodotti ed attrezzature per lagricoltura dai Paesi dell'Est. Produzione e vendita di sementi da orto, semi da prato e da fiore. Commercio all'ingrosso di bulbi e rizomi, piante e rose confezionate, concimi e terricci, attrezzature per l'orticoltura e la floricoltura.
Import/export of farm machines and products from/to Eastern countries. Production and trade of vegetable, grass and flower seeds. Wholesale trade of bulbs and rhizomes, ready-grown plants and roses, fertilizers and soil, gardening and flower-growing equipment.

SILVER SRL

indirizzo/address: Via Milano, 17 - 34132 TRIESTE
Tel.: 040.366390-366849 - Fax: 040.
attività/activity:
Fornitura merci di largo consumo, per supermarkets.
Company Supplying supermarkets with mass consumer goods.

SINCROTRONE TRIESTE

indirizzo/address: Padriciano, 99 - 34012 TRIESTE
Tel.: 040.3758500 - Fax: 040.226803
attività/activity:
Società di gestione della macchina di luce di sincrotrone "Elettra"; laboratorio di ricerca.
Company managing the "light machine, the syncrotron ELETTRA; research laboratory.

S. I. O. T. SPA

indirizzo/address: Piazza Unità dItalia, 7 - 34121 TRIESTE
Tel.: 040.3889111 - Fax: 040.3899191
attività/activity:
Società Italiana per l'Oleodotto Transalpino.
Italian Company managing the Transalpine Oil Pipeline.

S. I. T. I. SPA

indirizzo/address: Via Sempione, 82 - 28040 MARANO TICINO (NO)
Tel.: 0321.9781 - Fax: 0321.97183
attività/activity:
Impianti completi per l'industria ceramica (piastrelle, piatti, sanitari, rubinetteria).
Complete plants for the ceramics industry (tiles, plates, bathroom fixtures, taps).

STONE TEK

indirizzo/address: Via delle Mura Sud, 45 - 54100 MASSA
Tel.: 0585.810923 - Fax: 0585.811311
attività/activity:

Marmi; graniti; pietre.
Marbres and Stone.

STUDIO FRANDOLI SAS

indirizzo/address: Via Rittmeyer, 6 - 34134 TRIESTE
Tel.: 040.365398 - Fax: 040.368884
attività/activity:
Progettazione, studi di fattibilità e perizie per il settore edilizio industriale e turistico e per il settore distributivo.
Planning, feasibility studies and surveys in the industrial and tourist building sector, and in the distribution sector.

STUDIO SAVINO

indirizzo/address: Via San Francesco, 9 - 34133 TRIESTE
Tel.: 040.630270-639029 - Fax: 040.631068
attività/activity:
Consulenza societaria amministrativa e contrattuale, con particolare riguardo alla legislazione ceca e slovacca. Sede operativa distaccata in Praga.
Accounting, managment and contractual consulting company, with particular expertise in Czech and Slovac legislation; branch office in Prague.

UNITECH SRL

indirizzo/address: Via del Lavatoio, 2/A - 34132 TRIESTE
Tel.: 040.369693 - Fax: 040.361791 - Telex 460110
attività/activity: commercio / trade
Commercio all'ingrosso ed export di apparecchiature, componentistica, ricambi ed accessori per impianti di condizionamento, riscaldamento, refrigerazione, gas ed idrocarburi.
Wholesale trade and export of equipment, appliance components, spare parts and accessories for oil, fuel, conditioning, heating and refrigeration plants.

VENETA IMP. EXP. di R. PIZZI

indirizzo/address: Via Mazzini, 18 - 34121 TRIESTE
Tel.: 040.365965 - Fax: 040.368198 - Telex 461030
attività/activity: import/export
Import/export di prodotti agricoli, alimentari, carni, animali vivi, budella artificiali, generi vari.
Import/export of agricultural and food products, meat, live animals, artificial casings and sundry goods.

JEWELRY INDUSTRY: SELECTED COMPANIES

UNO A ERRE ITALIA

Uno A Erre ITALIA, which is based in Arezzo, is the largest company specializing in the manufacture, distribution and export of gold jewelry worldwide.

With 750 employees and consolidated turnover for the year 2000 of about ITL 580 billion, Uno A Erre alloys 44.5 metric tons of gold every year. In its production the company uses equipment designed to complement the traditional craftsmanship of the Arezzo goldsmiths with the latest in modern technology.

The study and creativity of product design, attention to detail, competitive pricing, quality control and the guarantee of the final product have always been Uno A Erre's distinctive characteristics.

ITALIAN LEADERSHIP

The Italian gold industry, traditionally fragmented into over 20.000 companies, is the world leader internationally with a production of 515 metric tons and exports accounting for over 75% of production. Arezzo, Vicenza, and Valenza are the leading manufacturing centers. Production is highly polarized with 2% of the manufacturers accounting for roughly 45% of production.

UNO A ERRE MARKET SHARE IN 2000

Uno A Erre held a leading world market share in 2000 thanks to sales in:
Middle East (11.4 tons), Europe (17.6 tons) and North America (8.3 tons). These results are evidence of the multi-market and multi-area position of Uno A Erre which has achieved a consolidated presence worldwide by offering all the carat ranges through diverse production technology allowing for a vast product range (necklaces, bracelets, rings, earrings, pendants, brooches, tie clips, cuff links, wedding bands, medals, zodiac charms and coins).

The mother company, Unoaerre Italia SpA, presides over : Unoaerre, Unoargeno, and Xenia.

UNOAERRE

This company's activity is gold production, which represents approximately 90% of volume and 95% of total sales. Its brand positioning offers classic styles with an innovative design showing great attention to the quality of the finished product at affordable prices.

UNOARGENTO

Founded in 1990 and employing about 50 people, Unoargento specializes in the production and distribution of silver jewelry and products. Its strength and its market position are based on its flexibility in product mix, on the service it gives its customers and on its design and manufacture of products made to order.

XENIA

Xenia, which caters to the high end of the jewelry and accessory market with its silver and gold collections proves to be highly attentive to the evolution of fashion. The company was established in 1998 as a partnership with two young Milanese designers with expertise in the fashion accessory sector. Marketing of the Xenia brand in Italy and abroad is highly selective and is mainly implemented through prestigious jewelers and boutiques.

Legal Company Name : UNO A ERRE ITALIA SpA
Legal offices : Arezzo
Principal Activity: manufacture, distribution and export of gold jewelry
Company founded: 1926
Share capital: ITL 50 billion
Shareholders: Morgan Grenfell Private Equity (51%), Zucchi Family (49%)
Consolidated turnover 2000: ITL 580 billion
Employees: 750

President: Mr. Federico Minoli
Uno A Erre is one of the most dynamic Italian gold manufacturing companies thanks to its professional organizational structure which guarantees full coverage of the markets both in Italy and abroad.

In particular, Uno A Erre can count on its own direct presence in 43 countries with representation in France, Germany, Japan, Korea, Scandinavia, the United Kingdom and the United States, employing over a hundred people that guarantee the company the export of 80% of its total production.

For information regarding Uno A Erre and its products, please contact the appropriate country area office or the headquarter office for all other countries not listed:

HEADQUARTERS:

ITALY
UNO A ERRE ITALIA S.p.A.
Via Fiorentina, 550
52100 Arezzo
Tel. 0039 0575 9251
Fax 0039 0575 925904
Emailinfo@unoaerre.it
www.unoaerre.it

SALES OFFICES:

FRANCE
SARL D.H.T.
14, Rue Clement Marot
75008 - Paris - France
Tel. 0033 1 4073 8469
Fax 0033 1 4720 1929
Emaillimon@unoaerre.it

GERMANY
ROLAND BINNINGER
Schlossberg 19
75175 Pforzheim - Germany
Tel. 0049 7231 568344
Fax 0049 7231 568345
Emailroland.binninger@t-online.de

JAPAN
UNOAERRE JAPAN
Hiroo Sk Bldg 5F
2-36-13 Ebisu Shibuya-Ku,
Tokyo - Giappone
Tel. 0081 3 5421 3301

Fax 0081 3 5421 3377
Emailimport@unoaerre.co.jp

SOUTH KOREA
DAVID & CO., LTD
1st Floor, FPS Building
897-10, Daechi 4-Dong
Kangnam-Ku, Seoul 135-284 South Korea
Tel. 0082 2 34533451
Fax 0082 2 34533455
Emailkjj@unoaerrekorea.co.kr
Webwww.unoaerrekorea.co.kr

SWEDEN
KJELLIN IMPORT AB
Frejgatan 87
113 26 Stockholm - Sweden
Tel. 0046 8 301596
Fax 0046 8 312145
Emailewak@algonet.se

U.K.
WILLIAM HASKEY
24-25 Nutford Place
London W1H 5YN - U.K.
Tel. 0044 207 5693298
Fax 0044 207 5693299

U.S.A.
AUREA JEWELRY CREATIONS LLC
516 Fifth Avenue
New York, NY 10036
Tel. 001 212 6293300
Fax 001 212 6293700
Emailsales@aureausa.com

ADVERTISING AGENCIES

ASSOCOMUNICAZIONE

The most important Italian advertising and communication trade association is ASSOCOMUNICAZIONE - Associazione delle Imprese di Comunicazione (Italian Association of Communication Companies). Established in 1949, ASSOCOMUNICAZIONE includes the major advertising agencies, which hold more than 70 percent of total market share. Presently, 71 agencies belong to ASSOCOMUNICAZIONE, with over 4,235 employees and total revenues of $522 million, a 15.78% increase over 1998.

ASSOCOMUNICAZIONE
Associazione delle Imprese di Comunicazione
(Italian Association of Communication Companies)
Via Larga, 23
20122 Milano
Tel: 011/39/02/5830.7450
Fax : 011/39/02/5830.7147
E-mail: info@assocomunicazione.it
www.assocomunicazione.it
Contact: Mr. Enrico Montangero, President Mr. Bepi Monico, General Manager

3. ASSOCOMUNICAZIONE SURVEY

According to a recent survey conducted by ASSOCOMUNICAZIONE, total Italian advertising expenditures amounted to approximately $13.7 billion in 2004, an 8% increase over 1998. The top ten advertising agencies hold more than 40 percent of the market for advertising services. American advertising agencies and their subsidiaries and joint-ventures do extremely well in the Italian market, holding a 30 percent share of total advertising revenue in 2004.

During the last decade, most advertising agencies limited their activities to traditional activities, with divisions specialized in direct marketing, sales promotion, and media communications. With the growing number of internet users and companies in Italy, recently many agencies have introduced special divisions devoted to the new electronic forms of advertising. Italian agencies, especially the largest ones, are embracing the new electronic medium and are developing new skills and initiating new divisions offering e-promotional services. For example, Armando Testa, the largest communications agency in Italy, is planning to open a new division called Testa Web, specialized in communications activities related to electronic commerce.

However, so far, in Italy few companies are specialized in offering electronic promotion services. On-line advertisement on public internet sites as well as company websites still plays only a minor role in the Italian market. The internet is still small in terms of the amount of advertising money it attracts in Italy. However, the advertising industry could change as much in the next five years as it did in the last thirty, with agencies persuading marketers of the internet's power to raise international awareness of brand names.

As a result, the Italian internet advertising market has strong growth potential and may offer many opportunities for U.S. companies wishing to expand their activities internationally.

TOP TEN ADVERTISING AGENCIES IN ITALY:

AD AGENCY REVENUES '99 EMPLOYEES
(IN MILLION $*)
1) ARMANDO TESTA 48.895 440
+2) YOUNG & RUBICAM 48.508 414
+3) MCCANN ERICKSON 48.046 302
4) BGS D'ARCY 34.135 288
+5) J.W. THOMPSON 33.330 248
6) LOWE LINTAS PIRELLA GOTTSCHE 32.716 231
+7) MILANO & GREY 29.732 200
+8) LEO BURNETT 22.907 179
9) EURO-RSCG 21.151 114
10) SAATCHI & SAATCHI 20.729 146

(LEGEND: + = U.S. ADVERTISING AGENCIES)
*1$= 2,000 LIRA

U.S. ADVERTISING AGENCIES

Several American advertising agencies are represented in the Italian market either through their Italian subsidiaries or through joint ventures with Italian advertising firms. U.S. companies are considered to be the most qualified by a general consensus in the marketplace.

In terms of market share American advertising agencies hold more than 30 percent of the total market, with Italian and European agencies holding the balance. In 2004, five American advertising firms were ranked on the top ten list in revenue.

In addition, American companies enjoy the reputation of being innovative, and of having wide expertise in all aspects of e-commerce, critical features for success in the new Italian market. This excellent reputation puts U.S. communication companies in a good position to boost activities in Italy.

MAJOR ADVERTISING AGENCIES IN ITALY

ARMANDO TESTA
Via Luisa del Carretto, 58
10131 Torino
Tel. 011/39-0118810111
Fax: 011/39-0118810367
www.testa.it

YOUNG & RUBICAN ITALIA
Piazza Eleonora Duse, 2
20122 Milano
Tel: 011/39/027732.1
Fax: 011/39/027600.0904
www.yr.com

MCCANN-ERICKSON ITALIANA S.P.A.
Via Albricci, 10
20122 Milano
Tel: 011/39/028529.1
Fax: 011/39/0285292557
www.mccann.com

BGS D'ARCY
Corso Galileo Ferraris, 24/A
10121 Torino
Tel: 011/39-0115601911
Fax: 011/39-0115175300

Via Correggio, 18
20149 Milano
Tel: 011/39/02/4679.1
Fax: 011/39/02/4818633

J. WALTER THOMPSON S.P.A.
Via Paolo Lomazzo, 19
20154 Milano
Tel: 011/39/02/336341
Fax: 011/39/02/33634400
www.jwalterthompson.com

LOWE LINTAS PIRELLA GOTTSCHE
Piazzale Biancamano, 8
20121 Milano
Tel: 011/39/02/290281
Fax: 011/39/02/6597722

MILANO & GREY S.P.A.
VIA Bertani, 6
20154 Milano
Tel: 011/39/02/349761
Fax 011/39/02/34530785

LEO BURNETT COMPANY
Via Fatebenefratelli, 14
20121 Milano
Tel: 011/39/02/6354.1

Fax: 011/39/02/2900.5229
www.leoburnett.it

EURO RSCG
Via Dante, 7
20123 Milano
Tel: 011/39-02802021
Fax: 011/39-0272000027

SAATCHI & SAATCHI
Corso Monforte, 52
20122 Milano
Tel: 011/39-0277011
Fax 011/39-02781196
www.saatchi_saatchi.it

TRAVEL & TOURISM INDUSTRY

TOUR OPERATORS

Acentro
Via Vittor Pisani, 7
20124 Milano
Phone: 0266711811
Fax: 026709370
Http://
E-mail:
Contact: Mr. Davide Piras

Agamare
Viale Tunisia. 38
20124 Milano
Phone: 026739721
Fax: 0267397299
Http://
E-mail:
Contact: Ms. Antonella Corradini

Aleramo Viaggi
Galleria Argenta, 7
14100 Asti
Phone: 0141595390
Fax: 0141599557
Http://
E-mail: aleramo@atlink.it
Contact: Mr. Valter Balsamo

Algorab Viaggi
Via Picasso - c/o Centro Morbella
04100 Latina
Phone: 0773620578
Fax: 0773620921
Http://
E-mail:
Contact: Si.ra Stefania Angelini

American Dream
Via Gordigiani, 72
50127 Firenze
Phone: 0553289245
Fax: 055365040
Http://
E-mail:
Contact: Mr. Giovanni Bertaccini

Ancona Viaggi
Corso Cavour, 205
70121 Bari
Phone: 0805237992
Fax: 0805242506
Http://
E-mail:
Contact: Mr. Giuseppe Ancona

Atitour - Dertour Italia
Viale Filippetti, 26/a
20122 Milano
Phone: 02582921
Fax: 0258320519
Http://
E-mail:
Contact: Ms. Elena Pasqualin

Beautiful Travel
Viale Garibaldi 46/B
30122 Mestre (VE)
Phone: 0415351795
Fax: 0412668539
Http:// www.beautifulcruises.com
E-mail:
Contact:

Bestway
Via San Marco, 14
85049 Potenza
Phone: 091471400

Fax: 0971471403
Http://
E-mail:
Contact: Ms. Antonia Pesce

Beverly Vacanze
Via A. Verdecchia, 2
63013 Grottammare
Phone: 0735735173
Fax: 0735735166
Http://
E-mail:
Contact: Mr. Lorenzo Rossi

Billabong Tour Operator
Via delle Porte Nuove, 17
50144 Firenze
Phone: 055367460
Fax: 055367145
Http://
E-mail: billabong@fol.it
Contact: Ms. Francesca Ballerini

Blue Marlin Viaggi e Turismo
Viale dei Colli Portuensi, 396/404
00151 Roma
Phone: 0665740704
Fax: 0665740767
Http://
E-mail:
Contact: Mr. Gianni Salvo

Bluewings
Via Incoronata, 20/27
80133 Napoli
Phone: 0815527233
Fax: 0815517605
Http://
E-mail: bwingslr@tin.it
Contact: Ms. Mirella Castagna

Boarding Pass
Piazzale Baracca, 1
20123 Milano
Phone: 024987861
Fax: 024813500
Http://
E-mail: info@boarding.pass.it
Contact: Mr. Mario Mangiarotti

Brevitours
Via Trieste, 22/a
25121 Brescia
Phone: 0303774900
Fax: 030290258
Http://
E-mail: info@brevitours.it
Contact: Mr. Marco Casati

Byblos Tour Operator
Via Val di Non, 39
00141 Roma
Phone: 068124600
Fax: 068125479
Http://
E-mail:
Contact: Ms. Roberta Cantu'

C.T.C. Viaggi
Via Matteotti, 169
60121 Ancona
Phone: 0712800121
Fax: 07155674
Http://
E-mail:
Contact: Mr. Ennio Di Foglio

Cts Viaggi
Via Nazionale 66
00184 Roma
Phone: 06441111
Fax: 0644111300
Http:// www.cts.it
E-mail: mcastriste@cts.it
Contact: Mr. Maurizio Casatriste

Cielo Azzurro Viaggi Vacanze
Via Btg. Val Leogra, 63/65
36015 Schio
Phone: 0445527300
Fax: 0445527610
Http://
E-mail:
Contact: Mr. Gianfranco Costeniero

Cisalpina Tours SpA
Corso Francia, 92
10123 Torino
Phone: 0117771777
Fax: 011771763
Http://
E-mail:
Contact: Mr. Luciano Baldi

Club Vacanze Spa\Comitour SpA
Viale Mentana, 150
43100 Parma
Phone: 0521288111
Fax: 0521239225
Http://
E-mail:
Contact: Mr. Walter David

Contea Viaggi
Via Privata de' Grassi, 12/a
20123 Milano
Phone: 0248558550

Fax: 0248022326
Http://
E-mail: contea@conteaviaggi.com
Contact: Mr. Roberto Chiesa

Crazy Tour
Via Alessandro Manzoni, 4
51100 Pistoia
Phone: 0573534199
Fax: 0573935077
Http://
E-mail:
Contact: Ms. Ambra Benedetti

Crossworld
Via A. Usodimare, 56
00154 Roma
Phone: 065748145
Fax: 065782245
Http://
E-mail: crossworld@adv.it
Contact: Mr. Carlo Sacchetti
De Franchi - International Travel Office
Via F.lli Rosselli, 86/88
19121 La Spezia
Phone: 0187735146
Fax: 0187731127
Http://
E-mail:
Contact: Mr. Paolo De Franchi

Dielleffe Agenzia Viaggi
Via XX Settembre, 300
19100 La Spezia
Phone: 0187734207
Fax: 018720232
Http://
E-mail:
Contact: Mr. Giovanni Petrini

Doorway Leading to Future
Via L. Alamanni, 32/r
50123 Firenze
Phone: 055260951
Fax: 055211738
Http://
E-mail:
Contact: Mr. Antonio Ballone

Durlindana
Via Papirio Pacedi 18
19100 La Spezia
Phone: 018520702
Fax: 0187564313
Http://
E-mail:
Contact: Ms. Miriana Rovaron

E. F. Education
Corso Vittorio Emanuele, 24
20122 Milano
Phone: 0277891
Fax: 02782733
Http://
E-mail:
Contact: Mr. Marco Urso

EffettoViaggi
Via Plinio, 39
20129 Milano
Phone: 0229523542
Fax: 0229523543
Http://
E-mail:
Contact: Mr. Ciro Fragale

Equinoxe Viaggi
Via dei Mille, 18
10123 Torino
Phone: 0118124089
Fax: 0118178387
Http://
E-mail:
Contact: Ms. Mariolina Longoni

Esotic Tour
Via Zaccherini Alvisi, 2/a
40138 Bologna
Phone: 051303651
Fax: 051345619
Http://
E-mail:
Contact: Ms. Lavinia Cugolli

Euganeatours
Via Stazione, 96
35036 Montegrotto Terme
Phone: 049793666
Fax: 049793367
Http://
E-mail:
Contact: Ms. Patrizia Buson

Evasioni
Via Ressi, 26
20125 Milano
Phone: 026705518
Fax: 026705674
Http://
E-mail:
Contact: Mr. Fulvio Badetti

F.lli Cosulich SpA
Stazione Marittima 61
80133 Napoli
Phone: 0817047563

Fax: 0815522803
Http:// www.cosulich.it
E-mail:
Contact: Mr. Leonardo Massa

Fabretto Viaggi
Corso Porta Nuova, 11
37122 Verona
Phone: 04558060101
Fax: 04558060105
Http:// www.fabretto.it
E-mail: penazzi@fabretto.it
Contact: Mr. Livio Penazzi

Falisca Travel
Via 4 Giornate di Napoli, 28
01033 Civita Castellana
Phone: 0761518044
Fax: 0761518020
Http://
E-mail:
Contact: Mr. Massimo Pompei

Garmon Viaggi
Corso delle Provincie, 41
95129 Catania
Phone: 0957221422
Fax: 095382354
Http://
E-mail:
Contact: Mr. Giovanni Raciti

Go & go Tour Operator
Via Petrarca, 161
80122 Napoli
Phone: 0815752442
Fax: 0815752099
Http://
E-mail:
Contact: Mr. Cesare Foa'

Godot Viaggi
Via Bodoni, 16
12037 Saluzzo
Phone: 017547258
Fax: 017547454
Http://
E-mail:
Contact: Mr. Riccardo Conte

Going spa Gruppo HIT
Viale Mentana, 150
43100 Parma
Phone: 0521288525
Fax: '0521228006
Http://
E-mail:
Contact: Ms. Paola Calore

Goldtravel
Piazza Gramsci, 14
15048 Valenza
Phone: 0131924971
Fax: 0131946707
Http://
E-mail:
Contact: Mr. Giovanni Ceva

Heron Travel
Via San Gregorio VII, 164/a
00165 Roma
Phone: 066390074
Fax: 066381874
Http://
E-mail:
Contact: Mr. Guido Trivero

High Performance Travel
Lungadige B. Rubele, 36/38
37121 Verona
Phone: 045597299
Fax: 0458009390
Http://
E-mail:
Contact: Ms. Elena Giardini

HIT - Holding Italiano Tourismo
Viale Mentana, 150
43100 Parma
Phone: 0521288111
Fax: 0521288357
Http:// www.clubvacanze.it
E-mail:
Contact: Mr. Dindo Florindo

I Tuoi Tours...nel Mondo
Via Dei Prati Fiscali, 221
00141 Roma
Phone: 0688640150
Fax: 0688641771
Http://
E-mail:
Contact: Mr. Ivano Pasetti

I Viaggi dell'Airone
Via XX Settembre, 4
00187 Roma
Phone: 064744333
Fax: 064818953
Http:// www.iviaggidellairone.com
E-mail: airon@itb.it
Contact: Mr. Sergio Uboldi

International Know How - I Viaggi di Qualita'
Corso Italia, 8
20122 Milano
Phone: 02876767

Fax: 028692961
Http://
E-mail:
Contact: Ms. Luciana Spelgatti

Island Tours SrL
Route 66, Viale Monza 149
20122 Milano
Phone: 022847208
Fax: 0226115287
Http://
E-mail:
Contact:

IVET
Corso Italia, 37
20122 Milano
Phone: 02583901
Fax: 0258301294
Http://
E-mail: info@ivet.it
Contact: Ms. Marisa Sironi

Kele & Teo
Corso del Popolo, 90
30172 Mestre
Phone: 0415316455
Fax: 0415310355
Http://
E-mail: kt.teo@iol.it
Contact: Mr. Michele Serafini

La Fabbrica dei Sogni
Via L'Aquila, 14
00176 Roma
Phone: 0670300273
Fax: 0670300272
Http://
E-mail:
Contact: Mr. Bruno Pallotta

La Grande Mela Viaggi di Ulisse 2000
Via Lorenzo Valla, 25
20141 Milano
Phone: 0289516870
Fax: 0289516880
Http://
E-mail:
Contact: Ms. Cristina Galimberti

La Via della Seta di Marco Polo
Via dei Fossi, 12
50123 Firenze
Phone: 055214686
Fax: 055288191
Http://
E-mail:
Contact: Mr. Mario Lapini

Levantur
Corso Italia, 1/3
19015 Levanto
Phone: 0187808039
Fax: 0187808331
Http://
E-mail:
Contact: Ms. Beatrice Serafini

Loisirs S.r.l.
Via Settembrini, 27
20124 Milano
Phone: 026713141
Fax: 026709024
Http://
E-mail:
Contact: Dottor Elio Bertolina

Madison Travel
Via San Biagio, 14
35121 Padova
Phone: 0498751882
Fax: 0498786015
Http://
E-mail:
Contact: Mr. Massimo Pierini

Marcelletti Tour Operator
Via G. Belluzzo, 1
00149 Roma
Phone: 065599672
Fax: 065581694
Http://
E-mail: mtoinfo@flashnet.it
Contact: Mr. Romano D'Antonio

Marea Viaggi e Turismo
Via Nazionale Adriatica Nord, 1
66023 Francavilla al mare
Phone: 0854913070
Fax: 0854912043
Http://
E-mail:
Contact: Ms. Andrea Buccini

Mobiltravel Agency
Via Montalbano, 28/e
51039 Quarrata
Phone: 0573737374
Fax: 0573739484
Http://
E-mail:
Contact: Mr. Antonio Sacchi

Neo Tours Cruise Center
Viale Sacco e Vanzetti, 54/56
00155 Roma
Phone: 064066666

Fax: 064066521
Http://
E-mail:
Contact: Mr. Gianfranco De Carolis

Nouvelles Frontieres
Via Tirone, 11
00146 Roma
Phone: 06551961
Fax: 065565279
Http://
E-mail:
Contact: Ms. Helga Schenke

Ocean Tour Operator
Via Garibaldi, 75
25017 Lonato sul Garda (BS)
Phone: 0309131461
Fax: 0309131464
Http://
E-mail:
Contact: Mr. Eliseo Capretti

Osservando il Mondo
Via Boves, 5
23100 Brescia
Phone: 0303541719
Fax: 0303541719
Http://
E-mail:
Contact: Mr. Ettore Francesconi

Oxbridge
Via Gianbattista Vico, 7
10128 Torino
Phone: 0115683864
Fax: 0115683664
Http://
E-mail:
Contact: Ms. Luisa Prandi

Ozanam Viaggi e Turismo
Via Federico Ozanam, 62
00152 Roma
Phone: 0658204725
Fax: 0658200710
Http://
E-mail:
Contact: Mr.Guglielmo Gammacurta

Pofinatours
Via Panisperna, 104
00184 Roma
Phone: 064828280
Fax: 064828283
Http://
E-mail:
Contact: Mr. Antonio Rigillo

Praga Viaggi
Via D. Fiasella, 15/r
16121 Genova
Phone: 010586141
Fax: 010584363
Http://
E-mail:
Contact: Ms. Franca Scontrino

Press Tours
Piazza Grandi, 9
20129 Milano
Phone: 02754121
Fax: 02714447
Http://
E-mail:
Contact: Mr. Carlo Cellamare

Programmi Alitur
Via Cusani, 5
20121 Milano
Phone: 02806771
Fax: 0280677299
Http://
E-mail:
Contact: Ms. Laura Rossi

Pulsar Viaggi
Viale Bezzi, 81
20146 Milano
Phone: 02468335
Fax: 024390837
Http://
E-mail:
Contact: Mr. Giovanni Di Benedetto

Punto Vacanze
Viale della Repubblica, 18/c
62029 Tolentino
Phone: 0733967467
Fax: 0733974177
Http://
E-mail:
Contact: Ms. Paola Cimarelli

Quickly
Via Sarsina, 101/a
00127 Roma
Phone: 0652372981
Fax: 0652372436
Http://
E-mail:
Contact: Ms. Anna Di Leo

Reimatours SrL
Via del Pianeta Venere, 85
00144 Roma
Phone: 065297146
Fax: 065297170
Http://
E-mail:
Contact: Ms. Laura Barberis
Reportage
Via Michelangelo Schipa, 44
80122 Napoli
Phone: 081669730
Fax: 081682341
Http://
E-mail:
Contact: Mr. Attilio Maurano

Sforzesco Viaggi
Via Caduti Liberazione, 7
27029 Vigevano
Phone: 038170442
Fax: 038177159
Http://
E-mail:
Contact: Mr. Dante Ferrari

Silbago Viaggi
Via Principe Amedeo, 12
10123 Torino
Phone: 0118126016
Fax: 0118123103
Http://
E-mail:
Contact: Mr. Franco Nosengo

Skipperviaggi
Corso G. Agnelli, 78
10137 Torino
Phone: 0113299357
Fax: 011351329
Http://
E-mail:
Contact: Ms. Lilia De Marino

Special Places by Vivitours
Via F. Crispi, 17
20121 Milano
Phone: 0229005444
Fax: 0229012875
Http://
E-mail: specialp@mail.dex-net.com
Contact: Mr. Luciano Bertelli

Springer Travel
Corso M. D'Azeglio, 76
10126 Torino
Phone: 0116690049
Fax: 0116503433
Http://
E-mail:
Contact: Mr. Rino Aglioti
Stat Viaggi
Via Roma, 191
15033 Casale Monferrato
Phone: 0142452814
Fax: 0142452004
Http://
E-mail:
Contact: Mr. Edoardo Chierotti

Suntur International
Via Lugano, 21/a
21016 Luino
Phone: 0332534300
Fax: 0332532300
Http://
E-mail:
Contact: Mr. Paolo Bonfino

Te-Ca Travels
Corso Amedeo, 60/64
57125 Livorno
Phone: 0586898444
Fax: 0586880932
Http://
E-mail:
Contact: Ms. Letizia Mazzanti

Terramia
Via Ariosto, 8
44100 Ferrara
Phone: 0532211621
Fax: 0532210578
Http://
E-mail:
Contact: Mr. Antonio Baldisserotto

Time Out
Via del Monte Oppio, 5
00184 Roma
Phone: 0648905590
Fax: 0648905570
Http://
E-mail:
Contact: Mr. Francesco Pizzardi

Topkapi srl
Viale P. Orlando 7
00122 Lido di Roma
Phone: 065600664
Fax: 0656304733
Http://
E-mail: topkapi@flashnet.it
Contact: Mr. Franco Libotte

Tramontana Viaggi TO
Via Ceccardi, 2/7
16121 Genova
Phone: 011586791
Fax: 010566468
Http://
E-mail:
Contact: Ms. Annalisa Damiano

V.V.S. Viaggi Vacanze Studio
Via Davila, 12
35100 Padova
Phone: 049664406
Fax: 049655693
Http://
E-mail:
Contact: Mr. Secondo Gastone Schiavon

Vacantioner Viaggi
Via Los Angeles, 185-Loc. Santa Maria degli Angeli
06081 Assisi
Phone: 0758012480
Fax: 0758012466
Http://
E-mail:
Contact: Ms. Simonetta Cianetti

Valtur T.O. SpA
Piazza della Repubblica, 59
00185 Roma
Phone: 064706811
Fax: 064706801
Http://
E-mail:
Contact: Mr. Riccardo Minozzi

Vela Turismo e Crociere
Corso Alfieri, 291
14100 Asti
Phone: 0141355035
Fax: 0141353830
Http://
E-mail:
Contact: Mr. Enrico Monari

Veratour
Viale Cesare Pavese, 8
00144 Roma
Phone: 065000661
Fax: 065004343
Http://
E-mail:
Contact: Ms. Silvana Tamburrino

Viaggi nel Mondo
Circonvallazione Gianicolense, 41
00152 Roma
Phone: 065816365
Fax: 065809540
Http://
E-mail:
Contact: Mr. Paolo Nugari

Viaggi Tigullio Marcone
Piazza Matteotti, 21
16043 Chiavari
Phone: 0185324949
Fax: 0185303750
Http://
E-mail:
Contact: Mr. Fabio Marcone

Viaggiare
Via San Nicola da Tolentino, 18
00187 Roma
Phone: 06421171
Fax: 0642117777
Http://
E-mail:
Contact: Mr. Fabrizio Cerio

Viaggidea
Via Biondelli, 1
20141 Milano
Phone: 02895291
Fax: 028467710
Http://
E-mail:
Contact: Mr. Walter Sala

Viva
Via San Tomaso, 7
20121 Milano
Phone: 0272001373
Fax: 0272023053 Http://
E-mail:
Contact: Ms. Ornella Magrini

World Arrow Tours
Via Quintino Sella, 55
00187 Roma
Phone: 064874020
Fax: 064874014
Http://
E-mail:
Contact: Ms. Frida Russo

TOUR OPERATORS MEMBERS OF THE VISIT USA COMMITTEE IN ITALY[2]

Aerocar Delta Holidays
Viale della Liberazione, 18
20124 Milano
Phone: 0267072000
Fax: 0267073406
Http:// www.aerocar.it
E-mail: ferretti@aerocar.it
Contact: Mr. Giuseppe Ferretti

Agiata SrL
Via Carroccio, 3
20123 Milano
Phone: 0289401857
Fax: 0289401857
www.galactica.it.aziende/agiata
E-mail: agiata@galactica.it
Contact: Ms. Simona Masiero

Alidays SrL
Via G. Carducci, 12
20123 Milano
Phone: 028900011
Fax: 028900619
Http:// www.alidays.com
E-mail: ali.america@flashnet.it
Contact: Mr. Biagio Di Sano

Alpitour SpA
Via Roccavione, 15
12100 Cuneo
Phone: 01713131
Fax: 0171313219
Http:// www.alpitour.it
E-mail: canesch@alpitour.it
Contact: Ms. Roberta Caneschi

Chiariva SpA
Via Dante, 8
20121 Milano
Phone: 0285041
Fax: 028504229
Http:// www.chiariva.it
E-mail: chiariva@chiariva.it
Contact: Ms. Isabella Garrone

Colony Srl
Via C. Cantu`, 50
47831 Dogana-San Marino
Phone: 0549909945
Fax: 0549909953
Http://
E-mail: colony@inthenet.sm
Contact: Ms. Silvia Brunetti

Factory Travel
Via Santa Brigida, 79
80132 Napoli
Phone: 0815511556
Fax: 0815510759
Contact: Mr. Massimo Pucci

Francorosso International SpA
Via Santa Chiara, 19
10122 Torino
Phone: 0114646111
Fax: 0115212740
Http://
E-mail: info/fri@francorosso.it
Contact: Mr.Giuliano Croci

Glamour Tour Operator
Via San Girolamo, 14
55100 Lucca
Phone: 0583495757
Fax: 0583495759
Http:// www.glamourviaggi.it
E-mail: itglam@tin.it
Contact: Ms. Gabriella Venturi

Grimaldi Viaggi e Crociere
Via M. Campodisola, 13
80133 Napoli
Phone: 081496212
Fax: 0815517716
Http:// www.grimaldi.napoli.it
E-mail: isler@grimaldi.napoli.it
Contact: Mr. Hans Ruedi Isler

Hotelplan
Corso Italia, 1
20122 Milano
Phone: 02721361
Fax: 028054580
Http:// www.hotelplan.it
E-mail: hotelplanit@gncomtex.com
Contact: Mr. Marco Cisini

I Grandi Viaggi
Via della Moscova, 36
20121 Milano
Phone: 0229046301
Fax: 0229046322
Http:// www.igrandiviaggi.it

[2] THE VISIT USA ITALIA COMMITTEE IS A CONSORTIUM OF COMPANIES DIRECTLY OR INDIRECTLY INTERESTED IN THE DEVELOPMENT OF ITALIAN TOURISM TOWARDS THE UNITED STATES. IN 2000 IT ASSOCIATES 34 TOUR OPERATORS, 7 AIR LINES, 5 HOTEL CHAINS, 1 RENT A CAR, 6 G.S.A./ REPRESENTATIVES, 1 CRUISE LINES, 2 DESTINATIONS AND 7 USA SPONSORS.

E-mail: igvti@tin.it
Contact: Mr. Gianluca Resmini

I Viaggi del Toghiro
Via Montevidio 1/4
16129 Genova
Phone: 0103622489
Fax: 0103620805
Http:// www.toghiro.com
E-mail: getoghiro@toghiro.com
Contact: Ms. Stefania Tedesco

I Viaggi del Ventaglio - Caleidoscopio
Via dei Gracchi, 35
20146 Milano
Phone: 0246754600
Fax: 0246754700
Http:// www.caleidoscopio/.it
E-mail: piero.ezhaya@ventaglio.com
Contact: Mr. Piero Ezhaya

KUONI Gastaldi Tours SpA
Via Mura di Santa Chiara, 1
16128 Genova
Phone: 01059991
Fax: 010594890
Http:// www.gastaldi.it
E-mail:
Contact: Ms. Graziella Limani

Meridiano Viaggi
Via Mentana, 2/b
00185 Roma
Phone: 0644700015
Fax: 0644700902
Http:// www.meridiano.it
E-mail: andrea@dol.it
Contact: Mr. Massimiliano Radi

NAAR Tour Operator
Piazzale Cadorna, 10
20123 Milano
Phone: 02583411
Fax: '0258341490
Http:// www.naar.com
E-mail: naar@iol.it
Contact: Mr. Frederic Naar

Nautilus Srl Viaggi E T.O.
Via Castiglione,31
09131 Cagliari
Phone: 070400678
Fax: 070493203
E-mail: nautilto@tin.it
Contact: Ms. Laura Crispo

Offshore di ITALIATOUR
Viale A. Marchetti, 111
00148 Roma
Phone: 06656151
Fax: 0665615342
E-mail: corrado_di_mario@alitalia.it
Contact: Mr. Corrado Di Mario

Oltremare Tour Operator
Via Privata Monterusso, 26
80078 Pozzuoli
Phone: 0815247777
Fax: 0815247781
Http:// www.connect.it
E-mail: oltremar@connect.it
Contact: Ms. Sandra Palmieri

Outgoing Tour Operator
Via Crati, 19
00199 Roma
Phone: 068416055
Fax: 068415864
Http:// www.jerrytravel.com
E-mail: outgoing@jerrytravel.com
Contact: Mr. Giancarlo Monti

Sandan Tour Operator Srl
Via L. Bissolati, 22
00187 Roma
Phone: 064885355
Fax: 064819476
Http://
E-mail: sandanto@tin.it
Contact: Ms. Annelisa Forcella

Simply Tour Operator by Teorema Tour
Largo Augusto1/a
20122 Milano
Phone: 02763021
Fax: 0576302704
Http://
E-mail: teorema@galactica.it
Contact: Mr. Giuseppe Gerevini

Sky Reps
Via Calabria, 17
00187 Roma
Phone: 0642884208
Fax: 0642882531
E-mail: sky1@uni.net
Contact: Mr. Saro Maggio

Sprintours Tour Operator
Lungomare P. Toscanelli, 52/a-b
00122 Roma Lido
Phone: 065621973
Fax: 0656181303
Http:// www.sprintours.it
E-mail: info@sprintours.it
Contact: Ms. Laura Bellini

T.A.B.B.
Piazza della Repubblica, 28
20124 Milano
Phone: 026571141
Fax: 026592934
E-mail: tabb@tin.it
Contact: Mr. Cesare Bassani

Tecnitravel Esperienza America
Via Pantano, 26
20122 Milano
Phone: 028053903
Fax: 028693351
Http:// www.betacom.it.ttvl
www.xperienceAlaska.com
E-mail: ttvlm@betacom.it
Contact: Mr. Guido Cassano

Tecno Tour Operator
Via L. Perna, 51
00142 Roma
Phone: 0659602411
Fax: 065413662
Http://
E-mail:
Contact: Ms. Laura Bitursi

Tour & Travel Italia S.p.a.
Piazza Lagrange, 21
10100 Torino
Phone: 0115596409
Fax: 0115596442
Contact: Ms. Laura Loffredo

Touring Club Viaggi
Corso Italia, 10
20122 Milano
Phone: 028526419
Fax: 028526362
Http:// www.touringclub.it
E-mail: amm.viaggi@iol.it
Contact: Mr. Marco Falsarella

Turisanda SpA
Via Poerio, 2/a
20129 Milano
Phone: 0275201
Fax: 02701245551
Http:// www.turisanda.it
E-mail: turisanda@turisanda.it
Contact: Ms. Patrizia Modonesi

Utat Viaggi SpA
Via Travnik, 14
34018 San Dorligo della Valle (TS)
Phone: 040389125
Fax: 0403891297
Http:// www.utat.it
E-mail: srebula@iol.it
Contact: Mr. Silvio Rebula

Uvet Viaggi Turismo
Via Vittor Pisani, 22
20124 Milano
Phone: 02675061
Fax: 0267506322
E-mail: Ppegolotti@uvet.it
Contact: Ms. Patrizia Pegolotti

Vespucci Tour Operator
Via Arno, 102
50019 Osmannoro (FI)
Phone: 055315855
Fax: 055315810
Http:// www.vespucci.it
E-mail: d.fani@vespucci.it
Contact: Mr. Daniele Fani

Viaggi del Mappamondo
Via IV Fontane, 109/b
00184 Roma
Phone: 0647699106
Fax: 064817506
E-mail: usavdm@tin.it
Contact: Mr. Mario Coin

G.S.A./REPRESENTATIVES

B.C.N. International Marketing
Corso Sempione 62
20154 Milano
Phone: 02-34538172
Fax: 0234932453
http//: www.virtualia.it
E-mail: brucatta@tin.it
Contact: Mr. Bruno Cattaneo

Interplanet
Via della Liberazione 18
20124 Milano
Phone: 02-67073186
Fax: 0267075011
http:// www.interplanet-gsa.it
e-mail: booking@interplanet-gsa.it
contact: mr.matteo pomini

Giocoviaggi Cruise & Tour Operator
Piazza Dante, 6
16121 Genova
Phone: 0105531169
Fax: 0105531191
E-mail: giocoviaggi@split.it
Contact: Mr. Roberto Agostini

Master Consulting srl
Via Crati 19

00019 Roma
Phone: 06-8414545
Fax: 068415570
E-mail: mastercons@tiscalinet.it
Contact: Mr. Massimo Loquenzi

Sundeck Viaggi
Via Festo Aveno, 59
00136 Roma
Phone: 0635347101
Fax: 0635347679
E-mail: sundeck.viag@flashnet.it
Contact: Mr.Tonio Colangelo

Airlines

American Airlines
Via Vittor Pisani 19
20124 Milano
Phone: 02-67914400
Fax: 0267071803
Http://: www.aa.com
Contact: Mr. Claudio Cavallari

Continental Airlines
Via S. Clemente 1
20121 Milano
Phone: 02-86463361
Fax: 0286463838
Http://: www.flycontinental.com
E-mail:
Contact: Mr. Ariel Klein

Delta Air Lines
Piazza Cavour 2
20121 Milano
Phone: 02-762581
Fax: 0276258300
Http://: www.delta-air.com
Contact: Mr. Camillo Bozzolo

Iberia
Via Bertoloni 3d
00197 Roma
Phone: 06-8083105
Fax: 068082662
Http://: www.iberia.es
Contact: Mr. Felix Gomez Perez

Lufthansa
Via Larga 23
20122 Milano
Phone: 02-5837285
Fax: 0258372288
Http://: www.lufthansa.it
Contact: mr. Enzo Gobbo

Trans World Airlines
Corso Europa 11
20121 Milano
Phone: 02-76250302
Fax : 0276014583
Http://: www.twa.com
E-mail: smichae@twa.com
Contact: Mr. Stephanos Michaelidis

United Airlines
Via della Liberazione 18
20100 Milano
Phone: 02-66984207
Fax: 0266984790
Http://: www.ual.com
Contact: Mr. Aldo Gallo

Rent a car

Avis
Via Arcangelo Corelli 150
20134 Milano
Phone: 02-70200140
Fax: 0270200442
Http://: www.avis.com
Contact: Mr. Paolo Pigni

Destinations

Boston & Massachusetts
Via Gherardini 2
20124 Milano
Phone: 02-33105841
Fax: 0233105827
Http://: www.massport.com
E-mail: mail@themasrl.it
Contact: Ms. Olga Mazzoni

Rocky Mountain International
Via Gherardini 2
20124 Milano
Phone: 02-33105841
Fax: 0233105827
Http://: www.rmi-realamerica.com
E-mail: mail@themasrl.it
Contact: Ms. Olga Mazzoni

Hotel chains:

Best Western International Inc.
Via Cechov 48
20151 Milano
Phone: 02-33428401
Fax: 0233403851
Http://: www.bestwestern.com
Contact: Ms. Eleonora Leccardi

Hilton Worldwide
Via Galvani 12
20124 Milano
Phone: 02-6697176
Fax: 0266987638
Http://: www.hilton.com
E-mail:
Contact: Ms. Francesca Viola

Inter-Continental & Crowne Plaza Hotel & Resorts
Via Vittor Pisani 12
20124 Milano
Phone: 02-6692541
Fax: 0266982377
Http://: www.crowneplaza.com
www.interconti.com
E-mail: milhs@interconti.com
Contact: Mr. Gabriele Ferola

Marriott hotels
Corso di Porta Romana 6
20122 Milano
Phone: 02-804368
Fax: 02804850
Http://: www.marriot.com
Contact: Ms. Maria Pinton

Starwood
Piazza della Repubblica 20
20100 Milano
Phone: 02-6266300
Fax: 026266333
Http://: www.starwood.com
Contact: Ms. Nandina Spagnuolo
CLOTHES AND APPAREL COMPANIES

MAJOR EXPORTERS

ANGELO ARENIELLO

LOCATION
ANGELO ARENIELLO is located in San Giuseppe Vesuviano, province of Naples, in Southern Italy. Full address:

MARKET
ANGELO ARENIELLO products are sold in Italy and in all the world, including Europe and Japan.

Main customers are wholesalers and retail chains, as well as clothing brands or companies willing to produce a quality product in Italy.

Recently ANGELO ARENIELLO focused its sales also to medium and large retail chains, selling directly or through some dedicated agents and representatives

ANGELO ARENIELLO Srl

via Astalonga 21/a	
San Giuseppe Vesuviano	Napoli, ITALY
Telephone	+39-081-5202946
Fax	+39-081-5292507

COMPANY
ANGELO ARENIELLO, established in 1947 by John Areniello, has been working for years with success in the field of the distribution of wholesale clothing. Today the firm spreads over a 22,000 square-metre surface, it deals with an average of 200 million goods yearly and has national and foreign customers. There are two basic features in the company strategy: a highly professional staff and a favourable quality-price ratio for all the company's products.

PRODUCTS

ANGELO ARENIELLO designs and manufactures a comprehensive range of men's wear, including suits, jackets, trousers and overcoats. All articles features a typical "Italian style" and are made from quality fabrics.

ANGELO ARENIELLO may match the needs of every type of customer, from mass distribution to specialised chains, even offering the possibility of manufacturing models other than those in its collections.

- Men's Suits
- Jackets
- Trousers
- Overcoats

PRODUCT GALLERY OVERVIEW

Below are a selection of articles manufactured and offered by ANGELO ARENIELLO.

MEN'S SUITS

OVERCOATS AND JACKETS

FINE MEN'S WEAR

Collections, Brands and Trademarks
Mr. ARANS's BARONE ROCCADORO

CONTACT

For more information, send an E-mail now to our sales reps at angelo@areniello.it
Our staff is fluent in English.
You may also reach Mr. Angelo Areniello, our sales manager, at +39-081-5202946 between 9:00 am - 1:00 pm and 4:00 - 8:00 pm GMT+1, Monday through Friday.

ACHILLE PINTO

In 1933, at the age of 27, Mr. Achille Pinto bought four second hand looms and started his own company with courage and foresight .
Today ACHILLE PINTO is one of the most important and dynamic dyeing and printing mills in the Como textile district. It extends over an area of 30,000 square meters and employs 140 people with an average turnover of 35 billion Itl. per year.
Research, quality, and customer service are the main elements of ACHILLE PINTO policy.

PRODUCTS

The ACHILLE PINTO product (clothing fabrics and fashion accessories) is the result of a consistent research of new fabrics, designs and printing/finishing processes. Each item is manufactured through steps requiring advanced knowledge and high skills.

All the products used in the manufacturing processes are environment-friendly. ACHILLE PINTO also collaborates with known designers to create exclusive collections and develop private label programs.

- Clothing Fabrics
- Scarves
- Shawls
- Fashion Fabrics

MARKET

The fashion accessories collection is worldwide distiributed to boutiques, duty frees and to the most prestigious department stores, such as Harrods, Fenwich, Liberty, Lafayette, Printemps, Saks, Nieman Marcus, Henry Bendell, and others.

ACHILLE PINTO's clothing fabrics are sold to qualified fashion apparel companies in all over the world.

LOCATION

ACHILLE PINTO is located in Casnate con Bernate, province of Como, in Northern Italy. Full address:

ACHILLE PINTO SpA
via Roma 9
Casnate con Bernate
Como, ITALY
Telephone+39-031-564686
Fax+39-031-565472

CONTACT

For more information, send an E-mail now to our sales reps at info@achillepinto.com
Our staff is fluent in English, German and French.
You may also reach our sales manager at +39-031-564686 between 9:00 am and 6:00 pm GMT+1, Monday through Friday.

PRODUCT GALLERY OVERVIEW

Below are a selection of articles manufactured and offered by ACHILLE PINTO.
Silk Scarves and Stoles

Silk satin scarf - waves design
Iridescent velvet and taffetas silk stole.

Fine Clothing Fabrics
Iridescent and printed velvet fabrics for women's wear
Pleated and printed fabrics for women's wear

Silk & Wool Stoles
Satin silk quilted stole
Patchwork stole in mohair/velvet/silk
Collections, Brands and Trademarks
All fashion accessories are entirely hand sewn and assembled by experienced local workers, real leaders in the hand crafted art, distinguishing the "Made in Italy" throughout the world.
Before shipment all products are inspected and carefully packed in order to guarantee high quality standars to the consumer. The entire production cycle is ISO 9002 certified.

ANTARTIDE

Established in 1990, ANTARTIDE is a young, dynamic, and totally quality oriented company which has made its way into the very center of the evolution of finest in Italian tradition. ANTARTIDE's winning secret is their ability to produce a continuous line of great styles, and very focused product research to meet the ever increasing demand of their very discriminating clientele.

PRODUCTS

All ANTARTIDE ties are all handmade. They each have very distinguishing marks of excellence, such as the loop on the reverse side being made of the same fine fabric, and the inside lining made from only very high-end fabrics (which can also be customized).

- Neckties
- Scarves
- Handkerchiefs

MARKET

The company manufactures ties in silk, or other natural fibres, such as linen, wool, and cashmere. ANTARTIDE produces the highest quality of necktie on the market. The main thrust of its sales are directed to overseas markets such as Europe, the USA, Australia and the Far East where its extreme care in quality, progressive style, and customer service is well appreciated.

LOCATION

ANTARTIDE Srl
via Alciato 17/a
Como (Como), ITALY
Telephone: 39031275125
Fax: 39031243920

CONTACT

Our sales staff is fluent in English and German. Ask for our sales manager, Mr.Angelo Donati with any type of request.

You may get in touch with ANTARTIDE by phone from 9.0 am to 6.00 pm, Monday-Friday,

PRODUCT GALLERY OVERVIEW

Below are a selection of some of the most important articles manufactured and sold by ANTARTIDE Srl.

Silk Neckties

Hand-made Neckties

Luxury Silk Ties

Collections, Brands and Trademarks

SEGNI & DISEGNI is the main brand of ANTARTIDE. The distinguishing marks of any SEGNI & DISEGNI neckties are their superb quality fabric and their superior stitching.

Whoever wears a SEGNI & DISEGNI tie has chosen a chic, yet elegant look because of the perfect balance of design and color. ANTARTIDE can design and deliver custom-made high-quality silk ties for prestigious corporate, or club gifts.

ATTEX

ATTEX is a long-experienced leader in silk fabrics for ties. The company may satisfy every request concerning up-to-date styling and promotional designs, thanks to the extensive use of advanced technologies

PRODUCTS

ATTEX delivers yarn-dyed Jacquard and printed fabrics for fine neckwear, as well as high quality silk neckties and men's scarves.

Luxury fabrics, special linings and tippings are used to manufacture ATTEX ties. Available products includes also more men's fashion accessories like silk hankyes and fabrics for dressing gowns.

- Jacquard Fabrics
- Printed Fabrics
- Silk Neckties
- Promotional Neckties

MARKET

ATTEX operates on the worldwide market directly and through agents. The currently most important markets are: Great Britain, Germany and France.

Corporations, advertising agencies, museums, and associations are typical customers of ATTEX promotional neckties: all requests for proposals and quotations are promptly complied.

LOCATION

ATTEX is located in Luisago, province of Como, the world capital of quality silk fashion accessories. Full address:

ATTEX SpA
via Adige 4
22070 Luisago
Como, ITALY
Telephone+39-031-88321
Fax+39-031-881035

CONTACT

For more information, send an E-mail now to our sales reps at sales@ATTEX.it
Our staff is fluent in English, German and French.
You may also reach Attilio Pascucci, our sales manager, at +003903188321 between 8.30 am and 5.30 pm GMT+1, Monday through Friday.

PRODUCT GALLERY OVERVIEW

Below are a selection of articles manufactured and offered by ATTEX.

NECKWEAR FABRICS

PRINTED & JACQUARD FABRICS

SILK NECKTIES

Collections, Brands and Trademarks

Cutting-edge CAD graphic systems allow ATTEX to provide customers with different colorways of its designs on paper or as digital images in standard file format delivered through Internet in very short times.

BEBA

BEBA is a 20-year company designing and manufacturing personal underwear, sexy lingerie, beachwear, costumes and other types of clothing. The whole manufacturing process is developed with great care and making use of the best materials available.

PRODUCTS

Trend Clothes with special and precious , elastic draper - man-made leather - varnish -

Sexy underwear in man-made leather - fantasy and paillettes shiny drapers Animation's Costumes Performance's

Available Sizes : European from 1° to 5°, including oversize and calibrated.

- Sexy Lingerie
- Beachwear
- Underwear
- Costumes

MARKET

BEBA's main customers are Shops of trendy clothing, qualified Sexy Shops and Department Stores.

LOCATION	
BEBA is located in Sesto San Giovanni, province of Milano, in Northern Italy. Full address:	
BEBALINE - Vilardi Maria Catia	
via Pisacane 15	
Sesto San Giovanni	Milano, ITALY
Telephone	+39-02-26224203
Fax	+39-02-26224203

CONTACT

For more information, send an E-mail now to our sales reps at bebaline@libero.it
Our staff is fluent in English.

You may also reach Mrs. Paola, our sales manager, at +39-02-26224203 between 8:30 am and 5:30 pm GMT+1, Monday through Friday.

PRODUCT GALLERY OVERVIEW

Below are a selection of articles manufactured and offered by BEBA.

Sexy Lingerie

Beachwear and Trendy Clothing

Sexy CLothing and Pareos

Collections, Brands and Trademarks

The main brand is BEBA.

Spring- Summer :

- 1st collection from Jannaury to March
- 2nd collection from April

Autumn - Winter :

- 1st collection from August to December
- 2nd collection additional at 20 October and at 31 December (collection Christmas and New Year)

to May
- 3rd collectio from 15 May
to July

BLU LINE

BLU LINE manufactures high quality fabrics for women's wear.

An in-house production allows a quick, timely, and versatile service, as well as on-demand custom products able to meet the need of every single client.

PRODUCTS

High quality and silk fabrics developed after a deep style and technological research.

Solid, fancy, Jacquard, and yarn-dyed fabrics, as well as fabrics featuring very special finishing processes. BLU LINE makes use of natural and blended yarns to create innovative looks and brand new tactile feelings.

- Plain Fabrics
- Jacquard Fabrics
- Special Finishing Fabrics
- "Fil-coupe'" Fabrics

MARKET

BLU LINE sells its fabrics through a network of agents working wit the most qualified women's wear manufacturers in Italy and in all over the world.

These agents are always available to show personally the BLU LINE fabric collections at any time.

LOCATION

BLU LINE is located in Lurago d'Erba, not far from Como, the famous district of quality fabrics production. Full address:

BLU LINE Srl
via Verdi 11
Lurago d'Erba
Como, ITALY
Telephone+39-031-697446
Fax+39-031-697429

CONTACT

For more information, send an E-mail now to our sales reps at info@bluline.it
Our staff is fluent in English and German.
You may also reach our sales staff at +39-031-697446 between 9:00 am and 6:00 pm GMT+1, Monday through Friday.

PRODUCT GALLERY OVERVIEW

Below are a selection of articles manufactured and offered by BLU LINE.

Silk Fabrics

Advanced Fine Fabrics

Jacquard and Plain Fabrics

E. BOSELLI & C.

E. BOSELLI & C. is specialized in polyester woven fabrics for intimate apparel and outerwear. Production is vertically organised from yarn twisting to fabric finishing through yarn texturizing, warping, warp-sizing, weaving, dyeing and printing. All the different processes are carried out within the company facilities and developed with its own know-how.

PRODUCTS

BOSELLI offers classic silky-looking fabrics and micro fibers fabrics, mono and bi stretch, fancy prints and Jacquard fabrics for corsetry, lingerie, and men's underwear, homewear, outerwear and sportswear. Width is from 95 to 180 centimeters. Weight goes from 50 to 170 grams/square meter. Content is 100% polyester or polyester/elastan.
BOSELLI also delivers a furnishing fabric collection with 280, 300 and 330 cms-wide fabrics, especially for curtains, bedsheeting, bedspreads. Silk-like fabrics, essentially addressed to wholesalers: georgettes, crêpes, satin, slubby yarns, taffetas and others. A flame retardant collection suitable for the contract market is also available, made of TREVIRA CS yarn.

- Lingerie Fabrics
- Underwear Fabrics
- Sportswear Fabrics
- Curtains & Bedspreads

MARKET

BOSELLI usually sells its fabrics to clothing manufacturers and fabric wholesalers in all around thew world, through an extensive network of sales agents. Companies and professionals interested in applying as a BOSELLI agent, please send an E-Mail with a detailed business profile.

BOSELLI has also subsidiaries in the markets where it is mostly strong: Germany & Holland, UK & Ireland, France, Spain, USA & Canada.

LOCATION
BOSELLI is located in Olgiate Comasco, province of Como, in Northern Italy. Full address:

E. BOSELLI & C. SpA
via Carducci 11
Olgiate Comasco
Como, ITALY
Telephone+39-031-944050
Fax+39-031-943017

CONTACT

For more information, send an E-mail now to our sales reps at marketing@boselli.it

Our staff is fluent in English, German and French.

You may also reach Dr. Giulio Balossi Restelli, our Sales General Manager, at +39-031-944050 between 9:00 am and 6:00 pm GMT+1, Monday through Friday.

PRODUCT GALLERY OVERVIEW

Below are a selection of articles manufactured and offered by BOSELLI.

Lingerie Fabrics

Outerwear Fabrics

Underwear Fabrics Polyester Printed Satin

CAMICERIA BOTTERI

CAMICERIA BOTTERI is a manufacturer of fine and made-to-measure men's shirts since more than 70 years.

An oustanding experience featuring the best of the appreciated Italian tradition in men's shirting.

PRODUCTS

All the shirts produced by CAMICERIA BOTTERI are made from high quality fabrics and well-finished with hand care.

Some features:

- the shirts monograms are rigorously hand made
- the buttons are in pure nacre and can be even monogrammed with the customer's name
- the buttonholes are hand-finished
- the side sections of our shirts are one-needle sewn

Our service for customized shirts is mostly targeted to the single client.

- Fine Cotton Shirts
- Customized Shirts
- Made-to-Measure

MARKET

CAMICERIA BOTTERI sells its superb Italian-style shirts to shops and boutiques. Made-to-measure shirts are sold to consumers directly.

CAMICERIA BOTTERI has also a strong experience in custom shirts and neckties for Clubs, Associations and Companies featuring their own logo.

LOCATION

CAMICERIA BOTTERI is located in Trieste, in the very North-East of Italy. Full address:

CAMICERIA BOTTERI Snc	
Corso Italia 8	
Trieste	Trieste, ITALY
Telephone	+39-040-631023
Fax	+39-040-660082

E-Mail

CONTACT

For more information, send an E-mail now to our sales reps at info@camiceriabotteri.com Our staff is fluent in English and German. You may also reach Mr. Lorenzo Fossi, our sales general manager, at +39-040-631023 between 8:30 am and 6:00 pm GMT+1, Monday through Friday.

PRODUCT GALLERY OVERVIEW

Below are a selection of articles manufactured and offered by CAMICERIA BOTTERI.

Fine Men's Shirts

Shirts made from the finest Cotton Fabrics

Italian Style and Tradition

Collections, Brands and Trademarks

CAMICERIA BOTTERI is also a qualified reseller of clothing items by LACOSTE, GANT, ZEGNA, VALENTINO and FRED PERRY.

CONFEZIONI CLAUDIA

CONFEZIONI CLAUDIA has been established in 1964. Since then the company got a terrific manufacturing and style experience, one of its main assets to give a timely and excellent service coupled with a great quality.

CONFEZIONI CLAUDIA has its own labels, but it manufactures also for other brands like Cotton Belt, Calvin Klein, and others. Ask for more info.

PRODUCTS

CONFEZIONI CLAUDIA designs and manufacturers a large range of women's clothing, both for ladies and girls.

Jersey fabrics are extensively used and usually enriched by embroderies, gorgeous prints and special washing, including a final treatment delivering a special feeling.

- Dresses
- Jackets
- Trousers
- Shirts - Blouses

MARKET

CONFEZIONI CLAUDIA's products are sold in all the world, and especially in the United States, Japan and Europe.

Main customers are wholesalers and retail chains, as well as clothing brands or companies willing to produce a quality product in Italy.

LOCATION

CLAUDIA is located in Agliana, province of Pistoia, very near to Florence, in Central Italy. Full address:

CONFEZIONI CLAUDIA Srl	
via G. La Pira 2	
Agliana	Pistoia, ITALY
Telephone	+39-0574-751063
Fax	+39-0574-751386
E-Mail	

CONTACT

For more information, send an E-mail now to our sales reps at claudiamoda@ego.it
Our staff is fluent in English.

You may also reach Mrs. Claudia, our sales manager, at +39-0574-751063 between 9:00 - 12:00 am and 3:00 - 7:00 pm GMT+1, Monday through Friday.

PRODUCT GALLERY OVERVIEW

Below are a selection of articles manufactured and offered by CONFEZIONI CLAUDIA.

Women's Wear

CLAUDIA E BASTA : wool and silk T-Shirt

WHITE ANGEL : T-Shirt made from modal and lycra, with paillettes at the neck line

CLOTHING FOR LADIES

CLAUDIA E BASTA : T-Shirt made of wool and silk with stretch throuser in the same print

WHITE ANGEL : shirt in wrinkled material

Italian Style and Quality

BASIC COLLECTION LONDON : jacket & trousers made from cotton with silicon touch

MARINA LANTE DELLA ROVERE : jacket and trousers made of velvet stretch fabric with special print

COLLECTIONS, BRANDS AND TRADEMARKS

BASIC COLLECTION LONDON-
A line designed for young teenagers, with simple style and happy colors. Targeted to an age from 15 to 25 years

CLAUDIA E BASTA -
Total look with a large choice of materials, usually more classic than the other lines, but targeted to an aggressive/sweet woman

WHITE ANGEL -
A line targeted to a very sexy and sophisticated young woman: all articles are enriched by embrodery or special treatments. Ideal for an age from 20 to 30 years.

MARINA LANTE DELLA ROVERE -
This line is produced under license: a very special collection of clothing for any special woman with a very strong and particular personality.

CONFEZIONI SILVANA,

CONFEZIONI SILVANA, established over 30 years ago, is specialized in manufacturing and selling clothes for children and young girls.
The company developed an outstanding experience in the search for accessories and high quality fabrics, in collaboration with skilled Italian designers.
CONFEZIONI SILVANA products are tailored and manufactured by a qualified staff taking advantage of the most advanced apparel machinery..

PRODUCTS

CONFEZIONI SILVANA production is entirely "made in Italy", and is covered by a full warranty.

Its elegant and sport clothes are targeted to a medium-high market of kids (2-7 years old) and young (8-16 years old) girls .

The main products are: dresses, skirts, trousers, T-Shirts, and pinafores, as well as blouses.

- Childrenwear

- Teenwear
- Knitted Dresses
- Skirts

MARKET

CONFEZIONI SILVANA sells its superb products to Italian and international wholesalers.

LOCATION

CONFEZIONI SILVANA is located in Muzza Cornegliano Laudense, province of Lodi, in Northern Italy. Full address:

CONFEZIONI SILVANA Srl
via Mazzini 12/14
Muzza Cornegliano Laudense
Lodi, ITALY
Telephone+39-0371-69010
Fax+39-00371-69020

CONTACT

For more information, send an E-mail now to our sales reps at conf.silvana@pmp.it
Our staff is fluent in English.
You may also reach our sales manager at +39-0371-69010 between 9:00 am and 6:00 pm GMT+1, Monday through Friday.

Product Gallery Overview

Below are a selection of articles manufactured and offered by CONFEZIONI SILVANA.

Pullovers

Sweaters

Collections, Brands and Trademarks

CONFEZIONI SILVANA develops three collections a year:

- Spring/Summer
- Autumn/Winter
- Christmas

CSP INTERNATIONAL

CSP INTERNATIONAL has been operating the hosiery field for 30 years: it has more than 1500 employees and produces more than 100 millions pairs of stockings and tights per year.

CSP INTERNATIONAL is the 2nd largest Italian Hosiery Company, the 3rd largest Hosiery Company in Europe. The buildings of CSP International are the most modern and have a complete automated production cycle. Ask for more info.

PRODUCTS

CSP INTERNATIONAL principally produces stockings and tights, but it also offers different products, such as men socks, knitwear, corsetry and pyjamas.

- Stockings & Tights
- Men's Socks
- Corsetry
- Knitwear - Pyjamas

MARKET & COLLECTIONS

CSP INTERNATIONAL's leading fashion products are distributed by departments stores, wholesalers and quality boutiques in all over the world.

The mission of CSP INTERNATIONAL is to produce and distribute the best products in the world as of quality/price ratio, and its motto is: "*Innovation in hosiery and underwear*" !

CSP INTERNATIONAL offers brands and collections for all the different market needs :

- "Sanpellegrino" is the brand with the best quality/price ratio
- "Oroblu'" is the brand with the highest quality and image level. It is sold in the best Department Stores
- "Starway" is the youngest brand. It is sold in the qualified retail and in the best Department Stores
- "Le Bourget" is the brand of great and consolidated tradition on the French market
- "Lepel" is the specialised brand for corsetry

LOCATION

CSP INTERNATIONAL is located in Ceresara, in the huge hosiery district of Castelgoffredo (province of Mantova), in Northern Italy. Full address:

CSP INTERNATIONAL SpA
via Piubega 5c

Ceresara Mantova, ITALY
Telephone+39-0376-8101
Fax+39-0376-810435

CONTACT

For more information, send an E-mail now to our export department at export.office@cspinternational.it

Our staff is fluent in English, German, Spanish, French and Russian.

You may also reach our sales managers, at +39-0376-8101 between 8:30 am and 5:30 pm GMT+1, Monday through Friday.

Product Gallery Overview

Below are a selection of articles manufactured and offered by CSP INTERNATIONAL.

Stockings and Tights

Fine Seamless Lingerie

Casual Socks and Fashion Collections

Collections, Brands and Trademarks

DIANA

DIANA, established in 1947, is one of the world's leaders in swim and beachwear. Most of the advancements in technical swimwear over the past thirty years has been developed as a result of DIANA research breakthroughs. DIANA sells mainly through a network of agents, distributors and department stores. Ask for more info.

PRODUCTS

All swim and beachwear is made from start to finish in Italy, and is covered by a full (remove "quality") warranty. DIANA products are manufactured from only the best and most advanced fabrics and materials available on the market. These products are designed by skilled Italian stylists in close collaboration with the manufacturers and the style bureau.
Minimum regular sale: 20 assorted pieces.

- Swimwear
- Beachwear
- Waterpolo Apparel
- Swim Accessories

MARKET

DIANA typically sells its superb products to wholesalers and department stores, but also serves retailers in various countries and regions. Ask for details.
Sports clubs and teams are very enthusiastic customers, because of affordable minimums for custom-made swim caps and swimwear.
DIANA also makes great items for Internet shops.

LOCATION

DIANA is located in Merate, province of Lecco, in Northern Italy. Full address:

Rue Royale Diana SpA
via Statale 24
Merate Lecco, ITALY
Telephone +39-039-9908551
Fax +39-039-9903761

CONTACT

For more information, send an E-mail now to our sales dept at info.diana@dianasport.it
Our staff is fluent in English, German and French.
You may also reach Mr. Antonello Goretti, our sales manager, at +390399908551 between 8.30 am and 5.30 pm (GMT+1)

PRODUCT GALLERY OVERVIEW

Below a selection of some of the most important articles manufactured and sold by DIANA.
A consumer product catalog may be viewed at DIANA SHOP online: click here.

SWIMWEAR

BEACHWEAR

WATERPOLO - ACCESSORIES

COLLECTIONS, BRANDS AND TRADEMARKS

DIANA offers five main collections:

- Swimwear
- Fun & Beachwear
- Basic Line
- Waterpolo
- Accessories

MACH 1 is a new, one-piece swimsuit, made from 100% silicone especially designed for the pros.

DIDI & BERT

DIDI & BERT was established in the beginning of 2000 after a nice and original idea of the owner, a very creative woman. DIDI & BERT realized the time was right for a new product: it PATENTED a new kind of nylon-fiber (Poliammide) and very cheap underwear, the ideal answer for our society's demand of quick and easy-to-use goods..

PRODUCTS

Very cheap line of underwear. DIDI & BERT's underwear has been designed just for a large range of uses and situations such as those requiring frequent underwear changes, without having to worry about washing, drying and ironing. Main consumers: frequent travellers, people into fitness (gym, tennis, swimming pool, football, disco, etc ...), boys and girls camping, etc ...

Our very cheap underwear is available in several fashionable colors and models.

DIDI & BERT offers also a second product line, featuring a superior quality and a seamless design for traditional wearing, made from advanced microfiber and lycra fabrics

• Cheap Underwear	• Better Underwear
• Gym Clothing	• T-Shirts and Socks

MARKET

DIDI & BERT sells to international wholesalers and importers of underwear clothing, offering a large choice of different qualities and prices, able to match any type of request.

Agents and distributors are welcome: click here to send us a profile of your company.

LOCATION

DIDI & BERT is located in Ciserano, between Milan and Bergamo, in Northern Italy. Full address:

DIDI & BERT Srl
Borgo San Marco 1

Ciserano	Bergamo, ITALY
Telephone	+39-035-871784
Fax	+39-035-4820747

CONTACT

For more information, send an E-mail now to our sales reps at info@didiebert.com
Our staff is fluent in English.
You may also reach Mrs. Anna Maria, our sales manager, at +39-035-871784 between 8:30 am and 5:30 pm GMT+1, Monday through Friday.

PRODUCT GALLERY OVERVIEW

Below are a selection of articles manufactured and offered by DIDI & BERT.

Cheap Women's Underwear

Underwear and Tops

Men's Underwear

LINEA DORI

LINEA DORI has been established in the '70s, as spin-off from a large knitting mill. The company's strategy emphasizes the product quality and a manufacturing cycle completely made in Italy, from weaving to packaging. Ask for more info.

PRODUCTS

All the products manufactured by LINEA DORI are made from high quality materials and closely inspected throughout all the production process.

LINEA DORI offers a broad range of women's and men's underwear in many models, materials, sizes and colors. Most items are regularly available in LINEA DORI's warehouse, allowing fast deliveries and an "on-demand" service to customers

- Women's Underwear
- Men's Underwear
- "High-Tec" Items
- T-Shirts

MARKET

LINEA DORI has been selling most of its production to wholesalers in Italy and all around the world.

During the '90s it focused its sales also to medium and large retail chains, selling directly or through some dedicated agents and representatives.

LOCATION

LINEA DORI is located in Solbiate Olona, province of Varese, in Northern Italy. Full address:

LINEA DORI Srl
via IV Novembre 133

Solbiate Olona	Varese, ITALY
Telephone	+39-0331-641291
Fax	+39-0331-643196

CONTACT

For more information, send an E-mail now to our sales reps at lidozz@tin.it
Our staff speaks English and French.
You may also reach Mr. Carlo Gallazzi or Miss Lucia Salmoiraghi, our sales manager, at +39-0331-641291 between 9:00 am and 6:00 pm GMT+1, Monday through Friday.

PRODUCT GALLERY OVERVIEW

Below are a selection of articles manufactured and offered by LINEA DORI.

Women's Underwear

Intimate Apparel

Men's Underwear

Collections, Brands and Trademarks

LINEA DORI has two main labels:

- UNDERMEN (men's underwear)
- DORINETTE (women's underwear)

FLOREAL

FLOREAL, established in 1969, is one of the world leaders in fashion bathing suits and bikinis, joining great

Italian style with a superb product quality.

PRODUCTS

All FLOREAL products are manufactured in Italy taking advantage of the most advanced production processes and quality controls.

All models are designed and manufactured after a continuous in-depth research of new materials, fashion trends, colors,as well as finishing processes.

- Women's Bathing Suits
- Fashion Bikinis

MARKET

FLOREAL usually sells its range of products to wholesalers, retail chains and department stores in all over the world.

New agents and distributors are always welcome. Please send a detailed business profile if you are interested to represent FLOREAL in your market.

LOCATION

FLOREAL is located in Milan. Full address:

FLOREAL Srl	
via Lorenteggio 39	
Milano	Milano, ITALY
Telephone	+39-02-472911
Fax	+39-02-4233818

CONTACT

For more information, send an E-mail now to our sales reps at info@florealmilano.com
Our staff is fluent in English.
You may also reach Mr. Alberto Zonescuti, our sales manager, at +39-02-472911 between 9:00 am and 6:00 pm GMT+1, Monday through Friday.

Product Gallery Overview

Below are a selection of articles manufactured and offered by FLOREAL.

Bikinis

Fashion Beachwear

Great Bathing Suits

Collections, Brands and Trademarks

FLOREAL offers two different collections:

- FLOREAL
- SHE

Both collections are enriched by coordinated accessories.

LE FOGLIE

Le FOGLIE has been successuflly manufacturing and selling underwear and swimwear/beachwear throughout the last eighteen years, getting a prominent market share.

PRODUCTS

Le FOGLIE collections are targeted to the medium/fine market of women's underwear, beachwear and swimwear. All products are manufactured with quality materials and carefully designed with the most charming Italian style.

The main consumer profile is woman between 24 and 45 years old, having a middle/high purchasing capacity, and loving to like herself and be pleased.

- Women's Underwear
- Women's Beachwear
- Swimwear

MARKET

The typical customers of Le FOGLIE are wholesalers and departments stores demanding for high quality Italian-style underwear and beachwear.

All the products proposed by Le Foglie are great items for Internet shops selling online.

LOCATION

LE GOCCE, the company producing "LE FOGLIE", is located in Corbola, province of Rovigo, in Northern Italy. Full address:

LE GOCCE Srl
via Lazzara 21
Corbola ovigo, ITALY
Telephone +39-0426-950123
Fax 39-0426-45607

CONTACT

For more information, send an E-mail now to our sales reps at lefoglie@tiscalinet.it

PRODUCT GALLERY OVERVIEW

Below are a selection of articles manufactured and offered by LE FOGLIE.

Women's Underwear

Beachwear

Bathing Suits

Collections, Brands and Trademarks

Women's Underwear

LE GOCCE has two more lines of underwear and beachwear:

"Le FOGLIE" is the main brand of the company LE GOCCE, while "Ognidì" is a special collection of underwear.

"Le FOGLIE MOVING" is the new packaging of all the products: glamorous black boxes in three different flavors, great for any kind of gift too.

- ENCHANTE' (comfort and fashion)
- FOGLIE YOUNG (the best for teenagers)

staff is fluent in English.
You may also reach Mr. Gianluca Levi, our marketing manager, at +39-0426-950123 between 8.30 am and 17.30 GMT+1, Monday through Friday.

HELEN

HELEN has been operating in the clothing industry for many years with the brand HELEN and private and/or commercial labels in the "ready-to-wear" women's fashion market.

We offer frequently new packages of products and delivery and re-stocking times usually do not exceed 10 working days . The quality of products is medium-high and created for young ladies for ages between 25 and 50.

PRODUCTS

The main HELEN's women's wear products :

suits, jackets, skirts, trousers, chemises, dresses and coats.

HELEN shows its collection for the Fall/Winter season at the end of June and July, while for the Spring season in January and for Summer season in April. During the seasons HELEN offers other new products matching the latest fashion trends.

- Suits
- Jackets
- Skirts & Trousers
- Coats

MARKET

HELEN successfully supplies retailers, retail chains, wholesalers, apparel companies, as well as department stores in all over the world.

LOCATION

HELEN is located in Bassano del Grappa, province of Vicenza, in North-East Italy. Full address:

HELEN Srl
via Colomba 1
Bassano del Grappa
Vicenza, ITALY
Telephone +39-0424-228139
Fax 39-0424-228149

ONTACT

For more information, send an E-mail now to our sales reps at info@helen.it
Our staff is fluent in English.
You may also reach Mr. Giampietro Calmonte, our sales manager, at +39-0424-228139 between 8:30 am and 6:30 pm GMT+1, Monday through Friday.

PRODUCT GALLERY OVERVIEW

Below are a selection of articles manufactured and offered by HELEN.

Coats and Dresses

WOMEN'S CLOTHING

Comfortable Clothing

LINEA AZZURRA

is a primary textile printing company working in the swimwear, sportswear and underwear market. It has been established in 1983. We design and produce a wide range of exclusive prints.

PRODUCTS

Linea Azzurra manufactures stretch printed fabrics, mainly with a composition of 20% Lycra and 80% polyamide, as well as any other cotton, viscose, or polyester textile fabric.

- Swimwear fabrics
- Underwear fabrics
- Ink-jet sampling

MARKET

Linea Azzurra fabrics are used domestically and internationally by the most prestigious swimwear, beachwear and underwear manufacturers.

Our large collection may be viewed in any moment through our network of sales reps placed all around the world.

LOCATION

Linea Azzurra Mare is located mid way between Como and Milano. Full address:

LINEA AZZURRA MARE Srl
via Pascoli 9
Verano Brianza
Milano, ITALY
Telephone+39-0362-991208
Fax+39-0362-991210

CONTACT

For more information, send an E-mail now to our sales reps at azzurtex@tin.it
Our staff is fluent in English, German, French and Spanish.
You may also reach Marco Vanzini, our sales manager, at +39-0362-991208 between 8.30 am and 17.30 GMT+1 of any week day.

PRODUCT GALLERY OVERVIEW

Below are a selection of articles manufactured and offered by Linea Azzurra Mare.

For more information about Linea Azzurra Mare products, please feel free to send an E-Mail message.

Fabrics for Beachwear

Printed Fabrics

Underwear & Swimwear Fabrics

Collections, Brands and Trademarks

Linea Azzurra develops some collections:

- swimwear, once in a year
- underwear, twice a year
- many special and fully exclusive customer collections

Thanks to a best-of-breed ink jet digital printer, the company can produce new designs, or customer's artworks in just thee days without any silkscreening involved. Low costs, quick service, superb results.

NODITALIA,

NODITALIA, established in 1997, is a manufacturer of fine ladies and men's wear accessories.

NODITALIA sells mainly through a world-wide network of specialty and department stores.

PRODUCTS

NODITALIA's entire production is based in Italy and all fabrics and material are of domestic origin.

Silk and other natural fibres are used to keep the product updated to satisfy the present consumer demands.

- Silk Neckties
- Scarves
- Shirts
- Men's Formalwear

MARKET

NODITALIA typically sells its superb products to specialty-stores and department stores, but also serves wholesalers in various countries and regions.

NODITALIA also makes great items for Internet shops. At the moment NODITALIA does not sell directly to consumers.

LOCATION

NODITALIA is located in Albavilla, province of Como, in Northern Italy. Full address:

NODITALIA Srl
via Civati 13
Albavilla Como, ITALY
Telephone +39-031-3353140

Fax +39-031-3353141

CONTACT

For more information, send an E-mail now to our sales reps at sales@NODITALIA.it
Our staff is fluent in English.
You may also reach Mr. Livio, our sales manager, at +39-031-3353140 between 9:00 am and 6:00 pm GMT+1, Monday through Friday.

Product Gallery Overview

Below are a selection of articles manufactured and offered by NODITALIA.

Silk Scarves - Women's Accessories

Scarves and Shawls

Formalwear Accessories

Collections, Brands and Trademarks

NODITALIA offers four main collections:

- Ladies' Fashion Accessories
- Men Neckwear Accessories
- Men's Formalwear
- Men's Shirts

NASTRI TESSUTI

NASTRI TESSUTI has over 30 years of experience in manufacturing fine woven ribbons. Its product is among the highest quality available on the market today, using the most advanced machinery available enabling the company to match any kind of product request.

PRODUCTS

The product range of NASTRI TESSUTI is quite broad including ribbons made from polypropylene, polyester, nylon, cotton or wool.

The company is continually developing new products together with their ever growing list of clientele.

- Jacquard Ribbons
- Printed Ribbons
- Polyester Ribbons
- Special Ribbons

MARKET

NASTRI TESSUTI tipically sells its best-of-breed range of ribbons to manufacturers of:
- fashion accessories
- portswear accessories
- handbags

- luggage
- furniture
- military supplies

LOCATION

NASTRI TESSUTI is located in Marano, province of Vicenza, in northeast Italy.

NASTRI TESSUTI Srl
via del'Artigianato 16
Marano Vicentino
Vicenza, ITALY
Telephone+39-0445-622889
Fax+39-0445-560164

CONTACT

For more information, send an E-mail now to our sales staff, at nastritessuti@schio.nettuno.it
Our staff is fluent in English, and French.
You may also reach Mrs. Raffaella Saccardoi, our sales manager, at +390445622889 between 8.30 am and 17.30 GMT+1

Product Gallery Overview

Below are a selection of articles manufactured and offered by NASTRI TESSUTI.

Jacquard & Luggage Ribbons

Special Ribbons

Ribbons and Tapes

OLIMPIA COMPANY

Over thirty years of experience, advanced technologies, highly skilled and motivated staff, along with production flexibility and a well tuned organization have made OLIMPIA one of the most qualified and specialized companies in the sector. OLIMPIA is recognized as having a well established international image in the marketplace.

OLIMPIA manufactures a wide range of men's and women's underwear in cotton, Lycra, microfibers and elastic fabrics.

All items are delivered in custom-made packaging with wide, transparent windows which allow immediate recognition of colors and patterns, along with a label indicating size and color, care instructions and barcode number.

- Women's Underwear
- Men's Underwear
- Bras
- Boxer Shorts

MARKET

OLIMPIA sells most of its production to international wholesalers.

The company guarantees a quick turnaround on all orders, plus a large assortment of styles, sizes, colors, and frequent updates of patterns based on current fashion trends.

OLIMPIA's style staff is committed to anticipate market indications and discuss customer's requests, delivering skilled consulting.

LOCATION

OLIMPIA is located in Cardano al Campo (province of Varese), close to the Malpensa International Airport in Milan.

OLIMPIA Srl
via Giovanni XXIII 60
Cardano al Campo
Varese, ITALY
Telephone+39 0331 261506, Fax+39 0331 730431

For more information, send an E-mail now to our sales dept at info@olimpia2000.it Our staff is fluent in English, and French.
You may also reach Mr. Remo Mazzetti, our sales manager, at +390331261506 between 9.00 am and 6.00 pm (GMT+1)

Product Gallery Overview

Below a selection of some of the most important articles manufactured and sold by OLIMPIA.

WOMEN'S UNDERWEAR

Collections, Brands, and Trademarks

OLIMPIA offers many different product lines for its great underwear:

WOMEN'S

- New Trends
- Microfibre
- Elastic Fiber

MEN'S

- Elastic Fabrics
- Jo 2001
- Classic

SAF

SAF was established in 1975 as a company specialized in selling stocklots of fashion designers' clothing. In 1995 the company started to design and manufacture its own fashion collection in close collaboration with some important Italian brands.

PRODUCTS

SAF offers a large range of branded and unbranded fine clothing, including business suits, shirts, trousers, knitwear, cachemire knitwear, leather jackets, sweatshirts, raincoats, and coats.

Besides original quality surplus from Italian fashion designers, SAF also sells the VALENTINO Men's Underwear line (VALENTINO BODY).

- Classic CLothing
- Activewear
- Sportswear
- Underwear

MARKET

SAF sells worldwide mainly to wholesalers and retail chains.

Its large and regular offer of branded clothing stocklots at bargain prices is a real business opportunity for many importers and wholesalers dealing with surplus and liquidation fashion merchandise of world-famous Italian fashion designers.

LOCATION

SAF is located in San Marino, the indipendent republic located in Central Italy. Full address:

SAF Sa
via C.Cantu' 104
Repubblica San Marino
Republic of San Marino
Telephone+378-0549-941092
Fax+378-0549-973612

CONTACT

For more information, send an E-mail now to our sales reps at saf@omniway.sm
Our staff is fluent in English.
You may also reach Nicola Cavani, our sales manager, at +378-0549-941092 between 9:00 am and 5:30 pm GMT+1, Monday through Friday.

PRODUCT GALLERY OVERVIEW

Below are a selection of articles manufactured and offered by SAF.

MEN'S WEAR

Women's Wear & Leatherwear

SHIRTS & ACTIVEWEAR

Collections, Brands and Trademarks

SAF proposes regular collections from the following brands:

- LAURA BIAGIOTTI
- VALENTINO BODY (Men's Underwear)
- BASILE
- BASILE SPORT

SAF also sells clothing branded by:

- FORNARINA
- CALVIN KLEIN JEANS
- PIERRE CARDIN
- KH
- UNGARO ITALY
- FRUIT OF THE LOOM
- CARISMA ROUGE (VALENTINO)
- GAI MATTIOLO

SAMAR

SAMAR, established in 1970, is a group of textile and clothing companies located in the surroundings of Biella, in northern Italy.

SAMAR is specialized in the production of ready-made garments for men, women and children and it is the market leader in Italy.
A highly efficient trading organization always takes care to satisfy all the particular requests of clients.

PRODUCTS

SAMAR's main product lines:

- Underwear
- Pyjamas
- Shorts and trousers
- Track-suits and sweat-shirts
- Swimming shorts
- T-shirts, polo
- Shirts
- Knitwear
- Jackets

The products are designed by internal skilled Italian stylists in close collaboration with the manufactures of the group.

Thanks to an excellent mix between quality and very competitive prices, SAMAR is a recognized leader in Italy

- Underwear
- Clothing
- Sleepwear
- T-Shirts - Shirts

MARKET

SAMAR typically sells its products to wholesalers, retail chains and department stores.

In order to meet the demands of chain distribution, SAMAR created IPERGEST (www.ipergest.com), a new company offering to its clients (organised chain distribution) a complete service, as well as pre- and post-sales assistance. IPERGEST can supply this channel respecting its developing times, stock needs, timing and all the related commitments.

IPERGEST is today the supplying leader of the Italian organized chain distribution, and is able to reach ambitious goals also on an international scale. The realization of private label projects are an important example of the confidence that an ever increasing number of clients place on IPERGEST.

Among the distributors' branded articles manufactured by SAMAR - IPERGEST, you can find some international key leaders, such as METRO (Timor), AUCHAN (In Extenso), CARREFOUR (Jackerton e Basic), COOP (Intimo Coop), and OVIESSE-COIN (Theorema).

LOCATION

SAMAR is located in Mottalciata, province of Biella, in Northern Italy. Full address:

SAMAR SpA
via Martiri Libertà 68
Mottalciata
Biella, ITALY
Telephone+39-0161-8721
Fax+39-0161-857585

Product Gallery Overview

Below are a selection of articles manufactured and offered by SAMAR.

WOMEN'S APPAREL, UNDERWEAR & PYJAMAS

Men's Apparel, Underwear & Pyjamas

CHILDREN'S APPAREL, UNDERWEAR & PYJAMAS

Collections, Brands and Trademarks

SAMAR offers different collections and five main brands:

- **SAMAR**: underwear and pyjamas
- **TIDEandSAIL** and **OCN-OCEANIC**: young and "fashion" wear - Total Look
- **SOLISTA**: "classic" casual wear - Total Look
- **GREEN-EARTH**: children's wear

SELEZIONE

SELEZIONE is a company from Como with a long experience in the market of promotional neckties and scarves.

The company staff helps customers to get the best product for their marketing and merchandise needs, thanks to skilled advice and a huge design archive.

PRODUCTS

SELEZIONE manufactures printed and Jacquard neckties made from silk or polyester.

In case of a promotional tie the custom logo or pattern may be delivered to SELEZIONE. Alternatively a new design can be developed or an existing one may be retrieved from our large archive (just adding a custom label on the back).

SELEZIONE also offer collections of scarves for ladies and gentlemen, as well as bow-ties, handkerchiefs, and any other kind of textile fashion accessory.

- Promotional Ties
- Promotional Scarves
- Silk Neckties
- Silk Scarves

MARKET

SELEZIONE typically works with:

- advertising agencies serving large corporations such as FORD, FIAT, L'OREAL, MACONALD'S, etc....

- smaller companies needing corporate gifts, brand merchandise, or promotional items for special events, in low minimum quantities.

- museums, club, and associations looking for fine silk custom-made neckties and scarves.

- wholesalers and retailers of fashion neckties and scarves made from silk and polyester.

LOCATION

SELEZIONE is located in Como, the internationally recognized capital of fashon accessories. Full address:

SELEZIONE Srl
via Oltrecolle 21
Como Como, ITALY
Telephone +39-031-283103
Fax +39-031-281238

CONTACT

For more information, send an E-mail now to our sales reps at selezione@betacom.it
Our staff is fluent in English.
You may also reach Mr. Rccardo Mason, our sales manager, at +39031283103 between 8.30 am and 17.30 GMT+1, Monday through Friday.

Product Gallery Overview

Below are a selection of articles manufactured and offered by SELEZIONE.

Promotional Neckties

Company and Museums Merchandise

Collections, Brands and Trademarks

VIGNONI

VIGNONI has been manufacturing producing and selling a wide range of tights, both for women and kids, since 1957. It is a hosiery leader always investing remarkable resources in its production units, supported by its constant success all over the world. Today its two plants cover an area of around 60,000 square meters, and employ 165 people.

PRODUCTS

VIGNONI production includes a full range of hosiery products featuring an excellent quality/price ratio, able to match most consumers' requirements.
In addition to the classic "Filanca" and "Stretch" product lines, there are also elasticised tights, knee-highs and hold-ups with covered, double-covered and "vanisée" yarns, an increased choice of deniers, soft opaque hosiery made from microfibre, acrylic and cotton, as well as gradual compression tights, the latest fashion trends and fantasy patterns.

Flexible marketing and marketing facilities, a factual customer-oriented commercial collaboration, as well as a timely and effectual service make VMC one of the major European hosiery manufacturing companies.

- Pantyhose
- Tights
- Knee-Highs
- Hold-Ups

MARKET

The company has achieved great results in the domestic market in terms of both the wholesale distribution channel and the large-scale retail trade. It has also consolidated its business relationships with EEC and Extra-EEC countries, currently getting about 70% of VIGNONI entire output.

Among the Italian clients there are:
"Gruppo Rinascente - Auchan", "Coop Italia", "Euromercato", "Continente", "Pam", "Finiper", "Conad", "Oviesse".

Among the best VIGNONI international clients are:
"Bomo" (France), "Metro, Kaufhof, Kaufhalle, C&A" (Germany), "Adler" (Austria), "Dia" (Spain), "Adria, Madison" (Great Britain).

At the moment Vignoni is mostly interested in the great distribution, international wholesalers and supermarkets.

LOCATION

VIGNONI is located in Brescia, in Northern Italy. Full address:

VIGNONI VMC
via Creta 21
Brescia Brescia, ITALY
Telephone+39-030-2423725
Fax+39-030-2425458

CONTACT

For more information, send an E-mail now to our International Marketing Office at info@vignoni-vmc.com
Our staff is fluent in English, Spanish, and Russian.

PRODUCT GALLERY OVERVIEW

Below are a selection of articles manufactured and offered by VIGNONI VMC.

"Made in Italy" Hosiery

Tights & Pantyhose

Collections, Brands and Trademarks

VIGNONI offers many different product lines, both for lady and baby.

LADY Line:

Classic	Opaque	Fashion
Benefit	Easy	

BABY GIRL Line:

Baby Joy	Baby City	Baby Luna
Soft Girl	Mini Fantasy	

SETERIE LADAVAS

SETERIE LADAVAS was established in 1953, now one of the world's leaders in silk neckwear fabrics. Mr. Bruno Ladavas, a man of great creativity and incomparable taste, was head of the company till 1988.
The new management kept offering great neckwear fabrics successfully, thanks to the development of new style choices, without forgetting the traditional classics. Now the team has been increased by further experienced people.

PRODUCTS

Jacquard yarn-dyed fabrics in different qualities (silk, silk blends, hi-tech man-made fibers) are SETERIE LADAVAS main production. However, the company features a remarkable printed silk know-how.

Besides the traditional production processes, SETERIE LADAVAS is developing new advanced technologies, including ink-jet printing on silk fabric.

- Jacquard Neckwear Fabrics
- Plain Neckwear Fabrics
- Printed Neckwear Fabrics

MARKET

SETERIE LADAVAS sells its neckwear fabrics in a wide range of designs, colroways and qualities to qualified necktie manufacturers all over the world, with a special focus in Europe.

Agents and distributors welcome! Please send a professiona profile by E-Mail.

LOCATION

SETERIE LADAVAS is located in Como, province of Como, in Northern Italy. Full address:

SETERIE BRUNO LADAVAS Srl
via Recchi 4
Como
Como, ITALY
Telephone+39-031-300148
Fax+39-031-300239

CONTACT

For more information, send an E-mail now to our sales reps at info@ladavas.it
Our staff is fluent in English, and native with German, Spanish and French. You may also ask for a sales rep at +39-031-300148 between 9:00 am and 6:00 pm GMT+1, Monday through Friday.

PRODUCT GALLERY OVERVIEW

Below are a selection of articles manufactured and offered by SETERIE LADAVAS.

Jacquard Fabrics for Neckwear

Silk Fabrics for Fine Neckwear

Supplies for Neckties Manufacturers

5SETA

5SETA is a young and dynamic company expressing the new wave of silk fabrics and fashion accessories with traditional Italian high-quality standards. This company is a real converter, able to interpret fashion and style at its best, while delivering products of exceptional quality at competitive prices.

PRODUCTS

5Seta offers a large collection of Jacquard and printed silk fabrics for fine neckwear, as well as gorgeous printed fabrics for scarves. It also manufactures printed and Jacquard neckties (including promotional ties). In addition, 5SETA produces fine leather goods including belts, keyholders, agendas, etc ...) with fine silk inserts.

- Neckwear Fabrics
- Fabrics for Scarves
- Promotional Ties
- Leather Goods

MARKET

5SETA offers its products to retailers and wholesalers, as well as, necktie manufacturers needing fast, reliable service. (Fabrics are delivered more quickly than most of its competitors). Tricot neckties ship in 5SETA's standard colors with no minimum quantity requirements.

Leather goods are also available on a ready-to-ship basis for retailers and wholesalers.

5SETA produces custom "promotional" neckties specifically for clubs, corporations, or associations incorporating their corresponding logo into the product, with fast service and low minimum orders.

LOCATION

5Seta is located next to Como, in Northern Italy. Their full address is:

5SETA Srl
via Verga 6
Montano Lucino
Como, ITALY
Telephone+39-031-470884
Fax+39-031-470638

CONTACT

For more information, send an E-mail now to our sales reps at info@5seta.it
Our staff is fluent in English.
You may also reach our sales manager at +39-031-470884 between 8.30 am and 17.30 GMT+1 of any week day.

Product Gallery Overview

Below are a selection of articles manufactured and offered by 5Seta.

Silk Fabrics for Neckwear

Promotional Neckties and Leather Goods

Collections, Brands and Trademarks

All fabric collections are developed after a careful evaluation of the markets where they will be traded, just to match the best sales opportunities for 5Seta's customers.

The company offers a design, and a color service to satisfy any kind of request from tie producers.

All the leather goods proposed by 5Seta are handcrafted with extreme care: they are precious gifts any retailer or wholesaler may sell very well in its own local market.

STUDIO FRANCA LEONARDI SRL

STUDIO FRANCA LEONARDI Srl has been supplying the largest multinational companies for many years with promotional leather articles. Now the company is expanding its sales to department stores and wholesalers, as a consequence of a success due to high product quality (all items made in full grain genuine leather processed by vegetable tanning), reliability, and timely deliveries.

PRODUCTS

Promotional, business, travel, and fashion leather products, including: briefcases, doctor bags, diaries, document holders, congress folders, travel wallets, flight ticket holders, credit cards holders, key holders. Any other leather article may be produced on request.

STUDIO FRANCA LEONARDI Srl has a great experience in special briefcases for pharmaceutical sales agents. Women may find the FL handbag line, designed by Franca Leonardi.
Each product has an excellent value for money.

- Leather Briefcases
- Doctor Bags
- Handbags
- Belts, Wallets, Accessories

MARKET

STUDIO FRANCA LEONARDI Srl sells its special and promotional products to a large range of Italian and international companies (including Nestlè, Fiat, Atlas Copco, Pharmacia, Schering, Schering Plough, Yamanouchi, Astra, Deutch Bank), while the business and fashion items are sold to qualified wholesalers and department stores (for example: Selfridges in London) in all over the world.

Minimum quantity per order: 50 to 100 pieces.

LOCATION

STUDIO FRANCA LEONARDI Srl is located in Milan. Full address:

FRANCA LEONARDI Srl
viale Papiniano 36
Milano Milano, ITALY
Telephone +39-02-4987643
Fax +39-02-4986644

CONTACT

For more information, send an E-mail now to our sales reps at info@francaleonardi.it
Our staff is fluent in English.
You may also reach Mrs. Franca Leonardi at +39-02-4987643 between 9:00 am and 6:00 pm GMT+1, Monday through Friday.

Product Gallery Overview

Below are a selection of articles manufactured and offered by FRANCA LEONARDI Srl.

For more information about FRANCA LEONARDI Srl products, please feel free to send an E-Mail message.

BRIEFCASES AND DOCTOR BAGS LEATHER HANDBAGS

MOTTA ALFREDO was established in 1912. Today it is the world leader in the production of leather for clothing.

MOTTA ALFREDO got this success by a daily relationship with the most important raw markets around the world, as well as by the most peculiar experiments in the leather treatment (thanks to its advanced laboratory facilities).

PRODUCTS

The raw sheep and goat skins come from the most important markets around the world. MOTTA ALFREDO produces finished skins of nappa (aniline and semi-aniline), suede, shearlings, printed leather, and pigs. There are thousands of colors and articles matching the needs of any clothing or fashion accessories manufacturer.

- Nappa Leather
- Suede

- Shearling
- Printed Leather

MARKET

MOTTA ALFREDO sells its quality leather to leatherwear manufacturers, fashion houses, and apparel companies all around the world.

Its huge offer of designs and colors, as well as its timely deliveries, are a warranty for all the buyers dealing with leather clothing.

MOTTA ALFREDO has a skilled tecnical staff closely supporting all the customers around the world and helping them to develop custom fashion leather collections.

LOCATION

MOTTA ALFREDO is located in Cinisello Balsamo, province of Milan, in Northern Italy. Full address:

MOTTA ALFREDO SpA
Via Luciano Manara 3
Cinisello Balsamo Milano, ITALY
Telephone +39-02-66049541
Fax +39-02-61290057

CONTACT

For more information, send an E-mail now to our sales reps at tannery@mottaalfredo.com
Our staff is fluent in English, German, Spanish, and French.
You may also our sales reps at +39-02-66049541 between 8:30 am and 5:30 pm GMT+1, Monday through Friday.

PRODUCT GALLERY OVERVIEW

Below are a selection of articles manufactured and offered by MOTTA ALFREDO.

ADVANCED LEATHER MANUFACTURING

XSPI

XSPI sells through Internet apparel for man, woman and kid, especially young fashion style. Most products are "made in Italy", and we sell in stock all items.]

PRODUCTS

Accessories, Jackets, Knitwear, T-shirts: all items are manufactured from quality fabrics and materials developed by qualified suppliers. XSPI makes extensive us of Tactel fabrics, that increase fit and clinging of clothes.

Minimum regular sale: generally starting at 100 pieces.

- Sweatshirts
- Pile
- Sweaters
- Jeans

MARKET

XSPI items are typically sold through a secure online Shop, but now XSPI is selling directly to wholesalers, department stores, and retailers in all of the world. Visit our stocklots offers at http://www.xspi.com/stock

Great prices and business opportunities for wholesale and retail purchases!

LOCATION

XSPI is located in Ispra (just on Lake Maggiore), province of Varese, in Northern Italy. Full address:

XSPI Srl
p.zza Madonnina del Grappa 17
Ispra Varese, ITALY
Telephone+39-0332-782596
Fax+39-0331-256480

CONTACT

For more information, send an E-mail now to our sales reps at stock@XSPI.com
Our staff speaks English.
You may also reach a XSPI sales rep at +39-0332-782596 between 9:00 am and 5:30 pm GMT+1, Monday through Friday.

PRODUCT GALLERY OVERVIEW

Below are a selection of articles manufactured and offered by XSPI.

SWEATSHIRTS

UNIONE CINQUE

UNIONE CINQUE is a company manufacturing all types of Jacquard and printed silk fabrics for fine neckwear

Our experienced staff is able to offer talented consulting for designing custom patterns, or offer the most in-demand items from the regular collections.

PRODUCTS

Most production is about silk Jacquard and printed fabrics for neckwear: UNIONE CINQUE has its own weaving mill in order to match any kind of request. Cutting edge technology is used to deliver gorgeous ink jet fabrics on silk, great for quick sampling and high quality small productions.

- **Jacquard fabrics**
- **Printed fabrics**
- **Silk ties**
- **Promotional ties**

MARKET

UNIONE CINQUE usually sells to necktie manufacturers all around the world, including retailers offering their own brands. We have a network of agents and resellers: if you want to share UNIONE CINQUE's business opportunities,

Clubs, companies and teams are satisfied customers of our expertise in promotional silk neckties. Great items printed by ink-jet technology in small quantities.

LOCATION

UNIONE CINQUE is located in Como, in Northern Italy. Full address:

UNIONE CINQUE Srl
via Castel Carnasino 22
Como ITALY

Telephone +39-031-576326, Fax +39-031-576327

CONTACT

For more information, send an E-mail now to our sales dept at info@unionecinque.com

Our staff is fluent with English, and French.

You may also reach Mr. Flavio Romanini, UNIONE CINQUE's President, at +39031576326 between 9.00 am and 6.00 pm (GMT+1)

PRODUCT GALLERY OVERVIEW

Below are various examples of silk fabrics manufactured and offered by UNIONE CINQUE.

PRINTED FABRICS

COLLECTIONS, BRANDS AND TRADEMARKS

UNIONE CINQUE develops several collections of silk fabrics for neckwear throughout the year, in addition to a selection of "readily available" fabrics coinciding with the current fashion trends.

The main collections are:

- SETA e DISEGNI
- SOLOSETA
- ARCADIA

Each collection is carefully targeted to a precise market in terms of consumers, designs, and colors.

"SETA e DISEGNI" is the most trendy collection, including (remove "also") fabrics made from silk blends and other natural fibers. "SOLOSETA" offers more innovative designs, while "ARCADIA" offers designs in polyester fabrics.

PRACTICAL INFORMATION FOR CONDUCTING BUSINESS IN ITALY[3]

LEADING SECTORS FOR EXPORTS AND INVESTMENTS

BEST PROSPECTS FOR NON-AGRICULTURAL GOODS AND SERVICES

Following is a listing of non-agricultural products and services which are considered to offer particularly good opportunities for U.S. exporters. Sectors are listed in rank order based on estimated import market size. Statistics are unofficial estimates based on best available data and industry sources. The Commercial Service in Italy organizes special trade promotion events in many of these and other sectors. For more information please contact the Commercial Service at the American Embassy in Rome or the American Consulate General in Milan, Italy (see chapter XI for contact information).

1. Computer Software
2. Computers and Peripherals
3. Computer Services
4. Franchising
5. Management Consulting Services
6. Airport and Ground Support Equipment
7. Insurance Services
8. Telecommunications Services
9. Pet Products
10. Automotive Parts & Service Equipment
11. Education & Training Services
12. Electric Power Systems
13. Medical Equipment
14. Pollution Control Equipment & Supplies
15. Travel & Tourism

COMPUTER SOFTWARE

ITA Industry Code: CSW

The Italian computer software market is estimated at over 3 billion dollars and is Europe's fourth-largest. Application software accounts for 58 percent of the total market, and systems software for 42 percent (middleware accounts for 57 percent of systems software).

The market for software products recorded another positive year in 2004 with an 11 percent growth over 1998 (due to currency fluctuations, it increased by 6 percent in dollar terms). This is the first time since 1990 that the Italian IT market reached double-digit growth.

Application software scored the best performance with a 14 percent growth while systems software grew by 7 percent. Although this trend is in line with the European average on an annual basis, Italian market growth was higher in the third and fourth quarters than in the rest of Europe. In the first half of the year, demand was largely driven by Y2K projects and by the Euro currency conversion. In the second half of 2004, a sharp reduction in orders was compensated by purchases from large organizations of Supply Chain Management, Customer Relation Management and Datawarehousing software, and near-boom conditions for e-commerce-and Internet-related software by large clients as well as by small and medium size businesses following free Internet access introduced by many operators.

[3] This sections based in part on materials of the US Department of Commerce

Market analysts forecast an annual growth of 10 percent over the next three years. Italy relies heavily on foreign production of software, which account for approximately 75 percent of the total market. The United States is the leading exporter of multiple platform and application software, with a share of around 73 percent of imports. The Italian climate for U.S. software will continue to remain favorable as the market recognizes the supremacy and innovative quality of American products.

DATA TABLE:

(USD Millions)	1998 (actual)	2004 (actual)	2000 (estimated)
Total Market Size	3051	3234	3557
*Total Local Production	1960	2070	2215
Total Exports	331	349	370
Total Imports	1422	1513	1712
**Imports from U.S.	1035	1134	1308
Exchange rate:	1737	1818	2000

*Sales by Italian subsidiaries of U.S. companies are included in Total Local Production and include sales to the captive market.
**Imports from U.S. refer to direct sales from U.S.-based suppliers or through Italian distributors.
Source: ASSINFORM for Total Market Size
The above statistics are unofficial estimates.

COMPUTERS AND PERIPHERALS

ITA Industry Code: CPT

The computer and peripherals sector is forecast to remain one of the very best prospects for U.S. imports in the next three years.

The current re-structuring of Italian business is greatly impacting the development of the market. Italian companies are increasingly investing in ICT technologies, which are recognized as a means of strategic innovation in order to implement business process re-engineering, improve communications and expand the company's clientele. Information systems are being upgraded or substituted in order to adopt the most innovative solutions, from networking and Internet/Intranet based applications to e-commerce applications.

The increasing need for networking and Internet/e-commerce technologies is the major driving force in the growth of this sector. The market for LANs and WANs is developing at very high rates, and the need for network systems offering increased resource sharing capabilities, advanced enterprise communications features, integration of data, as well as voice and images on standard platforms, is booming. Excellent prospects exist for intelligent hubs, LAN and ATM switches, bridges and routers, gateway products, remote access servers, network interface cards, network security systems, and protocol conversion hardware.

Good opportunities also exist for both UNIX-based mini-systems (mainly used for enterprise applications such as ERP and CRM solutions, database server solutions and data warehouse), and Wintel systems (used for workgroup and as an infrastructure environment). UNIX workstations are still in demand in the high and medium-end segments, while they are increasingly substituted by PC workstations in the low-end segments.

The number of personal computers sold is growing at a rate of over 20 percent yearly. PC servers are in very high demand, because of their widespread utilization for networking, e-mail and internet applications. Portable PCs have registered the highest growth in 2004, due to their wide acceptance as real working tools, especially from "mobile workers" in the insurance, financial and pharmaceutical sectors. Demand for desktop PCs, which include personal workstations and multimedia edutainment PCs, is also growing very rapidly. Demand for integrated CD-ROM and multimedia products is expected to become one of the most dynamic parts of the Italian computer hardware/multimedia market, with the consumer/home PC market as one of the major driving forces.

U.S. technology and standards are highly regarded. The best opportunities for success lie with American companies offering innovative and sophisticated products, and who are willing to team up with well-established Italian firms for distribution or joint venture agreements.

DATA TABLE:

(USD Millions)	1998 (actual)	2004 (actual)	2000 (estimated)
Total Market Size	5,190	5,805	5,780
Total Local Production	5,265	5,420	5,300
Total Exports	3,390	3,445	3,480
Total Imports	3,315	3,830	3,960
Imports from the U.S.	1,300	1,535	1,670
Exchange rate:	1737	1818	2000

COMPUTER SERVICES

ITA Industry Code: CSV

The computer services sector was the most dynamic sector within the Italian Information and Communication Technology (ICT) market in 2004, and is expected to remain so in the next three years. Italian companies are increasingly investing in ICT solutions as a means to implement renewed business strategies and face the challenges of the new Web Economy.

Internet-related services to support intranet/extranet and electronic commerce solutions represent the area with the highest development potential in the short term. Italian companies are investing heavily in solutions and services related to the improvement of systems and network design and integration; web hosting; integration of Web and e-commerce solutions with ERP, Supply Chain Management and Customer Relationship Management solutions; data warehousing solutions to support knowledge management, decision support systems, business intelligence, document management, integrated logistics, sales force automation, and customer care services. Other services that are developing rapidly are transaction and payment management, Internet customer service, e-procurement and security management, production procurement, maintenance, repair and operating (MRO) solutions, home banking, and online financial services.

The growing complexity of technologies, resulting from the convergence of information technology and telecommunications and from the widespread utilization of the Internet and Intranet, is leading Italian companies to resort increasingly to external service providers to supplement their in-house capabilities.

Global outsourcing and "selective" outsourcing services (data processing, hardware/software maintenance, applications management, network management, desktop management and disaster recovery services) will be increasingly utilized as tools to operate efficiently and cost-effectively.

The U.S. dominates the market and its superiority in this sector is widely recognized. Good opportunities exist for new-to-market U.S. companies offering highly specialized and integrated services and who are willing to team up with well-established Italian firms.

DATA TABLE:

(USD Millions)	1998 (actual)	2004 (actual)	2000 (estimated)
Total Market Size	7,125	7,740	8,100
Sales by Local Firms	4,985	5,060	5,250
Exports by Local Firms	215	310	320
Sales by Foreign-owned Firms	2,355	2,990	3,170
Sales by U.S.-owned Firms	1,765	2,230	2,360
Exchange rate:	1737	1818	2000

FRANCHISING

ITA Industry Code: FRA

Franchising plays a significant role in the Italian economy and is perceived as the most innovative way to introduce a new business concept in Italy. Franchising has been growing at an average annual rate of 11 percent over the last few years and forecasts for the next three years indicate that this same rate will be maintained.

The total number of franchisors is in the range of 550, while franchisees are estimated at over 27,000. In 2004, the total turnover of the franchising sector was in excess of $11 billion, representing close to 3 percent of the total retail and services in Italy. The total number of employees in franchising operations has risen to 73,000.

The highly fragmented Italian retail distribution system is gradually being replaced with more modern distribution methods. Some of the greatest obstacles to franchising are being removed, and despite complex bureaucratic hurdles, there has been continued expansion of new and existing franchising operations.

The most dynamic sectors are services, with 198 franchisors; personal items, with 117 franchisors; and food chains, with 27 franchisors. Adaptability to the Italian business and cultural environment and flexibility in setting master license fees are key factors for the successful introduction of a foreign franchise.

The number of U.S. companies operating through a master franchisee is 33, out of a total of 74 foreign franchisors present in Italy. France is second both in terms of franchisors and franchising units. The Italian business community views American franchise companies with a very open mind and recognizes their predominance in the sector.

DATA TABLE:

(USD Millions)	1998 (actual)	2004 (actual)	2000 (estimated)
Total Market Size	10,625	11,580	11,700
Sales by Local Firms	10,500	11,420	11,500

Exports by Local Firms	800	875	900
Sales by Foreign-owned Firms	925	1,035	1,100
Sales by U.S.-owned Firms	580	710	750
Exchange rate:	1737	1818	2000

MANAGEMENT CONSULTING SERVICES

ITA Industry Code: MCS

The Italian market for management consulting was estimated at USD 1.8 billion in 2004 (excluding earnings additional to fee income, such as revenues from outsourcing activities, software licenses, etc.). Consulting is having an unprecedented period of growth in Italy, with yearly increases of 15% or more. Corporate strategy consulting accounts for about 40% of total fee revenues (with strategic planning and organization development totaling 15% and 13% respectively). Information technology consulting follows with 32% of total revenues (with "pure" IT consulting totaling 13% and IT systems development/integration 16%). Operations management and human resources consulting total respectively 20% and 8% of total revenues. In 2004, the manufacturing sector was the biggest purchaser of management consulting services (32%), followed by the banking and insurance sectors (29%), the communication and transportation sectors (19%), and the central & local governments (8).

The market in Italy is comprised of about 800 firms with 22,000 people, and is divided among global competitors (most of which are of U.S. origin) offering a full-range of state-of-the-art products, a few "national champions", and a number of local or niche players and "gurus". Concentration is high, with the top 20 firms making up about 40% of overall fee revenues. Multinational firms are said to make up as much as 60% of the market.

Most big multinational consulting firms are well established in the Italian market. The largest consulting firm in Italy is Andersen Consulting, which recorded sales in excess of USD 370 million in 2004 and employs over 3,000 people. In addition to consulting, Andersen Consulting (like other important consulting firms) provides solutions and technology in the area of information services, as well as outsourcing services in the area of administration and financial control. The top Italian firms include Consiel, Praxi, Soges, Elea, Monitor, Value Partners, and GEA.

Issues such as e-business, implementation of ERP systems, globalization/internationalization, mergers and acquisitions are said to be key drivers for management consulting services in the near future. Both private and public organizations offer opportunities. Public service companies and government agencies are slowly but steadily re-organizing and reviewing their operations to achieve higher efficiency. In particular, utility companies -- which used to hold monopoly positions in the telecommunications, energy, and transportation sectors -- are now faced with challenging liberalization and privatization processes.

A solid knowledge of the local regulatory environment and market conditions, as well as unique know how in specialized sectors/functions and adequate international experience have become pre-conditions for effectively competing in this market. American consulting firms considering entering the Italian market should therefore explore the possibility of teaming up with Italian partners.

DATA TABLE:

(USD Millions)	1998 (actual)	2004 (actual)	2000 (estimated)
Total Market Size	1,580	1,750	1,850

Sales by Local Firms	700	770	815
Exports by Local Firms	60	70	75
Sales by Foreign-owned Firms	940	1,050	1,110
Sales by U.S.-owned Firms	660	740	780
Exchange rate:	1737	1818	2000

AIRPORT AND GROUND SUPPORT EQUIPMENT

ITA Code: APG

After a difficult period that lasted until 1997, the Italian market for airport and ground support equipment is showing signs of substantial recovery. This is due to resumption of expenditures for capital equipment by both central and regional governments, in order to face the increasingly stronger European competition. In addition, the preparation for the massive passenger traffic anticipated for the current Jubilee year has prompted increased public and private expenditures and near term investments for airport expansion, (i.e. traffic control systems at the new Milan International Airport "Malpensa 2000"), upgrading of existing infrastructures (i.e. Naples Capodichino airport, Rome Leonardo da Vinci airport) and purchase of ground support equipment and systems. All the above works were deemed necessary to meet world standards of safety, performance and system maintenance.

Among the 88 Italian airports, 14 have been selected for upgrading air transportation management and passenger/cargo terminal facilities. In addition to the central government and regional financing, USD 500 million are expected to be spent in the current year by private enterprises. Most of the activity is concentrated in the 7 largest Italian airports whose passenger traffic amounted to some 50 million (over a national figure of nearly 62 million), split as follows: Rome (Fiumicino and Ciampino): 24,000,000; Milan (Linate and Malpensa): 16,000,000; Naples: 3,000,000; Venice: 3,000,000; Turin: 2,000,000; Bari: 1,100,000; Genoa: 900,000.

As U.S. technology and design is highly regarded by Italian airport and ground support equipment operators, U.S. manufacturers should be able to successfully compete against the increasingly strong efforts of companies from European countries such as Germany, France and U.K. U.S. industry which supplies nearly 25% of the total market, is likely to improve its share in the next year.

DATA TABLE:

(USD Millions)	1998 (actual)	2004 (actual)	2000 (estimated)
Total Market Size	2530	2500	2550
Total Local Production	1880	1860	1900
Total Exports	780	775	795
Total Imports	1430	1415	1445
Imports from the U.S.	660	650	675

Exchange rate:	1737	1818	2000

INSURANCE SERVICES

ITA Industry Code: INS

Total direct insurance premiums (exclusive of reinsurance) collected in Italy in 2004 increased 20 percent in nominal terms, with an extraordinary 34 percent increase in the sale of life insurance, surpassing for the second consecutive time the total amount of casualty insurance premiums and representing almost 58% of the entire Italian insurance business.

This remarkable increase is a direct consequence of the increasing uncertainties regarding the guarantees offered by the Italian state pension and health systems. Among the factors which contributed to such a lively trend, is the necessity of Italian households to increase the proportion of savings set aside for retirement needs, and their reduced preference for cash assets (a result of the drop in interest rates together with the positive development of the financial markets). In addition to the greater attention paid by the population to welfare problems, the growth in life insurance is also due to the variety of distribution channels and the expansion of index-linked and unit-linked policies.

Among the first top ten companies operating in the sector are eight large Italian insurance companies led by "Assicurazioni Generali". Foreign-owned insurance companies, which have been quite aggressive in the market, maintain an estimated market share of 30 percent. Countries whose firms have the strongest market presence are Germany, Switzerland and France (e.g. "Ras", "Lloyd Adriatico", "Axa Assicurazioni", "Winterthur Assicurazioni", "Zurigo").

The handful of U.S. companies presently doing business in Italy (namely "AIG Europe", "Cigna Life Insurance", "Chubb Insurance", "Prumerica Life" -- former "Pricoa Vita" -- and "Allstate" -- new entry) are estimated to have increased their performance by 17%, but still only still represent approximately 0.3 percent of the market. Nonetheless, U.S. companies are expected to take advantage of greater opportunities in Italy due to the liberalization of the EU insurance services market, as well as to the upcoming Italian fiscal incentives for insurance covers involving individual supplemental allowance and long term care plans (Italian Legislative Decree 47/2000 effective as of January 1, 2001).

The insurance industry will thus be playing a major role in Italy's financial markets, both as a source of capital and management for the newly created private pension funds and as a complementary system for the national pension and health systems. U.S. firms, which have operated in highly competitive environments, and have a long history and expertise, especially in life insurance, pension funds, individual retirement accounts, and health insurance, should take advantage of increased Italian need for insurance products. There is ample ground to believe that the Italian insurance industry will experience a further increase of 17% during the year 2000, with life insurance growing at about 23%.

Italy allows non-EC based insurance companies access to its market through local subsidiaries, branches or representative offices. Thus, in order to sell insurance products, a U.S. insurance company must set up in Italy at least a representative office which has to be authorized by ISVAP (Supervisory Institute of private and public-interest Insurance companies which monitors insurance activities in Italy). The license can normally be obtained in six months.

DATA TABLE:

(USD Millions)	1998 (actual)	2004 (actual)	2000 (estimated)
Total Market Size	57,674	65,875	70,060
Sales by Local Firms	54,791	67,193	72,035

Exports by Local Firms	14,419	21,080	22,995
Sales by Foreign-owned Firms	17,302	19,762	21,020
Sales by U.S.-owned Firms	197	220	240
Exchange rate:	1737	1818	2000

TELECOMMUNICATION SERVICES

ITA Industry Code: TEL

The Italian telecommunication services market is estimated at over 25 billion dollars and is Europe's fourth largest. Results were strong in 2004, as the sector increased by an additional 15 percent, the third successive year of double-digit growth. (Due to currency fluctuations, it increased by 10 percent in dollar terms).
Once again, the mobile communications segment turned in the best performance, with an increase overall of 36 percent in value terms from 1998. As of December 31, 2004, there were 30 million active users of cellular telephones in Italy, a penetration rate of 53 percent of the population, compared with an average of 40 percent for Europe.

Fixed line traffic revenues remained stable, increasing by 0.7 percent from 1998.
Demand for data transmission services grew by 34 percent, as internet usage accelerated sharply during 2004, spurred by offers of free connectivity services by many operators. Non-corporate subscribers are estimated at 3.7 million (540,000 in 1998) and business subscribers at 1.5 million (246,300 in 1998). E-commerce is reported to have grown by 48 percent for the year; 79 percent of Italian companies are said to have a website.

In the value-added services sub-sector, internet services (i.e. access/subscriptions, hosting, housing, web sites, intranets, portals, etc.) reported a record-breaking growth of 234 percent over 1998.

Future market indicators:

- the demand for data transmission services will continue to grow as internet usage expands further;
- quicker, better data and value-added services at substantially lower prices will be offered by an increasing number of competing operators;
- the cost of voice telephony will continue to decrease as new providers enter the market;
- five UMTS cellular phone licenses are to be awarded during 2000, with services to be operational starting in 2002.

In consideration of the market conditions described above, there are good business opportunities for U.S. companies with technical skills and expertise in website design and in e-commerce consultancy. Business-to-business e-commerce opportunities include internet access services, specialized services such as intranet/extranet and financial services. As Wireless Application Protocol technology for UMTS cellular telephony develops, there will be good prospects for internet services in the business-to-consumer market for publishing, internet music and videos, bookings for entertainment events, vacation and travel.

DATA TABLE:

(USD Millions)	1998 (actual)	2004 (actual)	2000 (estimated)
Total Market Size	32,988	25,320	28,358
Sales by Local Firms	22,758	25,070	28,058
Exports by Local Firms	---	---	---

Sales by Foreign- *Owned Firms	230	250	300
Sales by U.S.-*Owned Firms	20	30	50
Exchange rate:	1737	1818	2000

PET PRODUCTS

ITA Industry Code: PET

The Italian pet market has recorded the highest growth rates in Europe over the past several years. At the same time, the market remains far from saturated. Research shows the role that pets play in Italy has become more important in recent years leading to the development of a strong and growing market for pet products.

The pet products market in Italy is estimated at USD 2.1 billion in 2000, increasing approximately 12 percent from the previous year. Trade sources have forecast increases of the same magnitude for the next few years.

Dog food is one of the sectors that is expected to increase the most, since the consumption rate of commercial food is still very low compared to other countries. While the "Mediterranean diet" (pasta and rice) is still prevalent in dog and cat diets, the market for industrial or commercial pet food has increased greatly in recent years. The pet care sector is experiencing remarkable growth. The trends towards "humanization" of pets has led owners to use specific products for their animal companions. In the pet accessories sector, the trend towards diversification is greater. The growth in this sector is due to the development of high technology products, as well as accessories that focus on the beauty, elegance and "personality" of pets and satisfy pet owner whims.

At the same time, imports play a major role in this market, especially in the pet food sector – with over one third of the total market. Over 50 percent of pet food and 20 percent of pet accessories are imported. U.S. brands are the leading imports, especially in the pet food sector, where they enjoy an excellent reputation and continue to be the market leaders.

Given these positive market conditions, the Italian pet products market has great growth potential and offers many opportunities for U.S. companies wishing to expand their sales internationally.

DATA TABLE:

(USD Millions)	1998 (actual)	2004 (actual)	2000 (estimated)
Total Market Size	1,890	2,060	2,100
Total Local Production	1,320	1,380	1,400
Total Exports	110	120	125
Total Imports	680	800	825
Imports from the U.S.	130	145	160
Exchange rate:	1737	1818	2000

AUTOMOTIVE PARTS AND SERVICE EQUIPMENT

ITA Industry Code: APS

The demand in the 2004 Italian auto market exceeded all forecasts despite the expiration of State automobile purchase incentives. Automobile sales amounted to 2,349,200 units, slightly decreasing by 1.2%; sales of commercial vehicles actually rose 9% during 2004, reaching sales of almost 200,000 units, while heavy truck sales topped the previous 1989 record to reach 34,904 units, an increase of 34.2% over 1998.

The market for automotive parts and service equipment experienced an estimated 8% increase during 2004, with domestic production covering approximately 67% of the demand (up 4% compared to the previous year), and imports covering the remaining 33% (up 7% compared to the previous year). Sales of original equipment (OE) experienced an overall increase of 7% and accounted for 71% of total components demand (16% of which were covered by imports, which in turn increased 11 percentage points). Noteworthy is the fact that Italian car manufacturers tend to use imported components to a much lower extent (approximately 12%) than commercial/industrial vehicle producers (about 39%). Therefore, if the production of cars declines while the production of commercial/industrial vehicles grows (as was the case in 2004), the share of OE demand covered by the domestic component production decreases and the share covered by imports increases.

Aftermarket (AM) sales increased by 6% and represented 29% of overall components demand (well over half of which - that is, 61%- were covered by imports, which themselves increased by 9%). The exceptional market share of AM imports is attributable to the development of modern distribution channels and transnational operators, improved performance of foreign automotive organizations and greater competitiveness of imported products, especially due to the fall in the exchange rates of the currencies in many southeast Asian countries.

The main country suppliers are Germany (33%) and France (25%). Imports from the U.S. represent only 3% of overall imports. Italy has reportedly the highest auto density in the world and still has one of the oldest circulating auto fleets in Europe with approximately 36 million vehicles currently on the road. In the near future, a further boost to the renewal of the automotive fleet (with positive effects on OE sales) will result from the need to eliminate some of the many vehicles (currently 15 million) not equipped with catalytic converters due to the ban on the sale of leaded fuel in Italy scheduled for January 1, 2002. The higher frequency of periodic compulsory motor vehicle inspections and stricter pollution control regulations are also likely to spur sales in Italy of spare parts and service equipment.

Growth in U.S. auto parts, accessories, components and service equipment shipments to Italy is expected to experience a 6% average annual increase for the next couple of years. The U.S. industry is also supplying the Italian market primarily from its European subsidiaries and pursuing several joint ventures and "greenfield" investments. Best prospects include a wide range of passive and active security components/accessories, environmentally-friendly features, diagnostic apparatuses and light weight/acoustic insulation/advanced materials.

DATA TABLE:

(USD Millions)	1998 (actual)	2004 (actual)	2000 (estimated)
Total Market Size	20,295	21,022	20,500
Total Local Production	28,033	27,839	26,800
Total Exports	14,450	13,657	13,050
Total Imports	6,712	6,840	6,750
Imports from the U.S.	213	213	210

Exchange rate:	1737	1818	2000

EDUCATION AND TRAINING SERVICES

ITA Industry Code: EDS

The education and training services sector includes: language training, comprising language courses in both Italy and abroad; post-university programs (master programs and doctorates); and executive management training programs. Language training, with an estimated value of $680 million in 2004, and postgraduate programs, with an estimated value of $400 million, are the largest segments.

It has been estimated that only ten percent of Italians have a sufficient command of the English language to be able to use it in business transactions. On the other hand, the importance of possessing adequate language skills is becoming increasingly recognized in the era of globalization, and more and more Italians, both companies and individuals, are ready to invest time and money in order to learn foreign languages, particularly English. Therefore, language study abroad is a market with great potential. Estimates are that this segment will grow over 30 percent in the next three years, bringing the number of Italians studying a foreign language abroad from 1.2 to 1.7 million.

English is the preferred language for studying abroad by 64 percent of young people aged between 12 and 28, while this percentage goes up to 86 percent of the segment aged 12-17. Italian families are sending their children overseas to study/practice a foreign language because they consider the level of language teaching in traditional schools to be inadequate. Programs in the United Kingdom hold the lion's share of this market. However, there is an increasing trend towards studying in the U.S, because of the growing demand for higher quality programs that also includes a wide range of extra curricula activities.

Another market in which the U.S. has a larger and increasing share, is that of postgraduate education. In 2004, approximately 3,000 Italians obtained a J1 visa, which is granted to such students. This figure is still low compared to other European countries. However, increasing cooperation between the U.S. and the European Union in educational exchange programs, as well as numerous bilateral agreements between Italian and U.S. universities is likely to increase the number of Italian students and young researchers who go to the U.S.

Finally, there is growing demand for executive management programs, both in the public and private sectors. Italian enterprises are increasingly recognizing the need to restructure their organizations to meet international competition and develop a global strategy for their markets. The public sector at national and regional levels is also seeking to reorganize its operations in order to reduce expenditures while providing services more efficiently.

DATA TABLE:

(USD Millions)	1998 (actual)	2004 (actual)	2000 (estimated)
Total Market Size	1170	1230	1170
Sales by Local Firms	580	600	550
Exports by Local Firms	30	30	30
Sales by Foreign-owned Firms	620	660	650
Sales by U.S.-owned Firms	125	140	145
Exchange rate:	1737	1818	2000

ELECTRIC POWER SYSTEMS

ITA Industry Code: ELP

Italy is heavily dependent (nearly 80% of energy requirements) on foreign sources of energy and this fact strongly influences its energy policy. The economic strain experienced in the past years slowed down the implementation of the National Energy Plan (PEN), including investments in energy equipment and systems. Nevertheless demand for electric power has continued to increase, resulting in substantial imports of electricity from neighboring countries such as France, Switzerland and Austria. Italy decided to ban nuclear power for energy production in 1994 and, as a consequence, both the government and the industry are seeking alternatives to traditional energy production systems.

In the last few years there has been a shift from oil/coal to oil/gas for energy production. Government policy is focusing on investments in energy production (including incentive to self producers), diversification of energy sources, promotion of energy conservation technologies and utilization of alternative renewable sources. Consequently, and as a result of the EU Directive on Electricity, ENEL, the National Electricity Company, which still produces and distributes almost 80% of total electricity, is being privatized, and the country will open its market to both domestic and foreign competition. Although market liberalization is expected to stimulate increased demand for electric power systems, independent power producers have being holding off major investments until the new regulations governing the market are clarified.

Although still comparatively small (representing only 5-6% of the total market) there is growing interest in alternative sources of energy, especially for high-tech and sophisticated design in sectors like wind energy generation equipment, solar energy generation equipment (especially photovoltaic) and biomass. These renewable sources should reach 10% of the total energy production by 2003. There is good market potential also for advanced fuels systems, peak-load gas turbines and cogeneration systems.

European competition is strong and growing through a number of mergers and acquisitions aimed at acheiving increasingly larger market shares. U.S. firms should concentrate their efforts on innovative products/systems while strengthening their leadership in licensing and technical cooperation, since the majority of Italian manufactured heavy electrical machinery is made under U.S. licenses.

DATA TABLE:

(USD Millions)	1998 (actual)	2004 (actual)	2000 (estimated)
Total Market Size	5790	5730	5560
Total Local Production	6020	5960	5780
Total Exports	1930	1910	1880
Total Imports	1700	1680	1660
Imports from the U.S.	320	320	310
Exchange rate:	1737	1818	2000

MEDICAL EQUIPMENT

ITA Industry Code: MED

The National Healthcare System (SSN) is by far the major healthcare provider in Italy and it guarantees almost totally free medical care to all 57 million Italians. The Ministry of Health establishes the fundamental objectives of healthcare, including preventive care and rehabilitation, defines the level of healthcare guaranteed to all citizens and issues guidelines for the organization, delivery and funding of healthcare services paid by the SSN. The 20 Italian Regions, which now have the primary role in setting and implementing healthcare policies, are responsible for developing regional health plans and for organizing and delivering healthcare services through local "Health Units".

Public hospitals account for 75 percent of total expenditures for medical equipment and products, with the balance being held by private healthcare facilities. Private healthcare expenditures are increasing at a higher pace than public expenditures. In addition, the SSN purchases a significant portion of healthcare services from private providers. The SSN has jurisdiction over 1,005 public hospitals with a total of 311,000 beds. The private healthcare service providers account for 790 private and independently operated clinics, with a total of 75,000 beds. The latest trend shows an increase in the number of private healthcare facilities over public hospitals.

The Italian market for medical equipment relies heavily on imports. Major suppliers are the United States and Germany. The domestic production is limited for most of the more sophisticated and hi-tech medical equipment and products, those for which investments in R&D are of critical importance. Local production is good in such areas as radiology, dental and ultrasonic equipment. A large percentage of the medical equipment in use is obsolete, with potentially adverse effects on patients. In recent years, the local health care market has suffered from drastic cuts in public expenditures in an effort to reduce overall public expenditures. Prices are considered to be the primary factor in purchasing decisions. Effective June 1998 Italy has implemented a special certification program, known as CE mark, which is an EU-wide certification standard covering the majority of medical products, equipment and services.

DATA TABLE:

(USD Millions)	1998 (actual)	2004 (actual)	2000 (estimated)
Total Market Size	2,580	2,610	2,550
Total Local Production	1,056	1,065	1,040
Total Exports	279	285	280
Total Imports	1,803	1,830	1,790
Imports from the U.S.	996	1,020	1,000
Exchange rate:	1737	1818	2000

POLLUTION CONTROL EQUIPMENT AND SERVICES

ITA Industry Code: POL

The Italian pollution control equipment and services market continues to be one of the best prospects for U.S. products, technologies and services. Italy is giving increasing attention to the protection of the environment. Although Italy has lagged behind its industrialized European neighbors in safeguarding the environment, it has recently stepped up its efforts.

The government has implemented EU directives on waste, hazardous waste, and waste packaging and is moving forward in their application. Italy has also enacted a "Water Safeguard Law," a comprehensive reform of Italy's water quality/discharge, and more restrictive air pollution control legislation. The more stringent water legislation and higher water and waste water charges are likely to stimulate the modernization of industrial water and waste water treatment plants. Recent legislation also requires the creation of monitoring networks by utilities and industries which have major environmental impact, such as power plants, oil refineries, and chemical industries. Opportunities exist in the industrial applications market for air analysis equipment, as well as for continuous monitoring systems, control instruments, dust collectors and other pollution control equipment. Waste-to-Energy systems and technologies are also likely to represent an excellent market for air pollution control equipment.

The Italian industry is largely dependent on foreign expertise for know-how. In particular, U.S. products and technologies are very highly regarded. Competition in the marketplace is fierce, but demand is strong for truly innovative products and services. Moreover, Italy's strategic position in the Mediterranean Basin makes it an ideal gateway to other emerging markets. Italian companies specializing in turnkey operations have strengthened their position in foreign markets. American companies that team up with well-established local firms will have the greatest opportunities for success.

DATA TABLE:

(USD Millions)	1998 (actual)	2004 (actual)	2000 (estimated)
Total Market Size	4,292	4,390	4,170
Total Local Production	3,893	3,982	3,783
Total Exports	475	485	461
Total Imports	874	893	848
Imports from the U.S.	388	397	377
Exchange rate:	1737	1818	2000

TRAVEL AND TOURISM

ITA Industry Code: TRA

Italy ranks fourth among the world's top tourism destinations, and second in total receipts. At the same time, Italy is a country where taking a vacation is a must and a national tradition. In 1998, Italian residents made almost 93 million trips with at least one night out, and 85 percent of these trips were for vacation purposes.

Italy is also becoming an important source for international tourism. The number of outgoing flows has significantly increased in recent years. Italy recorded a boost of 30 percent from 1995 to 1998 in outgoing, bringing the number of Italians travelling abroad every year to over 20 million. Since 1997, Italy is also the fifth largest spender in international travel.

Italians travel abroad to get acquainted with different cultures, learn languages, seek new ideas, experiment new technologies, and use their leisure time to its fullest. For this reason, the number of Italian visitors to the U.S. keeps growing, despite an increasingly unfavorable exchange rate. In 2004, the arrivals exceeded 626,000, a three percent increase over 1998. Consequently, Italy remains the sixth most important overseas market for the U.S. tourism industry.

The U.S. is the most preferred long haul destination for Italian tourists. The number of repeat visitors is also increasing steadily. In addition to New York, California and Florida, which are the states most visited by Italians, there are several emerging destinations such as Nevada, the Rocky Mountain Region, and New England. The success of the latter destinations is directly related to the targeted marketing and promotional efforts that the tourism authorities of those states have devoted to the Italian market.

DATA TABLE:

(USD Millions)	1998 (actual)	2004 (actual)	2000 (estimated)
Total Holiday expenditures	64,500	62,000	59,600
Domestic Travel	47,100	45,400	43,700
Incoming Travel	29,800	28,400	28,100
Outgoing Travel	17,400	16,600	15,900
Travel to the U.S.	2,600	2,450	2,400
Exchange rate:	1737	1818	2000

B. BEST PROSPECTS FOR AGRICULTURAL PRODUCTS

The Italian diet has become an international reference point as it combines both Continental and Mediterranean eating habits. Italians have access to a broad range of fresh foods due to their own wealth of agricultural production. However, they remain fairly traditional in their food habits. While the per capita volume figures paint a picture of a fish and vegetable hungry Mediterranean nation, the per capita value figures also point to a group of health conscious modern consumers willing to pay a premium for quality food products. While the recent economic recession put a damper on luxury food sales and expensive restaurant visits, Italy still spends more per capita on food than any other EU country except Portugal.

Both American style fast food chains and American style buffet/salad bars are establishing themselves more firmly in the Italian market. This move toward cheaper and more convenient dining has led Italian importers to seek out U.S. food products adapted to self-service eateries. Many bars, restaurants and food service companies also are seeking foods that microwave easily. While home use of microwaves is still low, microwaves sales are increasing. Families with two working parents in the cities are relying more and more on microwaves to reheat food and prepare frozen foods.

Italy imports and produces a large quantity of "American style" foods such as breakfast cereals, organic foods and snack foods. The Italian youth market is especially interested in lifestyle foods such as American beer and salted corn chips. Finally, American packaging is perceived as being more sophisticated and more consumer (and environment) friendly.

Trade journals predict that Italian companies will be seeking more foods that meet U.S. standards of quality control and FDA labeling. American style innovations in food marketing (i.e. cross brand marketing) is predicted to be a U.S. driven trend in Italy within several years. Finally, Italians are looking to the U.S. for a better understanding of organic and low fat foods.

Finally, U.S. origin products do very well in the Italian seafood market (i.e. fresh lobster and frozen squid, etc.) and U.S. exports of bulk and packaged dried fruits and nuts including popcorn are on the upswing and expected to rise in the next year.

In addition to high-value products, U.S. companies also should look for opportunities to supply Italian export industries with raw materials. Forest products remain the most important U.S. export to Italy. While the value has increased slightly, the volume of imports decreased as a direct result of the higher value of the U.S. dollar versus the Italian lira. The Italian forest product market is characterized by the import of raw materials for manufacturing finished products for export. The Italian economy also affects domestic purchases of these products, but a strong foreign demand is compensating for the weak demand in the domestic market.

Forestry Products

(USD Millions)	1998 (actual)	2004 (actual)	2000 (estimated)
Total Market Size	na	na	na
Total Local Production	na	na	na
Total Exports	180	182	182
Total Imports	3,518	3,508	3,500
Imports from the U.S.	245	233	240
Exchange rate:	1737	1818	2000

PET FOOD

(USD Millions)	1998 (actual)	2004 (actual)	2000 (estimated)
Total Market Size	na	na	na
Total Local Production	na	na	na
Total Exports	5	5	5
Total Imports	236	214	230
Imports from the U.S.	31	17	20
Exchange rate:	1737	1818	2000

SEAFOOD

(USD Millions)	1998 (actual)	2004 (actual)	2000 (estimated)
Total Market Size	na	na	na
Total Local Production	na	na	na
Total Exports	34	32	33
Total Imports	2,222	2,167	2,200
Imports from the U.S.	48	47	49
Exchange rate:	1737	1818	2000

C. SIGNIFICANT INVESTMENT OPPORTUNITIES

The Italian Government will spend 90,000 billion lire (US$ 45 billion) in EU "objective one" structural funds and matching national funds in southern Italy as part of the 2000-2006 EU spending program. Additional EU funds will be spent in disadvantaged parts of Italy under "objective two" funding, for certain areas in Northern and Central Italy.

The Italian government's overall strategy for southern Italy focuses on reducing barriers to domestic and foreign private sector investment: strengthening law and order, fostering the spirit of innovation, reducing the underground economy, and boosting tourism. Natural resources will receive 19.7% of total funding (4.2 billion Euros and service networks (security, transportation, telecommunication, and sanitation infrastructure) are slated for 18.9% (4 billion Euros). The tourism infrastructure sector is to receive some 800 million Euros. Environmental protection projects are slated to receive 7.7% for a total of 1.6 billion Euros from the natural funding for resources.

The Italian government, which has had to return unused EU funds in the past, is determined to ensure that it can program its full share of funds allocated by the EU.

Some 50% of the EU funds for southern Italy will be spent in 2 regions – the Campania region, including Naples, and Sicily. Campania will receive over 25% of the funds for southern Italy or almost 4 billion Euro. That region, home to Capri, the Amafi Coast and the Sorrento peninsula, boasts significant tourism sector opportunities and environmental projects. Another 25% will go to Sicily where, thanks to its special autonomous status, U.S. firms participating in investment projects in Sicily can benefit from additional regional grants from the Sicilian regional government.

The Italian Government's determination to make full use of EU funds provides opportunities for U.S. firms to partner with European firms and regional governments on realizable projects. U.S. firms can also partner with Italian firms on investment projects in under-developed areas. In these cases, the venture can receive up to 50% of the funds required for land, buildings, equipment, and feasibility studies in grant form from the EU. Promising areas for American firms include franchising of lodging facilities, airport expansion projects, theme park, and golf course developments. Opportunities are also available for firms with advanced environmental technologies for waste disposal and soil and water clean up.

For information on infrastructure projects in southern Italy, American firms should contact the Commercial Service at the U.S. Consulate in Naples.

MARKETING PRODUCTS AND SERVICES IN ITALY

DISTRIBUTION AND SALES CHANNELS

American business representatives will find that selling in Italy offers new challenges, but it presents no over-whelming problems. Over 7,500 American com-panies are actively represented in Italy, with approximately 850 of them having subsidiaries there. U.S. executives may find that some commercial practices differ from those in the United States, but most will be very familiar. The system of retail and wholesale distribution, for instance, centers on small family-operated stores, although the supermarket-type operation has gained importance and there are a number of substantial department store operations.

RETAIL DISTRIBUTION IN ITALY

As Italy has a population of 57.6 million, its retail distribution sector is large in total sales and serves the consumer at the retail level through numerous small, family-owned, retail outlets rather than large, mass market operations. The market offers many commercial opportunities because of the large sales volume and a lack of competitive companies. Many large retail stores have recently been opening on Sundays. Recent legislation has liberalized the range of products and hours of operation permitted at retail outlets and should promote a more modern, competitive retail system.

In order to satisfy Italian consumers, firms operating in the Italian retail distribution sector find that they must invest large amounts of money in new techniques, management, research, media promotion, and equipment. The industry's average return on investment is approximately 13 percent. In terms of existing points of sale, there is a trend away from the family-type stores and street vendors to the distribution chains. Italian distribution systems include small family-owned stores, street vendors, hypermarkets, shopping malls, specialized stores and discount stores.

Horizontal points of sale such as general stores, which had experienced boom conditions in the early 1980s, have begun to lose ground to specialized stores, franchising chains, and hypermarkets. In order to create a unique business identity, department stores have begun a process of realignment and now tend to attract the more affluent, quality-oriented consumers, as well as compete on price and product selection. Supermarket chains now look toward further expansion, particularly in creating and operating large shopping malls. Where such shopping centers exist, they are proving to be successful.

The Italian retail distribution system is faced with the new challenges of competition and technology. It is in the process of being reorganized in terms of number of points of sale and of marketing strategies. The small traditional retail outlets are considered obsolete, but the Italian distribution groups are still too small in many cases to compete effectively with large chains operating in some of the other European nations. A process of internationalization is now taking place among Italian and foreign chains with some agreements already signed. There is, however, room for more.

The marketing of products in Italy is accomplished through a variety of channels, depending on the nature of the product, the sales territory to be covered, the type of buyer, and the sales promotional activities required. Brokers, commission merchants, and independent representatives are used extensively for the sale of raw materials, semifinished products, and capital goods to the larger manufacturing organizations. However, well-established distributors are normally employed to reach industrial firms as well as the large number of wholesalers and retailers engaged in the marketing of consumer goods.

If the product normally has a high sales volume and low profit margin, the Italian firms seek to deal directly with the manufacturer. Sales to a department store, chain store, or end-user often yield the best sales results, but require greater promotional effort by the American exporter. The direct sales method eliminates the added shipping and warehousing expenses, but the U.S. exporter and Italian importer must handle the shipping formalities and expend greater effort to ensure a successful business relationship.

USE OF AGENTS/DISTRIBUTORS; FINDING A PARTNER

Italy represents a large and affluent market where language and personal relationships are valued when conducting business transactions. Consequently some form of local presence is generally required to be successful. American firms have found that relying on local Italian sales agents or distributors, who have the contacts and understand the market, can most effectively develop sales.

There are important distinctions in Italian law between distribution and agency agreements:

Agency: Agency contracts are governed by the Italian Civil Code and by a number of other legislative decrees. An Italian agent for a foreign firm is generally regarded as being authorized to act for the firm. Depending on the contract, the principal may be subject to termination compensation payments and to income taxes and other levies on sales effected through the agent.

Distributorship: Under this arrangement the local distributor takes title of the merchandise and assumes the risks, and has the obligation to pay any taxes. Distribution agreements are subject only to the terms of the contract itself. There are no laws or regulations currently in effect in Italy providing for advance notice of termination, termination compensation, or social security payments in connection with these agreements.

Frequently, a distributorship agreement provides for exclusive sales rights. There is nothing in Italian law preventing exclusive arrangements in all or part of Italy. However, if these agreements provide for exclusive sales rights in all or part of the EU, they should be examined carefully, and with the assistance of a competent international lawyer, in light of the antitrust provisions of the EU regulations.

APPOINTING AN AGENT OR A DISTRIBUTOR

It is important to obtain specific legal advice on appointing an agent or distributor. However, some general guidelines apply and are outlined here. Italy implemented the EU directive 86653 in October, 1991. As a result, Italian agency law is now in conformity with EU requirements. All agent agreements should be in writing and state the marketing area and any exclusivity arrangements. Termination of the relationship is the area that most frequently causes problems for American exporters.

Generally, the civil code protects the interests of the representative. In the absence of termination provisions in a written agreement, the law provides for a minimum notice of termination of one month during the first year of the agreement, two months during the second year, three months for the third year, four months for the fourth year, five months for the fifth year, and six months for the sixth and additional years. Parties may agree to other terms, provided the notice of termination is not less than the above. An agreement with a definite period terminates on the agreed expiration date. If the parties continue to operate under the agreement after that date, the agreement becomes an agreement of indefinite term, which can be terminated in accordance with the aforementioned notice periods. If the American principal wants to terminate the relationship, notice of termination should be given, even with a definite term contract.

The termination of an agreement without the required notice makes a U.S. principal liable for compensation. The Italian sales agent could seek to claim the amount of the commissions that would have been earned during the termination period or for the amount of actual damages suffered. In exceptional cases, and only for just cause (such as competition or fraud), an agreement may be terminated without notice provided the other party is immediately advised of the reason. In such cases, the courts may be requested to terminate the contract.

At the expiration or termination of an agreement, by whatever means, an agent who has increased the value of the business is entitled, in principle, to an adequate remuneration which cannot exceed the average of the commissions in 1 year. Such claims by agents are subject to an expiration period of 1 year.

Three kinds of distribution agreements are commonly used:

- Exclusive distributorships, where the distributor has the sole right to sell specified goods within a defined area.

- Quasi-exclusive distributorships, where the distributor sells almost all the specified products within a defined area.

- Informal distributor arrangements, under which the grantor imposes heavy obligations on the distributor and which would cause damage to the distributorship if the grantor terminated the agreement.

In the absence of mutual agreement, or the failure to meet contract obligations, a distribution agreement of indefinite term cannot be terminated by the grantor without reasonable notice or fair compensation. In general, grantors should consider protecting themselves by entering into agreements for definite periods rather than an indefinite period. Also, specific minimum performance clauses should be considered, such as percent of distributor's sales, minimum annual sales, and number of business contacts to be made, and grantors should propose that U.S. law and courts have jurisdiction.

A continued and close working contact between the American firm and the agent or distributor is very desirable and should be developed early in the relationship. Certain products and equipment require servicing to maintain their useful life. The U.S. exporter should determine if servicing is needed and develop a distribution network to include such servicing by qualified personnel. To build trust, loyalty, and marketing skills, U.S. producers frequently bring their agents or distributors to the United States for training and marketing assistance.

FRANCHISING

Franchising in Italy has been growing a very fast pace. Latest figures available indicate that at in 2004 Italy had approximately 550 franchisors and over 27,000 franchisees, ranking it among the highest in Europe in terms of franchises operating. The franchising sector has continued to thrive total turnover for the franchising sector was in excess of $11 billion, representing close to 3 percent of all retail and services sales in Italy. Employment of the sector reached 73,000 in 2004.

Market Demand

The Italian population has shown itself to be receptive to the fast and efficient services provided by franchises. At the same time, the Italian end-user is not always open to franchises for those services that are traditionally strong and consolidated. Nevertheless, the Italian market's receptivity to the franchising concept appears to be steadily growing. The Italian business community has accepted the concept that franchising is the most innovative way to introduce a business concept.

End-User Profile

There is a vast difference in the economic makeup of the geographic regions of the country, as the north is predominantly industrial and the south is primarily agricultural. The north has a large number of commercial, financial, and industrial enterprises and has double the per capita income rate of the south. Similarly, the local geographic distribution of franchising is disparate, with a concentration of franchising networks in Northern Italy. However, recently, there are some indications that franchising is also gaining momentum in Southern Italy, where it is perceived as a way to alleviate the effects of chronic unemployment.

Competitive Situation

Italy has an extremely fragmented distribution system. The predominance of small, family-owned stores and the disproportionately large number of point-of-sale outlets are viewed as cause of market inefficiency, The present retail system survives mainly due to the complexity and protective nature of existing regulations. However, there is now a noticeable move towards concentration in retail distribution, which creates economies of scale and more efficient management. Thus franchising seems to be increasingly a system well suited to Italy.

While franchising is relatively new in Italy, there are local companies which have been in operation for a number of years and which have achieved both success and profitability. The most developed franchising sector is the services sector, with 11,000 franchisees and 198 franchisors, while the personal products sectors ranks second, with 4,600 franchisees and 117 franchisors. Another very strong sector is specialty retail stores, with 77 franchisors and 3,800 franchisees.

The Italian business community views American franchising companies with a very open mind and recognizes their predominance in the sector. However, smaller American franchisors trying to find Italian master licensees have to face obstacles related to their lack of name recognition in Italy and to inexperience with local business practices. The price for the master license is almost always set too high and the assistance to be provided by the franchisor is never spelled out clearly enough.

Best Sales Prospects

The sectors that appear to have the best potential are in the services area. They are travel and tourism, education and training, fast delivery services, management and consulting services, automotive services. Other good prospects are offered in fast food and hotels with a good brand recognition, and to personal items and fashion.

Legal Requirements

The development of the European Union has stimulated harmonization of trade, tariffs, legal requirements, standards and procedures. There is no specific legislation in Italy defining or regulating franchising. Rules governing franchising are those issued by the EU Commission. In Italy a franchising agreement is governed by general contract law principles and is considered a bilateral agreement between separate business enterprises resulting in "collaboration", not "association", between parties. Franchising agreements are subject to the laws governing commercial contracts in general, and to those governing sales of trademark licensing agreements in particular. The Italian Franchising Association (Assofranchising) has established a set of rules which reflect standards prevailing in the Italian business community and often taken into consideration in legal proceedings.

There are no trade barriers or limitations to the importation of US franchise business methods in Italy. However, due to the lack of specific Italian norms on franchising agreements, it is advisable that contracts be written in great detail when entering into an agreement with a master licensee

The average validity of a franchising contract in Italy is 5 years in 39 percent of cases, 3 years in 24 percent and 6 years in 10 percent. An entry fee is required by 51 percent of franchisors, while royalties are requested by 70 percent of master franchisors. Eighty-four percent of the standard contracts provide comprehensive training programs, manuals and programs of regularly scheduled workshops for franchisees.

FINANCING

Financing tailored to franchising activities is a concept which is still alien to Italian banks. However, one leading bank has very recently announced that it will offer loans to franchising systems and has set up a specialized department to this end. Nevertheless, the prevailing practice remains that financing is generally negotiated privately on a case-by-case basis between the master franchisor and the franchisees. Over 50 percent of the franchisors offer financing and leasing programs. Virtually all franchisees pay entry fees, royalties and contribute to advertising expenditures.

More than 80 percent of franchisor grant exclusive area contracts, while 46 percent require total inventory turnover with a contractually based mark-up.

More than 70 percent of the large companies offer assistance in the way of operations manuals, computerized management programs, assistance for the opening of the points of sale, as well as training seminars. Most companies hold annual conventions and provide newsletters and comprehensive assistance programs.

The cost of a franchise varies from a minimum of $ 50,000 to an average cost of $ 150,000 and escalates to $ 350,000 and more.

DIRECT MARKETING

There are many logistical problems of operating a nation-wide sales network as well as managing the growing personnel and promotion costs. Part-time employment is presently restricted, although there are now some moves to liberalize regulations governing part-time employment. Marketing firms are developing new distribution techniques designed to employ the casual worker and to target groups of consumers by catalog, door-to-door sales, teleshopping or telemarketing. The most widely used methods of direct marketing are:

- Direct selling, mainly used in the nonfood sector.

- Mail order, catalog sales, or orders placed directly with the supplier.

Mail order marketing has been in Italy for approximately 15 years. Although direct marketing is considered a very effective marketing technique, it still remains a modest channel of distribution for Italian companies. One of the disadvantages of this technique, which may be overlooked by foreign investors, is frequent delays by the postal system. However, the establishment of a semiprivate nationwide express mail service, the proliferation of couriers, and the arrival of foreign parcel delivery services now offer alternatives to the national mail system.

Telephone direct marketing is growing faster than any other selling technique. With the development of new telephone equipment, the business world has turned to the use of the facsimile, making Italy the second largest per capita user in the world.

Teleshopping (home shopping through TV) is becoming a popular sales approach to reach the consumer. There are a number of privately owned television stations which mainly host telemarketing programs.

Telecommunications technologies are playing an increasing role in the process of restructuring the distribution system. Scanners, electronic cash registers, and display management systems are now common while computerized stock control systems, customer databases, and inventory control programs are being used only by the large distribution networks. The more sophisticated groups have also resorted to consulting services, resulting in technical cooperation agreements between a number of Italian and international chains.

ELECTRONIC COMMERCE

2004 represented a turning point for the Italian Internet market. Italian businesses connected to the Internet were estimated at 1.5 million at the end of 2004 -- out of a total of 3.4 million – and are expected to reach at least 2 million by the end of 2002. Internet subscriptions in the consumer segment grew from 540,000 in 1998 to over 3.7 million in 2004. Internet penetration -- which is comparatively lower than in other European countries -- is predicted to double by the end of this year. The number of Internet access providers and Internet content and service providers increased from about 150 in 1996 to about 900 in 2004, with over 3,000 Points of Presence (POP).

Although electronic commerce applications in Italy are still in their early stages, all trade sources concur that they will boom in the next two years. Many Italian companies still utilize their Web home pages to create brand awareness, offer product information and generate leads, but this trend is rapidly changing. It is estimated that a growing number of companies are implementing web sales and web purchasing applications. Business-to-business transactions are expected to have a dramatic impact on the Italian economy, similar to what is happening in other countries.

BUSINESS-TO-BUSINESS TRANSACTIONS

According to IDC, the total market value for e-commerce transactions in Italy in 1998 was approximately $360 million, of which $290 million were business-to-business. In 2004, this value grew to approximately $1.1 billion, of which over $970 million were business-to-business. It is expected that this value will quadruple in the year 2000, reaching $4 billion. On-line trading of financial services boomed in 2004, totaling 4 percent of all traded securities, a share which could increase to even 20 or 30 percent in the next two to three years. Virtually all major Italian industrial groups -- as well as the public administration -- are organizing for e-procurement, and it is predicted that in a three years time at least half of all company purchases will be via e-procurement.

The main factors fueling the development of e-commerce in Italy are: 1) the increasing recognition of e-commerce as a means to provide better support to customers/suppliers; 2) recent Italian legislation which recognizes the legal validity of digital signatures and digital contracts; 3) improved consumer protection legislation; 4) and recent agreements between Italian banks and credit card operators to introduce the SET-Secure Electronic Transaction protocol.

In business-to-business e-commerce, the most successful sectors are expected to be computers and software, financial and banking services, and general procurement services by larger companies. The development of e-business in Italy will create superb opportunities for companies specializing in this sector. Consulting services to assist the customer in developing an e-business strategy and custom development services for e-commerce applications in the areas of marketing, sales, post-sales, and purchasing are expected to boom in the next two years. The greatest opportunities for American exporters and especially for American trading companies and virtual market places, are likely to be in the e-procurement area.

BUSINESS-TO-CONSUMER TRANSACTIONS

Business-to-consumer transactions via the Internet are still marginal in Italy, with $70 million in 1998, and $195 million in 2004. It is worth noting, however, that imports of foreign products via the internet were estimated to account for 45 percent of total sales to consumers, a much higher share than the European 13 percent average.

The relatively low diffusion of personal computers (less than 20 percent of Italian families) has represented one of the major obstacles to the development of the Internet consumer market and of business-to-consumer e-commerce transactions. High telephone tariffs and cultural factors have also hindered a faster development of this market segments. The increasing availability of inexpensive personal computers and set-top-boxes, the possibility of accessing the Internet free-of-charge, and the expected fall in the prices of Internet-related telephone calls are all acting as a strong driving force. More importantly, as the diffusion of mobile phones in Italy is among the highest in the world, the Internet consumer market is expected to be driven by the availability of web-enabled mobile phones, which, through the WAP technology, should allow Italy to catch up quickly.

In the business-to-consumer e-commerce, the most promising sectors are computers and software, publishing, internet music and videos, and bookings for entertainment events, vacation and travel. However, cultural resistances are still strong, and it is not likely that the Internet will soon become a real alternative to traditional distribution channels for consumer goods.

LEASING

It has become common to lease, rather than buy, certain types of machinery. The leasing of foreign machines is usually arranged with Italian clients through local branch offices or agents of foreign manufacturers established to provide this type of service. Leasing is complicated by the fact that the importation, payment of customs duties, and other related business formalities must be taken care of by a firm established in Italy. Such tasks would usually be done by either an agent of the foreign manufacturer or by the Italian lessee. Because the lessee is often not willing to assume the inconvenience of handling importation of leased equipment, local representation is usually necessary.

JOINT VENTURES / LICENSING

A joint venture (Associazione in Partecipazione) involves the participation by a supplier of capital in the profits of the business. The operator manages the business and is solely responsible for the obligations he or she assumes toward third parties. The person furnishing the capital is responsible for any loss in direct proportion to his or her share in the net profit, limited to the amount of his/her original investment.

Joint ventures can be for one-time defined transactions with a definite duration (contractual joint venture) or a permanent cooperation between separate groups through the incorporation of a joint-stock company (corporate joint venture). Corporate joint ventures are now seen frequently in Italy.

Licensing in Italy allows foreign entities to profit from technology transfers of a formula, process or patent without the need to invest substantial capital. The Italian government imposes no exchange control limitations on the transfer of royalties abroad. Protection over the use and ownership of the technology transferred should be included in the terms of the licensing agreement.

STEPS TO ESTABLISHING AN OFFICE

A foreign citizen wishing to establish temporary or permanent residence in Italy to administer a business or to manage a corporation should obtain a business visa for this purpose from one of the Italian Consulates in the United States. All individuals or firms in business in Italy must be registered with the local Chamber of Commerce, Industry and Agriculture. This is a quasi-government office, operat-ing essentially as a field office of the Ministry of Industry and Commerce. To register with this office, an agent for a foreign company must produce a power of attorney duly notarized by Italian consular or diplomatic official in the country of the principal.

ADVERTISING AND TRADE PROMOTION

Advertising in Italy has grown rapidly in volume, importance, and sophistication. This growth in advertising has been accompanied by a proliferation of advertising agencies and an expansion of services. Along with Italian--owned agencies, there are joint ventures with other European or American firms. While some agencies specialize in specific services and media, a large number of full service agencies deal with all advertising aspects and have market research capabilities.

Media use for advertising is as follows: newspapers, 35 percent; magazines, 35 percent; radio and television, 22 percent; movies, 2 percent; other methods, 6 percent.

Newspapers and magazines: The main means of product advertising in Italy is through daily newspapers. Newspapers work closely with advertising firms, both Italian and foreign. However, since the newspapers themselves do not maintain advertising departments, advertising firms must place their ads with special agencies commissioned by the papers to receive advertising for them.

Of about 90 daily newspapers in Italy, only a dozen or so are distributed throughout the country. While some 230 Italian and foreign periodicals are on sale in Italy, only about 20 have a large circulation (see list below).

Television: Italy is served by three public television networks operated by Radiotelevisione Italiana (RAI), a government-regulated company in which the state owns a majority interest. The three networks carry commercials in programs all day long. There are also 4 major nationwide privately-owned television stations. In addition, some 100 private television stations are licensed for local broadcasting.

Radio: There are three radio stations owned and operated by RAI. These are on the air for more than 340 hours weekly, and commercial time is available. In addition to the three networks, there are hundreds of local radio stations and several national private stations.

Motion Picture Theaters: Wide use of film clips is made for advertising purposes. There are some 10,000 motion picture theaters in Italy and many regularly show advertising. The rates for advertising vary according to the showing time and class of the theater. Advertising is shown during every intermission. Therefore, this medium may be used to reach a wide market and cuts across economic strata.

Posters and Billboards: Poster advertising is handled by a number of specialized companies, as is electric sign advertising, which is subject to special regulations. Poster advertisement on walls, along streets, in street cars, buses, and other means of transportation are used to reach the consumer market. Both posters and billboards are subject to the approval of provincial authorities and to payment of a tax on poster advertising.

Show Windows and Flyers: Show window advertising is extensively used in Italy. Displays are usually attractively done and show prices of the items for sale. Advertising flyers are in common use, and street banners are used also for special occasions. Loudspeakers are used for advertising at sporting events. Direct advertising, through the distribution of gifts, samples, and price reduction coupons, is frequently used to motivate consumers.

Trade Fairs: Exhibitions are a cost-effective method to enter a foreign market and meet a wide range of buyers interested in a particular industry sector. Sales professionals find that trade fairs attract extensive buyer attendance and frequently can be used to gauge acceptance and pricing of new products and to observe the competition. In the course of a few days, a new market entrant may be able to generate more qualified and motivated prospects than by using any other sales approach. Also, fairs are useful for finding an agent, distributor, or representative. The U.S. Department of Commerce frequently organizes U.S. pavilions at events that are identified as providing excellent prospects for American exporters. Information on participating in Italian trade fairs can be obtained from Department of Commerce Export Assistance Centers located throughout the United States.

For information about trade fairs at Fiera Milano, the large international trade fair site in Europe, firms can contact Fiera Milano's U.S. representative for information by calling 1-800 524-2193. Fiera Milano organizes an extensive variety of international shows each year, and the U.S. Department of Commerce participates in some of these events.

PRICING PRODUCT

When providing the Italian buyer with a price quote, American firms most frequently provide a quote that includes sales price plus packing costs, insurance, and freight to the named point of destination. This is called the c.i.f. price. The average Italian business representative can then usually determine the charges for customs, taxes, and local transportation to arrive at the final landed cost to the importer. The customary terms of sale in Italy are either cash on delivery (which is rare) or settlement 60-120 days after invoice date (more common).

Sales made on cash terms call for payment before delivery, on delivery, or shortly after delivery -- usually within 10 days from the date of delivery. A 2 to 5 percent discount is made for payment of the full amount of the transaction at the end of the specified period from 1 to 4 months from the date of the invoice. The length of the period depends on the commodity involved, the credit standing of the buyer, and the marketing and sales objective of the seller. A period of up to 2 years is often allowed for payment of capital goods, store equipment, trucks, and similar heavy equipment.

Italian firms indicate that some American suppliers are too rigid in their payment terms and have thus lost business to other suppliers because of their rigidity. Financing is considered as much a competitive factor as the product itself, the delivery date, or after-sales service.

While some U.S. manufacturers request payment upon receipt of the goods, more successful sellers are offering terms allowing settlement of the account from 60 to 120 days following date of invoice, which is the most common practice in Italy.

The use of irrevocable letters of credit for the Italian market has declined appreciably in recent years. Although such instruments are still required by American exporters, especially when the Italian customer's credit reputation is not well known, the growing reluctance of Italian firms to provide letters of credit has required American exporters to turn to other methods to assure payment or lose the sale to other suppliers in the competitive Italian market. The Italian businessperson is reluctant to pay a high fee for a letter of credit when other suppliers or means of payment are available. American firms have put to greater use the export credit insurance and guarantee programs available through the Foreign Credit Insurance Association (FCIA).

QUOTES AND PAYMENT TERMS

Italian importers generally prefer price quotes on a c.i.f. basis since they are usually familiar with the Italian customs charges and value-added taxes levied on the product at the time of importation, but may not be acquainted with U.S. costs for trucking, ocean, or air freight. Large Italian firms and department stores, however, may prefer to buy on other terms when they arrange for the shipping and insuring the goods. Quotes- and invoicing are usually in terms of the currency of selling country.

American quotes, usually stated in dollars and on a f.o.b. basis, are completely acceptable to Italian buyers. The usual practice of American firms selling to a new customer is to require cash against documents for the first sale or two. After establishing credit, the importer will expect to pay by 30-, 60-, or 90-day letter of credit. In all cases, the American exporter will have to decide how to strike a balance between making the sale perhaps more easily with liberal financing terms versus striking a sale by seeking more secure payment terms. When first starting out, American firms may often find it necessary to offer their best price and payment terms in order to land the sale in the competitive international market. Later, prices may be adjusted as sales and volume permit.

The Italian buyer may request a quote or shipment of goods under INCOTERMS. This is a set of international rules defining the important commercial terms and practices. By referencing INCOTERMS in contracts or invoices, both buyer and seller will have a uniform understanding of their responsibilities in an agreement. Copies of the 90-page publication Guide to INCOTERMS are obtainable from ICC Publishing, 156 Fifth Avenue, New York, NY 10010, (212) 206-1150. Exporters can also obtain information from the Dun & Bradstreet Exporters' Encyclopedia.

Merchandise may be examined by the Italian importer before customs clearance for inventory purposes. Goods cannot clear customs without shipping documents and payment of any required customs duty, applicable value-added taxes, and excise taxes. These formalities must be undertaken by the importer at the time of clearing customs. Import licenses, if required, should be presented by the importer within the period for which they were issued.

SELLING TECHNIQUES/SERVICE / CUSTOMER SUPPORT

An American company that is successful in Italy becomes so because its products are marketed with the same diligence employed in the U.S. market. Whether the firm establishes a manufacturing operation or a sales branch, or appoints a commission agent, a stocking distributor, or a combination agent/distributor, the American exporter must make a long-term commitment to exporting and follow sound marketing practices in order to sell successfully in the Italian market. A key factor in this commitment to serving the overseas buyer is the local stocking of parts and giving priority to immediate air shipments on request of the European customer.

An American company that is entering the competitive Italian market is advised to commit the resources needed to market the products properly and establish long-term sales to achieve maximum sales volume. The appointment of a resident representative is extremely important. For business promotion and market knowledge, there is no effective alternative to a resident representative who is part of the local business community and readily available to customers. Having a local representative is particularly important when the product is complex and may be expected to require follow-up servicing or modification. Local representatives are familiar with the product and needs of the customer and are in a position to solve problems. Personalized service is frequently demanded by customers, creates goodwill, and often stimulates repeat sales. Technical manuals and promotional literature should be in Italian. Italy is a competitive market where reliability is important. Local representatives with solid reputations and promotional material in Italian reflects a commitment to customer service and enhances the prestige of the American firm.

A number of U.S. firms maintain their own sales organizations in Italy. Still others sell through specialized importers or appoint sales agents who often are manufacturers' brokers. A large, well-established Italian firm with an efficient nationwide sales organization is likely to insist on an exclusive arrangement. About 7,500 U.S. firms are represented in the Italian market through agents, branches, subsidiaries, or licenses. Of these, nearly 850 have a substantial direct capital investment in the form of stock as a sole owner or partner in an enterprise. Generally, the sales territory includes all of Italy. In other cases, the territory also covers the entire European Union, depending on the type of product and degree of technical support needed. Italian distributors also have excellent contacts with Eastern Europe and the Mediterranean Basin.

SELLING TO THE GOVERNMENT

The Italian government does not typically purchase goods and services abroad unless they cannot be procured locally through domestic sources, which would include subsidiaries, branches and agents of American companies. In order to be considered as a source for Italian government purchases, it is recommended that the American firm be represented by an agent/distributor rather than try to deal directly with Italian government agencies.

Each of the Italian agencies maintains its own list of contractors and suppliers. Therefore, U.S. firms need to contact each agency directly to establish their eligibility. U.S. companies must first establish their financial and technical capabilities by presenting them directly to the Italian agencies.

NEED FOR A LOCAL ATTORNEY

American companies which are interested in setting up agencies, distributorships, licenses or joint ventures are encouraged to seek professional legal advice and counsel. The American Embassy in Rome, as well as the individual Consulates, maintain a list of lawyers (according to geographic jurisdiction) which is available to the public.

PERFORMING DUE DILIGENCE

Information on specific Italian firms is available from a variety of private agencies. American companies can contact their local U.S. Department of Commerce Export Assistance Center for a listing of firms offering this service. In addition, this section includes a list of Italian private sector firms which provide this service. American banks also provide credit information services.

Just as the terms of any sales offer should be presented in a clear and detailed manner, shipments should conform to the contract and to any samples which may have been sent to the Italian importer. Special attention should be given to the prompt observance of agreed delivery schedules, as prompt delivery may be a decisive and possibly an overriding consideration of the importer in placing additional orders. When shipping on letter of credit, all terms specified on the letter of credit must be strictly observed. If the terms are not followed, the letter of credit may not be honored by the issuing bank.

ITALIAN PRIVATE SECTOR FIRMS PROVIDING BACKGROUND INFORMATION CHECKS:

DUN & BRADSTREET KOSMOS SpA
Via di Valtorta, 48
20127 Milano
Tel: 39-02-284-551
Fax: 39-02-287-2181

EUROINFORM ITALIA srl
Via Roma, 108/F
20060 Cassina de' Pecchi MI
Tel: 39-02-954-291
Fax: 39-02-9530-1869

LINCE SpA
Corso Vittorio Emanuele, 22
20122 Milano
Tel: 39-02-77541
Fax: 39-02-7602-0458

PONZI SpA
Corso Monforte, 9
20122 Milano
Tel: 39-02-7600-2821
Fax: 39-02-781-515

MARKETING U.S. AGRICULTURAL PRODUCTS AND SERVICES

Although demand for food products in the domestic market is changing slowly, the Italian food sector is dynamic. In the early 1990s the transformation was far reaching, with the sector moving closer to U.S. norms for products, packaging and services. However, Italy still lags behind some of the other major European countries with similar socioeconomic parameters in restructuring its food distribution system, but progress in this area has accelerated.

There is a slow, but steady movement towards the consolidation of both processors and distributors which will favor increased cooperation with foreign firms, particularly in the north. Higher unemployment rates and lower incomes are slowing changes in the south. Family run shops are in a decline as a result of the growing consumer preference for modern distribution formats, the increased importance of price in consumer decision making, new stricter tax regulations and higher space rental costs. However, strong traditional preferences in food and shopping mean that this trend will develop slowly. It is estimated that in Italy is at least 5 years behind other European countries such as France and Germany in its marketing trends.

The relationship between the Italian food processing industry and food distributors is changing dramatically. There are now over 6500 supermarkets and hyper-markets in Italy. Many of the larger companies have become vertically integrated, while the smaller entities have closed their doors or made significant changes to become more competitive. Sales receipts for larger chain stores are increasing rapidly.

Hard discount stores have become firmly established in the Italian market, particularly in the north. The soft consumer demand has forced price into the forefront although Italians remain quality conscious. New research and expanded promotion trials have been undertaken to improve market share. Private labels are becoming more and more popular. This trend tends to favor least-cost suppliers.

There are over 30 retail food chains in Italy. As with most other agricultural sectors, no single chain or company commands more than 2% or 3% of the market. They can be divided into two main categories: chains owned by individuals, corporations or cooperatives; and networks of individually owned independent stores that share in group purchasing and logistical, marketing and (sometimes) financial services. Some networks incorporate a form of vertical integration by including one or more wholesalers. Most retail outlets in Italy are still individually owned and operated.

Important differences exist in Italian style supermarkets versus U.S. food chains. For example, Italian shoppers still prefer to walk to their local supermarket, thus packaging is smaller and lighter. Brand loyalty is high and Italy has one of the lowest levels of penetration of private labels in Europe. However, private labels are on the rise and represent a real opportunity for U.S. companies.

Many of the larger supermarket chains have centralized buying offices and attend foreign food shows to seek new products. In addition, supermarkets, hypermarkets and hard discounts stores (which have increased in numbers as a result of the recession) have their own logistics departments and can, although infrequently, act as direct importers. Wholesale marketing channels vary greatly according to the commodity (i.e. fish versus dried fruit). Regional wholesale markets continue to be important distribution points for fresh foods.

Most imported food products still enter the Italian market through brokers or specialized traders. Price is an increasingly important basis for import purchases, although quality and novelty alone does move some products. Imported products enter Italy indirectly from Rotterdam or directly via air, although 95% of all freight inside of Italian borders is transported via truck.

Northern Italy remains the country's most important economic region. The north accounts for almost 55 percent of national income and 45 percent of the population. The large difference in average income means that household expenditures on food and drink vary considerably by region. For example, the average family in northern Italy spends less than 19 percent of their income on food, while a southern family spends over 24 percent of total income on food items.

The importance of the tourist industry in Italy cannot be underrated. Approximately 30 million tourists visit Italy every year, and it is estimated that an additional 10 million will come for the Catholic Jubilee in the year 2000. Food service outlets vary greatly and bars and cafes are becoming increasingly important for American type foods. The popularity of snack foods has pushed up demand for fast food outlets and the typical Italian coffee bar now stocks a broad selection of sweet and salty snacks and ice creams, in addition to serving hot and cold plates.

The institutional food sector has consolidated and become much more efficient in recent years. Institutional cafeterias and restaurants are most interested in semi-prepared foods, frozen foods, ready to cook pasta or individual dishes and snacks. Roughly 12% of all frozen food purchases are frozen french fries, many of which are prepared in the microwave.

Consolidation of small companies and an increasing number of joint ventures is also continuing in the food processing sector. Selling strategies are more aggressive and marketing/PR spending is on the upswing in order to survive the price competition inspired by the advent of hard discount stores.

Italian food processors are seeking specialized ingredients such as whole grain flours and organic cereal products. Food processors are using an increasing amount of dried fruits and nuts (i.e. in the bakery and ice cream industry) in order to develop new products. Products with technical advantages such as sugar substitutes and exotic fruits and vegetables also are in increasing demand.

TRADE REGULATIONS, CUSTOMS AND STANDARDS

TRADE BARRIERS

Broadcast Directive and Motion Picture Quotas

Italy passed legislation in 1998 to significantly tighten European content requirements (TV quotas). The new law replaces Italy's previous requirement that a majority of television broadcast time for feature films be reserved for EU-origin films, and that half of the European quota be dedicated to Italian films. The new quota goes beyond the EU "Broadcast without Frontiers" Directive by applying quotas specifically to prime time broadcasting, and by excluding talk shows from the types of programming that may be counted towards fulfilling the quota. (The Directive excludes only news, sports, game shows, advertising, teletext and teleshopping. The Italian law excludes these categories as well, but additionally excludes talk shows.)

A separate but related issue concerns films shown in Italian theaters. After eliminating obligatory screen quotas for Italian films in 1994, Italy reinstituted EU content quotas specifically for multiplex cinemas in Fall 1998, at the same time including building restrictions on new multiplexes in order to minimize competition with existing cinemas. The quotas require that multiplexes devote 15-20% of seats, in at least three theaters per multiplex, to EU content on a "stable" (daily) basis. The United States continues its efforts both to obtain elimination of discriminatory laws and regulations in the audiovisual sector and to limit their impact in the interim.

Civil Aviation

Italy and the United States agreed on an "Open Skies" civil aviation regime in 2004. This is expected to liberalize the Italy-U.S. air travel market dramatically and, indeed, within the first eight months after the agreement was signed, several U.S. air carriers began new passenger or cargo service linking Italy with Chicago, Detroit and other cities.

Government Procurement

In Italy, fragmented, often non-transparent government procurement practices and previous problems with corruption have created obstacles to U.S. firms' participation in Italian government procurement. However, Italy has made progress in making the laws and regulations governing government procurement more transparent, although Italy has not yet fully updated its government procurement code, nor has it completely implemented EU directives on government procurement. In addition, the pressure to reduce government expenditures while increasing efficiency is resulting in increased use of competitive procurement procedures and greater emphasis on best value rather than automatic reliance on traditional suppliers. This trend is benefiting U.S. firms; to successfully meet the bureaucratic requirements, however, most firms rely on experienced local representatives and/or agents.

CUSTOMS REGULATIONS/TARIFF RATES/IMPORT LICENCE REQUIREMENTS

Prior to signing a long-term contract or sending a ship-ment of considerable value, it may be prudent for a U.S. exporter to first obtain an official ruling on the customs classification, duty rate, and taxes. Such requests should be sent to the Ministry of Finance's Customs Department, Rome, Italy (see "Customs Contact Information" at the end of this Section). The request should describe the product, the material it is made from, and other details needed by customs authorities to classify the product correctly. While customs will not provide a binding decision, the advance ruling usually will be accepted if the imported goods are found to correspond exactly to the full description provided when requesting the ruling.

With exception of a small group of largely agricultural items, practically all goods originating in the United States and most other free-world countries can be imported without import licenses and free of quantitative restrictions. There are, however, monitoring measures applied to imports of certain sensitive products. The most important of these measures is the automatic import license for textiles. This license is granted to Italian importers when they provide the requisite forms.

Various apparel and textile products, and controlled items such as arms and munitions are the most frequently regulated items. Import licenses are generally rapidly granted for goods of U.S. origin and delays are usually from lack of proper documentation or information.

Licenses are not transferable. They may be used to cover several shipments within the total quantity authorized. In general, the goods involved are indicated on the license by the Harmonized System classification number and the corresponding wording of the tariff position.

VALUE-ADDED TAXES

While customs duty rates are the same for all 15 EU countries, the value-added tax (VAT) and excise tax on products and services usually differ from country to country. These taxes are levied in the country of final destination. Following is the schedule of VAT rates presently applicable in Italy:

Zero rate: Applies to exports outside the EU and supplies of goods to entrepreneurs in other EU states, sales of ships and aircraft and related parts, and supplies (with certain limitations) and specified services relating to international operations;

4%: Applies to numerous basic agricultural products, basic foodstuffs (i.e. bread, milk and fruits), certain medical aids, books and newspapers;

10%: Applies to certain agricultural products, transportation services for individuals, most foodstuff, livestock and meat, most pharmaceutical products, energy for private use, telecommunication services rendered through public phones (tlc for private use are at 20% rate), services rendered by hotels and restaurants and the cost of domestic airline tickets;

20%: As the standard rate, applies to all goods and services not subject to other rates (including most of the goods previously subject to the 12% rate – i.e., shoes, textiles, records and tapes).

TEMPORARY GOODS ENTRY REQUIREMENTS

Temporary Imports

Material may temporarily be imported into Italy without payment of duties and tax if such material is to be used in the production or manufacture of a product that is to be exported. The importer gives security, usually in the form of a guarantee from a bank or insurance company, for the amount of the usual duties and taxes. Upon exportation of the finished product, the guarantee is released or the deposit returned.

Temporary entry of goods intended to be reexported in the same condition is permissible free of import duties and taxes upon approval of an application by Italian Customs.

Samples without commercial value are admitted free of duty and taxes. Product literature should be marked "product Literature - no commercial value". Samples with commercial value are also admitted duty and tax free, provided that the following conditions are complied with:

(a) The samples are accompanied by a representative of the U.S. firm with a statement, notarized by an Italian Consulate, identifying the commercial traveler and attesting to the intention that the samples are being imported into Italy for the purpose of being shown or demonstrated and they are to be reexported in due course.

(b) A certificate of origin from a recognized chamber of commerce is submitted to identify the source of the goods.

(c) A deposit or bond, in the amount of the applicable customs duties and taxes, is made at the point of entry. This will be refunded when the goods are reexported.

(d) A list (in duplicate) with a full description of each sample, including weight and value, is submitted. It is helpful to have such a list in Italian.

U.S. traders should be aware of another and more simplified procedure in the form of a carnet for the temporary importation of samples without posting guarantees. See the "Carnets" section located in Chapter IX: Business Travel (under Temporary Entry of Goods).

In practice, samples valued in excess of lira 1 million (or about 1,250 USD) are practically impossible to clear through Italian customs. In such cases, it is advisable to engage the services of a local freight forwarder.

Goods in Transit:

Goods may clear customs with an EU transit procedure that provides for the issuance of a single transit document under which the goods may be easily shipped across frontiers of the EU member states. These transit documents are completed for the importer by a freight forwarder in Italy. The EU transit document provides the basis for a single, comprehensive procedure covering the goods within the EU. Since single transit document is an EU form, the European importer, customs house broker, freight forwarder, or shipper must prepare the document at the point of entry.

Inward and Outward Processing
Inward processing is the temporary importation of raw material or products for additional manufacture or processing. Merchandise imported for additional processing and eventual reexport out of the EU is eligible for custom-free treatment.

The reexported goods may be partly or totally processed. The import duty and taxes are levied only on those goods that are not reexported and are finally sold in the EU.

To qualify for inward processing, an Italian (or EU) firm must satisfy customs that it is necessary to use imported goods instead of EU goods; state an intention to export products manufactured from the imported goods (or equivalent goods available in the EU); and assure that, upon reexportation, the conditions set forth in the authorization are satisfied, the exported products are accounted for, and the entered goods are identifiable and relate to specific importations.

In outward processing, a firm in Italy may export goods for further manufacture or processing from the EU customs area and then reimport the final product. Duties and taxes are levied only on the increased value added by the expatriate manufacturing or processing when the goods are returned to Italy and not to the total value of the product. Only firms located in Italy or another EU country are eligible to take advantage of this option, and they should first gain approval of the Customs authorities.

SPECIAL IMPORT/EXPORT REQUIREMENTS AND CERTIFICATIONS

Documents required for exporting include the usual shipper's commercial invoice and the bill of lading or air waybill, none of which require consular legalization. For textiles and apparel, it is good practice to provide a certificate of origin, available through most state chambers of commerce. For other products, however, if substantive proof of U.S. origin is provided through other accompanying documents as well as through characteristic trademarks, a certificate of origin is not normally necessary. For additional information or assistance on export documentation, readers should consult publications such as the Exporter's

Encyclopedia, published by Dun's Marketing Services or contact a local U.S. Department of Commerce International Trade Administration Export Assistance Center.

LABELING REQUIREMENTS

There is no general requirement that imports be marked as to country of origin. Under Italian legislation, the origin of imported merchandise is established through documentation accompanying the shipments arriving in Italy and not through marking of products or their containers. Certain specified commodities, however, must be marked or labeled to show composition, and name and location of manufacturer, in accordance with various laws and regulations. The following articles are subject to special marking or labeling regulations: lime, cement and similar binding agents; pianos, automatic pianos, harmonicas and similar instruments; clinical thermometers; ethical medicines; cosmetics. Hallmarking of gold and silver articles is required before they can be offered for sale. Only small tolerances are allowable for manufacturing errors. The hallmarking may be done by a hallmarking office after importation.

Italy uses the metric system of weights and measures, which is called the International System of Units (SI). The European Community has established standardized packaging units for numerous products which should be consulted by U.S. exporters. Labeling must be in metric units for all imported products to be sold in Italy. Products are allowed to be imported and then labeled in SI metric units prior to sale. Dual labeling information is permitted, but the non-metric information must not predominate.

Imports of certain commodities such as packaged foods, distilled spirits, beer, wine, vinegar and foodstuffs are subject to special regulations regarding the manner in which they must be labeled to show manufacturer, composition, content (in metric units), and country of origin. In view of the complexity of these regulations and changing requirements, information should be requested from the importer prior to shipment. When the services of an importer are not available, information can be obtained directly from the appropriate Italian Government authority listed at the end of this publication. For agricultural and food products, see "Trade Regulations and Standards for Agriculture" below.

PROHIBITED IMPORTS

There are a number of Italian regulations and European Community directives that prohibit certain foodstuffs, food colorings, drugs and narcotics, animal products, plants, seed grains, alcohol, cosmetics and toiletries, etc. It is therefore recommended American exporters contact the Italian importer prior to the shipment or use their freight forwarder to make the determination.

WARRANTY AND NON-WARRANTY REPAIRS

Import duties and taxes are not imposed on products exported from Italy, if the item which is shipped back is the same to return to Italy.

Shipments of replacement parts to Italy, however, are subject to duties plus VAT, even if shipped for a product under warranty.

EXPORT CONTROLS

For the purpose of national security, foreign policy, or the short supply of materials, the United States controls the export of goods and technology by two broad categories of export licenses -- general and validated.

The vast majority of U.S. exports are shipped abroad under general licenses that do not require formal application or approval. To determine which kind of export license is required, exporters should consult the U.S. Export Administration Regulations for complete details or obtain assistance from the local U.S. Department of Commerce district office.

As an overview, the first step in the export licensing process is to determine whether a product requires a general or validated license. Determine what is being exported, the destination of the product, its end-use, and the organization that will be using the product. Check the schedule of Country Groups listed in the U.S. Export Administration Regulations to determine the destination category; check the Commodity Control List to determine if the product requires a validated license for shipment to that particular country; and determine if any special restrictions are in effect.

If the product is not on the control list, then it can be exported under a general license. The U.S. exporter simply completes the "U.S. Shippers Export Declaration", Form 7525-V, providing details of the shipment; includes a commercial invoice; and exports the goods. If the product is on the control list, a validated license is needed. An application must be made and an export license granted. As a general rule, an exporter will need a validated license (1) if the products are controlled or in short supply regardless of the country of destination; (2) for any commodity to a destination with foreign policy concerns; or (3) for unpublished technical data to certain destinations. Certain special licenses are also issued to cover large projects or repeated sales through a foreign distributor.

For assistance in determining what type of license is needed and to initiate the processing of an application, contact your local Department of Commerce district office or the Bureau of Export Administration, Office of Export Assistance, Room H-1099D, U.S. Department of Commerce, Washington, DC 20230, (202) 482-4811.

STANDARDS

As a member of the EU, Italy applies the product standards and certification approval process developed by the European Community. Italy is required by the Treaty of Rome to incorporate approved EU directives into its national laws. However, there is frequently a long lag in implementing these directives at the national level. In addition, in some sectors such as pollution control, the uniformity in application of standards may vary according to region, further complicating the certification process. Italy has been slow in accepting test data from foreign sources, but is expected to adopt EU standards in this area. U.S.-EU negotiation of mutual recognition agreements should, over time, reduce problems in this area. In the Spring of 1997 the U.S. and EU concluded mutual recognition agreements in the following areas: network and electromagnetic compatibility (EMC) for telecommunications and information technology equipment and radio transmitters; EMC and electrical safety for electrical and electronic products; good manufacturing practices inspections for pharmaceutical products and certain medical devices; product assessment for medical devices; and safety of recreational craft.

As part of the unification program to establish common standards for all member countries, key product areas are being regulated by the EU. Mandatory requirements to protect the health and safety of consumers, as well as the environment are constantly being developed and implemented. To indicate conformance to the mandatory EU requirements, a CE mark must be placed on all regulated products by the manufacturer or a representative before they can be sold on the EU market. The applicable product testing and certification requirements for individual product categories are specified in the various EU directives. The CE mark relates only to the mandatory health, safety, and environmental requirements established by the EU; it does not indicate conformity to European product standards. Thus, national marks of conformity with product standards remain compatible with the CE mark and both may be applied to the product. It should be noted, however, that the CE mark does replace all national safety marks for the regulated products.

U.S. firms exporting to Italy are confronted with both national and EU standards for many products. Further, these regulations occasionally change to meet new technology and more stringent demands. Exporters can stay fully informed of the latest EU technical standards activities by contacting the Standards Information Service of the National Institute of Standards and Technology (NIST) at (301) 975-4040. A part of the U.S. Department of Commerce, NIST offers industry an in-depth reference system on EU standards information gathered from the two European standards bodies tasked to write the EU norms --the European Committee for Standards (CEN) and the European Committee for Electrotechnical Standardization (CENELEC). NIST also can provide updated information from the EU which will elaborate on directives and provide assistance in identifying EU and member state standards and regulations. For more information, contact NIST at (301) 975-4038.

Other valuable sources of information with regard to Italian standards include: the American National Standards Institute, 1430 Broadway, New York, NY 10018, (212) 354-3300; the Department of Commerce's National Technical Information Service, Springfield, VA 22161, (703) 557-4733; UNI, Ente Nazionale Italiano di Unificazione, Via Battistotti Sassi, 20133 Milan (Italian National Bureau of Standards); or through the various trade associations that follow international activities for their membership.

FREE TRADE ZONES / WAREHOUSES

There are two free trade zones in Italy located in Trieste and Venice. Goods of foreign origin may be brought in without payment of taxes or duties, as long as the material is to be used in the production or assembly of a product that will be exported.

Benefits of a free-trade zone include:

- customs duties deferred for 180 days from the time that the goods leave the free-trade zone to enter another EU country;
- the goods may undergo any transformation free of any customs restraints;
- absolute exemption from any duties on products coming from a third country.

The free-trade zone law also allows a company, of any nationality, to employ workers of the same nationality, under that country's labor laws and social security.

Italy also has numerous general warehouses that are located throughout Italy in all the port areas and cities. There are no limitations as to the type or origin of merchandise that can be stored in free trade zones or bonded or customs warehouses. The time limit for such storage is 5 years. Merchandise deteriorated while in storage can be destroyed without payment of duty.

The advantage of a free trade zone or bonded warehouse to American firms is having a European base of supply to assure customers prompt delivery and service. Being able to maintain inventory at low cost with a minimum of customs paperwork is also a distinct advantage.

MEMBERSHIP IN FREE TRADE ARRANGEMENTS

Italy has been a member of the European Union (EU) since its inception in 1958. The other EU members are Belgium, Denmark, France, Germany, Greece, Ireland, Luxembourg, the Netherlands, Portugal, Spain, the United Kingdom, Austria, Finland and Sweden. Other countries have applied for membership. The EU forms a customs union and a large unified market having free trade among the member states. It levies a common tariff on imported products coming from non-EU countries such as the United States, Japan, and Canada. The EU also has a common agricultural policy, joint transportation policy, and free movement of goods and capital within the member states. Other aspects of commercial activity are being harmonized.

The EU grants tariff preferences to more than 100 developing countries and about 40 overseas territories under the EU's Generalized System of Preferences (GSP). Imports of nearly all semi-manufactured and manufactured goods originating in these countries and territories enter the EU duty free. Annual duty-free quotas are established for those products and a system of providing certificates of origin has been established to ensure that goods are not diverted through the GSP countries to take advantage of the lower tariff concessions.

Free trade agreements have been developed between the European Union and the European Economic Area (EEA), which includes Norway, Iceland, Liechtenstein, and Switzerland. Under the terms of these agreements, most industrial products and certain processed agricultural products are exempt from import duties if traded within this trading bloc. The result of the agreements reached between the EU members and the EEA members is an open trading area for most industrial products of 19 nations with an affluent population of 380 million.

CUSTOMS CONTACT INFORMATION

Ministero delle Finanze
(Ministry of Treasury)
Dipartimento delle Dogane
(Customs Department)
Via M. Carucci 71
00143 Rome
Tel. 39-06-50241

TRADE REGULATIONS AND STANDARDS FOR AGRICULTURE

Since Italy is a member of the European Union (EU), virtually all of its agricultural sector is governed by the Common Agricultural Policy (CAP). Similarly, Italy employs the same tariffs, levies and other EU regulations as the other fourteen member states. For example, Italy imposes variable levies (on grain products) and quotas (on meat, cheese, bananas) as required by the European Union. Italy also applies a value added tax on most food/agricultural items (ranging from 4 percent for semi processed commodities to 19 percent for "luxury" high value food items).

In general, if a U.S. food product is imported into one EU member state it can be transhipped to Italy, provided it has a label written in Italian, and provided the product does not present a public or animal/plant health risk. However, if the product is directly imported into Italy it must meet all Italian food safety and quality standards, as well as Italian labeling and packaging regulations. Many of these standards and regulations have been harmonized within the European Union. For example, the EU has adopted a number of regulations covering production standards, analytical characteristics, product specifications, allowable additives, and labeling. Specific EU regulations exist for cocoa and chocolate products, sugars, fruit juices, fruit jams and jellies, milk and casein products.

However, where EU standards do not exist, Italy can set its own national requirements and some of these have been known to hamper imports of game meat, processed meat products, frozen foods, alcoholic beverages, and snack foods/confectionary products. U.S. exporters of "health" foods, weight loss/diet foods, baby foods and vitamins should work closely with an Italian importer, since Italy's labeling laws regarding health claims can be particularly stringent.

Italian legislation sets forth orders, obligations and criminal sanctions for violations. Food law is divided into two basic categories: rules dealing with hygiene/sanitary issues and rules governing labeling and packaging. All laws apply equally to domestically produced and imported goods.

Italy is still working on specific sectors of the food law to bring the regulations up to date scientifically in the areas of hygiene/sanitation. In the case of food additives, coloring and modified starches, Italy's laws are considered to be close to current U.S. laws, albeit sometimes more restrictive.

Basic labeling requirements in the EU/Italy:

Name of products (physical condition or specific treatment)
Name/address of manufacturer, packer, seller or importer in
EU Local language
Country of origin
Ingredients in descending order of weight
Metric weight and volume
Additives by category name
Special storage conditions
Minimum shelf life date
Special preparation instructions

U.S. exporters should be aware that any food or agricultural product transhipped through Italian territory must meet Italian requirements, even if the product is transported in a sealed and bonded container and is not expected to enter Italian commerce.

CUSTOMS AND CURRENCY REGULATIONS

There are no limits on importing lire or other currencies. Exporting currency from Italy is free up to a maximum of 20 million lire or the equivalent in foreign currency. Customs authorization is required for higher sums.

Italian currency in circulation consists of coins of 5, 10, 20, 50, 100, 200, and 500 lire and banknotes of 1,000, 2,000, 5,000, 10,000, 50,000 and 100,000 lire.

The Italian customs authorities allow duty-free importation of the following articles (for non-commercial reasons and subject to declaration at the frontier): 200 cigarettes or 100 small cigars or 50 cigars or 250 gr. of loose tobacco: 1 litre of alcohol over 22 degrees or 2 litres of alcohol under 22 degrees; 2 litres of wine; 50 cc of perfume; 500 gr. of coffee.

Tourists from EC countries can import larger quantities of duty-free goods (enquire at customs).

In addition to personal effects, visitors are also allowed to bring in jewellery, two cameras, one video camera, one radio, one television, one tape recorder, one bicycle, one boat (with or without motor), two pairs of skis, two tennis rackets, one canoe, one surf board. These limits apply only to non-EU citizens.

TRADE AND PROJECT FINANCING

DESCRIPTION OF BANKING SYSTEM

There are numerous banking offices located throughout the country, with over 800 banks and 22,000 branches performing commercial services. Among the most impor-tant are the Istituto Bancario San Paolo di Torino, Banca di Roma, Cassa di Risparmio delle Provincie Lombarde (CARIPLO), Banca Commerciale Italiana, Credito Italiano, Banco di Napoli and Banca Nazionale del Lavoro. These banks are a principal source of credit information. The banking sector is undergoing consolidation involving mergers and acquisitions among the major banks. This process is expected to continue over the next several years as the Italian banking sector seeks to become more competitive in the European market.

Several U.S. banks perform banking services in Italy through branches, subsidiaries, or representatives. Many American banks can also provide their commercial customers with bank reports on an overseas buyer as well as provide assistance on letters of credit and foreign exchange. U.S. banks with offices in Italy include Chase, Citibank, Morgan Guaranty Trust, Bank of New York, and Bank of America and numerous smaller, regional banks.

Banks in Italy that have the authority to participate in foreign exchange usually have an U.S. correspondent. Foreign currency transfers and foreign exchange transactions must be channeled via authorized intermediaries (the Bank of Italy, the Italian Foreign Exchange Office, and authorized banks). The larger Italian banks have branches in one or more U.S. cities.

The Bank of Italy, Italy's central bank, is widely respected both nationally and internationally as a non-political overseer of the Italian economy responsible for controlling inflation and balance of payments pressures.

FOREIGN EXCHANGE CONTROLS AFFECTING TRADING

Italy has no restrictions on the amount of foreign exchange instruments, currency, or checks that may be brought into the country. Normally, lire 20 million may be taken out of the country, but any amount declared on entry may be reexported.

Italian exchange regulations are issued by the Italian Exchange Office (Ufficio Italiano dei Cambi--UIC), Via Quattro Fontane 123, Rome 00184, Italy under authority of the Ministry of Foreign Trade. Foreign exchange may be sold or acquired from the Bank of Italy or any of the banks authorized by the Bank of Italy. In practice, all commercial banks are authorized to conduct foreign exchange transactions.

Dollar currency, travelers checks, and, in some cases, personal checks, may be exchanged at banks, exchange offices, and authorized tourist offices and hotels. Major credit cards are accepted with proper identification. It is best to first confirm what form of payment is accepted.

GENERAL AVAILABILITY OF FINANCING

Italy has a well-developed banking and credit system with numerous correspondent U.S. banks. Italian banks are subject to close government supervision. The Bank of Italy must authorize the establishment of a new bank.

Until 1993, the Italian banking system was divided into two categories, differentiated by length of lending authorized. The Single Banking Law passed in 1993 abolished this division, effectively allowing all Italian banks to lend at any maturity. Due to this historical legacy, those institutions that focused on longer-term lending remain at the forefront for this type of finance. Short-term business and trade finance is available from a wide range of Italian and U.S. banks.

U.S. firms desiring to finance major portions of their capital investment outside the United States may find capital available in the Eurodollar market. U.S. bank branches in Italy can assist in financing capital investment.

HOW TO FINANCE EXPORTS / METHODS OF PAYMENT

When providing the Italian buyer with a price quote, American firms most frequently provide a quote that includes packing costs, insurance, and freight. This is called the c.i.f. price.

The average Italian business representative can then usually determine the charges for customs, taxes, and local transportation to arrive at the final landed cost to importer. The customary terms of sale in Italy are either cash or net. Sales made on cash terms call for payment before delivery, on delivery, or shortly after delivery -- usually within 10 days from the date of delivery. A 2 to 5 percent discount is made for payment of the full amount of the transaction at the end of the specified period from 1 to 4 months from the date of the invoice. The length of the period depends on the commodity involved, the credit standing of the buyer, and the motivation of the seller. A period of up to 2 years is often allowed for payment of capital goods, store equipment, trucks, and similar heavy equipment.

Italian firms indicate that some American suppliers are too rigid in their payment terms and have thus lost business to other suppliers because of their rigidity. Financing is considered as much a competitive factor as the product itself, the delivery date, or after-sales service. While some U.S. manufacturers request payment upon receipt of the goods, more successful sellers are offering terms allowing settlement of the account from 60 to 120 days following receipt of the order.

The use of irrevocable letters of credit for the Italian market has declined appreciably in recent years. Although such instruments are still required by American exporters, especially when the Italian customer's credit reputation is not well known, the growing reluctance of Italian firms to provide letters of credit has required American exporters to utilize other methods to assure payment or lose the sale to other suppliers in the competitive Italian market. The Italian businessperson is reluctant to pay a high fee for a letter of credit when other suppliers or means of payment are available. American firms have put to greater use the export credit insurance and guarantee programs available through the Foreign Credit Insurance Association (FCIA).

Just as the terms of any sales offer should be presented in a clear and detailed manner, shipments should conform to the contract and to any samples that may have been sent to the Italian importer. Special attention should be given to the prompt observance of agreed delivery schedules, as prompt delivery may be a decisive and possibly an overriding consideration of the importer in placing additional orders. When shipping on letter of credit, all terms specified on the letter of credit must be strictly observed. If the terms are no followed, the letter of credit may not be honored by the bank.

EXPORT FINANCING AND INSURANCE

As a member of the G-7, Italy as a market for U.S. exporters does not warrant any special USG credit assistance. The network of Italian banks with branches in the U.S. will offer limited export credit assistance. Similarly, large U.S. banks and/or local banks located in the exporter's state can offer factoring; exchange fluctuation hedging and limited exporter's credit services. The Export-Import Bank of the United States (Exim Bank) and FCIA consider Italy a low political risk country. Italy is classified as a "rich" country under the OECD rate classification. Small business exporters may obtain assistance under the SBA's Export Revolving Line of Credit (ELRC) loan program.

AVAILABILITY OF PROJECT FINANCING

The Italian government has for decades promoted development in poorer parts of the country, particularly the southern "Mezzogiorno", through incentives such as tax reductions and financial assistance for private investment projects. A number of American companies have taken advantage of these incentives over the years to establish facilities in Italy. The government is trying to promote the "one office" concept so that potential investors have one place to go for all the information and permits they may require. At present, however, a company seeking information on these incentives should inquire at all of the following agencies:

1. Istituto per la promozione industriale
Viale Maresciallo Pilsudsky, 124
00197 Rome
Tel. 39-06-809721
Fax 39-06-8072898

2. Ministero dell' Industria, Commercio ed Artigianato
(Ministry of Industry and Commerce)

Direzione Generale per il Coordinamento degli Incentivi alle Imprese
(Directorate for Coordination of Enterprise Incentives)
Via del Giorgione, 2
00111 Roma
Tel. 39-06-5401-633
Fax 39-06-5960-1226

3. Sviluppo Italia
Via Molise
00187 Rome
Tel. 39-06-42129-1
Fax 39-06-41219-232

4. Ministero del Tesoro, Bilancio e Programmazione Economica
(Ministry of the Treasury, Budget and Economic Planning)
Dipartimento delle politiche di Sviluppo ed di Coesione
Responsabile Servizio Contrattazione Programmata
Tel. 39-06-4816-1242
Fax 39-06-4745-327

BASIC TITLES ON ITALY

IMPORTANT!

All publications are updated annually!

Please contact IBP, Inc. at ibpusa3@gmail.com for the latest ISBNs and additional information

title
Italy A "Spy" Guide - Strategic Information and Developments
Italy A Spy" Guide"
Italy Air Force Handbook
Italy Air Force Handbook
Italy Army Weapon Systems Handbook
Italy Army Weapon Systems Handbook
Italy Army Weapon Systems Handbook
Italy Aviation and Aerospace Industry Handbook
Italy Aviation and Aerospace Industry Handbook
Italy Banking & Financial Market Handbook
Italy Business and Investment Opportunities Yearbook
Italy Business and Investment Opportunities Yearbook
Italy Business and Investment Opportunities Yearbook Volume 1 Strategic Information and Opportunities
Italy Business Intelligence Report - Practical Information, Opportunities, Contacts
Italy Business Intelligence Report - Practical Information, Opportunities, Contacts
Italy Business Law Handbook - Strategic Information and Basic Laws
Italy Business Law Handbook - Strategic Information and Basic Laws

title
Italy Business Law Handbook - Strategic Information and Basic Laws
Italy Business Law Handbook - Strategic Information and Basic Laws
Italy Clothing & Textile Industry Handbook
Italy Clothing & Textile Industry Handbook
Italy Company Laws and Regulations Handbook
Italy Constitution and Citizenship Laws Handbook - Strategic Information and Basic Laws
Italy Country Study Guide - Strategic Information and Developments
Italy Country Study Guide - Strategic Information and Developments
Italy Country Study Guide - Strategic Information and Developments Volume 1 Strategic Information and Developments
Italy Customs, Trade Regulations and Procedures Handbook
Italy Customs, Trade Regulations and Procedures Handbook
Italy Diplomatic Handbook - Strategic Information and Developments
Italy Diplomatic Handbook - Strategic Information and Developments
Italy Ecology & Nature Protection Handbook
Italy Ecology & Nature Protection Handbook
Italy Ecology & Nature Protection Laws and Regulation Handbook
Italy Economic & Development Strategy Handbook
Italy Economic & Development Strategy Handbook
Italy Education System and Policy Handbook
Italy Energy Policy, Laws and Regulation Handbook
Italy Export-Import Trade and Business Directory
Italy Export-Import Trade and Business Directory
Italy Foreign Policy and Government Guide
Italy Foreign Policy and Government Guide
Italy Government and Business Contacts Handbook
Italy Government and Business Contacts Handbook
Italy Immigration Laws and Regulations Handbook - Strategic Information and Basic Laws
Italy Industrial and Business Directory
Italy Industrial and Business Directory
Italy Intelligence & Security Activities & Operations Handbook
Italy Intelligence & Security Activities & Operations Handbook
Italy Intelligence ,Security Activities & Operations Handbook
Italy Intelligence ,Security Activities & Operations Handbook
Italy Internet and E-Commerce Investment and Business Guide - Strategic and Practical Information: Regulations and Opportunities
Italy Internet and E-Commerce Investment and Business Guide - Strategic and Practical Information: Regulations and Opportunities
Italy Investment and Business Guide - Strategic and Practical Information
Italy Investment and Business Guide - Strategic and Practical Information
Italy Investment and Business Guide - Strategic and Practical Information
Italy Investment and Business Guide - Strategic and Practical Information
Italy Investment and Trade Laws and Regulations Handbook
Italy Justice System and National Police Handbook
Italy Justice System and National Police Handbook
Italy Labor Laws and Regulations Handbook - Strategic Information and Basic Laws
Italy Land Ownership and Agriculture Laws Handbook
Italy Medical & Pharmaceutical Industry Handbook
Italy Medical & Pharmaceutical Industry Handbook

title
Italy Mineral & Mining Sector Investment and Business Guide - Strategic and Practical Information
Italy Mineral & Mining Sector Investment and Business Guide - Strategic and Practical Information
Italy Mining Laws and Regulations Handbook
Italy Parliament Guide
Italy Parliament Guide
Italy Recent Economic and Political Developments Yearbook
Italy Recent Economic and Political Developments Yearbook
Italy Recent Economic and Political Developments Yearbook
Italy Research & Development Policy Handbook
Italy Research & Development Policy Handbook
Italy Research & Development Policy Handbook
Italy Space Agency and Programs Handbook
Italy Space Agency and Programs Handbook
Italy Space Programs and Exploration Handbook
Italy Space Programs and Exploration Handbook
Italy Starting Business (Incorporating) in....Guide
Italy Tax Guide
Italy Tax Guide
Italy Taxation Laws and Regulations Handbook
Italy Telecom Laws and Regulations Handbook
Italy Telecommunication Industry Business Opportunities Handbook
Italy Telecommunication Industry Business Opportunities Handbook
Italy Transportation Policy and Regulations Handbook
Italy Wine Industry Investment and Business Opportunities Yearbook
Italy: Economic Development of Italian Regions Yearbook

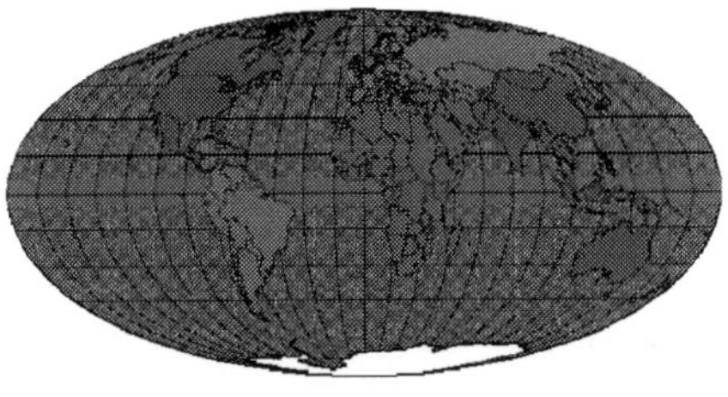

TITLE
Belgium Business and Investment Opportunities Yearbook Volume 1 Strategic, Practical Information and Opportunities
Belize Business and Investment Opportunities Yearbook Volume 1 Strategic, Practical Information and Opportunities
Benin Business and Investment Opportunities Yearbook Volume 1 Strategic, Practical Information and Opportunities
Bermuda Business and Investment Opportunities Yearbook Volume 1 Strategic, Practical Information and Opportunities
Bhutan Business and Investment Opportunities Yearbook Volume 1 Strategic, Practical Information and Opportunities
Bolivia Business and Investment Opportunities Yearbook Volume 1 Strategic, Practical Information and Opportunities
Bosnia and Herzegovina Business and Investment Opportunities Yearbook Volume 1 Strategic, Practical Information and Opportunities
Botswana Business and Investment Opportunities Yearbook Volume 1 Strategic, Practical Information and Opportunities
Brazil Business and Investment Opportunities Yearbook Volume 1 Strategic, Practical Information and Opportunities
Brunei Business and Investment Opportunities Yearbook Volume 1 Strategic, Practical Information and Opportunities
Bulgaria Business and Investment Opportunities Yearbook Volume 1 Strategic, Practical Information and Opportunities
Burkina Faso Business and Investment Opportunities Yearbook Volume 1 Strategic, Practical Information and Opportunities
Burundi Business and Investment Opportunities Yearbook Volume 1 Strategic, Practical Information and Opportunities
Cambodia Business and Investment Opportunities Yearbook Volume 1 Strategic, Practical Information and Opportunities
Cameroon Business and Investment Opportunities Yearbook Volume 1 Strategic, Practical Information and Opportunities
Canada Business and Investment Opportunities Yearbook Volume 1 Strategic, Practical Information and Opportunities
Cape Verde Business and Investment Opportunities Yearbook Volume 1 Strategic, Practical Information and Opportunities
Cayman Islands Business and Investment Opportunities Yearbook Volume 1 Strategic, Practical Information and Opportunities
Central African Republic Business and Investment Opportunities Yearbook Volume 1 Strategic, Practical Information and Opportunities
Chad Business and Investment Opportunities Yearbook Volume 1 Strategic, Practical Information and Opportunities
Chile Business and Investment Opportunities Yearbook Volume 1 Strategic, Practical Information and Opportunities
China Business and Investment Opportunities Yearbook Volume 1 Strategic, Practical Information and Opportunities
Colombia Business and Investment Opportunities Yearbook Volume 1 Strategic, Practical Information and Opportunities
Comoros Business and Investment Opportunities Yearbook Volume 1 Strategic, Practical Information and Opportunities
Congo Business and Investment Opportunities Yearbook Volume 1 Strategic, Practical Information and Opportunities
Congo, Democratic Republic Business and Investment Opportunities Yearbook Volume 1 Strategic, Practical Information and Opportunities
Cook Islands Business and Investment Opportunities Yearbook Volume 1 Strategic, Practical Information and Opportunities
Costa Rica Business and Investment Opportunities Yearbook Volume 1 Strategic, Practical Information and Opportunities

TITLE
Cote d'Ivoire Business and Investment Opportunities Yearbook Volume 1 Strategic, Practical Information and Opportunities
Croatia Business and Investment Opportunities Yearbook Volume 1 Strategic, Practical Information and Opportunities
Cuba Business and Investment Opportunities Yearbook Volume 1 Strategic, Practical Information and Opportunities
Cyprus Business and Investment Opportunities Yearbook Volume 1 Strategic, Practical Information and Opportunities
Czech Republic Business and Investment Opportunities Yearbook Volume 1 Strategic, Practical Information and Opportunities
Denmark Business and Investment Opportunities Yearbook Volume 1 Strategic, Practical Information and Opportunities
Djibouti Business and Investment Opportunities Yearbook Volume 1 Strategic, Practical Information and Opportunities
Dominica Business and Investment Opportunities Yearbook Volume 1 Strategic, Practical Information and Opportunities
Dominican Republic Business and Investment Opportunities Yearbook Volume 1 Strategic, Practical Information and Opportunities
Ecuador Business and Investment Opportunities Yearbook Volume 1 Strategic, Practical Information and Opportunities
Egypt Business and Investment Opportunities Yearbook Volume 1 Strategic, Practical Information and Opportunities
El Salvador Business and Investment Opportunities Yearbook Volume 1 Strategic, Practical Information and Opportunities
Equatorial Guinea Business and Investment Opportunities Yearbook Volume 1 Strategic, Practical Information and Opportunities
Eritrea Business and Investment Opportunities Yearbook Volume 1 Strategic, Practical Information and Opportunities
Estonia Business and Investment Opportunities Yearbook Volume 1 Strategic, Practical Information and Opportunities
Ethiopia Business and Investment Opportunities Yearbook Volume 1 Strategic, Practical Information and Opportunities
Falkland Islands Business and Investment Opportunities Yearbook Volume 1 Strategic, Practical Information and Opportunities
Faroes Islands Business and Investment Opportunities Yearbook Volume 1 Strategic, Practical Information and Opportunities
Fiji Business and Investment Opportunities Yearbook Volume 1 Strategic, Practical Information and Opportunities
Finland Business and Investment Opportunities Yearbook Volume 1 Strategic, Practical Information and Opportunities
France Business and Investment Opportunities Yearbook Volume 1 Strategic, Practical Information and Opportunities
Gabon Business and Investment Opportunities Yearbook Volume 1 Strategic, Practical Information and Opportunities
Gambia Business and Investment Opportunities Yearbook Volume 1 Strategic, Practical Information and Opportunities
Georgia Business and Investment Opportunities Yearbook Volume 1 Strategic, Practical Information and Opportunities
Germany Business and Investment Opportunities Yearbook Volume 1 Strategic, Practical Information and Opportunities
Ghana Business and Investment Opportunities Yearbook Volume 1 Strategic, Practical Information and Opportunities
Gibraltar Business and Investment Opportunities Yearbook Volume 1 Strategic, Practical Information and Opportunities
Greece Business and Investment Opportunities Yearbook Volume 1 Strategic, Practical Information and Opportunities

TITLE
Greenland Business and Investment Opportunities Yearbook Volume 1 Strategic, Practical Information and Opportunities
Grenada Business and Investment Opportunities Yearbook Volume 1 Strategic, Practical Information and Opportunities
Guam Business and Investment Opportunities Yearbook Volume 1 Strategic, Practical Information and Opportunities
Guatemala Business and Investment Opportunities Yearbook Volume 1 Strategic, Practical Information and Opportunities
Guernsey Business and Investment Opportunities Yearbook Volume 1 Strategic, Practical Information and Opportunities
Guinea Business and Investment Opportunities Yearbook Volume 1 Strategic, Practical Information and Opportunities
Guinea-Bissau Business and Investment Opportunities Yearbook Volume 1 Strategic, Practical Information and Opportunities
Guyana Business and Investment Opportunities Yearbook Volume 1 Strategic, Practical Information and Opportunities
Haiti Business and Investment Opportunities Yearbook Volume 1 Strategic, Practical Information and Opportunities
Honduras Business and Investment Opportunities Yearbook Volume 1 Strategic, Practical Information and Opportunities
Hungary Business and Investment Opportunities Yearbook Volume 1 Strategic, Practical Information and Opportunities
Iceland Business and Investment Opportunities Yearbook Volume 1 Strategic, Practical Information and Opportunities
India Business and Investment Opportunities Yearbook Volume 1 Strategic, Practical Information and Opportunities
Indonesia Business and Investment Opportunities Yearbook Volume 1 Strategic, Practical Information and Opportunities
Iran Business and Investment Opportunities Yearbook Volume 1 Strategic, Practical Information and Opportunities
Iraq Business and Investment Opportunities Yearbook Volume 1 Strategic, Practical Information and Opportunities
Ireland Business and Investment Opportunities Yearbook Volume 1 Strategic, Practical Information and Opportunities
Israel Business and Investment Opportunities Yearbook Volume 1 Strategic, Practical Information and Opportunities
Italy Business and Investment Opportunities Yearbook Volume 1 Strategic, Practical Information and Opportunities
Jamaica Business and Investment Opportunities Yearbook Volume 1 Strategic, Practical Information and Opportunities
Japan Business and Investment Opportunities Yearbook Volume 1 Strategic, Practical Information and Opportunities
Jersey Business and Investment Opportunities Yearbook Volume 1 Strategic, Practical Information and Opportunities
Jordan Business and Investment Opportunities Yearbook Volume 1 Strategic, Practical Information and Opportunities
Kazakhstan Business and Investment Opportunities Yearbook Volume 1 Strategic, Practical Information and Opportunities
Kenya Business and Investment Opportunities Yearbook Volume 1 Strategic, Practical Information and Opportunities
Kiribati Business and Investment Opportunities Yearbook Volume 1 Strategic, Practical Information and Opportunities
Korea, North Business and Investment Opportunities Yearbook Volume 1 Strategic, Practical Information and Opportunities
Korea, South Business and Investment Opportunities Yearbook Volume 1 Strategic, Practical Information and Opportunities

TITLE
Kosovo Business and Investment Opportunities Yearbook Volume 1 Strategic, Practical Information and Opportunities
Kurdistan Business and Investment Opportunities Yearbook Volume 1 Strategic, Practical Information and Opportunities
Kuwait Business and Investment Opportunities Yearbook Volume 1 Strategic, Practical Information and Opportunities
Kyrgyzstan Business and Investment Opportunities Yearbook Volume 1 Strategic, Practical Information and Opportunities
Laos Business and Investment Opportunities Yearbook Volume 1 Strategic, Practical Information and Opportunities
Latvia Business and Investment Opportunities Yearbook Volume 1 Strategic, Practical Information and Opportunities
Lebanon Business and Investment Opportunities Yearbook Volume 1 Strategic, Practical Information and Opportunities
Lesotho Business and Investment Opportunities Yearbook Volume 1 Strategic, Practical Information and Opportunities
Liberia Business and Investment Opportunities Yearbook Volume 1 Strategic, Practical Information and Opportunities
Libya Business and Investment Opportunities Yearbook Volume 1 Strategic, Practical Information and Opportunities
Liechtenstein Business and Investment Opportunities Yearbook Volume 1 Strategic, Practical Information and Opportunities
Lithuania Business and Investment Opportunities Yearbook Volume 1 Strategic, Practical Information and Opportunities
Luxembourg Business and Investment Opportunities Yearbook Volume 1 Strategic, Practical Information and Opportunities
Macao Business and Investment Opportunities Yearbook Volume 1 Strategic, Practical Information and Opportunities
Macedonia Business and Investment Opportunities Yearbook Volume 1 Strategic, Practical Information and Opportunities
Madagascar Business and Investment Opportunities Yearbook Volume 1 Strategic, Practical Information and Opportunities
Madeira Business and Investment Opportunities Yearbook Volume 1 Strategic, Practical Information and Opportunities
Malawi Business and Investment Opportunities Yearbook Volume 1 Strategic, Practical Information and Opportunities
Malaysia Business and Investment Opportunities Yearbook Volume 1 Strategic, Practical Information and Opportunities
Maldives Business and Investment Opportunities Yearbook Volume 1 Strategic, Practical Information and Opportunities
Mali Business and Investment Opportunities Yearbook Volume 1 Strategic, Practical Information and Opportunities
Malta Business and Investment Opportunities Yearbook Volume 1 Strategic, Practical Information and Opportunities
Man Business and Investment Opportunities Yearbook Volume 1 Strategic, Practical Information and Opportunities
Marshall Islands Business and Investment Opportunities Yearbook Volume 1 Strategic, Practical Information and Opportunities
Mauritania Business and Investment Opportunities Yearbook Volume 1 Strategic, Practical Information and Opportunities
Mauritius Business and Investment Opportunities Yearbook Volume 1 Strategic, Practical Information and Opportunities
Mayotte Business and Investment Opportunities Yearbook Volume 1 Strategic, Practical Information and Opportunities
Mexico Business and Investment Opportunities Yearbook Volume 1 Strategic, Practical Information and Opportunities

TITLE
Micronesia Business and Investment Opportunities Yearbook Volume 1 Strategic, Practical Information and Opportunities
Moldova Business and Investment Opportunities Yearbook Volume 1 Strategic, Practical Information and Opportunities
Monaco Business and Investment Opportunities Yearbook Volume 1 Strategic, Practical Information and Opportunities
Mongolia Business and Investment Opportunities Yearbook Volume 1 Strategic, Practical Information and Opportunities
Montserrat Business and Investment Opportunities Yearbook Volume 1 Strategic, Practical Information and Opportunities
Montenegro Business and Investment Opportunities Yearbook Volume 1 Strategic, Practical Information and Opportunities
Morocco Business and Investment Opportunities Yearbook Volume 1 Strategic, Practical Information and Opportunities
Mozambique Business and Investment Opportunities Yearbook Volume 1 Strategic, Practical Information and Opportunities
Myanmar Business and Investment Opportunities Yearbook Volume 1 Strategic, Practical Information and Opportunities
Nagorno-Karabakh Republic Business and Investment Opportunities Yearbook Volume 1 Strategic, Practical Information and Opportunities
Namibia Business and Investment Opportunities Yearbook Volume 1 Strategic, Practical Information and Opportunities
Nauru Business and Investment Opportunities Yearbook Volume 1 Strategic, Practical Information and Opportunities
Nepal Business and Investment Opportunities Yearbook Volume 1 Strategic, Practical Information and Opportunities
Netherlands Business and Investment Opportunities Yearbook Volume 1 Strategic, Practical Information and Opportunities
New Caledonia Business and Investment Opportunities Yearbook Volume 1 Strategic, Practical Information and Opportunities
New Zealand Business and Investment Opportunities Yearbook Volume 1 Strategic, Practical Information and Opportunities
Nicaragua Business and Investment Opportunities Yearbook Volume 1 Strategic, Practical Information and Opportunities
Niger Business and Investment Opportunities Yearbook Volume 1 Strategic, Practical Information and Opportunities
Nigeria Business and Investment Opportunities Yearbook Volume 1 Strategic, Practical Information and Opportunities
Niue Business and Investment Opportunities Yearbook Volume 1 Strategic, Practical Information and Opportunities
Northern Cyprus (Turkish Republic of Northern Cyprus) Business and Investment Opportunities Yearbook Volume 1 Strategic, Practical Information and Opportunities
Northern Mariana Islands Business and Investment Opportunities Yearbook Volume 1 Strategic, Practical Information and Opportunities
Norway Business and Investment Opportunities Yearbook Volume 1 Strategic, Practical Information and Opportunities
Oman Business and Investment Opportunities Yearbook Volume 1 Strategic, Practical Information and Opportunities
Pakistan Business and Investment Opportunities Yearbook Volume 1 Strategic, Practical Information and Opportunities
Palau Business and Investment Opportunities Yearbook Volume 1 Strategic, Practical Information and Opportunities
Palestine (West Bank & Gaza) Business and Investment Opportunities Yearbook Volume 1 Strategic, Practical Information and Opportunities
Panama Business and Investment Opportunities Yearbook Volume 1 Strategic, Practical Information and Opportunities

TITLE
Papua New Guinea Business and Investment Opportunities Yearbook Volume 1 Strategic, Practical Information and Opportunities
Paraguay Business and Investment Opportunities Yearbook Volume 1 Strategic, Practical Information and Opportunities
Peru Business and Investment Opportunities Yearbook Volume 1 Strategic, Practical Information and Opportunities
Philippines Business and Investment Opportunities Yearbook Volume 1 Strategic, Practical Information and Opportunities
Pitcairn Islands Business and Investment Opportunities Yearbook Volume 1 Strategic, Practical Information and Opportunities
Poland Business and Investment Opportunities Yearbook Volume 1 Strategic, Practical Information and Opportunities
Polynesia French Business and Investment Opportunities Yearbook Volume 1 Strategic, Practical Information and Opportunities
Portugal Business and Investment Opportunities Yearbook Volume 1 Strategic, Practical Information and Opportunities
Qatar Business and Investment Opportunities Yearbook Volume 1 Strategic, Practical Information and Opportunities
Romania Business and Investment Opportunities Yearbook Volume 1 Strategic, Practical Information and Opportunities
Russia Business and Investment Opportunities Yearbook Volume 1 Strategic, Practical Information and Opportunities
Rwanda Business and Investment Opportunities Yearbook Volume 1 Strategic, Practical Information and Opportunities
Sahrawi Arab Democratic Republic Volume 1 Strategic Information and Developments
Saint Kitts and Nevis Business and Investment Opportunities Yearbook Volume 1 Strategic, Practical Information and Opportunities
Saint Lucia Business and Investment Opportunities Yearbook Volume 1 Strategic, Practical Information and Opportunities
Saint Vincent and The Grenadines Business and Investment Opportunities Yearbook Volume 1 Strategic, Practical Information and Opportunities
Samoa (American) A Business and Investment Opportunities Yearbook Volume 1 Strategic, Practical Information and Opportunities
Samoa (Western) Business and Investment Opportunities Yearbook Volume 1 Strategic, Practical Information and Opportunities
San Marino Business and Investment Opportunities Yearbook Volume 1 Strategic, Practical Information and Opportunities
Sao Tome and Principe Business and Investment Opportunities Yearbook Volume 1 Strategic, Practical Information and Opportunities
Saudi Arabia Business and Investment Opportunities Yearbook Volume 1 Strategic, Practical Information and Opportunities
Scotland Business and Investment Opportunities Yearbook Volume 1 Strategic, Practical Information and Opportunities
Senegal Business and Investment Opportunities Yearbook Volume 1 Strategic, Practical Information and Opportunities
Serbia Business and Investment Opportunities Yearbook Volume 1 Strategic, Practical Information and Opportunities
Seychelles Business and Investment Opportunities Yearbook Volume 1 Strategic, Practical Information and Opportunities
Sierra Leone Business and Investment Opportunities Yearbook Volume 1 Strategic, Practical Information and Opportunities
Singapore Business and Investment Opportunities Yearbook Volume 1 Strategic, Practical Information and Opportunities
Slovakia Business and Investment Opportunities Yearbook Volume 1 Strategic, Practical Information and Opportunities

TITLE
Slovenia Business and Investment Opportunities Yearbook Volume 1 Strategic, Practical Information and Opportunities
Solomon Islands Business and Investment Opportunities Yearbook Volume 1 Strategic, Practical Information and Opportunities
Somalia Business and Investment Opportunities Yearbook Volume 1 Strategic, Practical Information and Opportunities
South Africa Business and Investment Opportunities Yearbook Volume 1 Strategic, Practical Information and Opportunities
Spain Business and Investment Opportunities Yearbook Volume 1 Strategic, Practical Information and Opportunities
Sri Lanka Business and Investment Opportunities Yearbook Volume 1 Strategic, Practical Information and Opportunities
St. Helena Business and Investment Opportunities Yearbook Volume 1 Strategic, Practical Information and Opportunities
St. Pierre & Miquelon Business and Investment Opportunities Yearbook Volume 1 Strategic, Practical Information and Opportunities
Sudan (Republic of the Sudan) Business and Investment Opportunities Yearbook Volume 1 Strategic, Practical Information and Opportunities
Sudan South Business and Investment Opportunities Yearbook Volume 1 Strategic, Practical Information and Opportunities
Suriname Business and Investment Opportunities Yearbook Volume 1 Strategic, Practical Information and Opportunities
Swaziland Business and Investment Opportunities Yearbook Volume 1 Strategic, Practical Information and Opportunities
Sweden Business and Investment Opportunities Yearbook Volume 1 Strategic, Practical Information and Opportunities
Switzerland Business and Investment Opportunities Yearbook Volume 1 Strategic, Practical Information and Opportunities
Syria Business and Investment Opportunities Yearbook Volume 1 Strategic, Practical Information and Opportunities
Taiwan Business and Investment Opportunities Yearbook Volume 1 Strategic, Practical Information and Opportunities
Tajikistan Business and Investment Opportunities Yearbook Volume 1 Strategic, Practical Information and Opportunities
Tanzania Business and Investment Opportunities Yearbook Volume 1 Strategic, Practical Information and Opportunities
Thailand Business and Investment Opportunities Yearbook Volume 1 Strategic, Practical Information and Opportunities
Timor Leste (Democratic Republic of Timor-Leste) Business and Investment Opportunities Yearbook Volume 1 Strategic, Practical Information and Opportunities
Togo Business and Investment Opportunities Yearbook Volume 1 Strategic, Practical Information and Opportunities
Tonga Business and Investment Opportunities Yearbook Volume 1 Strategic, Practical Information and Opportunities
Trinidad and Tobago Business and Investment Opportunities Yearbook Volume 1 Strategic, Practical Information and Opportunities
Tunisia Business and Investment Opportunities Yearbook Volume 1 Strategic, Practical Information and Opportunities
Turkey Business and Investment Opportunities Yearbook Volume 1 Strategic, Practical Information and Opportunities
Turkmenistan Business and Investment Opportunities Yearbook Volume 1 Strategic, Practical Information and Opportunities
Turks & Caicos Business and Investment Opportunities Yearbook Volume 1 Strategic, Practical Information and Opportunities
Tuvalu Business and Investment Opportunities Yearbook Volume 1 Strategic, Practical Information and Opportunities

TITLE
Uganda Business and Investment Opportunities Yearbook Volume 1 Strategic, Practical Information and Opportunities
Ukraine Business and Investment Opportunities Yearbook Volume 1 Strategic, Practical Information and Opportunities
United Arab Emirates Business and Investment Opportunities Yearbook Volume 1 Strategic, Practical Information and Opportunities
United Kingdom Business and Investment Opportunities Yearbook Volume 1 Strategic, Practical Information and Opportunities
United States Business and Investment Opportunities Yearbook Volume 1 Strategic, Practical Information and Opportunities
Uruguay Business and Investment Opportunities Yearbook Volume 1 Strategic, Practical Information and Opportunities
Uzbekistan Business and Investment Opportunities Yearbook Volume 1 Strategic, Practical Information and Opportunities
Vanuatu Business and Investment Opportunities Yearbook Volume 1 Strategic, Practical Information and Opportunities
Vatican City (Holy See) Business and Investment Opportunities Yearbook Volume 1 Strategic, Practical Information and Opportunities
Venezuela Business and Investment Opportunities Yearbook Volume 1 Strategic, Practical Information and Opportunities
Vietnam Business and Investment Opportunities Yearbook Volume 1 Strategic, Practical Information and Opportunities
Virgin Islands, British Business and Investment Opportunities Yearbook Volume 1 Strategic, Practical Information and Opportunities
Wake Atoll Business and Investment Opportunities Yearbook Volume 1 Strategic, Practical Information and Opportunities
Wallis & Futuna Business and Investment Opportunities Yearbook Volume 1 Strategic, Practical Information and Opportunities
Western Sahara Business and Investment Opportunities Yearbook Volume 1 Strategic, Practical Information and Opportunities
Yemen Business and Investment Opportunities Yearbook Volume 1 Strategic, Practical Information and Opportunities
Zambia Business and Investment Opportunities Yearbook Volume 1 Strategic, Practical Information and Opportunities
Zimbabwe Business and Investment Opportunities Yearbook Volume 1 Strategic, Practical Information and Opportunities

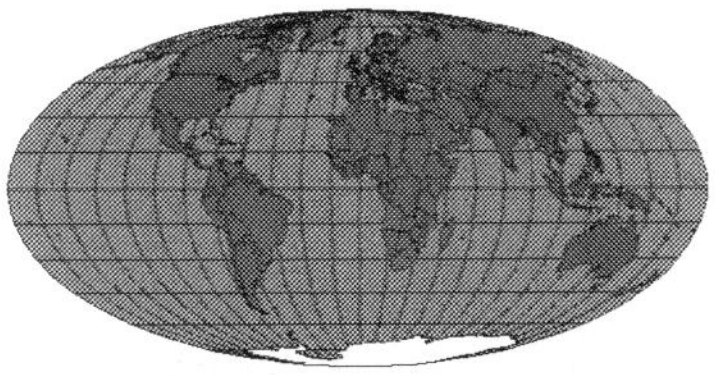

WORLD EXPORT-IMPORT, TRADE AND BUSINESS DIRECTORIES LIBRARY

Price: $149.95 Each

International Business Publications USA
P.O. Box 15343, Washington DC 20003, Email: ibpusa@comcast.net
Phone: 202-546-2103, Fax: 202-546-3275
World Business Information Catalog: http://www.ibpus.com

1.	Albania Export-Import, Trade and Business Directory
2.	Algeria Export-Import, Trade and Business Directory
3.	Andorra Export-Import, Trade and Business Directory
4.	Angola Export-Import, Trade and Business Directory
5.	Antigua & Barbuda Export-Import, Trade and Business Directory
6.	Antilles (Netherlands) Export-Import, Trade and Business Directory
7.	Argentina Export-Import, Trade and Business Directory
8.	Armenia Export-Import, Trade and Business Directory
9.	Australia Export-Import, Trade and Business Directory
10.	Austria Export-Import, Trade and Business Directory
11.	Azerbaijan Export-Import, Trade and Business Directory
12.	Bahamas Export-Import, Trade and Business Directory
13.	Bangladesh Export-Import, Trade and Business Directory
14.	Barbados Export-Import, Trade and Business Directory
15.	Belarus Export-Import, Trade and Business Directory
16.	Belgium Export-Import, Trade and Business Directory
17.	Belize Export-Import, Trade and Business Directory
18.	Bermuda Export-Import, Trade and Business Directory
19.	Bolivia Export-Import, Trade and Business Directory
20.	Bosnia and Herzegovina Export-Import, Trade and Business Directory
21.	Botswana Export-Import, Trade and Business Directory
22.	Brazil Export-Import, Trade and Business Directory
23.	Brunei Export-Import, Trade and Business Directory
24.	Bulgaria Export-Import, Trade and Business Directory
25.	Cambodia Export-Import, Trade and Business Directory
26.	Cameroon Export-Import, Trade and Business Directory
27.	Canada Export-Import, Trade and Business Directory
28.	Cayman Islands Export-Import, Trade and Business Directory
29.	Chile Export-Import, Trade and Business Directory
30.	China Export-Import, Trade and Business Directory
31.	Colombia Export-Import, Trade and Business Directory
32.	Comoros Export-Import, Trade and Business Directory
33.	Cook Islands Export-Import, Trade and Business Directory
34.	Costa Rica Export-Import, Trade and Business Directory

For additional analytical, business and investment opportunities information, please contact Global Investment & Business Center, USA at (202) 546-2103. Fax: (202) 546-3275. E-mail: rusric@erols.com

35.	Croatia Export-Import, Trade and Business Directory
36.	Cuba Export-Import, Trade and Business Directory
37.	Cyprus Export-Import, Trade and Business Directory
38.	Czech Republic Export-Import, Trade and Business Directory
39.	Denmark Export-Import, Trade and Business Directory
40.	Dominica Export-Import, Trade and Business Directory
41.	Dominican Republic Export-Import, Trade and Business Directory
42.	Dubai Export-Import, Trade and Business Directory
43.	Ecuador Export-Import, Trade and Business Directory
44.	Egypt Export-Import, Trade and Business Directory
45.	El Salvador Export-Import, Trade and Business Directory
46.	Equatorial Guinea Export-Import, Trade and Business Directory
47.	Estonia Export-Import, Trade and Business Directory
48.	Falkland Islands Export-Import, Trade and Business Directory
49.	Fiji Export-Import, Trade and Business Directory
50.	Finland Export-Import, Trade and Business Directory
51.	France Export-Import, Trade and Business Directory
52.	Georgia Export-Import, Trade and Business Directory
53.	Germany Export-Import, Trade and Business Directory
54.	Gibraltar Export-Import, Trade and Business Directory
55.	Greece Export-Import, Trade and Business Directory
56.	Grenada Export-Import, Trade and Business Directory
57.	Guam Investment & Business Guide
58.	Guatemala Export-Import, Trade and Business Directory
59.	Guernsey Export-Import, Trade and Business Directory
60.	Guyana Export-Import, Trade and Business Directory
61.	Haiti Export-Import, Trade and Business Directory
62.	Honduras Export-Import, Trade and Business Directory
63.	Hungary Export-Import, Trade and Business Directory
64.	Iceland Export-Import, Trade and Business Directory
65.	India Export-Import, Trade and Business Directory
66.	Indonesia Export-Import, Trade and Business Directory
67.	Iran Export-Import, Trade and Business Directory
68.	Iraq Export-Import, Trade and Business Directory
69.	Ireland Export-Import, Trade and Business Directory
70.	Israel Export-Import, Trade and Business Directory
71.	Italy Export-Import, Trade and Business Directory
72.	Jamaica Export-Import, Trade and Business Directory
73.	Japan Export-Import, Trade and Business Directory
74.	Jersey Export-Import, Trade and Business Directory
75.	Jordan Export-Import, Trade and Business Directory
76.	Kazakhstan Export-Import, Trade and Business Directory
77.	Kenya Export-Import, Trade and Business Directory
78.	Kiribati Export-Import, Trade and Business Directory

79. Korea, North Export-Import, Trade and Business Directory
80. Korea, South Export-Import, Trade and Business Directory
81. Kuwait Export-Import, Trade and Business Directory
82. Kyrgyzstan Export-Import, Trade and Business Directory
83. Laos Export-Import, Trade and Business Directory
84. Latvia Export-Import, Trade and Business Directory
85. Lebanon Export-Import, Trade and Business Directory
86. Libya Export-Import, Trade and Business Directory
87. Liechtenstein Export-Import, Trade and Business Directory
88. Lithuania Export-Import, Trade and Business Directory
89. Luxemburg Export-Import, Trade and Business Directory
90. Macao Export-Import, Trade and Business Directory
91. Macedonia, Republic Export-Import, Trade and Business Directory
92. Madagascar Export-Import, Trade and Business Directory
93. Malaysia Export-Import, Trade and Business Directory
94. Malta Export-Import, Trade and Business Directory
95. Man Export-Import, Trade and Business Directory
96. Mauritius Export-Import, Trade and Business Directory
97. Mauritius Export-Import, Trade and Business Directory
98. Mexico Export-Import, Trade and Business Directory
99. Micronesia Export-Import, Trade and Business Directory
100. Moldova Export-Import, Trade and Business Directory
101. Monaco Export-Import, Trade and Business Directory
102. Mongolia Export-Import, Trade and Business Directory
103. Morocco Export-Import, Trade and Business Directory
104. Myanmar Export-Import, Trade and Business Directory
105. Namibia Export-Import, Trade and Business Directory
106. Netherlands Export-Import, Trade and Business Directory
107. New Caledonia Export-Import, Trade and Business Directory
108. New Zealand Export-Import, Trade and Business Directory
109. Nicaragua Export-Import, Trade and Business Directory
110. Nigeria Export-Import, Trade and Business Directory
111. Northern Mariana Islands Export-Import, Trade and Business Directory
112. Norway Export-Import, Trade and Business Directory
113. Pakistan Export-Import, Trade and Business Directory
114. Panama Export-Import, Trade and Business Directory
115. Peru Export-Import, Trade and Business Directory
116. Philippines Export-Import, Trade and Business Directory
117. Poland Export-Import, Trade and Business Directory
118. Portugal Export-Import, Trade and Business Directory
119. Romania Export-Import, Trade and Business Directory
120. Russia Export-Import, Trade and Business Directory
121. Samoa (American) Investment & Business Guide
122. Samoa (Western) Export-Import, Trade and Business Directory

123. Saudi Arabia Export-Import, Trade and Business Directory
124. Scotland Export-Import, Trade and Business Directory
125. Singapore Export-Import, Trade and Business Directory
126. Slovakia Export-Import, Trade and Business Directory
127. Slovenia Export-Import, Trade and Business Directory
128. South Africa Export-Import, Trade and Business Directory
129. Spain Export-Import, Trade and Business Directory
130. Sri Lanka Export-Import, Trade and Business Directory
131. St. Helena Export-Import, Trade and Business Directory
132. Sudan Export-Import, Trade and Business Directory
133. Suriname Export-Import, Trade and Business Directory
134. Sweden Export-Import, Trade and Business Directory
135. Switzerland Export-Import, Trade and Business Directory
136. Syria Export Import & Business Directory
137. Taiwan Export-Import, Trade and Business Directory
138. Tajikistan Export-Import, Trade and Business Directory
139. Thailand Export-Import, Trade and Business Directory
140. Tunisia Export-Import, Trade and Business Directory
141. Turkey Export-Import, Trade and Business Directory
142. Turkmenistan Export-Import, Trade and Business Directory
143. Uganda Export-Import, Trade and Business Directory
144. Ukraine Export-Import, Trade and Business Directory
145. United Arab Emirates Export-Import, Trade and Business Directory
146. United Kingdom Export-Import, Trade and Business Directory
147. United States Export-Import, Trade and Business Directory
148. Uruguay Export-Import, Trade and Business Directory
149. US Export-Import, Trade and Business Directory
150. Uzbekistan Export-Import, Trade and Business Directory
151. Venezuela Export-Import, Trade and Business Directory
152. Vietnam Export-Import, Trade and Business Directory
153. Yugoslavia Export-Import, Trade and Business Directory

Made in United States
Orlando, FL
04 November 2026

90207786R00175